False Science: Underestimating the Soviet Arms Buildup

False Science: Underestimating the Soviet Arms Buildup

An Appraisal of the CIA's Direct Costing Effort, 1960–80

STEVEN ROSEFIELDE

Foreword by Patrick Parker

Transaction Books
New Brunswick (U.S.A.) and London (U.K.)

For My Daughter
Justine Danielle

Library of Congress Catalog Number: 81-1050
ISBN: 0-87855-868-3 (paper)
Printed in the United States of America

Library of Congress Cataloging in Publication Data

Rosefielde, Steven.
  False science.

  Bibliography: p.
  Includes index.
  1. Soviet Union—Armed Forces—Appropriations and expenditures.
2. United States. Central Intelligence Agency. I. Title.
UA770.R6   355.6′22′0947   81-1050
ISBN 0-87855-868-3 (pbk.)

Contents

List of Tables and Figures

FIGURES   **PAGE**

Sponsorship

This study is an entirely independent, self-financed, scholarly endeavor, supported neither by government grants nor private consultantships. The author's only affiliations during the years in which this volume was written were with the University of North Carolina, and the U.S. Naval Postgraduate School where he taught summer school in 1978–80 as a visiting professor of national security affairs.

Foreword

Ten years ago, when I was deputy assistant secretary of defense for intelligence, I discovered that the CIA's estimates of Soviet weapon expenditures were implausibly low and failed to reflect the rapid quantitative and qualitative improvements which we were seeing in Soviet weapon systems and technology. Since these estimates were directly relevant to my own work, I endeavored on numerous occasions to learn how the agency performed its calculations, and why the magnitude and growth of Soviet procurement expenditures appeared to be so far out of line with the size and quality reflected in Soviet force developments. My inquiries ended in frustration. While the agency assured me of its high confidence in the estimates and described the general procedures used to make them, it failed to provide the detailed calculations required for a responsible audit.

During the seventies the disparity between my own judgment (and that of most interested and properly qualified military officers) of the resources required to support the Soviet arms buildup and the CIA's estimates of those resources continued to widen. My own estimates, supported by those of most military intelligence organizations, indicated that the real value of Soviet weapons production was growing at roughly 10 percent per annum, while the agency put the figure variously between 2 and 4.5 percent per annum.

Matters appeared to come to a head in 1976, when the DIA and CIA obtained information from the Soviet Ministry of Defense that showed that the agency's estimate of Soviet military procurement expenditures was about one-third the actual level. This evidence strongly suggested that the CIA's cost estimating methodology was flawed.

Nonetheless, despite the very large disparity between actual Soviet weapons outlays and its estimates, the CIA reasserted its confidence in the reliability of its direct cost estimating methodology and its estimates of real Soviet procurement growth, explaining the discrepancy between its estimate and actual Soviet weapons outlays largely on the basis of hidden Soviet inflation; that is, changes in weapon prices unaccounted for in official Soviet price statistics.

1

Most students of national security affairs appear to have accepted this explanation without serious reservation, endorsing by default the perception of Soviet behavior it sustained. By and large scholars continue to believe that the United States maintains a substantial margin of military superiority over the Soviets; that if the Soviets are catching up they are merely seeking parity; and that should the Soviets actually attain superiority that disadvantage can be quickly reversed because of the superior productive capability of the United States.

The merit of these beliefs and the CIA's estimates upon which they rest are all thoroughly and skillfully examined in the present volume by Professor Rosefielde. By rigorous application of scientific method Professor Rosefielde demonstrates that the inconsistencies in the CIA's estimates of Soviet weapon production costs, which I tried to resolve a decade ago, are caused by a fundamental error in the agency's direct cost estimating methodology. This error, which is confirmed by an important classified study, systematically understates technological growth and biases the agency's estimates downward.

Professor Rosefielde's calculations show that the Soviets have not only endeavored to catch up and overtake the United States in terms of quality adjusted military procurement expenditures but that they have already done so. This finding, which is consistent with military intelligence, discredits a wide variety of theories purporting to describe the dynamics of Soviet-American military competition and places American national security options in the eighties in a disturbing perspective. Contrary to the usual view that time and production potential are on our side, Professor Rosefielde's calculations indicate that the United States will have to proceed rapidly and efficiently just to maintain the unsatisfactory present military balance. This book shows that the Soviets have constructed a formidable military-industrial base which will enable them to produce more than a trillion dollars worth of new weapons during the current decade, roughly three times foreseeable U.S. outlays.

Asymmetries of this dimension are likely to be politically and militarily destabilizing. If Professor Rosefielde is right, and I believe he is, a revolution in American national security analysis and policy is needed, and needed quickly, to cope effectively with the rapidly growing margin of Soviet arms superiority. The magnitude and structure of Soviet forces in the coming years must be accurately forecast, their purposes understood, and the necessary U.S. strategy and forces required to counter them must be swiftly put in place.

To accomplish this objective, scholars of national security affairs will want to reassess the record of the past twenty years carefully, both to discover why the agency's error went undetected for so long, and to determine for themselves whether the new estimates are reliable. Professor Rosefielde's pathbreaking monograph has the merit of satisfying both these requirements and therefore is the essential point of departure for all those who wish to participate effectively in the national security debates of the eighties.

Patrick Parker

Preface

Most of the analytical techniques utilized in this volume are familiar to specialists and require no special discussion. One aspect of my research has been unconventional, however, and warrants elaboration. Both the details of the CIA's direct costing methodology and its data are classified. This posed a substantial impediment to the serious assessment of the agency's direct costing effort. Various contradictions evident in official publications and congressional testimony indicated that important aspects of the record were being suppressed but it was impossible to discern in the open literature precisely what they were. I attempted to sort these contradictions out in a series of unpublished papers, one of which was delivered at the Military Operations Research Society meetings in the winter of 1976, and subsequently forwarded to the CIA in revised form for comment.

In 1978, after being denied access to the agency for four years because I did not have a need to know, Patrick Parker, former principal deputy assistant secretary of defense for intelligence arranged a meeting for me with Donald Burton, chief of the Military Economic Analysis Center and five of his deputies. I was given what in retrospect could be called a "congressman's" briefing on the rudiments of direct costing practice. Basically, I was told that my conjectures about the inadequate handling of technical progress were wrongheaded and that the agency possessed irrefutable proof that the prices of Soviet weapons were continuously rising due to hidden cost push inflation.

For the next several months I tried to reconcile what I had been told with my prior research. This process continued at the U.S. Naval Postgraduate School where I taught the summer session in 1978. With the assistance of two operations research specialists, Commander John Scott Redd and Lieutenant Alexander Callahan (students in my national security seminar), I was able to identify several important defects in the agency's characterization of its direct costing procedures and its hidden inflation hypothesis. Commander Redd, possessing the necessary special access clearances, went to Washington where he spent several days trying to obtain information clarifying these perplexities. When he returned the agency's replies were scrutinized, discussed, and evaluated.

The new information resolved several issues but raised others. Commander Redd recontacted the agency, initiating a dialogue that culminated with a visit by James Steiner and a coworker to Monterey.

The results of our summertime investigations were then transformed into two working papers, both of which were sent to the agency for further comment. A direct response was not immediately forthcoming, but I did receive a highly critical review from an anonymous source who Jeremy Azrael had asked to evaluate my findings. Although I did not agree with many of his points, this critic forced me to recognize that my perception of the historical record was seriously incomplete. The agency apparently had in its possession a wide range of unpublished direct cost estimates which could be pulled out of the hat as the circumstances dictated. As a consequence the merit of the CIA's direct costing effort could not be evaluated without an understanding of how its published ruble estimates differed from those that were suppressed, and why the agency had chosen the series it did as the one meriting publication.

For six months I tried in vain to discuss these matters with the agency. Finally, Patrick Parker once again came to the rescue by arranging a meeting in August 1979 with Donald Burton and his deputy Donald Swain at the Naval Postgraduate School. It was only then that I discovered that the agency's original direct cost estimates showed that Soviet procurement expenditures had been static from 1960 to 1970 instead of growing at an annual rate of 4 percent as the official record indicated. This piece of information unravelled the puzzle of the CIA's direct costing effort for me. Within four months I had written or rewritten all the chapters appearing in the first part of this volume.

A second breakthrough occurred in August 1980 when Commander Redd apprised me of his own independent study comparing the CIA's estimates of Soviet procurement costs with analogous estimates computed with the Defense Department's parametric costing relationships. These findings differed insignificantly from my own, but were derived with an entirely different methodology. This helped me refine my understanding of the deficiencies of the CIA's direct costing methodology, and greatly increase the power of my exposition.

S.R.

Acknowledgments

My greatest debt is to Patrick Parker, former principal deputy assistant secretary of defense for intelligence, and chairman of national security affairs at the U.S. Naval Postgraduate School. He not only provided the encouragement that prompted me to seriously undertake this investigation in the fall of 1976, but he arranged a series of crucial interviews with the CIA that I could not have secured on my own.

Commander John Scott Redd and Lieutenant Alexander Callahan worked intensively with me during the summer of 1978 on the statistical and econometric aspects of direct costing. Their detailed knowledge of military cost estimating procedures, weapons systems, and operations research greatly facilitated the progress of this investigation.

Donald Burton, former chief of the Military and Economic Analysis Center, OSR, CIA; Deputy Chief Donald Swain; James Steiner, chief, Economic Implications Branch, OSR; Robert Huffstutler (director, OSR); and numerous other members of the MEAC technical staff patiently explained the intricacies of direct costing and hidden inflation to me on various occasions. Hans Heymann, Abraham Becker, and Herbert Levine made me aware of difficulties impeding a full assessment of direct costing in their critiques of an early draft of my essay, "Real Soviet Arms Procurement Expenditures 1960–1980." Jeremy Azrael commented on this same paper and transmitted it to an anonymous critic whose review prodded me to redirect my efforts along more fruitful lines.

William Lee, Jan Rylander, Andrew Marshall, Leonard Sullivan, James Kehoe, Kenneth Brower, James Herd, Quinn Mills, Peter Vigor, Les Aspin, Richard Anderson, Michael Kaser, Alec Nove, Martin Shubik, Harry Rowen, Abram Bergson, Martin Spechler, Gur Ofer, Gregory Grossman, Morris Bornstein, Stanley Cohn, Franklyn Holzman, David Yost, Jerry Hough, William Reese, Michael Sovereign, Sherman Blandin, Donald Daniels, Katherine Herbig, William Manthorpe, Frederick Giessler, Lance Lord, William Pfouts, James Leutze, Dietrick Schroeer, Edward Azar, Elizabeth Samonds, Frank Trager, and Irving Louis Horowitz provided invaluable insights on a host of technical problems.

Quinn Mills and William Reese read the first draft of the manuscript in its entirety. Their comments, as well as the suggestions of Jan Rylander, Frederick Giessler, William Manthorpe, Lance Lord, Frank Trager and Irving Louis Horowitz prompted me to rethink and rewrite Parts 4, 5 and 6 to focus my analysis on the technical issue of the Soviet arms buildup, instead of the more speculative question of the Soviet military threat. Commander Redd played a critical role in shaping the second draft. In the spring of 1980, he independently discovered that the CIA's fixed vintage parametric cost estimating equations generated estimates of *American* weapons that substantially understated their actual cost. We discussed these matters that summer, and in the fall worked closely together to determine whether valid reasons could be found to explain why the CIA's estimates understated the production cost both of American weapons and "Sovietized" American weapons. The results of our collaborative effort, more than anything else, dispelled my concern that the findings reported in this volume might be invalidated by classified information that had been withheld from my purview.

To Commander Redd, to Sarah Mason who carefully typed both drafts of the book, to George Brown who drew the graphics, to all those who have assisted me in this endeavor, and most especially to my wife Susan, I wish to express my great appreciation and gratitude. I alone, of course, take full responsibility for any and all deficiencies that may still mar the text.

Two chapters in this volume have been previously published in scholarly journals, and are included here with the kind permission of the publishers. Chapter 6 appeared under the title "On the Interpretation of Soviet Arms Procurement Expenditures Under Conditions of Rapid Technical Progress," in *Osteuropa Wirtschaft*, vol. 25, March 1980, pp. 41–52. Chapter 8 appeared as "Are Soviet Industrial Production Statistics Significantly Distorted by Hidden Inflation?" in the *Journal of Comparative Economics*, vol. 5, no. 2, June 1981, pp. 185–99.

Research Summary

Subject to the reservations set forth at the conclusion of this summary, and to the large, unknown standard errors that may beset any and all estimates of Soviet arms expenditures, this monograph demonstrates that because the CIA neglected to systematically test and confirm the theorems and subordinate hypotheses of its direct cost estimating methodology it failed to detect a fundamental specification error in its dollar parametric cost estimating equations. This has biased its estimates of the size, growth, and momentum of the Soviet arms buildup significantly downward, and has prevented it from discovering that the Soviets quietly achieved a small margin of arms superiority in the late seventies, an advantage rapidly increased thereafter (see chapter 16 for the definition of *superiority*).

The principal findings of this study, which can be classified under four headings, are:

A. *Real Soviet Procurement Trends*
   1. The real rate of Soviet procurement growth measured either in dollars or rubles exceeds the CIA's estimates, 1960–79, by a factor of three (chapters 13 and 16).
   2. The real rate of Soviet procurement growth is 9.6 percent per annum measured in dollars, and 12.9 percent per annum measured in rubles, 1960–79. During the same time period, American arms procurement declined .7 percent per annum (chapter 13).
   3. Cumulative Soviet weapons production, 1960–79, exceeds the CIA's estimate by 14 percent measured in dollars and 57 percent in rubles (chapters 13 and 16).
   4. Cumulative Soviet procurement production, 1960–79, exceeds U.S. outlays by 25 percent valued in dollars and 122 percent in rubles (chapters 13 and 16). [N.B.: The author's ruble estimate of *U.S.* procurement relies on the CIA's implicit ruble-dollar ratio.]
   5. Cumulative Soviet procurement, 1970–79, exceeded U.S. outlays in all major weapons categories including: strategic forces, in-

tercontinental attack, general purpose forces, land forces, tactical air forces, and naval procurement (chapter 13).

6. Current CIA dollar estimates of Soviet procurement in 1979 that show Soviet outlays exceeding American expenditures by 74 percent substantially understate the true disparity—121 percent (chapter 13).

7. Current CIA ruble estimates of Soviet procurement in 1979 that show Soviet outlays exceeding American expenditures by 94 percent substantially understate the actual disparity—316 percent (chapters 13 and 16). [N.B. The ruble estimates of U.S. procurement is derived with the CIA's implicit ruble-dollar ratio.]

8. Foreseeable cumulative Soviet procurement production during the eighties is likely to exceed the agency's forecast by at least a factor of two, measured either in dollars or rubles (chapter 15).

9. Foreseeable cumulative Soviet procurement production during the eighties is likely to exceed U.S. outlays by at least a factor of three, valued either in dollars or rubles, even if American arms production grows 4 percent per annum from 1980 to 1989 (chapter 15).

B. *The Arms Balance*

1. Since cumulative Soviet procurement outlays exceed U.S. expenditures measured both in dollars and rubles in the aggregate and for all major mission categories, and because it can be shown that in "Sovietizing" its direct cost estimates the CIA makes a substantial adjustment for the putative qualitative inferiority of Soviet weapons, it can be demonstrated, assuming ordinal transitivity, that the Soviets achieved a margin of arms superiority over the United States in the late seventies (chapter 16).

C. *National Security Implications*

1. All theories purporting to show that the Soviets could not or would not attempt to overtake and surpass the U.S. militarily are falsified by the empirical findings of this study (chapter 17).

2. All arms race theories of the Richardson-Cournot-Stackelberg type based on the supposition that the actions of the leader determine the reactions of the followers are falsified by the empirical findings of this study. When U.S. procurement outlays declined from 1968 to 1979, the Soviets did not follow the American lead but instead increased their weapons production at a double digit rate even after a margin of arms superiority was achieved in the late seventies (chapter 17).

3. All theories purporting to show that the Soviets do not intend to use force as a basic instrument of their foreign policy because

the economic burden of Soviet defense has been declining, and is low by past standards, are empirically falsified by the empirical findings of this study (chapters 14 and 17).

4. All theories purporting to show that the high economic burden of Soviet defense reflects the inefficiency of the Soviet military machine-building sector, and therefore implies Soviet weakness rather than strength, are empirically falsified by the empirical findings of this study (chapters 1, 17, and 18).

5. All theories purporting to show that the high economic burden of Soviet defense is caused by hidden ruble price inflation and does not reflect the magnitude of the Soviet arms buildup are empirically falsified by the findings of this study (chapters 1, 3, 5, 7–11, 17, and 18).

6. All theories purporting to show that the Soviets prefer arms control to arms superiority are falsified by the empirical findings in this study. When the Soviets rejected President Carter's disarmament initiatives in 1977 and 1978, after having achieved effective arms parity, the Soviet leadership revealed by its actions that it considered arms superiority to be preferable to arms control and disarmament (chapter 17).

7. Recent Soviet assertions that the United States is responsible for reviving the arms race are falsified by the empirical findings of this study.

8. The CIA's failure to provide the national security community with a timely assessment of the real dimensions of the Soviet arms buildup preempted a wide range of policy responses that might have prevented the Soviets from achieving arms superiority and might have induced them to seek genuine arms control.

D. *False Science*

1. The CIA could have discovered the specification error in its cost estimating equations as early as 1965 if it had scientifically tested the theorems and subordinate hypotheses of its direct costing methodology (chapter 18).

2. Correct estimates can be readily computed using the Department of Defense's variable vintage cost estimating equations (chapter 4 and the postscript).

3. Since the CIA's estimates are not scientifically tested and evaluated, they are determined de facto by a variety of nonscientific theoretical, bureaucratic, political, and social factors (chapter 19).

4. Soviet counterintelligence manipulated the level and growth trend of the published Soviet defense budget to conceal the size

of its defense expenditures, to persuade the CIA to believe its own estimates, and more speculatively to facilitate the public dissemination of the agency's low procurement estimates (chapter 19).

The validity of conclusions B–D depend heavily on the empirical calculations underlying the findings reported under heading A. These calculations (partially summarized in Tables S1, S2, and Figures S1 and S2) in turn are contingent on the merit of the adjustments that have been made to the CIA's direct cost estimates of Soviet procurement for the cost of qualitative improvements in Soviet weapons technology not captured in the agency's computations. The justification for these adjustments, which implicitly assume that with the exception of the lapses to be described the CIA's direct costing methodology is logically consistent and its weapons counts reasonably accurate, is predicated on the following considerations:

1. Data obtained directly from the Soviet Ministry of Defense in 1975 conclusively demonstrated that the ruble cost of Soviet weapons procured in 1970 was 209 to 236 percent higher than the CIA had estimated: 17–18.5 billion rubles versus 5.5 billion rubles (chapter 1).

2. The CIA's explanation that this discrepancy had to be attributed to hidden inflation because its weapons count was correct is not empirically supportable (chapters 7–11).

3. If the agency's weapon count is accepted and its hidden inflation conjecture rejected, it can be shown that the only reasonable explanation for the 236 percent ruble cost estimating discrepancy is the technological improvement of the weapons contained in the CIA's inventory of Soviet procurement (chapter 12).

4. This inference is supported by the behavior of the CIA's official Paasche dollar series published during the seventies, which give no indication of having been meaningfully adjusted to take account of the rapid advances that have occurred in Soviet weapons technology.

5. This deduction is also supported by the Department of Defense's variable vintage parametric cost estimating equations for American weapons both in "pre-Sovietized" and "Sovietized" form (Sovietization refers to adjustments made by the Central Intelligence Agency to the dollar cost of American weapons for their putative technological inferiority—see chapter 4).

6. The estimates referred to above, as well as the empirical results of another independent study, cannot be reported, but the existence and magnitude of intervintage technological progress is verified by

TABLE S1
Summary of Soviet and American Military Procurement Trends and Projections, 1960–79

	Actual			Projected		
	1960–69 (1)	1970–79 (2)	1960–79 (3)	(4)	1980–89 (5)	(6)
A. *Procurement Growth* Compound annual dollar rates (percent)						
1. Soviet (Rosefielde)	8.7	10.6	9.6	10.6	0	4.0
2. Soviet (CIA)	0	3.3	3.0	3.3		
3. American	1.2	−2.8	−.7	4.0	23.5	4.0
B. *Procurement* Cumulative dollar expenditures (billions)						
1. Soviet (Rosefielde)	199.2	509.2	708.4	1,374.9	758	984.3
2. Soviet (CIA)	264.5	354.6	619.1	492.1		
3. American	331.3	233.5	564.8	299.4	758	295.4
C. *Procurement Burden* GNP share valued in currency of the designated country						
1. Soviet (Rosefielde)	4.2	7.5	5.9	15.8	7.6	9.6
2. Soviet (CIA)	2.3	4.6	3.5	5.0		
3. American	1.7	1.1	1.4	1.1	2.6	1.1

Sources:
A.1: Actual (Table 13.2, column 5). The estimates of projected Soviet procurement growth represent in turn (4) the trend of the seventies, (5) steady state expenditure growth, (6) procurement growth with a constant procurement burden (assuming GNP grows 4 percent per annum 1980–89).

A.2: Actual (Table 13.2, columns 1–3). Procurement growth is projected at the trend rate of the seventies. The actual value 1960–69 is the author's estimate of either the CIA's hypothetical Paasche or Laspeyres dollar growth series. See chapter 4, section IX and chapter 13, note 5.

A.3: Actual (Table 13.2, column 7). Procurement is defined according to the CIA's conventions. The estimates of projected American procurement growth represent (4 and 6) recent Congressional forecasts, (5) the rate of growth needed to maintain cumulative parity with the Soviets assuming no growth in the current dollar value of annual Soviet procurement outlays.

TABLE S1 (Continued)

B.1: Actual (Table 13.2, column 5). Projected cumulative procurement expenditures are extrapolated from the 1979 value (75.8 billion dollars) reported in Table 13.2, column 5 at the growth rates listed in A.1, columns 4, 5, and 6.

B.2: Actual (Table 13.2, column 2). Projected cumulative procurement expenditures are extrapolated at 3.3 percent per annum from the 1979 value (24.2 billion dollars) reported in Table 13.2, column 2.

B.3: Actual (Table 13.2, column 7). Projected cumulative procurement expenditures are extrapolated from the 1979 value (23.6 billion dollars) reported in Table 13.2, column 7 by 1.041 1979–1980 (the actual rate from DOD sources), and thereafter at the rates shown in A.3, columns 4, 5, and 6.

C.1: Actual estimates refer to the years 1965 and 1975 shown in Table 14.1, column 5. The projected procurement burden for 1985 is estimated by assuming real Soviet GNP in rubles reported in *Narodnoe Khoziaistvo* for 1979, 496 billion rubles (NMP in 1970 prices adjusted by the Greenslade GNP/NMP coefficient 1.17) grows at 4 percent per annum to 627.6 billion rubles, and that procurement during the same time interval grows at ruble rates of (4) 12.9 percent per annum, (5) zero, (6) 4 percent per annum from a base of 55.2 billion rubles (see Table 13.1, column 2).

C.2: Actual estimates refer to the years 1965 and 1975 shown in Table 14.1, columns 1 and 2. GNP is projected in the same manner described in C.1, but at a slower rate of growth 2.5 percent per annum, in accordance with recent CIA forecasts. Procurement is extrapolated at a ruble rate of 4 percent per annum from a base of 24.2 billion rubles.

C.3: Actual estimates refer to the years 1965 and 1975 shown in Table 14.1, column 6. The projected burden for 1985 is estimated by assuming real U.S. GNP in constant 1978 prices grows at 3.4 percent per annum 1979–85 (the postwar average rate) to 2,697 billion dollars, and that procurement grows at the rates indicated in A.3 from the 1980 base of 24.6 billion dollars (valued in 1978 prices).

TABLE S2
Summary of Soviet and American Military Procurement Trends and Projections, 1960–79
(Valued in 1970 Ruble Prices)

	Actual			Projected
	1960–69 (1)	1970–79 (2)	1960–79 (3)	1980–89 (4)
A. *Procurement Growth* Compound annual ruble rates (percent)				
1. Soviet (Rosefielde)	12.9	12.9	12.9	12.9
2. Soviet (CIA)	0	4	4	4
3. American	1.2	−2.8	−.7	4.8
B. *Procurement* Cumulative ruble expenditures (billions)				
1. Soviet (Rosefielde)	100.8	339.2	440	1,012.9
2. Soviet (CIA)	57.2	221.9	279.1	290.4
3. American	74.3	123.6	197.9	155.9

TABLE S2 (Continued)

A.1: Actual (Table 13.1, column 6).

A.2: Actual (Table 13.1, columns 1 and 2). The estimate 1960–69 is the agency's unpublished prerevision figure. The estimates 1970–79 and 1960–79 are its published postrevision figures.

A.3: Actual (Table 16.1, columns 3 and 4). The projected rate is computed by applying the ruble-dollar index number growth disparity for Soviet weapons 4/3.3 to U.S. procurement growth: $\dot{g} = 1.21$ (4).

B.1: Actual (Table 13.1, column 6). The projected estimate is computed by extrapolating the 1979 procurement output level (55.2 billion rubles) with the growth rate shown in A.1, column 4.

B.2: Actual (Table 13.1, columns 1 and 2). The projected estimate is computed by extrapolating the 1979 CIA procurement output level (24.2 billion rubles) with its postrevision long term growth estimate. See A.2, column 4.

B.3: Actual (Table 16.1, columns 3 and 4). The projected estimate is computed by extrapolating the 1979 American procurement output level (12.5 billion rubles) with the growth rate shown in A.3, column 4.

a comprehensive study undertaken by Leonard Sullivan, assistant secretary of defense for program analysis and evaluation in 1975 (chapters 4, 8, and appendix 1).

7. Table S3 and Figures S3A and S3B demonstrate how the level and growth of American and Soviet procurement, 1960–79, are affected if American intervintage technological progress (derived from Sullivan's estimates of "technical growth") are not taken into account. Instead of growing 1.2 percent per annum 1960–69, and −2.8 percent per annum 1970–79, American procurement unadjusted for intervintage technological progress falls −2.2 and −8.8 percent per annum respectively. Soviet procurement estimates are similarly downward biased.

8. The CIA's use of fixed vintage parametric dollar cost estimating relationships instead of variable vintage CERs (valued in constant prices) violates its congressional mandate. The CIA is charged with the responsibility of computing dollar cost estimates of Soviet weapons that are comparable with the dollar cost of newly procured American weapons. By failing to take intervintage technological progress into account the agency not only calculates low estimates but these estimates neither satisfy the ground rules established by Congress nor embody the meanings usually placed upon them (chapter 4, and postscript).

9. Strictly speaking, while the CIA's fixed vintage dollar parametric cost estimates violate the congressional mandate, there can be no assurance that Soviet intervintage technological progress can be inferred from American intervintage technological change. Given the highly publicized "scientific and technical revolution" in Soviet

FIGURE S1
Soviet and American Military Procurement, 1960–79 (Billions of 1978 Dollars)

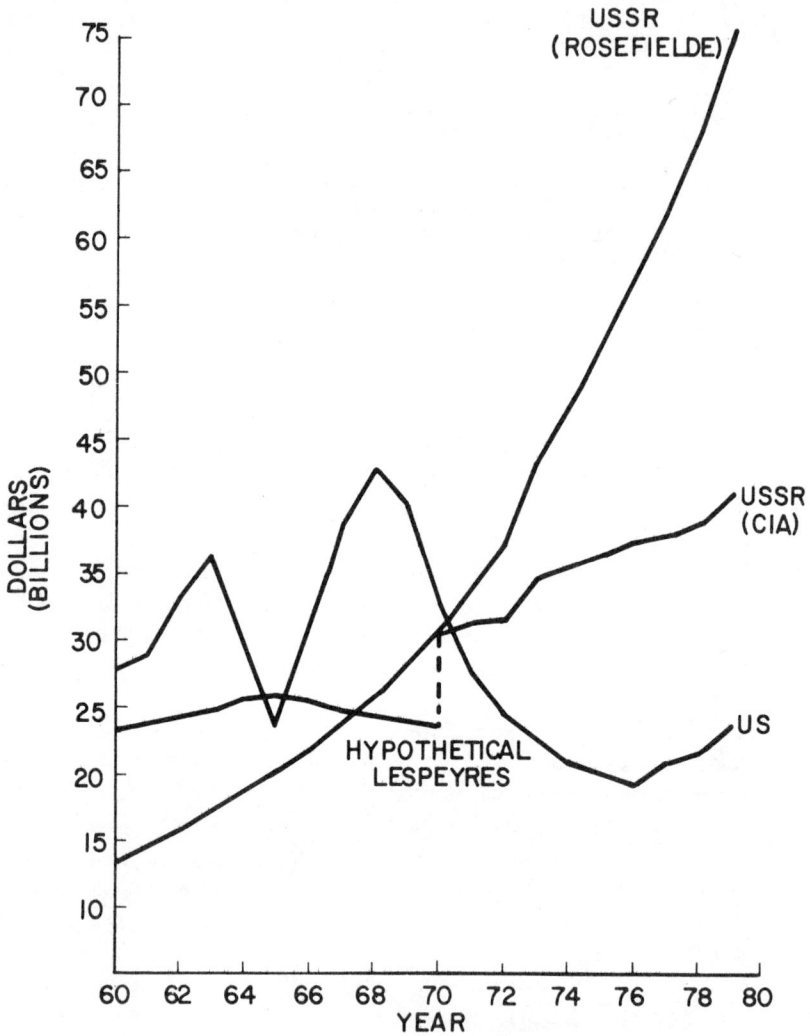

FIGURE S2
Soviet and American Military Procurement, 1960–79 (Billions of 1970 Rubles)

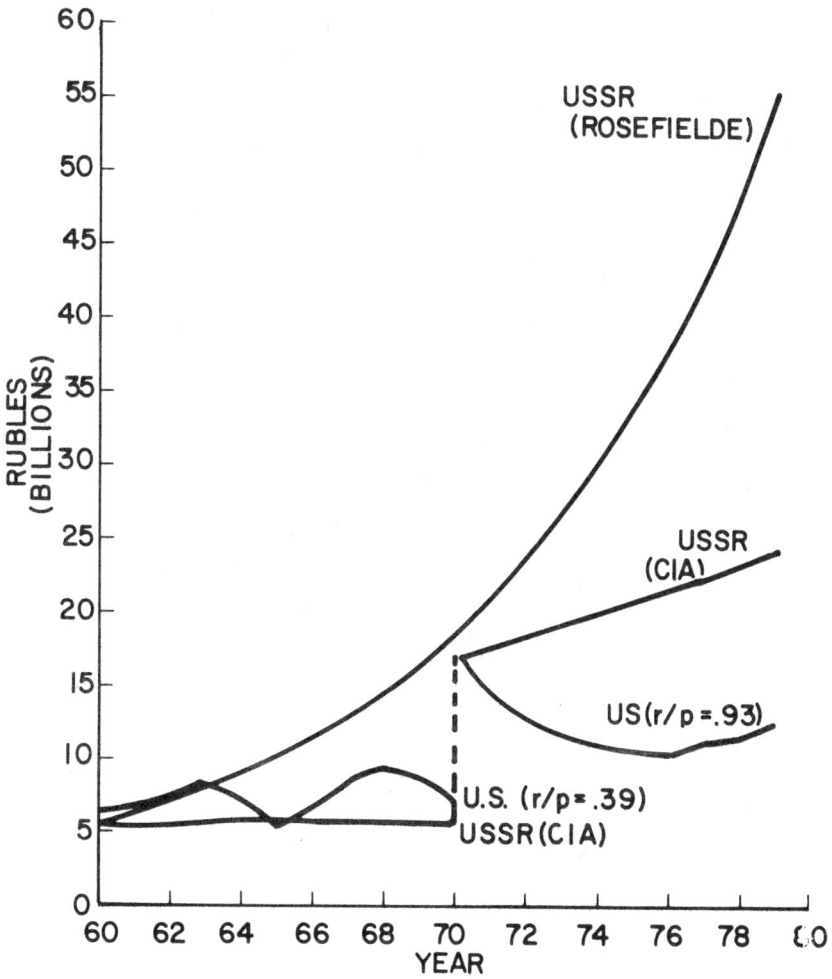

TABLE S3
Soviet and American Military Procurement, 1960–79: Fixed Vintage Versus Variable Vintage Parametric Estimates
(Billions of 1978 Dollars)

| | American | | Soviet | |
	Fixed Vintage Parametric CER	Actual	Fixed Vintage Parametric CER	Actual
1960	27.8	27.8	13.3	13.3
1961	27.9	28.7	13.6	14.5
1962	31.3	33.0	13.8	15.7
1963	33.1	36.2	14.1	17.1
1964	26.4	29.7	14.4	18.6
1965	20.4	23.6	14.7	20.2
1966	25.8	30.8	14.4	21.9
1967	31.4	38.6	14.1	23.8
1968	33.8	42.8	13.8	25.9
1969	30.7	40.1	13.6	28.2
1970	(24.3)	32.7	(13.3)	30.6
1971	26.1	27.7	31.4	34.1
1972	21.8	24.5	31.6	37.2
1973	19.1	22.7	34.5	43.3
1974	16.6	20.9	35.5	47.8
1975	14.9	20	36.4	52.5
1976	13.5	19.1	37.7	57.5
1977	13.9	20.9	37.7	62.3
1978	13.4	21.4	38.6	68.1
1979	14	23.6	41	75.8

Sources:
Column 1: Fixed vintage estimates are computed by adjusting actual U.S. procurement outlays (Column 2) for intervintage technological progress (see appendix 1):
1) $y_t^{F1960-69} = y_t^{A1960-69}/(1.03)^{t-1}$ t = 1,. . .,9
2) $y_t^{F1970-79} = y_t^{A1970-79}/(1.06)^{t-1}$ t = 1,. . .,9
Column 2: Table 13.2, column 7.
Column 3: Table 13.2, column 1. The subseries 1960–69 is the hypothetical CIA Paasche or Laspeyres dollar series adjusted with its ex-post ruble-dollar ratio for 1970. See the bracketed entry for 1970 in Table 13.2n, column 6.
Column 4: Table 13.2, column 5.

FIGURE S3A
American Procurement: Actual Cost and Fixed Vintage Cost
Estimates, 1960–79

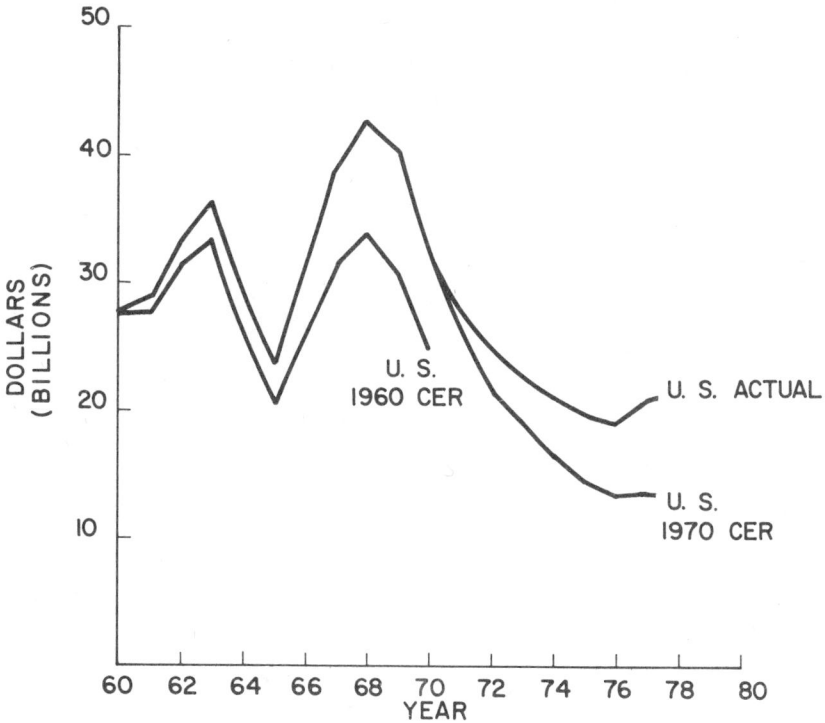

weapons technology and the possibilities for "catching up" latent in the relative backwardness of the Soviet economy, it could be surmised that Soviet intervintage technological progress is growing at least as fast as American intervintage technological progress (chapter 4).

10. This surmise is supported by the unclassified portions of a comprehensive classified six-volume DIA study on Soviet weapons technology (*U.S. and Soviet Weapon Systems Design Practice* (*U*), May, 1980); by the judgment of other competent intelligence analysts, including Leonard Sullivan (chapter 4 and appendix 1); and by the independent evaluation of foreign weapons analysts (see Royal United Services Institute and Brassey's *Defense Yearbook*, 1981).

11. The magnitude of Soviet intervintage technological progress can be estimated in rubles by utilizing the information obtained from the

FIGURE S3B
Soviet Procurement: Actual Cost and Fixed Vintage Cost Estimates,
1960–79

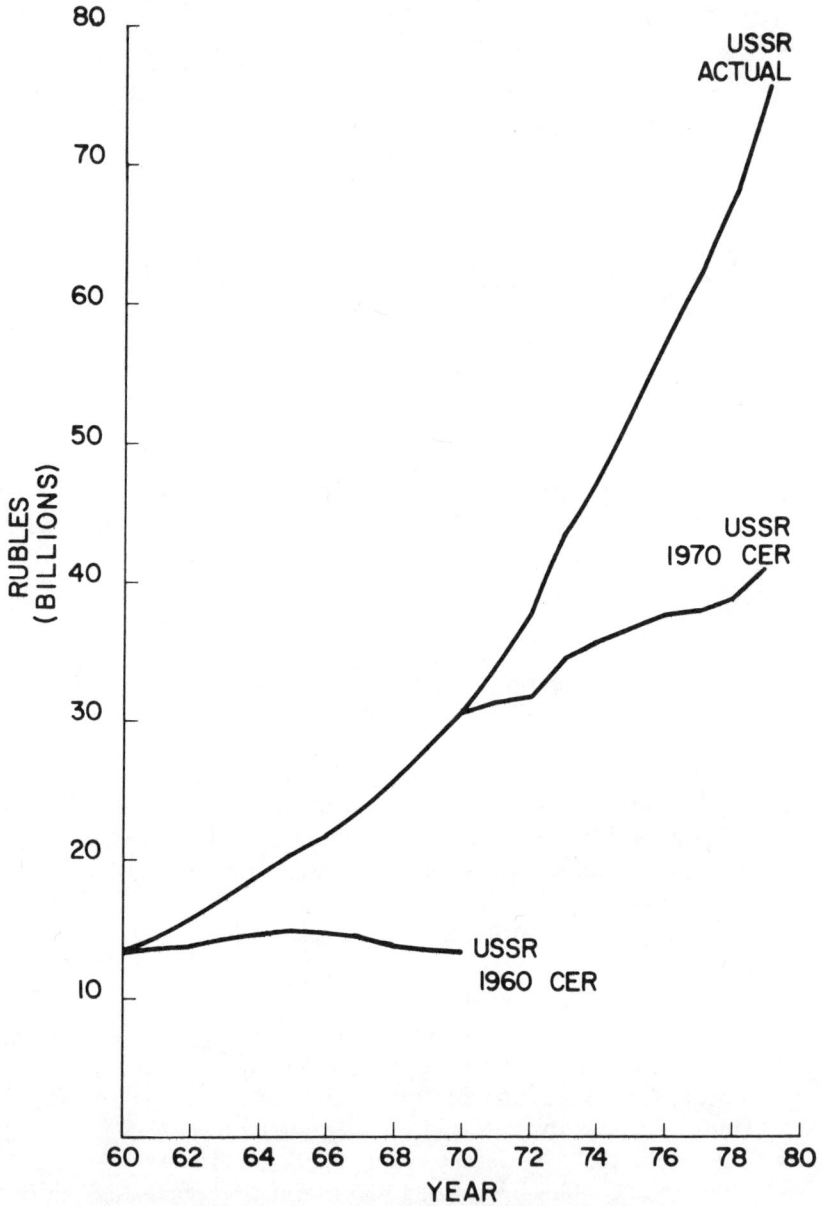

Soviet Ministry of Defense on the ruble cost of Soviet procurement in 1970. Accepting the CIA's postrevision estimate of the ruble rate of Soviet procurement growth, excluding intervintage technological progress (4 percent) from 1960 to 1970, as a reasonably accurate measure of the quantitative growth of Soviet weapons, intervintage technological progress can be computed as the difference between the rate implied by the information obtained from the Soviet Ministry of Defense and the growth of the agency's weapon count: 8.9 percent per annum (chapter 13).

12. This estimate—which exceeds the U.S. rate of intervintage technological progress, 1970–79, by nearly half unadjusted for index number relativity (the dollar differential is negligible, 6.3 versus 6 percent)—is supported by the fact that the statistics obtained from the Soviet Ministry of Defense were independently estimated by William Lee using the "residual method" as early as 1974, and were reconfirmed by the agency's own subsequent "residual method" calculations (chapter 12). In addition, DIA estimates that Soviet military machine building grew 12 percent per annum, 1965–78.

13. Convincing proof that the estimates of Soviet procurement reported in this study are reliable is also provided by analyzing the internal consistency of the diverse ruble and dollar series found in the text. The CIA's series contain 12 major internal contradictions. These contradictions are chronicled in chapter 18. It is then demonstrated that once intervintage technological progress is taken into account all the internal inconsistencies in the agency's series are resolved.

14. The CIA has just acknowledged that its ruble estimate of Soviet arms expenditures for *1980* calculated with the residual method coincides with Lee's and exceeds its published direct cost estimate by approximately 140 percent, replicating the discrepancy that occurred in 1970 and confirming the estimates computed in this study (chapter 13). [N.B. As in the case of the *1970* ruble cost underestimate, the agency attributes the present discrepancy to hidden inflation, even though it is admitted that no ruble weapon prices have been acquired since the early 1970s.]

If these 14 points, which support the empirical estimates of Soviet procurement presented in this volume, are deemed to adequately sustain the contention that the CIA's estimates of the size, growth, and momentum of the Soviet arms buildup are significantly understated, then the rest of the conclusions drawn under headings B-D regarding Soviet arms superiority, American national security analysis, and the CIA's false approach to scientific hypothesis testing and evaluation follow straightforwardly. The reader is invited to verify this by perusing chapters 16–19. Readers interested in learning how the CIA's existing methodology can be reformed should consult the postscript where it is shown that reliable estimates of Soviet procurement expenditure satisfying Congress's mandate that American and Soviet dollar procurement estimates be directly comparable can be readily computed with variable vintage American parametric cost estimating relationships available at the material acquisition departments of the U.S. Navy, Army, and Air Force.

Reservations

The estimates of Soviet procurement computed in this study and the policy inferences they sustain are vulnerable in complex ways to three sorts of uncertainties:

1. Uncertainty about the behavior of the CIA's classified current dollar value estimates of Soviet procurement 1960–74, and the associated real Paasche and real Laspeyres dollar series the agency maintains it has never computed (see chapter 4, section IX).
2. Uncertainty about the exact nature of the qualitative improvements in all weapons systems that have been lumped by the author under the rubric of "intervintage technological progress."
3. Uncertainty about the ruble weapon prices covertly obtained in 1968–73 that the agency still asserts conclusively confirm its "hidden inflation" hypothesis.

The first class of uncertainty primarily affects the credibility of the CIA's direct dollar costing effort during the sixties. Having scrutinized the internal consistency of the pertinent data, and having studied in a limited way classified information on "Sovietization" factors, parametric models, and learning curve adjustments for this period, I cannot rule out the possibility that the agency's current value estimates are so incommensurable that they cannot be employed to reliably measure the level and trend of real Soviet procurement.

The second class of uncertainty concerns the identification of the specific factors which explain why the documented DOD acquisition costs exceed the CIA's "pre-Sovietized" parametric estimates (equivalently defined) both before and after learning curve phenomena are taken into consideration. It is conceivable that some of the disparity between documented DOD acquisition costs and the CIA's "pre-Sovietized" parametric estimates is explicable in conceptual terms akin to index number relativity or other yet undetermined causes.

Finally, the possibility cannot be completely ruled out that the 236 discrepancy between the agency's pre- and postrevision ruble procurement estimates for 1970 is explained by "hidden inflation." New evidence could surface, or the CIA might succeed where it has hithertofore failed in confirming its hypothesis with the data already at its disposal.

Under the most adverse circumstances I can foresee, uncertainties 1 and 2 might significantly qualify but should not reverse the fundamental trends delineated in this study. Uncertainty 3 could in principle invalidate my central thesis, but this contingency appears remote at the moment.

Introduction

Most Western assessments of the Soviet arms buildup depend critically on the accuracy of the CIA's direct cost estimates of Soviet arms expenditures. These estimates not only measure the cost of Soviet defense programs, they also provide essential information on the real rate of Soviet procurement growth, serving in this way as a summary indicator of the aggregate annual improvement in the quantity and quality of Soviet weaponry.

Until quite recently, confidence in the reliability of the CIA's direct cost estimates and by extension our perception of the real dimension of the Soviet arms buildup was very high. This confidence reflected the agency's own appraisal of the quality of its work, a judgment broadly supported in the national security community. New information obtained from covert sources in 1975 strongly disconfirmed this evaluation, compelling the agency to abruptly revise its estimates of Soviet procurement for 1970 from 5.5 to 18.5 billion rubles, and its estimate of total defense spending from 25 to 50 billion rubles.

These revisions redressed the specific inconsistency between the agency's ruble estimates of Soviet defense expenditures and the actual values as they appeared on the books of the Soviet Ministry of Defense, but they also raised serious doubts about the adequacy of the CIA's direct costing effort for the entire period from 1960 to 1980. Was the discrepancy between the agency's estimates for 1970 and the true values fortuitous, or did it reflect fundamental deficiencies inherent in direct costing? If fundamental deficiencies existed were they artifacts of the methodology, or were they attributable to other factors such as inadequate data, inept calculation, or discretionary manipulation?

This book attempts to assess these important issues both to judge the merit of the CIA's direct costing effort and to determine the probable magnitude of the Soviet arms buildup. The assessment is carried out in six parts. Part I reviews the history of the CIA's direct costing effort, explicates the methodology, analyzes the inconsistencies between the agency's published and unpublished procurement series, identifies and proves the existence of a fundamental error in the specification of the CIA's parametric cost estimating equations, evaluates the potential sig-

nificance of the discovery that actual ruble outlays on Soviet procurement were 236 percent higher than the agency estimated for 1970, and
explains why ruble and dollar estimates of Soviet growth should not
diverge as greatly from one another as they did from 1929 to 1955. Part
II scrutinizes the theoretical and empirical research on the subject of
hidden inflation in order to assess what proportion of the 236 percent
discrepancy between actual Soviet procurement outlays in 1970 and the
CIA's estimate should be attributed to price phenomena. This analysis
demonstrates that virtually no credible empirical evidence exists supporting the hypothesis that a significant portion of the observed discrepancy is explained by hidden inflation.

Part III utilizes the finding in part I that the CIA's parametric cost
estimating equations do not take account of intervintage technological
progress and the finding in part II that hidden inflation at most explains
only a small portion of the 236 percent discrepancy between the agency's
pre- and postrevision estimates of Soviet procurement to compute conceptually sound ruble and dollar estimates of Soviet arms procurement
adjusted for intervintage technological progress. These series are then
employed to study the level and trend of the Soviet procurement burden
from 1960 to 1979 and forecast cumulative Soviet procurement outlays
in the eighties. Part IV builds on this foundation by demonstrating that
strong inferences can be drawn about the potential military utility of
Soviet weapons, and Soviet arms superiority merely by assuming ordinal
transitivity.

Part V places these results in a coherent national security perspective
identifying those theories of Soviet behavior confirmed by the adjusted
series, and those theories that are disconfirmed. Part VI completes the
analysis by simultaneously demonstrating that the CIA has failed to
systematically test the theorems and subordinate hypotheses sustaining
its methodology, and by showing that if intervintage technological progress is taken into account all the major inconsistencies in its ruble and
dollar series are eliminated. These demonstrations are then supplemented with an assessment of how the agency actually goes about determining its published estimates of Soviet procurement and how Soviet
counterintelligence has exploited the CIA's procurement underestimates. Finally, a simple method for calculating reliable estimates of
Soviet procurement with the Defense Department's variable vintage
parametric cost estimating equations is elaborated in the postscript.

The fundamental conclusion that emerges from this comprehensive
investigation is that the Soviet Union has managed to conduct a massive
arms buildup during the last twenty years that enabled it to achieve arms
superiority over the United States without the CIA's discerning either

its scope or its momentum. This finding has profound implications for American national security policy in the eighties, but does not entail a uniquely optimal set of American national security policy responses. The issue of optimal American national security policy in the eighties of course is immensely important, but it is far too complex a matter to be dealt with in the confines of the present study. The task of determining how the United States should meet the burgeoning Soviet military challenge is left as a problem for other scholars to resolve.

Part I

DIRECT COSTING

CHAPTER 1

The Origins of the Soviet Arms Procurement Cost Estimating Controversy

The origin of the present controversy over the size, growth, and momentum of the Soviet arms buildup goes back a quarter of a century to the mid-fifties when the Central Intelligence Agency began experimenting with a novel cost estimating methodology. This technique, dubbed the direct cost estimating method, was predicated on the supposition that newly produced Soviet weapons could be reliably counted with national technical means, valued in constant dollars (and/or rubles), and aggregated to obtain value estimates which could be meaningfully compared with U.S. procurement outlays, and used to compute the weapons component of the Soviet defense burden.

The early history of the CIA's experience with direct costing is classified, and difficult to reconstruct. Available evidence indicates, however, that the agency's confidence in direct costing increased gradually during the sixties, and that by 1970 the technique had completely displaced its rivals.[1]

The CIA's current dollar estimates of Soviet military procurement calculated during the sixties and early seventies which governed its perception of the real rate of weapons growth from 1960 to 1973 have never been published, and remain highly classified. Its ruble estimates however have been recently released and are illustrated in Figure 1.1.[2] They exhibit no growth from 1960 to 1970 measured point to point, increasing thereafter from 5.5 to 5.8 billion rubles (measured in prerevision 1970 prices).[3] For the full period 1960–73, Soviet procurement appears to grow only .6 percent per annum.

These estimates, derived as they were with a methodology the agency held in high esteem, indicate that the CIA had good objective reasons

31

FIGURE 1.1
Unpublished Prerevision CIA Ruble Estimates of Soviet Procurement
Valued in 1970 Prices

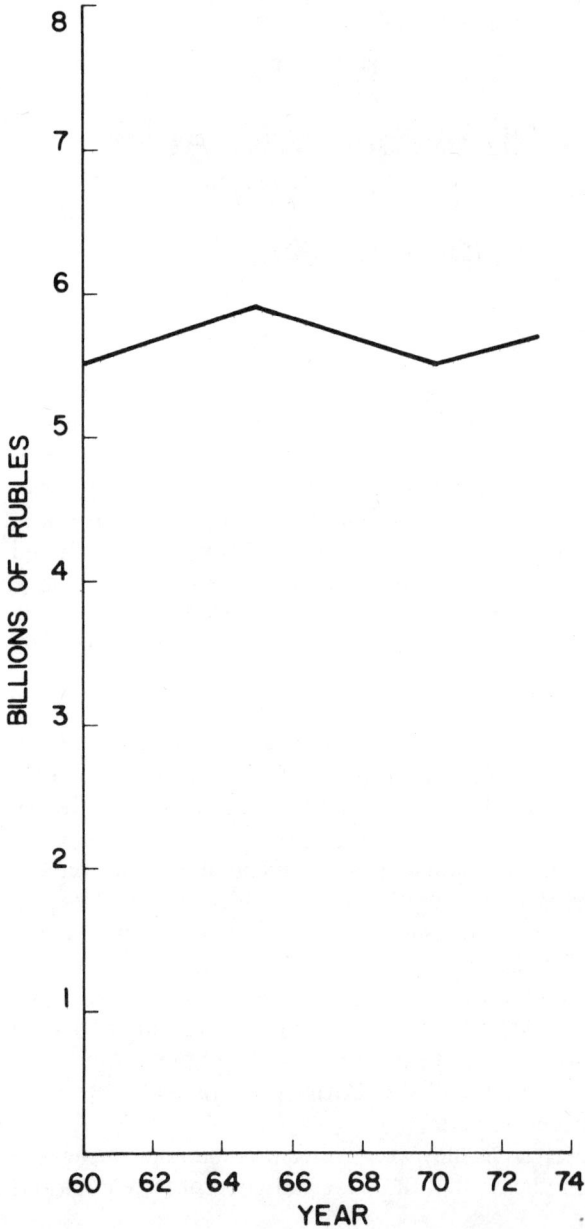

for believing that the Soviet Union had adopted a policy of arms restraint during the sixties and early seventies; and for concluding that the Soviets were neither attempting to build up their arsenal, nor actively seeking to achieve arms superiority. However, not all available evidence at the time pointed in this direction. Procurement estimates calculated with the residual method indicated that Soviet arms production was growing more than 10 percent per annum,[4] a rate consistent with the growth of total defense outlays reported in the official defense budget, which rose from 9.3 billion rubles in 1960 to 17.9 billion rubles in 1970, or at 6.8 percent per annum.[5]

Although, in the agency's eyes the intrinsic superiority of the direct costing methodology countervailed the dubious results obtained with the residual method, or the trend displayed by the official Soviet defense budget, the tension between these disparate indicators was intensified in the late sixties and early seventies by covertly acquired data that demonstrated that Soviet weapons were much more expensive than had been previously thought. This covert information was ambiguous and lent itself to a variety of interpretations. It could have implied that the number of components in Soviet weapon systems were increasing, that Soviet weapons were improving qualitatively, or that production costs were being affected by inflation which somehow was not reflected in the Soviet machine-building and metalworking price index.

These alternative explanations no doubt were heatedly debated within the agency. That they caused considerable consternation is plainly evidenced by the contradictory testimony given to the Joint Economic Committee of Congress by CIA director Colby in 1974.[6] According to Colby Soviet procurement expenditures valued in constant prerevision 1970 rubles grew during the sixties at the same rate as all Soviet defense expenditures, 4 percent per annum. This assertion, however, is strikingly contradicted elsewhere in his testimony where it is claimed that procurement expenditures in 1960 and 1970 were virtually the same, 5.5 billion rubles in constant 1970 prices.[7] Clearly, real Soviet procurement valued in constant ruble prices could not grow at 4 percent and remain unchanged at the same time.

Although Colby's testimony has now been repudiated in response to my criticisms,[8] it is easy to see in retrospect that his error was not fortuitous. It reflected a profound division of opinion within the agency. The agency's own direct ruble cost estimates showed that Soviet procurement growth was zero in the sixties, whether valued in 1955 or prerevision 1970 prices.[9] The cost data collected covertly in the late sixties and early seventies suggested a much higher rate of growth, however. The schism created by these disparate perceptions must have been very great because the evidence in the agency's possession was both contestable and portentous. The data were contestable partly for the conceptual reasons mentioned above, and partly because they implied rates of real procurement growth far in excess of the 4 percent suggested in Colby's testimony.[10] If the 4 percent figure was actually derived with direct cost methods in 1973, that estimate must have been informal because it received no official sanction.[11] As a consequence those who doubted the authenticity of the cost data could criticize the insurgents for drawing inferences from information that actually implied rates of Soviet procurement growth thought at the time to be completely implausible.

The cost data were portentous for precisely the reason they were believed to be implausible. If Soviet procurement were really growing substantially faster than 4 percent since 1960, then everything thought to be known about Soviet defense expenditures and Soviet intentions would be called into question. Whereas it was formerly believed that the Soviets had exhibited admirable self-restraint for the sake of detente, SALT I, and world peace, the possibility emerged that they had done no such thing. Whereas it was firmly believed that the direct cost estimating method provided a reliable technique for measuring Soviet procurement growth, the possibility had to be faced that the method failed even to correctly determine the direction of the trend.

The situation circa 1973 therefore was fluid, and riven with contradiction. CIA estimates of total Soviet defense expenditures for 1970 were almost 40 percent higher than the figure stated officially by the Soviets,[12] but the agency's estimate of the growth of aggregate Soviet defense spending from 1960 to 1970 was 40 percent less than the rate reported in the Soviet defense budget.[13] The official CIA direct cost estimate of Soviet procurement growth during the sixties was zero. But new evidence, not yet formally validated by the direct costing method, suggested that Soviet procurement had been growing at least 4 percent per annum and perhaps faster. If the latter view were confirmed it would not only cast doubt on the reliability of the direct cost method, but it would indicate that the Soviets were deliberately manipulating their reported defense expenditures—which were virtually unchanged from 1969 to 1973 and have remained unchanged ever since.[14]

To the best of my knowledge no coherent attempt was ever made by the agency to come to terms systematically with these contradictions. Partial explanations, however, were tentatively put forward to rationalize two sensitive political issues. High defense department officials (who did not know that the CIA's prerevision real procurement series grew only .6 percent per annum from 1960 to 1973) were bothered by the disparity between the arms growth they perceived in physical terms (confirmed subsequently by the CIA's published dollar procurement growth rate) and the impression conveyed both by the CIA (1960–70) and the official Soviet defense budget (1969–73) which implied that Soviet procurement growth in *current* ruble prices was zero. How, it was asked, could aggregate defense expenditures be constant (1969–73), as indicated by the Soviet defense budget, and how could the procurement share be declining, as shown in Colby's testimony (from 40 percent to 20 percent, 1960–70), if procurement were increasing? The answer widely circulated in the early seventies was that the Soviet military machine-building sector was hyperproductive. Because the defense sector had priority access to the best resources, personnel, and technology, unit production costs were declining rapidly. As a consequence, while real procurement was rising, total procurement costs were not. The putative inconsistency therefore was not a real one; it was an illusion.[15]

This explanation gained broad currency at the time because the facts needed to evaluate its merit were not generally known. Few knew that prerevision 1970 prices were really cosmetically adjusted 1955 prices.[16] Fewer still understood that the real ruble Laspeyres growth rate valued in 1955 prices was zero. This made it easy, if nonetheless unpalatable, to accept the authority of the CIA which stated that the nominal costs of Soviet weapons were falling.

The other issue that demanded an answer was why the CIA believed that estimates of Soviet procurement growth in excess of 4 percent per annum were unthinkable when covert cost data indicated otherwise. The reason put forward was illuminating. Soviet procurement costs, it was contended, were rising due to hidden inflation.[17] The Soviet machine-building and metalworking sector was not hyperproductive, it was hypoproductive, and as a result, weapon prices paid by the Ministry of Defense were rising, not falling! Although this explanation of Soviet arms price behavior flatly contradicted the first rationale no attempt was ever made to reconcile the inconsistency.

Had an informant not arrived on the scene in 1975 who had personally inspected the expenditure data on the books of the Soviet Ministry of Defense,[18] the standoff within the agency between the contending factions would probably remain unresolved today.[19] Those who believed it unreasonable to suppose that Soviet procurement could significantly exceed levels supportable by the official defense budget would undoubtedly continue to dispute the validity of covert cost data, while those who had confidence in the cost data would have found it politically inexpedient to challenge the official position based on direct cost estimates in constant 1955 and 1970 prerevision ruble prices.[20]

Be this as it may, the informant did arrive, followed shortly thereafter by the discovery that weapon procurement costs were not included in the official Soviet defense budget after all. They were paid for out of the fund for the national economy.

The figures reported by the informant were entirely out of proportion to anything previously supposed. Instead of total defense spending for 1970 being 17.9 billion rubles as officially claimed, or 25 billion rubles as estimated by the CIA, it was 50 billion rubles.[21] Instead of procurement being 5.5 billion rubles, as stipulated in Colby's testimony, or 8.1 billion rubles, as implied by prior covert cost data,[22] it was 18.5 billion rubles. The conclusion seemed inescapable. Sometime in the early sixties the Soviets decided to embark on a massive arms buildup, increasing real procurement expenditures 12.9 percent per annum,[23] and concealing their intentions by publishing misleading information on their defense expenditures which fortuitously corresponded with agency's secret direct cost estimate of real Soviet procurement growth.

The CIA, however, found an escape. In May 1976 the agency published *Estimated Soviet Defense Spending in Rubles, 1970–1975* in which it publicly admitted that Soviet defense expenditures were double those previously reported in Colby's testimony. But it was unequivocally asserted that this change had no significant effect on the CIA's perception of real Soviet procurement growth:

> The revised estimate of the ruble costs of Soviet defense has had a major effect on some important intelligence judgments but not others. Specifically, because the changes are largely the result of estimates of higher ruble prices rather than discovery of larger programs, the revised estimate:
>
> —Does not affect our appraisal of the size or capabilities of Soviet military forces. Such estimates are based mainly on direct evidence.[24]

Did the agency therefore acknowledge that their direct cost estimate of Soviet procurement growth had been close to zero from 1960 to 1973? The CIA was more circumspect than that.

Instead of analyzing the question of procurement directly the agency focused on total defense expenditures. These expenditures, it asserted, grew 4 percent per annum from 1970 to 1975, just as Colby's had from 1960 to 1970, so "the revised estimate" was unaffected by the new information.[25] Only on page 13 in the section on resource analysis does the CIA's estimate of real procurement growth emerge. It is stated there that "investment, operating and RDT & E" "has accounted for the same portion of the total" since 1970, implying that procurement grew at the same rate as the rest of Soviet defense expenditures—4 percent per annum![26]

By burying its procurement revision inconspicuously in the text and confining the time frame to the period 1970–75, the CIA very cleverly and effectively contrived to bury the contradictions of the past. Completely ignored is the fact that the agency's direct costing method indicated that real Soviet procurement did not grow at all during the sixties and crept upwards at about 1 percent per annum during the period 1970–73 valued in prerevision 1970 prices. This is an omission of some moment. Not only did it conceal the real situation, but it allowed the agency to establish the continuity of its estimates with Colby's testimony without having to acknowledge: that Colby's testimony was internally inconsistent, that the direct costing methodology was unreliable, that real Soviet procurement growth could be vastly greater than it was willing to publicly admit,[27] and that the underestimate of 1970 was apt to recur, as it has in 1980.[28]

Notes

1. The principal alternative was the residual method. See William Lee (1977a).
2. Private letter from Donald Swain, deputy chief for analysis, Military-Economic Analysis Center, Office of Strategic Research, dated August 9, 1979, confirming discussions held at the U.S. Naval Postgraduate School, August 3, 1979 with Swain, Donald Burton, chief for analysis, MEAC, and Patrick Parker, former principal deputy assistant secretary of defense for intelligence. On October 24, 1980 I wrote Swain again to confirm his letter of August 9, 1979 because Abraham Becker asserted at the Air Force conference "The Soviet Union: What Lies Ahead?" Reston, Virginia, September 26, 1980 that Swain had repudiated the figures cited in the text. James Steiner, chief, Economic Implications Branch, OSR/MEAC, responding for Swain in a letter dated November 10, 1980 neither affirmed nor denied the position taken by Swain in the August 1979 letter, but stated somewhat ambiguously that because the agency has not made an updated estimate of Soviet defense spending in the sixties valued in prerevision prices since 1972, the old series is outdated and not directly comparable to Swain's estimate of 1960–70 valued in postrevision 1970 prices. This interpretation, however, is contradicted by the testimony given in *Estimated Soviet Defense Spending in Rubles, 1970–1975*, p. 1, where it is asserted that the discovery of new programs has had only minor effect on the agency's calculations.

    Other interpretations of Steiner's comments, however, are possible. The full text of his letter is: "The following is in response to your letter to Derk Swain dated 24 October. CIA has not made an estimate of Soviet defense spending in pre-1970 ruble prices since 1972. Further, because we review and revise the entire data base and its structure on an annual basis, the pre-1972 estimates are neither consistent nor comparable to today's estimate (in 1970 prices). In brief, we do not have an estimate of Soviet defense spending in pre-1970 prices." Also note that Swain has asserted that the prerevision series was calculated through early 1974, not 1972.
3. Prerevision 1970 ruble prices were computed by revising 1955 prices upward across the board 6 percent to make allowance for the change in the Soviet

industrial price level brought about by the price reform of 1966–67. According to Swain the core 1955 price set was supplemented with updated information in the early sixties so that the underlying data can best be thought of as characterizing Soviet weapon prices circa 1960, often designated in the text as 1955/60 prices.

4. Lee (1977a).
5. *Narodnoe Khoziaistvo, 1971*, p. 724,
$$\dot{q} = 100\,[(1.92)^{1/10} - 1] = 6.76 \text{ percent.}$$
6. *Allocation of Resources in the Soviet Union and China (1974)*.
7. According to testimony provided by CIA director William Colby, Soviet procurement in 1970 was roughly 20 percent of total Soviet defense expenditures, or 5 billion rubles. See *Allocation of Resources in the Soviet Union and China (1974)*, pp. 68–69. Donald Burton, chief of the Military-Economic Analysis Center, Office of Strategic Research, informs me in a letter dated February 21, 1979 that Colby's testimony was in error. The prices underlying the figures he reported pertained to 1955. Adjusting Colby's estimate for this factor and allowing for some small error puts the estimate for 1970 at approximately 5.5 billion rubles. This figure is the same as Colby's estimate for 1960, a fact confirmed by Swain. It follows from this that nominal procurement growth from 1960 to 1970 was
$$\dot{g} = 100\,[(1.06)^{1/10} - 1] = .58 \text{ percent.}$$
8. Swain, personal correspondence (op. cit.).
9. Ibid.
10. Burton, personal correspondence (op. cit.). The CIA has vigorously denied my suggestion that the agency would not have revised its estimates as it did if the informant who saw the statistics on the books of the Soviet Ministry Defense had not appeared. If Burton is correct the data at the agency's disposal already indicated that Soviet procurement circa 1970 was in a range between 15.3 and 18.7 billion rubles. Since the CIA's estimate for Soviet procurement in 1960 was roughly 5.5 billion rubles, it would have been easy to suppose that during the sixties Soviet procurement had grown far faster than 4 percent.
11. Swain has indicated that the CIA ceased using the prerevision data at the beginning of 1974. Swain, op. cit.
12. The official Soviet figure was 17.9 billion rubles in 1970 prices. The CIA estimate valued in their prerevision prices was 25 billion rubles. See *Allocation of Resources in the Soviet Union and China (1974)*.
13. Ibid. The CIA estimated that total Soviet defense expenditures grew 4 percent during the sixties. The Soviets stated that it had grown 6.8 percent.
14. *Narodnoe Khoziaistvo, 1977*, p. 559.
15. *Economic Impact of Soviet Military Spending*, ER-IR-75-3, April 1974, pp. 6, 12. I have discussed this theory with Stephen Enke, Patrick Parker, and a host of other knowledgeable defense department officials. They all confirm its currency. Enke attributed the theory to Rush Greenslade, chief of the Office of Economic Research of the CIA. I was never able to confirm this although I was told it was so by others. I discussed the subject briefly with Greenslade at the First World Conference on Slavic Studies at Banff, Canada in 1974. He supported the hypothesis, but did not claim its authorship.
16. See note 3.
17. The concept of hidden inflation predates the present controversy. The phenomenon was documented by Soviet scholars before the Second World War

when it was rampant. Many American scholars have commented on it in the postwar period. A revival of interest in the subject became manifest in the early seventies. See Rush Greenslade, "Industrial Production Statistics in the USSR," in Treml and Hardt, eds., *Soviet Economic Statistics*, and Abraham Becker (1974).

18. "Assessing the Soviet Economy," (1977), p. 97; *Allocation of Resources in the Soviet Union and China—1976*, p. 82; Joseph Alsop (1977), pp. 7–21.

19. Burton and Swain vehemently deny this. Their opinion should be given considerable weight. However, I personally remain skeptical. My impression is that the political pressures on the CIA to keep their estimates low are very strong. Cf. Franklyn Holzman (1980a).

20. Perhaps those who participated directly in these discussions will soon be stimulated to clarify the record and correct any unintentional distortions that may blemish my account.

21. *Estimated Soviet Defense Spending in Rubles, 1970–1975*, p. 1.

22. $[(1.04)^{10}]\, 5.5 = 8.1$ billion rubles.

23. $\Sigma r_{70}^* q_{70} / \Sigma r_{55} q_{70} = 18.5/5.5.\ \dot{g} = 100\,[(3.36)^{1/10} - 1] = 12.9$ percent. Cf. *Soviet Military Power*, DOD, September 1981.

24. *Estimated Soviet Defense Spending in Rubles, 1970–1975*, p. 1. Cf. note 6.

25. Swain indicates that the CIA switched to some form of revised 1970 prices in 1974. Swain, op. cit.

26. *Estimated Soviet Defense Spending in Rubles, 1970–1975*.

27. Abraham Becker, a specialist on Soviet military expenditures estimates, downplays the significance of the new information, and the agency's interpretation of its meaning in *CIA Estimates of Soviet Military Expenditure* (1980). Becker contends that the agency's estimates and explanations are correct, but this cannot be effectively conveyed to the public because of the "security screen imposed by the intelligence community." As a consequence he argues that estimates made by outsiders are given more weight than they should and laments that "technical complexity also means that an honest effort to evaluate competing claims by experts requires painstaking examination of sources and methods. Unfortunately, this does not take place" (p. 4).

To prove his point that the skepticism prompted by the 1976 revelations is unwarranted he then provides a series of examples demonstrating that all such criticism is politically motivated. "Participants in the public debate on Soviet military expenditure have often taken explicit and controversial positions on the reality of the Soviet 'threat' and the desirability of increased U.S. defense spending, so that conceptual and methodological issues have seemed incidental to the main bout. In the early 1970s the principal concern with the validity of CIA procedures came from those who were convinced that the estimates were too low" (p. 5). "The basic criticism from the other end of the spectrum has been that estimates of Soviet military outlays are used as political instruments by what Daniel Yergin has called the 'arms coalition' " (p. 6). "The differences in outlook from which the estimates of Soviet military expenditure are viewed were sharply established by the varying reaction to the CIA's 1976 announcement. To 'hawkish' critics, this was not only confirmation that they were correct all along, but fresh confirmation of the Soviet dedication to drive for military superiority over the United States. To Representative Les Aspin, on the other hand, the revised figure showed that 'it will be much more difficult for [the Soviets] to expand much further without pushing their people to the wall.' " (p. 6). Apparently, Becker believes that the motives of CIA (and MEAP) critics demonstrate that the agency's estimates are sound.

28. At Norbert Michaux's Price Methodologies Working Group, CIA Conference on Price Change in the Soviet Defense Sector, Northern Virginia, December 8, 1981, Donald Swain acknowledged that the CIA's residual method estimate of Soviet defense spending in 1980 corresponded closely with William Lee's, that the burden of defense calculated with the residual method was approximately 20 percent of Soviet GNP, and that the residual method estimate of military procurement exceeded the agency's direct cost estimate by nearly 140 percent. This disclosure does not mean that the CIA has rejected its direct cost estimate for 1980 calculated in constant 1970 ruble prices in favor of its residual estimate. The agency still believes that real Soviet military procurement grew 4 percent per annum 1970–80, not 12.9 percent per annum. This belief does not extend to current value estimates. The CIA appears to be moving toward the position that the residual estimates provide a reasonable impression of nominal growth, including hidden inflation, while the direct cost estimates accurately measure real growth. If this assessment is correct, the agency should announce shortly that the burden of Soviet defense in 1982 ruble prices is in the neighborhood of 20 percent.

CHAPTER 2

The Anomalous Behavior of the CIA's Indices of Soviet Procurement Growth, 1960–70

The CIA's assertion that neither improvements in the quality of Soviet weapons, nor the discovery of new arms programs explains the discrepancy between its prerevision 1970 estimate of Soviet procurement and the actual value obtained covertly from the Soviet Ministry of Defense can be evaluated by identifying and testing the latent implications of its hidden inflation theory. This can be accomplished by noting that hidden inflation according to the agency's calculations does not merely entail a change in the ruble price level, but affects the measured rate of procurement growth. Figure 2.1 illustrates this distinction. The total discrepancy between the agency's prerevision estimate of Soviet procurement, and the actual value obtained from the Soviet Ministry of Defense is the vertical distance AC. CIA calculations utilizing the new price information acquired covertly in the late sixties and early seventies imply that 52 percent of this distance, the line segment AB, is imputable to a 109 percent increase in the price level 1955/60–70, and 48 percent to the effect relative price changes have on the measured rate of growth (the line segment BC).

The analytic merit of the first attribution depends on whether the new price data refer to money price inflation or reflect the real cost of qualitative improvements in Soviet weapons systems during the sixties. This is an empirical matter which will be thoroughly investigated in part II. The validity of the agency's assertion that 48 percent of the discrepancy is explained by the effect late year price relatives have on the measured rate of growth can be appraised more directly.

As is widely understood physical output series valued in late year prices almost invariably grow more slowly than outputs valued in early year prices.[1] The CIA's procurement series displayed in Figure 2.1 constitute a rare exception to this rule. Instead of its Laspeyres index valued in 1955/60 prerevision prices increasing more rapidly than its Paasche index, the reverse relationship prevails with the prerevision series growing .6 percent per annum from 1960 to 1973, and the Paasche series growing 4 percent per annum. Behavior of this sort is manifestly implausible and raises fundamental questions about the internal consistency of the agency's series.

The issue of internal consistency posed by the Laspeyres-Paasche relative growth rate reversal can be probed by expanding the analytic framework to encompass all the CIA's procurement series, including its published dollar estimates. If no other anomalies are uncovered, then the extraordinary behavior of the agency's postrevision ruble procurement series may be an exception that proves the rule. If additional inconsistencies do emerge, however, it can safely be concluded that 48 percent of the discrepancy between the agency's estimate of Soviet procurement and the actual values should be imputed to aberrations in the CIA's data, rather than to exotic relative price effects.

Table 2.1 presents the agency's unclassified estimates of Soviet procurement growth.[2] As is easily seen, not only is the expected ruble Laspeyres-ruble Paasche ordering reversed, but the dollar-weighted Paasche rate of growth inexplicably exceeds the ruble Laspeyres rate, 1960–70 and 1970–75.[3] Instead of observing the normal growth rate rank order:

ruble Laspeyres > ruble Paasche > dollar Paasche

transitivity runs in the opposite direction:[4]

ruble Paasche > dollar Paasche > ruble Laspeyres

I. The Common Basis[5]

For those unfamiliar with the rudiments of index number relativity theory, the extreme perversity of this ordering can be brought out by recognizing that all the CIA's direct cost estimates have a common basis. They rely on the same physical output series and employ prices linked to the agency's dollar price series. The output data are compiled using a "building bloc" approach. Individual weapons and weapon systems are classified according to a standard nomenclature and counted. They are then valued in dollars, aggregated, and indexed. Conventional Laspeyres and Paasche indices are employed.

FIGURE 2.1
CIA Ruble Estimates of Soviet Procurement Valued in Pre- and
Postrevision 1970 Prices

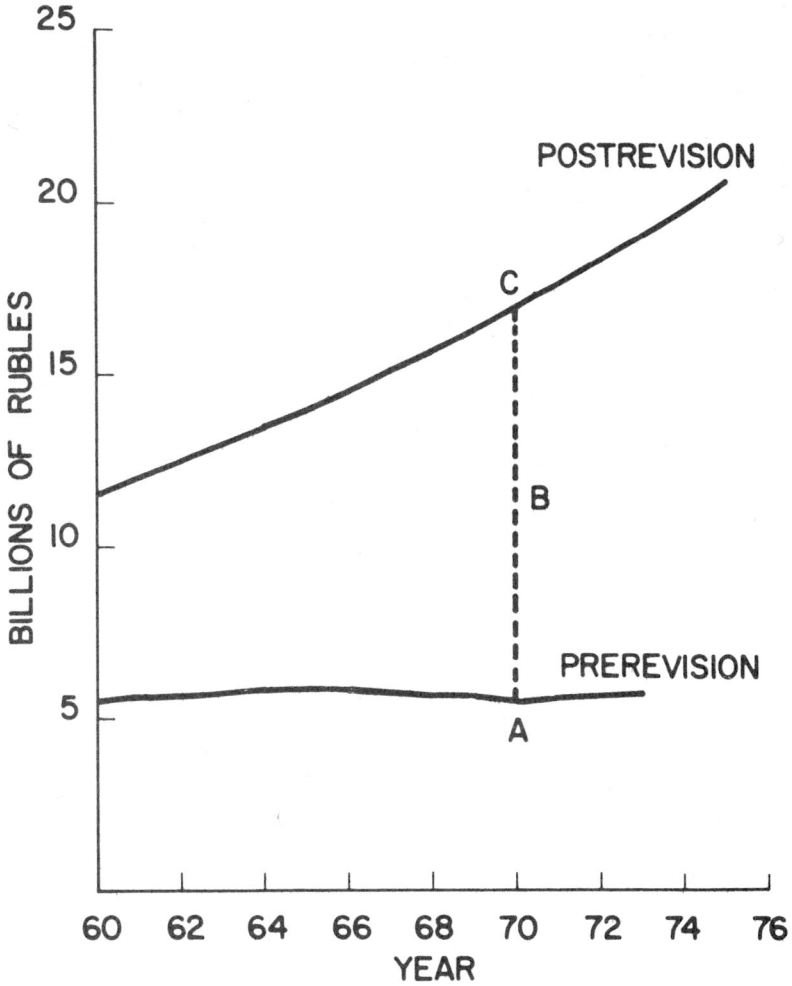

TABLE 2.1
CIA Estimates of Soviet Procurement Growth, 1960–75

	1960–70	1970–75*
Index Measure		
1. Prerevision (ruble weighted Laspeyres)	0	1.2
2. Postrevision (ruble weighted Paasche)	2.9–5.0	4–5
3. Dollar weighted Paasche	2.5–2.9	3.7

* The Laspeyres series according to CIA sources ceased being computed in 1972 (Steiner), or 1974 (Swain). The figure reported for 1970–1975 was computed from agency data pertaining to the difference between its pre and postrevision estimate for 1975, and can therefore be interpreted as an extrapolated rate after 1972, or 1974. The derivation of all estimates is provided in footnote 2.

1.
$$L = \frac{\sum_{i=1}^{n} r_i^{55} q_i^{t}}{\sum_{i=1}^{n} r_i^{55} q_i^{60}}$$

2.
$$P = \frac{\sum_{i=1}^{n} r_i^{70} q_i^{t}}{\sum_{i=1}^{n} r_i^{70} q_i^{60}}$$

3.
$$D = \frac{\sum_{i=1}^{n} p_i^{70} q_i^{t}}{\sum_{i=1}^{n} p_i^{70} q_i^{60}}$$

Ruble and dollar prices are designated by the symbols r and p, quantities by q, and the superscripts represent time. The q's (quantities) used for all three measures are identical. The indices differ only with regard to price weights.

In actual practice the dollar estimates are computed first. The dollar cost of each Soviet weapon and/or weapon system is calculated from engineering data, parametric models, and analogue techniques, and then summed. Ruble procurement estimates are computed similarly. Soviet prices of varying quality are collected for weapons, or goods thought to be close weapon substitutes. Because the number of such prices in the agency's inventory is relatively small, data valuation cannot be carried out in the same detail as dollar costing. Weapons and weapon systems are aggregated with dollar weights into groupings of composite goods and converted to rubles by means of ruble dollar ratios.

The use of ruble dollar ratios rather than the true ruble prices means that the actual ruble procurement index computed by the CIA has the following form:

4.
$$L^* = \frac{\sum\limits_{j=1}^{m} \frac{r_j^{55}}{p_j^{60}} p_j^{60} q_j^{t}}{\sum\limits_{j=1}^{m} \frac{r_j^{55}}{p_j^{60}} p_j^{60} q_j^{60}}$$

and

$$P^* = \frac{\sum\limits_{j=1}^{m} \frac{\hat{r}_j^{70}}{p_j^{70}} p_j^{70} q_j^{t}}{\sum\limits_{j=1}^{m} \frac{\hat{r}_j^{70}}{p_j^{70}} p_j^{70} q_j^{60}}$$

For the period 1970–75 the hybrid

$$L^{**} = \frac{\sum\limits_{j=1}^{m} \frac{r_j^{55}}{p_j^{70}} p_j^{70} q_j^{t}}{\sum\limits_{j=1}^{m} \frac{r_j^{55}}{p_j^{70}} p_j^{70} q_j^{60}}$$

was probably employed. The symbol ˆ indicates that 1970 prices were actually 1955 prices slightly adjusted to make allowance for the 1967 price reform.

The integral relationship exhibited in equations 4-6 between ruble and dollar weapons prices makes it apparent that the anomalous behavior of the CIA data cannot be attributed to the utilization of inconsistent datasets. The dollar and ruble series are not separable. The dollar series drives the ruble series.

II. Plausible Explanations and Rank Order Transitivity

It follows directly from the fact that all three procurement indices are derived from the same physical output data that if a reasonable explanation exists for the anomalous behavior of the agency's series it must repose in the structure of the ruble and dollar prices employed as aggregation weights. Let us define a reasonable explanation as one in which the agency's results are replicated simultaneously for all three indices, without entailing assumptions that are palpably implausible.

In order to ascertain whether a reasonable explanation exists in this sense it is necessary to construct a series of concrete examples based on what appear to be sensible assumptions. The key assumptions used in the examples which follow are:

A. If Soviet weapons are partitioned into two categories, conventional and advanced, conventional weapons should represent the larger share in the base year, 1960.[6]
B. Dollar cost estimates of Soviet conventional weapons will be relatively high because they are produced with technologies no longer in widespread use in the United States. Dollar cost estimates of advanced Soviet weapons will be comparatively low because weapons which are advanced in the Soviet Union are well down the U.S. learning curve. As a consequence, the conventional/advanced weapons dollar price ratio will be lower than either the early or late year ruble price ratio.[7]

The ruble-weighted Laspeyres and Paasche indices shown in equations 7 and 8 obey assumption A and are consistent with the agency's ruble procurement growth rates, 0 percent and 4 percent.

$$7. \quad L = \frac{r_1^0 \, q_1^1 + r_2^0 \, q_2^1}{r_1^0 \, q_1^0 + r_2^0 \, q_2^0} = \frac{2(1.088)3 + 3(.824)}{2(3) + 3(1)} = 1; \; 0 \text{ percent}$$

$$8. \quad P = \frac{r_1^1 \, q_1^1 + r_2^1 \, q_2^1}{r_1^1 \, q_1^0 + r_2^1 \, q_2^0} = \frac{3(1.088)3 + 2(.824)}{3(3) + 2(1)} = 1.04; \; 4 \text{ percent}$$

Conventional weapons are represented by q_1, advanced weapons by q_2.[8] The ratio of conventional to advanced weapons is set for didactic purposes at $q_1/q_2 = 3/1$ in accordance with assumption A. It is further assumed as is customary in index theory that scarce, advanced weapons are relatively expensive in the base year, but become comparatively cheaper as production expands in subsequent years.[9] In the base year the ratio of conventional to advanced weapons prices is set at $r_1/r_2 = 2/3$; in time 1 the proportionality is reversed, $r_1/r_2 = 3/2$.

Given this information, rates of growth for conventional and advanced weapons must be found that satisfy the conditions $L = 1$, $P = 1.04$. When $L = 1$ procurement growth is zero, then $P = 1.04$ the annual rate is 4 percent. With two linear, independent equations and two unknowns, if a solution exists it will be unique.[10] The solution values for this example are 1.088 and .824, which converted to growth rates imply that conventional weapons in physical units grew 8.8 percent annually while advanced weapons declined 17.6 percent per annum.

The objective facts of the Soviet military buildup during the sixties indicate that growth rates of this sort are unreasonable. The scientific technical revolution in Soviet weapons technology, which commenced in the early sixties and continued throughout the period under discussion, is inconsistent with absolute declines in Soviet advanced weapons production. Moreover, when the dollar index is computed using the solution values for equations 7 and 8 the agency's growth rate rank ordering is violated; the dollar rate of procurement growth inadmissibly exceeds the Paasche ruble rate (6.2 percent versus 4 percent):

$$9. \quad D = \frac{p_1^1 q_1^1 + p_2^1 q_2^1}{p_1^1 q_1^0 + p_2^1 q_2^0} = \frac{3(1.088)3 + .824(1)}{3(3) + 1(1)} = 1.062; 6.2 \text{ percent}$$

This result, which is predicated on the agency's assertion that the rate of unit physical procurement growth is identical in all its indices, is computed straightforwardly. In accordance with assumption B the ratio of conventional to advanced weapons dollar prices is set at $p_1/p_2 = 3/1$. All the other elements of the dollar-weighted Paasche index are the same as before. The inadmissibly high dollar procurement growth rate therefore is solely the consequence of the dollar price relatives the CIA itself considers reasonable.[11] The solutions for equations 7 and 8 thus must be rejected not only because they are implausible, but because they violate the rank order of the agency's own procurement rates.[12]

Another potentially viable set of solution values are illustrated in equations 10 and 11,

$$10. \quad L = \frac{r_1^0 q_1^1 + r_2^0 q_2^1}{r_1^0 q_1^0 + r_2^0 q_2^0} = \frac{3(.952)3 + 2(1.216)}{3(3) + 2(1)} = 1; 0 \text{ percent}$$

$$11. \quad P = \frac{r_1^1 q_1^1 + r_2^1 q_2^1}{r_1^1 q_1^0 + r_2^1 q_2^0} = \frac{2(.952)(3) + 3(1.216)}{2(3) + 3(1)} = 1.04; 4 \text{ percent}$$

which differ from equations 7 and 8 only by the assumption that the relative cost of advanced weapons increased rather than decreased as scarce advanced weapons production expanded. The ratio of conventional to advanced weapons prices in the base year is set at $r_1/r_2 = 3/2$, and at $r_1/r_2 = 2/3$ in the final year.

Once again, one of the components of the procurement index declines absolutely, a phenomenon mandated by the fact that the growth rate of both subgroups cannot be positive if the Laspeyres rate is zero. This time it is conventional weapons which decline, decreasing 5 percent annually while advanced weapons grow 21.6 percent per annum. Since it is difficult to determine without a close inspection of the agency's quantity series whether conventional weapons did indeed decline steadily in absolute terms from 1960 to 1970, equations 10 and 11 at least have the virtue of not being manifestly implausible.

Equation 12, which expresses the dollar-weighted Paasche procurement growth rate, demonstrates that the rank-ordering condition is strongly violated.

$$12. \quad D = \frac{p_1^1 q_1^1 + p_2^1 q_2^1}{p_1^1 q_1^0 + p_2^1 q_2^0} = \frac{3(.952)3 + (1.216(1))}{3(3) + 1(1)}$$

$$= .98; \; -2.0 \text{ percent}$$

According to assumption B dollar costed advanced weapons prices should be lower than their ruble counterparts in either the base or the final year. These weights, however, generate an overall 2.0 percent decline in aggregate procurement growth, behavior incompatible with the CIA transitivity conditions.

The underlying explanation for this apparent inconsistency is especially revealing. While a weak case could perhaps be made for the proposition that advanced weapons costs were rising in rubles,[13] which might ostensibly explain the observed index order reversal, no such argument can be sustained for constant dollar prices. As a consequence, the agency is caught between Scylla and Charybdis: it can either rationalize its ruble procurement growth rates infringing its own transitivity ordering, and forcing the dollar procurement growth rate below zero; or it can maintain the proportionality between the ruble and dollar Paasche procurement rates violating assumption B. In either case a reasonable and consistent explanation of the anomalous behavior of the agency's series cannot be sustained.

Although the examples above, of course, are not definitive because the exact values used for r_1/r_2, p_1/p_2 and q_1/q_2 were chosen arbitrarily, they are indicative of a class of solutions. Any set of meaningful numbers preserving the direction of the price-quantity proportionalities employed in equations 7-12 will display the same anomalies. The inferences drawn from our examples are therefore very powerful.

One lacuna, however, remains, which can be easily closed. Suppose assumption A were invalid. What effect would a reversal of quantity proportions have on our conclusions? As with any alteration of the exact price-quantity values, the reversal of assumption A will change the solution values. But they will not alter the inferences that have been drawn. Equations 13-15, which duplicate equations 7-9 but reverse the quantity proportions, demonstrate that while the growth rates are altered the rank ordering of the indices is preserved:

13. $\quad L = \dfrac{r_1^0 q_1^1 + r_2^0 q_2^1}{r_1^0 q_1^0 + r_2^0 q_2^0} = \dfrac{2(1.216) + 3(.952)3}{2(1) + 3(3)} = 1;\ 0$ percent

14. $\quad P = \dfrac{r_1^1 q_1^1 + r_2^1 q_2^1}{r_1^1 q_1^0 + r_2^1 q_2^0} = \dfrac{3(1.216) + 2(.952)3}{3(1) + 2(3)} = 1.04;\ 4$ percent

15. $\quad D = \dfrac{p_1^1 q_1^1 + p_2^1 q_2^1}{p_1^1 q_1^0 + p_2^1 q_2^0} = \dfrac{3(1.216) + (.952)3}{3(1) + 1(3)} = 1.084;\ 8.4$ percent

This finding shows beyond reasonable doubt that 48 percent of the line segment AC in Figure 2.1 should not be attributed to the effect hidden inflation has on the measured rate of real Soviet procurement growth, but is the consequence of profound anomalies besetting the CIA's unclassified procurement series.[14] The existence of these anomalies, of course, does not resolve the further issue of whether the 5.5 billion rubles (line segment BC) the agency has misattributed to hidden inflationary growth effects should be ascribed to hidden inflationary changes in the price level of the military machine-building sector, or to real increases in the number and quality of Soviet weapons. To establish causality the implications of these anomalies must be analyzed in a greater detail, a task addressed in the next two chapters.[15]

Notes

1. The CIA explicitly discusses index number issues in annual reports on ruble defense expenditures. For a typical statement on this matter see Donald Burton (1979), p. 6. More specifically, pp. 6–8: "The estimated dollar costs of Soviet procurements showed a monotonic upward trend in the 1970s, averaging about 3.5 percent per year. (In ruble terms, the growth rate was 4 to 5 percent, reflecting the comparatively high costs to the Soviets of producing high technology weapons and equipment.)"
2. The sources for these figures are:
   a. The ruble-weighted Laspeyres rate: Donald D. Swain, deputy director of the Military and Economic Analysis Center, CIA in a letter dated August 9, 1979 has written me as follows: ". . . the implication that Soviet procurement did not grow at all in the 1960s is indeed erroneous. Our estimates at that time indicated no growth, end year to end year, 1960 to 1970. Corrected cyclically, however, there was an upward growth

trend averaging 1 percent to 2 percent. As indicated below, we now believe that the average rate of growth was substantially higher." This statement is ostensibly confirmed by the testimony of CIA Director Colby in *Allocation of Resources in the Soviet Union and China* (1974), pp. 68–69. I have demonstrated elsewhere that this testimony is internally inconsistent (see chapter 1). Donald Burton, chief of the Military and Economic Analysis Center, and Mr. Swain have subsequently explained to me that Colby's testimony was indeed inconsistent, but the statement that Soviet procurement did not grow from 1960 to 1970 in real terms was correct. "The Allocations testimony was based on our 1973 estimates which were wrong for the many reasons we have discussed" (Swain, August 9, 1979).

The estimate for the period 1970–75 is derived from *Estimated Soviet Defense Spending in Rubles, 1970–1975*, where the following information is provided: total Soviet defense spending rose 3 percent per annum in prerevision prices; total defense spending "about" doubled valued in postrevision prices, total defense spending as the "Soviets might account for their defense effort" rose from 45-50 billion rubles for 1970 "to about 55-60 billion rubles in 1975," postrevision defense spending grew 4–5 percent per annum (p.1). These data imply that the agency's prerevision 1970 Laspeyres estimate (the underlying prices are slightly adjusted 1955 prices) for total defense spending was 23.75 billion rubles (half the mean 45-50). The corresponding figure for 1975 is $23.75 (1.03)^5 = 27.5$ billion rubles, and the total change from 1970 to 1975 is 3.78 billion rubles.

To compute the rate of growth of procurement, 1970–75, the procurement share of these 3.78 billion rubles must be estimated and related to prerevision procurement in 1970. This is accomplished by noting that the total change in Soviet defense spending valued in postrevision prices is 10 billion rubles. The procurement component of these 10 billion postrevision rubles, using the agency's best direct cost procurement estimate for 1970, 17 billion rubles (*USSR: Toward a Reconciliation of Marxist and Western Measures of National Income*, CIA, ER 78-10505, p. 14) can be estimated at $17 (1.045)^5 - 17 = 4.2$ billion rubles. Subtracting this figure from the 10 billion total change in postrevision defense spending leaves a best estimate residual of 5.8 billion rubles. Of this residual, 2.38 billion is imputable to "changes in national intelligence estimates of the size of Soviet forces" (*Estimated Soviet Defense Spending in Rubles, 1970–1975*), i.e., 10 percent of 23.75 billion rubles.

The remaining 3.42 billion rubles represents the CIA's estimate of nonprocurement growth from 1970 to 1975, before it obtained new information on the size of Soviet forces. Subtracting this implicit prerevision estimate of nonprocurement expenditures from the total change estimated above implies that the prerevision change in procurement was .36 billion rubles (3.78 − 3.42 = .36). Since prerevision procurement in 1970 valued in prerevision 1970 prices was roughly 5.8 billion rubles, prerevision procurement for 1975 can be set at 6.16 billion rubles, which produces a compound Laspeyres rate of growth of 1.2 percent per annum $(6.16/5.8) = (1.062)^{1/5} = 1.2.$, a figure consistent with Swain's cyclically corrected estimates for the sixties. (According to Don Burton, Colby's figures were in 1955 prices; private correspondence, February 21, 1979. Prerevision 1970 prices were 6 percent higher than 1955 prices; private correspondence with Donald Swain, August 9, 1979.) Note that Swain contends that the agency stopped computing its prerevision series in 1974. Steiner asserts 1972 was the last year in the series. In Table 13.1 and Figure 2.1 I split the difference assuming that the prerevision series terminated in 1973.

b. The ruble-weighted Paasche rate for the 1960s was roughly 4 percent. ". . . it should be noted we have no official estimates of procurement growth in the 60s but the roughly 4 percent figure (closer to 4.5 percent by current definitions) applies since 1965. We think this will probably hold up for the early 60s as well" (Donald Swain, August 9, 1979). The 4-5 percent Paasche procurement growth trend is partially confirmed and extended to the late seventies (more exactly the indicator is Paasche up to 1970 and Laspeyres thereafter) in *Estimated Soviet Defense Spending: Trends and Prospects*, where it is stated that Soviet procurement grew at an annual rate of 4 percent from 1967 to 1977 (p. 2).

The 4 percent estimate can be interpreted as a "best" estimate. The range of the Paasche procurement growth rate is considerably broader. It can be estimated with reasonable accuracy by assuming that the "best" growth rate estimate is derived from the agency's "best" procurement estimate for 1970, 17 billion rubles (*USSR: Toward a Reconciliation of Marxist and Western Measures of National Income*, p. 14). If Soviet procurement expenditures in 1970 were 17 billion postrevision rubles, and procurement grew 4 percent per annum, it follows that in constant 1970 postrevision prices procurement in 1960 was 11.5 billion rubles (q_{60} = $17/(1.04)^{10}$ = 11.48). CIA estimates of Soviet procurement in 1970 range from 13 billion to 21 billion, with a mean of 17 billion. This band of uncertainty is substantially larger than the confidence interval usually favored by the CIA in its dollar cost estimates of procurement. A 10 percent confidence interval of 15.3 billion to 18.7 billion rubles therefore may provide a better impression of the high probability range. The growth rates implied by these bounds are 2.9 percent and 5 percent, i.e., $(15.3/11.48$ = 1.33; $(1.33)^{1/10}$ = 1.029 and $(18.7/11.48)$ = 1.63; $(1.63)^{1/10}$ = 1.05).

The Paasche ruble-weighted growth rate for the period 1970–75 is 4–5 percent (*Estimated Soviet Defense Spending in Rubles 1970–1975*, "Defense spending in rubles is now estimated to have increased at an average annual rate of 4–5 percent. . . ."—p. 2; "Another way of analyzing Soviet defense spending is to break it down into three principal resource categories—investment, operating, and RDT & E. Since 1970, each of these categories has accounted for about the same portion of the total" p. 13).

c. The dollar-weighted Paasche rate for the sixties can be inferred from two types of information. First, data on Soviet military investment from 1966 to 1976 are provided in a graph found in *A Dollar Cost Comparison of Soviet and US Defense Activities, 1966–1976*. Investment can be considered as a reliable indicator of procurement because throughout the period in question CIA dollar estimates show that procurement has been a constant share of investment, comprising approximately 90 percent of total investment expenditures. (Procurement valued in 1978 dollars was 36.5 billion in 1975. The analogous figure for investment was 40 billion dollars. See the appropriate graphs in *A Dollar Cost Comparison of*

Soviet and US Defense Activities, 1968–1978, p. 10, and Burton, 1979, Chart 2.) The investment proxy for procurement exhibits a 2.9 percent rate of growth $(40/30 = 1.33; (1.33)^{1/10} = 1.029)$.

Second, as has already been demonstrated, Swain and Burton both believe that the rate of procurement growth has been relatively constant from 1960 to 1979, with a slight upward trend since 1965. It follows that the dollar-weighted Paasche growth for the sixties in the agency's opinion is close to, but slightly less than 2.9 percent.

The dollar-weighted Paasche procurement growth rate from 1970 to 1975 is approximately 3.7 percent. See Burton (1979), Chart 2. Procurement in 1970 was roughly 30.5 billion dollars and in 1975, 36.5 billion dollars; $36.5/30.5 = (1.197); (1.197)^{1/5} = 1.037$.

3. The least reliable estimate is the ruble-weighted Laspeyres figure for the period 1970–75. Its derivation is described in footnote 2. The uncertainty surrounding this number stems from the agency's low prerevision procurement estimate, approximately 5.8 billion rubles. Since the postrevision best estimate of 17 billion rubles is so vastly higher than the initial figure, the use of the latter in deriving the former could be affected by rounding errors. The reasonableness of the ruble-weighted Laspeyres rate for the seventies, however, is supported by the proportionality exhibited by all series across time and among trends, and is buttressed by Mr. Swain's assertion that, "Corrected for cyclicality . . . there was an upward growth trend averaging 1 to 2 percent" in Soviet procurement valued in 1955 prices during the sixties (Swain, August 9, 1979).

4. The reader may wish to note that a zero rate of growth in procurement expenditures does not mean that procurement expenditures were zero. Based on the agency's prerevision numbers, the Soviets were adding about 5.5 billion rubles in arms annually to their arsenal during 1960–75. Allowing for depreciation, this figure probably implies that the stock of Soviet weapons was either being maintained, or increased at a very slow rate.

5. The agency appears to be taking the position that the calculations which follow are invalid because the ruble data for the sixties valued in pre- and postrevision prices are incompatible. See note 7, chapter 1. According to Steiner's letter of November 10, 1980, Soviet procurement valued in 1955 and prerevision 1970 prices, which relied on old data, ceased being calculated after 1972. Swain's estimates in postrevision prices by contrast were not computed until much later, and employed updated quantity data. Differences in the physical output series, it is implied, therefore account for the nominal inconsistencies I have discovered exist in the agency's real procurement growth series.

Although the differences in the quantity series underlying the CIA's estimates of real procurement growth from 1960 to 1970 may partially affect the findings in the text, it should be noted that Steiner's explanation is not consonant with the published record. CIA estimates showing procurement growing at 4 percent per annum go back to Colby's testimony in 1974. The calculations underlying this estimate were probably made in 1973 and should not have deviated importantly from the same estimates made in prerevision prices in 1972, especially when it is explicitly stated in *Estimated Soviet Defense Spending, 1970–1975,* p. 1, that the discovery of new military programs (additional weapons) had little effect on the agency's revisions. Also, while it is true that subsequent calculations made after 1976 in response to

my queries may have benefited from additional information, it is unlikely
that quantity data for the sixties were significantly affected because Swain's
later calculations merely confirmed Colby's earlier estimates.

A more plausible explanation of the internal inconsistencies in the CIA's
series is provided in chapter 4, section VII.

6. This assumption is introduced for didactic purposes. As will be shown, it
can be relaxed without affecting the inferences that will be drawn from this
analysis.

7. This assumption is a commonplace of CIA analysis and underlies its contention that dollar procurement growth rates will be slower than ruble rates.

8. Quantities in the equations above are expressed in base year physical units
and a growth coefficient where appropriate. For example, the quantities in
equation 7 are $q_0^1 = 3$, $q_1^1 = 1.088\ (3)$, $q_2^0 = 1$, $q_2^1 = .824\ (1)$. The growth
coefficients $\delta_1 = 1.088$ and $\delta_2 = .824$ are initially unknown. They are
determined by solving a pair of simultaneous equations.

9. The ruble prices used here are:

$$r_1^0 = 2,\ r_1^1 = 3,\ r_2^0 = 3,\ r_2^1 = 2.$$

10. Prices and base year quantities are known. The unknowns are the rates of
growth in physical units of conventional and advanced weapons. The solution values for equations 7 and 8 are determined as follows:

7. $$\frac{6}{9}\delta_1 + \frac{3}{9}\delta_2 = 1$$

8. $$\frac{9}{11}\delta_1 + \frac{2}{11}\delta_2 = 1.04$$

From equation 7:

$$\delta_1 = \frac{9}{6} - \frac{1}{2}\delta_2$$

Substituting in equation 8:

$$\frac{27}{22} - \frac{9}{22}\delta_2 + \frac{4}{22}\delta_2 = 1.04$$
$$\delta_2 = .824$$
$$\delta_1 = 1.088$$

11. If the ratio of conventional to advanced weapons dollar prices were less
than the ruble rate then the dollar growth rate would normally exceed the
ruble Paasche rate. This would not only be in conflict with the facts but
would violate normal expectations based on the theory of international
index number analysis.

12. Instead of solving equations 7 and 8, equations 8 and 9 could be solved for δ_1 and δ_2. The solution values are $\delta_1 = 1.022$, $\delta_2 = 1.12$. Substituting these values in equation 7 yields a Laspeyres growth rate of 5.5 percent. This rate is sensible from the standpoint of conventional index number theory since the Laspeyres rate exceeds the Paasche, but it violates the transitivity order established by the agency's empirical calculations. Note an average dollar procurement growth rate of 3.2 percent was used in solving equations 8 and 9.

13. "The *Allocations* testimony was based on our 1973 estimates which were wrong for the many reasons we discussed" (Donald Swain, private correspondence, August 9, 1979). This statement refers to CIA director Colby's representation of Soviet ruble defense expenditure statistics in 1974. See *Allocation of Resources in the Soviet Union and China* (1974), pp. 68–69; and Rosefielde, "Real Soviet Arms Procurement Expenditures 1960–1978," footnote 6 in Rosefielde, ed. (1980g), p. 49.

14. "Your question 4 would require substantial additional research which we are not willing to undertake. It is of no interest to the government what calculations using obsolete data might show." The obsolete data referred to above are the 1955 price and quantity procurement figures. Donald Swain, private correspondence, August 9, 1979. Also see Donald Burton, (1979), where it is stated that "Where possible, we check the ruble estimates against other intelligence information as well as published Soviet economic statistics. We believe they pass these tests" (p. 3).

15. Revisions in the CIA's methodology after 1970 distort its growth series for the seventies. A full analysis of these biases is provided in Rosefielde (1982c). These distortions do not materially alter the findings presented in this chapter which pertain primarily to the sixties.

CHAPTER 3

Inconsistent Procurement Estimates and the Hidden Inflation Hypothesis

To determine whether the 5.5 billion rubles misattributed by the CIA to hidden inflationary changes in relative military machine-building prices should be imputed to hidden inflationary changes in the price level or real increases in the quantity and quality of Soviet weapons, the aggregate rates of hidden inflation implied by these alternatives can be calculated and appraised in the Soviet institutional setting. In the first instance, assuming that the entire vertical distance AC in Figure 2.1 should be ascribed to a neutral 209 percent increase in the ruble price level,[1] hidden inflation can be estimated by dividing the agency's nominal procurement estimates for 1960 and 1970 with its Laspeyres real weapons growth index:

1.
$$\frac{\Sigma r_{70}q_{70}}{\Sigma r_{55}q_{70}} = \frac{\Sigma r_{70}q_{70}}{\Sigma r_{55}q_{60}} \cdot \frac{\Sigma r_{55}q_{60}}{\Sigma r_{55}q_{70}}$$

$$= 17/5.5 \div 1$$

$$= 3.09$$

which (remembering that many of the CIA's 1955 prices were actually collected in the early sixties)produces a compound annual inflation rate of

2.
$$\dot{p} = 100[(3.09)^{1/10} - 1] = 11.9 \text{ percent.}$$

In the second instance, assuming that the line segment BC reflects real procurement growth, hidden inflation can be computed by dividing nominal procurement with an adjusted prerevision Laspeyres real procurement index:

3.
$$\frac{\Sigma r_{70}q_{70}^*}{\Sigma r_{55}q_{70}^*} = \frac{\Sigma r_{70}q_{70}^*}{\Sigma r_{55}q_{60}} \cdot \frac{\Sigma r_{55}q_{60}}{\Sigma r_{55}q_{70}^*}$$

$$= 17/5.5 \div 5.5/5.5(1.04)^{10}$$

$$= 2.09$$

yielding a compound annual inflation rate of

4.
$$\dot{p}^* = 100[(2.09)^{1/10} - 1] = 7.6 \text{ percent.}$$

Both these rates appear implausibly high.[2] Ruble prices in the Soviet Union, as is generally understood, are not determined in the market by the forces of supply and demand. All military and civilian machine-building prices are set administratively by the State Price Committee and exhibit a declining rather than a rising trend. While it is of course conceivable that price discipline is infringed in sundry ways by enterprise managers in the Soviet military machine-building sector, inflation rates of the magnitude estimated above must be viewed with considerable skepticism suggesting that the deficiency of the agency's hidden inflation hypothesis is not confined to the relative price effect measured by the line segment BC.[3]

Notes

1. I use the agency's best direct cost 1970 ruble procurement estimate, 17 billion rubles, instead of its best residual estimate 18.5 billion rubles because the CIA employs this value in the published series graphed in Figure 2.1.
2. "We are convinced, and we have published a number of studies on this, that there is measurable inflation in Soviet machinery as a whole and in defense machinery in particular. Specifically, we believe that in 1967, when the Soviets undertook a major price reform, one of the things that they did was remove substantial subsidies on military procurement . . . and to change the profit rates that they charged on defense products to better reflect real resource cost. We think this primarily explains the discrepancy between the estimates that we made before 1976 and the revised estimates that we came out with later" (James Barry, Chief Economic Implications Branch, OSR, CIA; testimony to Congressman Les Aspin, *CIA Estimates of Soviet Defense Spending,* House Select Committee on Intelligence, September 3, 1980, Washington, D.C., pp. 78–79).

   Before 1976 the CIA allowed 6 percent for this effect (see chapter 12, note 1). James Steiner and I discussed the issue of weapons subsidies and profits in Monterey. Barry's testimony to the House Select Intelligence Committee greatly exaggerates the explanatory significance of this factor, and conceals the speculative nature of the evidence supporting his conjecture. For an analysis of the various alternative theories advanced by the agency to explain hidden inflation see part II.

3. "Essentially what happens with Professor Rosefielde's argument is because the 1960 values he cites from the public literature are too low and the 1970 values are too high, this yields an implied rate of growth in Soviet procurement expenditures which he believes cannot be explained by our analysis of price changes in the Soviet Union. If those figures he cites were correct, that would indeed be the case, but they are not correct figures. Rather, the correct figures show that the difference between our estimates, when we made them for 1960 and those that we make in 1970 can be explained by real growth in procurement on the order of 4 or 5 percent, and inflation in Soviet defense procurement of a similar order of magnitude, 4 or 5 percent." Barry, ibid. Barry's remarks to Congressman Aspin are misleading. He does not realize that the values I cite were not only given to me in 1979 by Derk Swain and Don Burton, but that Swain used them himself to derive precisely the same 4 to 5 percent rate of inflation to which Barry alludes. Thus if my estimates are inconsistent or wrong, so are his because they are taken from the same source. Note in addition that the growth rate Barry refers to is computed from the vertical line DE in Figure 2.1. Although Barry appears to believe that DE is explained by the discovery in 1976 of new weapons programs undertaken in 1970, his surmise is disconfirmed by the agency's official position in *Estimated Soviet Defense Spending in Rubles, 1970–1975*, p. 1; a point confirmed privately by Swain and Burton. See chapter 7, note 6.

Barry also inexplicably seems to believe that my estimates of real procurement growth are in current prices.

CHAPTER 4

Parametric Cost Estimation and the Downward Bias in the CIA's Dollar and Ruble Estimates of Soviet Procurement Growth

I. Direct Cost Underestimation

The perverse behavior of the agency's procurement series and the implausibly high rates of hidden inflation implied by its explanation of the discrepancy between its pre- and postrevision 1970 estimates of Soviet procurement indicate that the CIA's direct cost estimating methodology is seriously flawed. It appears that *dollar* estimates derived from *fixed vintage* American parametric cost estimating models do not satisfactorily measure all relevant dimensions of real Soviet procurement growth. The reasons for this failure are elaborated below and an empirical test is developed which demonstrates that the CIA's underestimation of both the Laspeyres and Paasche rates of procurement can cogently be attributed to the misestimation of qualitative improvements in Soviet weaponry that have occurred during the last two decades. A related argument is also advanced which shows why the order reversal exhibited by the agency Laspeyres and Paasche ruble procurement growth indices is explained by the same cause.

II. The Hypothesis

The downward bias in the CIA's direct cost estimates of Soviet procurement growth can largely be explained by the inadequate specification of its cost functions, which systematically bias ruble price estimates when technological change is concentrated in automated subsystems, the weapons suit, navigation, guidance, and design.

This hypothesis contains two distinct theorems. The first states that the specification of the agency's cost functions used to estimate ruble prices are inadequate and cause systematic biases to arise when technological change has certain specified characteristics. The second asserts that these systematic biases necessarily cause the CIA's estimates of Soviet procurement growth to be downward biased.

Theorem 1 contains two axioms (necessary implications of the agency's costing procedures), and one factual assertion. Axiom 1 shows that the specification of the cost function used to estimate ruble prices is restrictive. Axiom 2 demonstrates that this restrictive specification may generate biased results when used to estimate prices for certain weapon vintages. Evidence is then advanced to show that the conditions needed to generate these biases have prevailed in the Soviet defense sector during the sixties. Theorem 2 follows directly from the principles of index construction.

III. Theorem 1

Ruble price estimates of Soviet weapons with very few exceptions are derived from estimates of the dollar cost of American weapons judged to be close analogues of similar types of Soviet equipment.[1] These analogues are determined in three ways:[2] (1) weapons are individually matched, tank for tank, submarine for submarine, etc.; (2) composite analogues are calculated by using dollar cost estimating models derived from ex-post data on the production cost of American weapons to estimate the dollar cost of weapons with Soviet performance characteristics; and (3) engineering analogues are determined by computing the dollar cost of producing weapons to Soviet product specification with American production technology.

Most of the analogues used by the agency to compute ruble prices are of the second variety, composite analogues.[3] They are derived from functions of the following form:

1.
$$c_i^t = D_i^t (\beta_{i1}^t, \beta_{i2}^t, \ldots, \beta_{is}^t)$$

where c_i^t represents the ith composite analogue of vintage t expressed as the dollar cost of the ith weapon; D_i^t is the dollar cost estimating function derived from ex-post dollar cost data for vintage t American weapons of the ith type; and $\beta_{i1}, \beta_{i2}, \ldots, \beta_{is}$ are indicators of the physical-cum-macroperformance characteristics such as weight, size, velocity for vintage t Soviet weapons of the ith type.[4] Equation 1 indicates that the composite analogues utilized in the CIA's ruble price estimating procedures are expressed as the dollar cost of a vintage t American weapon, built with *American* technology in year t, but meeting Soviet macroperformance characteristics.

Ruble price estimates are calculated from these dollar cost composite analogues by means of purchasing power parity ratios. Ratios of the ruble and dollar cost of diverse composite goods are computed and used to convert dollar to ruble magnitudes:

2. $$r_i^t \simeq c_i^t \cdot \frac{r_j^t}{c_j^t}$$

where r_i^t represents the ruble price of the ith weapon of the t vintage and r_j^t/c_j^t is the ruble dollar ratio of composite goods judged appropriate for valuing weapons of the ith type.

With the exception of a few ruble weapon prices obtained directly through covert means, most of the CIA's ruble price estimates used in its procurement growth indices are derived from composite analogues. The remaining estimates are calculated with simple analogues and engineering analogues computed as:

3. $$r_i^t = E_i^t(\alpha_{i1}^t, \alpha_{i2}^t, \ldots, \alpha_{iv}^t)$$

where the engineering dollar costing function E_i^t replaces the parametric function D_i^t, and detailed product characteristics $\alpha_{i1}, \alpha_{i2}, \ldots, \alpha_{iv}$ replace the macroperformance indicators $\beta_{i1}, \beta_{i2}, \ldots, \beta_{is}$.

Axiom 1 asserts that the cost functions employed by the agency to estimate these ruble prices are restrictive because they do not include all the diverse factors which determine the actual ruble production cost of Soviet weapons. Ruble prices computed from composite analogues are based on very sketchy data. The performance indicators employed describe a few aggregate characteristics of a weapon or weapon subsystem, but provide little technical detail. The cost functions for composite analogues therefore restrictively assume that the contents of a weapon system or subsystem valued at dollar factor cost can always be accurately estimated from the external physical characteristics of its container. The restrictiveness of the agency's cost functions is most extreme in the case of simple analogues which are not determined by Soviet characteristics at all, except impressionistically. It is least pronounced for engineering analogues, but these estimates are only infrequently computed, and seldom updated.[5]

Axiom 2 stipulates that if composite analogues are employed to estimate constant ruble prices for Soviet weapons in vintages other than the one for which the dollar cost estimating model is defined, those prices will be biased when technological change is concentrated in the "contents" of the "weapon container"; that is, in the engineering characteristics of automated subsystems, the weapons suit, navigation, guidance, and design.[6] The CIA computes constant ruble prices for the most part with equations of the following type,[7]

4. $$r_i^{60} = R_i^{70}(\beta_{i1}^{60}, \beta_{i2}^{60}, \ldots, \beta_{is}^{60})$$

where R_i^{70} represents a dollar cost estimating function converted to rubles with a ruble-dollar ratio.[8] Equation 4 indicates that the ruble price r_i^{60} of the ith weapon of the 1960 vintage is determined by the cost estimating relationships for 1970 vintage American weapons (R_i^{70}) and the macroperformance characteristics of 1960 vintage Soviet equipment $(\beta_{i1}^{60}, \beta_{i2}^{60}, \ldots, \beta_{is}^{60})$. These ruble price estimates will be unbiased if, and only if, the technology embodied in the ith Soviet weapon produced in 1960, $(\alpha_{i1}^{60}, \alpha_{i2}^{60}, \ldots, \alpha_{iv}^{60})$ is reflected on average by the macroperformance indicators such that:

5. $$R_i^{70}(\beta_{i1}^{60}, \beta_{i2}^{60}, \ldots, \beta_{is}^{60}) = r_1^{70}f_1^{70}(q_i^{60}) + r_2^{70}f_2^{70}(q_i^{60}), \ldots, + r_g^{70}f_g^{70}(q_i^{60})$$
$$= E_i^{70}(\alpha_{i1}^{60}, \alpha_{i2}^{60}, \ldots, \alpha_{iv}^{60})$$

where the first set of terms on the right hand side of the equation represent the ruble factor cost of producing one more unit of the weapon q_i^{60} at 1970 ruble factor prices r_j^{70} and 1970 input usage $f_j^{70}(q_i^{60})$.[9]

Should equation 5 be violated because the technology expressed in the engineering variables $\alpha_{i1}^{60}, \alpha_{i2}^{60}, \ldots, \alpha_{iv}^{60}$ is significantly inferior to the technology $\alpha_{i1}^{70}, \alpha_{i2}^{70}, \ldots, \alpha_{iv}^{70}$ implicit in parametric cost estimating function R_i^{70}, the agency's constant 1970 ruble price estimates for the 1960 vintage, r_i^{60}, will be overstated $(R_i^{70}(\beta_{i1}^{60}, \beta_{i2}^{60}, \ldots, \beta_{is}^{60}) > E_i^{70}(\alpha_{i1}^{60}, \alpha_{i2}^{60}, \ldots, \alpha_{iv}^{60}))$. Likewise, if constant 1970 ruble price estimates for Soviet weapons produced in 1980 that possess superior engineering characteristics $\alpha_{i1}^{80}, \alpha_{i2}^{80}, \ldots, \alpha_{iv}^{80}$ are implicitly computed with the technology $\alpha_{i1}^{70}, \alpha_{i2}^{70}, \ldots, \alpha_{iv}^{70}$, they will be understated $(R_i^{70}(\beta_{i1}^{80}, \beta_{i2}^{80}, \ldots, \beta_{is}^{80}) < E_i^{70}(\alpha_{i1}^{80}, \alpha_{i2}^{80}, \ldots, \alpha_{iv}^{80}))$.

These systematic intervintage parametric cost estimating functional biases are illustrated in Figure 4.1. CIA constant 1970 ruble estimates of Soviet weapons for any year are calculated from the cost estimating relationship $R_i^{70,70}(\beta_{i1})$, where the superscripts indicate that the cost estimating function R_i is derived with 1970 prices and 1970 technology α_{i1}^{70}, α_{i2}^{70}, . . ., α_{iv}^{70}, and β_{i1} is a macrovariable used to determine the cost of individual weapons. The cost of a Soviet ship produced in 1960 weighing β_{i1}^{60} tons and valued in 1970 prices using the costing relationship $R_i^{70,70}(\beta_{i1})$, for example, will be r_i^{60}. If the same estimate, however, is made using the engineering technology prevailing in 1960 the ship would actually cost only r_i^{*60}, indicated by the true parametric cost estimating relationship $E_i^{70,60}(\beta_{i1})$.

It is especially important to recognize that the difference between these estimates expressed by the downward shift of the parametric cost estimating curve is caused entirely by intervintage changes in technology omitted from the CIA's cost estimating relationship $R_i^{70,70}(\beta_{i1})$. This is the fundamental deficiency endemic to the agency's method.[10] Changes in the engineering technology of Soviet weapons uncorrelated with macroparameters such as weight, velocity, etc. find no expression in the CIA's estimates making it appear as if the cost estimating relationship $R_i^{70,70}(\beta_{i1})$ is invariant across vintages when in fact the entire cost estimating curve has shifted. Cost estimates in this way are overstated for early years, understated for later years, regardless of the exact set of prices used to compute the cost estimating function.

There are three good reasons for believing that conditions prevailing during the sixties biased the CIA's constant 1970 ruble estimates in the manner illustrated in Figure 4.1. First, the scientific and technical revolution in Soviet weapons technology, as the Soviets themselves refer to it, is a widely recognized and well documented phenomenon.[11] Second, the static macroperformance indicators used in American parametric cost estimating models are not especially sensitive to the kind of technological improvements that have characterized the scientific and technical revolution in Soviet weaponry. They were designed merely to obtain rough estimates of the production cost of standard, modified or new weapons with similar technologies of a specified vintage, taking little account of costly improvements in automated subsystems, the weapons suit, navigation, guidance, and design.[12] Third, Defense Department data show that estimated average intervintage technological progress for American weapons grew approximately 3 percent per annum during the sixties and 6 percent per annum in the seventies.[13] Given the opportunities afforded by their relative technological backwardness in the sixties, intervintage Soviet technical progress should have been at least as rapid as the U.S. experience during the seventies.[14]

It thus appears based on our axioms and available evidence regarding recent Soviet advances in weapons technology, that the CIA's constant ruble price estimates should be downward biased.

FIGURE 4.1
Intervintage Parametric Cost Estimating Bias

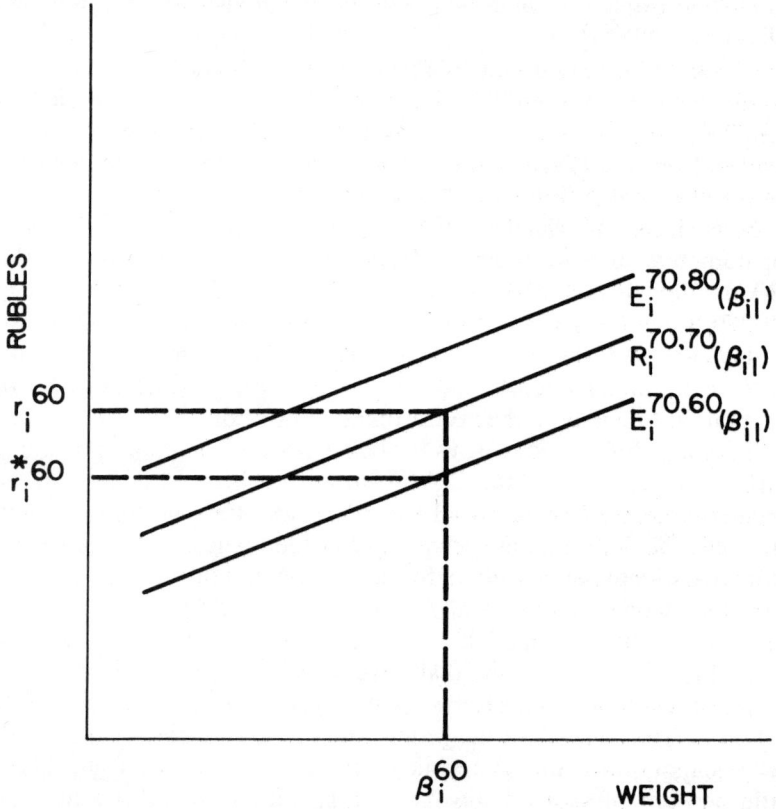

IV. Theorem 2

The real growth of Soviet procurement can be computed from data on the volume of Soviet weapons production and constant ruble prices. These indices are commonly calculated either in constant base year prices, or constant final year prices. Theorem 2 asserts that regardless of whether base or final year prices are employed, the biases in the agency's estimated constant ruble prices will cause the rate of Soviet procurement growth to be understated.

This assertion follows from the way in which procurement growth indices are constructed. Assume for simplicity that the ruble price estimates of the current year r_i^t are unbiased because the technology embodied in the cost estimating equations R_i^t is the same as that embodied in the macroperformance indicators β_{i1}^t, β_{i2}^t, . . ., β_{is}^t.[15] Since $\Sigma r_i^{60} q_i^{60}$ and $\Sigma r_i^{70} q_i^{70}$ are unbiased by construction, the direction of the bias in the agency's indices of Soviet procurement growth necessarily depends on the bias in the ruble price estimates for weapons of other vintages.[16] In the Laspeyres case,

6.
$$L = \frac{\Sigma R_i^{60}(\beta_{i1}^{70}, \beta_{i2}^{70}, \ldots, \beta_{is}^{70})q_i^{70}}{\Sigma R_i^{60}(\beta_{i1}^{60}, \beta_{i2}^{60}, \ldots, \beta_{is}^{60})q_i^{60}}$$

the numerator will be underestimated because the cost estimating relationship R_i^{60} does not take account of the technological improvements embodied in weapons of the 1970 vintage, q_i^{70}.

In the Paasche case,

7.
$$P = \frac{\Sigma R_i^{70}(\beta_{i1}^{70}, \beta_{i2}^{70}, \ldots, \beta_{is}^{70})q_i^{70}}{\Sigma R_i^{70}(\beta_{i1}^{60}, \beta_{i2}^{60}, \ldots, \beta_{is}^{60})q_i^{60}}$$

the denominator will be overestimated because the cost estimating relationship R_i^{70} falsely imputes the embodied technology of American (and/or Soviet) weapons in 1970 to Soviet weapons in 1960, q_i^{60}.

In both instances the results are exactly the same. The CIA's estimates of Soviet procurement growth are downward biased, as asserted in Theorem 2. Moreover, these findings are unaffected by the time period chosen for purposes of example. If the assumptions specified in Theorem 1 remain valid, agency estimates of Soviet procurement growth during the seventies would likewise be downward biased.

8.
$$L = \frac{\Sigma R_i^{70}(\beta_{i1}^{80}, \beta_{i2}^{80}, \ldots, \beta_{is}^{80})q_i^{80}}{\Sigma R_i^{70}(\beta_{i1}^{70}, \beta_{i2}^{70}, \ldots, \beta_{is}^{70})q_i^{70}}$$

as is easily verified by inspection.[17]

V. Empirical Confirmation

The biases postulated in Theorem 1, which govern the behavior of the CIA's procurement indices, can be tested by means of a simple empirical experiment. According to Theorem 1, the numerator of the agency's Laspeyres index $\Sigma R_i^{60}(\beta_{i1}^{70}, \beta_{i2}^{70}, \ldots, \beta_{is}^{70})q_i^{70}$ should be downward biased and the denominator of the Paasche index $\Sigma R_i^{70}(\beta_{i1}^{60}, \beta_{i2}^{60}, \ldots, \beta_{is}^{60})q_i^{60}$ should be upward biased. To check whether these correspondences are empirically observable, limit values must be determined which serve as benchmarks for establishing the existence of the postulated biases. These limit values can be inferred from the fundamental axiom widely employed in index number theory that base year quantities valued in final year prices, and final year quantities valued in base year prices will both exceed current year values.[18] More specifically, this axiom implies that:

9. $\Sigma R_i^{60}(\beta_{i1}^{70}, \beta_{i2}^{70}, \ldots, \beta_{is}^{70})q_i^{70} \geq \Sigma r_i^{70}q_i^{70} = 18.5$ billion rubles.[19]

and

10. $\Sigma R_i^{70}(\beta_{i1}^{60}, \beta_{i2}^{60}, \ldots, \beta_{is}^{60})q_i^{60} \geq \Sigma r_i^{60}q_i^{60} = 5.5$ billion rubles.[20]

If Theorem 1 is valid, inequality 9 should be violated and inequality 10 preserved. These predictions are easily verified. $\Sigma R_i^{60}(\beta_{i1}^{70}, \beta_{i2}^{70}, \ldots, \beta_{is}^{70})q_i^{70}$ equals 5.5 billion rubles,[21] which is 13 billion rubles less than the lower limit established for $\Sigma r_i^{70}q_i^{70}$, 18.5 billion rubles. $\Sigma R_i^{70}(\beta_{i1}^{60}, \beta_{i2}^{60}, \ldots, \beta_{is}^{60})q_i^{60}$ is 11.5 billion rubles,[22] which is 6 billion rubles above the lower limit set for $\Sigma r_i^{60}q_i^{60}$, 5.5 billion rubles. These are dramatic results. The CIA's estimate of Soviet procurement for 1970 valued in 1960 prices is 70 percent below the limit established by the current value of Soviet procurement. The agency's estimate of Soviet procurement for 1960 valued in 1970 prices is 109 percent greater than the corresponding current value. The disparity in the former can be explained entirely by bias; the disparity in the latter may be attributed in part to the fact that $\Sigma r_i^{70}q_i^{60}$ should normally exceed $\Sigma r_i^{60}q_i^{60}$, but the gap is very large and must to a substantial degree indicate the presence of an upward bias. The biases predicted by Theorem 1 thus are empirically confirmed.

VI. Empirical Confirmation: Parametric Dollar Cost Estimating Bias

Ruble values were employed in section V to demonstrate that the CIA's estimates of Soviet procurement were impaired by fixed vintage parametric cost estimating bias because the "new information" provided an objective basis for evaluating the agency's calculations. However, rearranging terms in equations 1, 2, and 5 discloses that if the CIA's fixed vintage parametric ruble cost estimates are biased, its dollar estimates must be biased as well,

11. $$D_i^t(\beta_{i1}^{t+i}, \beta_{i2}^{t+i}, \ldots, \beta_{is}^{t+i}) = \frac{c_j^t}{r_j^t} R_i^t(\beta_{i1}^{t+i}, \beta_{i2}^{t+i}, \ldots, \beta_{is}^{t+i})$$

because the agency's dollar estimates are scalar transforms, c_j^t/r_j^t (the dollar-ruble ratio) of its ruble estimates.

This implication can be tested either by comparing "Sovietized" CIA fixed vintage estimates with "Sovietized" variable vintage estimates computed by the DOD's material procurement branches:

12. $$D_i^{80,70}(\beta_{i1}^{80}, \beta_{i2}^{80}, \ldots, \beta_{is}^{80}) \gtrless D_i^{*80,80}(\beta_{i1}^{80}, \beta_{i2}^{80}, \ldots, \beta_{is}^{80})$$

or by directly comparing the agency's pre-"Sovietized" fixed vintage estimates (adjusted for certain accounting differences) with the DOD's pre-"Sovietized" variable vintage estimates (or more simply the actual ex-post dollar cost of weapon q_i):

13. $$D_i^{80,70}(b_{i1}^{80}, b_{i2}^{80}, \ldots, b_{is}^{80}) \gtreqless D_i^{*\,80,80}(b_{i1}^{80}, b_{i2}^{80}, \ldots, b_{is}^{80}) \gtreqless c_i^{80}$$

Tests performed by the author on equations 12 and 13 demonstrate that both the agency's "Sovietized" and pre-"Sovietized" fixed vintage parametric dollar cost estimates of *American* weapons are greatly downward biased.[23] The exact value of these biases, which are consistent with the ruble bias discussed in section V, cannot be reported at present, but they are compatible with the 6 percent compound annual rate of "technical growth" from 1942 to 1980 for all U.S. weapons estimated in 1975 by Leonard Sullivan, assistant secretary of defense for program analysis and evaluation.[24] This measure which subsumes intervintage technological progress as a constituent part when adjusted to conform with our definitions produces estimates of *American* intervintage technological progress for the sixties of 3 percent per annum (see appendix 1):

14. $$100\left[\left(\frac{\sum_{i=1}^{k} D_i^{74,69}(b_{ij}^{69})}{\sum_{i=1}^{k} D_i^{74,60}(b_{ij}^{60})}\right)^{1/9} - 1\right]$$

$$\simeq 100 \left[\left(\frac{\sum\limits_{i=1}^{n} \hat{D}_i^{74,69} (b_{ij}^{69})}{\sum\limits_{i=1}^{n} \hat{D}_i^{74,60} (b_{ij}^{60})} \right)^{1/9} - 1 \right] = 3 \text{ percent per annum}$$

and 6 percent per annum for the seventies:

$$15. \quad 100 \left[\left(\frac{\sum\limits_{i=1}^{k} D_i^{74,79} (b_{ij}^{79})}{\sum\limits_{i=1}^{k} D_i^{74,70} (b_{ij}^{70})} \right)^{1/9} - 1 \right]$$

$$\simeq 100 \left[\left(\frac{\sum\limits_{i=1}^{n} \hat{D}_i^{74,79} (b_{ij}^{79})}{\sum\limits_{i=1}^{n} \hat{D}_i^{74,70} (b_{ij}^{70})} \right)^{1/9} - 1 \right] = 6 \text{ percent per annum.}$$

These findings corroborate the hypothesis that the anomalous behavior of the CIA's estimates is attributable to a specification error in its dollar parameter cost estimating equations, that fails to take *Soviet* intervintage technological progress into account either directly, or derivatively using *American* intervintage technological progress as a surrogate.

VII. Other Sources of Downward Bias

Although confirmation of the biases predicted by Theorem 1 demonstrate that the agency's use of fixed vintage parametric cost estimating relationships provides a cogent explanation of the 236 percent error in its 1970 estimate of Soviet procurement expenditures, this does not imply that other factors did not contribute to the underestimate. In theory, CIA estimates could also have been biased downward because (1) allowance was not made for retrofitting (upgrading) old equipment;[25] (2) weapons were undercounted; (3) procurement estimates were arbitrarily adjusted; and (4) Soviet prices might have been distorted by hidden inflation.

It is easily shown, however, that these ancillary factors are subordinate causes because they cannot adequately explain the behavioral anomalies associated with equations 9 and 10. Retrofitting and weapons undercounts obviously will not suffice because the quantities (qs) on the right and left hand side of both weak inequalities are the same and cannot account either for the underestimate ΣR_i^{60} (β_{i1}^{70}, β_{i2}^{70}, . . ., β_{is}^{70}) q_i^{70} in equation 9, or the overestimate ΣR_i^{70} (β_{i1}^{60}, β_{i2}^{60}, . . ., β_{is}^{60}) q_i^{60} in equation 10. Arbitrary adjustment, and price inflation could conceivably constitute partial alternative explanations but neither is especially compelling. Military machine-building price inflation, if it existed at all (see chapter 3, and part II), was too small to produce the anomalous effects actually observed in weak inequalities 9 and 10. It thus seems reasonable to deduce that even if parametric cost estimating bias was not the only cause of the discrepancy between the agency's 1970 pre- and postrevision estimates of Soviet procurement, it was the principal cause.

VIII. Laspeyres-Paasche Order Reversal

This deduction is buttressed by the fact that fixed vintage parametric cost estimation is apt to generate a Laspeyres-Paasche order reversal under conditions of rapid technological change. The likelihood of such a reversal arises because the cost savings that would normally be achieved in standard, modified, or new weapons (produced in the base year) undergoing rapid expansion (down the learning curve) might well be offset by costly qualitative improvements in their subsystems, while obsolete weapons that cannot be easily upgraded and are in the process of being phased out continue to achieve small production economies. Under these circumstances, late year prices, estimated from late year cost estimating relationships, embodying late year ex-post technology, will make it appear as if the prices of weapons experiencing rapid expansion are high (because changes in quality are misconstrued as changes in average factor costs) compared with the prices of these same weapons in the base year. Likewise, the prices of weapons that are growing slowly, or even declining will appear to be low relative to base year prices. The positive association of high relative prices (in comparison with base year prices) with rapid volume increases, and low relative prices with slow volume increases necessarily causes procurement growth computed in late year prices to be faster than in early year prices; that is, causes a Laspeyres-Paasche order reversal.

This reversal, which is a direct consequence of substituting fixed vintage parametric cost estimating techniques for engineering estimates and which could easily be misattributed to "hidden inflation," is, of course, likely to be an accounting illusion.[26] If qualitative improvements were properly distinguished from cost savings achieved in the production of weapons undergoing rapid expansion (see chapter 6), adjusted late year prices of these weapons would almost certainly decrease instead of rising and the Laspeyres rate would once again exceed the Paasche rate of growth as theory dictates. It follows therefore that a clear understanding of the bias likely to be induced by parametric cost estimation not only explains why the CIA's estimates exhibit a Laspeyres-Paasche reversal, it also elucidates why a valid, quality-adjusted Laspeyres index of Soviet procurement growth should rectify this anomaly.

IX. Underestimated Soviet Procurement Growth, 1960–70: The Agency's Dollar Series

The foregoing analysis should leave little doubt that the most probable explanation of the 236 percent discrepancy in the agency's 1970 pre- and postrevision estimates of Soviet procurement and the anomalous behavior of its ruble Laspeyres and Paasche indices is fixed vintage, parametric cost estimating bias. One perplexity however remains. Did the behavior of the real dollar Laspeyres procurement growth series 1960–70 correspond with the ruble series as the intervintage parametric cost estimating hypothesis would appear to suggest? The answer to this question unfortunately may never be known. The CIA has informed me that it does not possess and has never calculated a real Laspeyres dollar procurement series in 1960 prices. Dollar estimates computed before 1970 I was told were made exclusively in current prices, and were not used to evaluate the plausibility of the ruble procurement series.

X. Conclusion

The CIA routinely maintains that its estimates of real Soviet procurement cannot be seriously in error because the methodological procedures it employs are beyond reproach. This premise has been disconconfirmed by the evidence compiled in the preceding sections. Contrary to the agency's claims, it has been demonstrated that its real ruble procurement series behave aberrantly judged from the perspective of index number theory. This aberrant behavior cannot be adequately explained by the CIA's "hidden inflation" theory, but is entirely consistent with the hypothesis that the agency's fixed vintage parametric cost estimating method systematically underestimates embodied technological progress.

Additional confirmation of the fixed vintage parametric cost estimating bias hypothesis has been provided by diverse DOD studies which document the phenomenon in U.S. weapons systems and demonstrate that the CIA's "pre-Sovietized" dollar estimates for one major class of U.S. weapons produced in 1979 was inordinately low; a shortcoming that has not as yet been rectified in the agency's "Sovietized" real procurement series. And just recently the agency has acknowledged that its residual method ruble estimate of Soviet procurement for *1980* exceeds its published direct cost estimate by 140 percent, replicating its underestimate for 1970.[27]

It seems reasonable to deduce that the disparity between the CIA's prerevision ruble estimate of Soviet procurement in 1970 and the figure obtained from the books of the Soviet Ministry of Defense should not be attributed to unobservable causes like "hidden inflation," but to deficiencies in the agency's estimating procedures that have severed the link between documented DOD procurement acquisition costs and the cost data embodied in the CIA's parametric costing models. Although further research is required to determine the exact degree to which documented DOD acquisition costs diverge from CIA estimates for all U.S. weapons, the evidence at hand is sufficient to establish the general order of magnitude. Likewise, while it is true that a full appreciation of the dynamics of Soviet procurement is clouded by the fact that the agency does not calculate Laspeyres dollar growth series—the behavior of its Paasche dollar indices and its Laspeyres pre- and postrevision ruble series provide an adequate basis for concluding that real Soviet procurement growth, measured in dollars or rubles, is significantly faster than the agency's statistics suggest.

Notes

1. Donald Burton (1979), p. 3.
2. "The Metaphysics of Dollar Estimates of Soviet Defense Activities," CIA, 1978. Also Burton (1979), p. 2–3.
3. The agency claims to have a large sample of ruble weapon prices. "The sample of prices is especially good for the most expensive Soviet weapon systems—aircraft, missiles, ships, etc." (Burton, 1979). This assertion should not be construed to mean that most ruble weapons prices for 1960 and 1970 are obtained covertly from Soviet sources. The agency's sample is a heterogeneous collection assembled for diverse years. For the most part the CIA uses these prices to form composite ruble/dollar ratios employed to transform dollar subaggregates into ruble subaggregates.
4. The CIA has chosen to develop its own parametric costing models of Soviet weapons independently from those computed by the procurement departments of the navy, army, and air force. These models are derived from American production data for some given year, and are very infrequently reestimated with an entirely fresh dataset for later years because it is assumed that U.S. weapons being more advanced, contain all feasible new Soviet observations. From time to time special engineering studies are undertaken for isolated weapons, or a new costing model is developed, but in all cases the fixed vintage approach is preserved because these new models are not continuously updated with revised production data for all observations in subsequent years. The procurement departments of the U.S. Navy, Army and Air Force by contrast employ variable vintage parametric

models that are continuously updated for all weapons in current production. The variable vintage parametric approach has the distinct advantage of always reflecting current ex-post production cost. If Soviet weapons were computed with these relationships they would be strictly comparable with U.S. procurement expenditures. Fixed vintage models do not possess this property, however. They quickly become obsolete, understating real cost compared with weapons produced in a later vintage. For a further discussion of this issue see the postscript.

Abram Bergson has pointed out that for some purposes weight and size are best construed as physical rather than performance characteristics. The reader should interpret the term *macroperformance indicators* accordingly.

5. Engineering analogues constitute only a small proportion of the agency's dollar estimates, despite its assertion that ". . . we have good data, our cost estimates capture the 'austerity or complexity' of the Soviet weapon" (Burton, 1979, p. 2). The precise share is classified.

6. The use of fixed vintage parametric cost estimating relationships to value weapons produced at a later date is equivalent to using engineering estimates of early models as proxies for valuing improved late vintage models. Both procedures ignore the effects of technological change.

7. Note that the CIA does not publish, or compute Soviet procurement series in current rubles (Swain, personal correspondence).

8. The symbol R_i^{70} is used instead of $\frac{r_i^t}{p_j^i} \cdot D_i^{70}$ for expository convenience since the discussion which follows deals principally with ruble values. R_i^{70}, however, should not be misconstrued as representing ruble cost estimating relationships derived directly from ex-post data on ruble weapon costs. Also note that the superscript 70 does not imply that the database underlying each and every cost estimating relationship is 1970. It merely indicates that most of the equations in force during the seventies are circa 1970 when the last major revision of the database took place. The superscript 1960 should be interpreted in the same sense. The CIA costing effort began in the mid-1950s. I do not know the exact dates when the majority of its costing equations for the sixties came into effect, but presume that the designation circa 1960 is a reasonable one.

9. $r_i^{70} = r_1^{70}f_1^{70} (q_i^{60}) + r_2^{70}f_2^{70} (q_i^{60}), \ldots, + r_z^{70}f_z^{70} (q_i^{60})$

where factor usage x_j^{70} is

$x_j^{70} = f_j^{70} (q_i^{60})$.

10. See note 4. Although the general problem of intervintage technological change is widely discussed in the cost estimating literature, the phenomenon is seldom treated in the present context because aside from the CIA, parametric cost estimation is almost never used to calculate "constant" prices for the purpose of computing real procurement growth series. Costing specialists from the U.S. Naval Postgraduate School, NAVMAT, and Rand have informed me directly (and in one instance indirectly) that the agency nonetheless should have anticipated the problem, but never broached the issue with experts at these institutions. It thus may well be the case that the difficulties posed by intervintage technological change simply escaped the agency's attention. Alternatively, the CIA may have been aware of the problem, but believed that the benefits of using its own costing models

rather than those of the navy, army, and air force procurement agencies outweighed the costs, assuming that most technological progress would be embodied in new weapons captured along the regression line.

On the general issue of intervintage technological change in the professional costing literature see J. P. Large and K. M. S. Gillespie (1977), esp. pp. 28–33; William L. Stanley and Michael D. Miller (1979); William Stanley (1980); James Daniels and George Kreisel, Jr. (1975); J. R. Nelson and F. Timson (n.d.); Robert Shisko (1973); Alvin J. Harman (1970), esp. p. 22 ff.

11. Patrick Parker, "Soviet Military Objectives and Capabilities in the 1980s," in Steven Rosefielde, ed. (1980g). The most comprehensive work on this subject is the classified six-volume DIA study *U.S. and Soviet Weapon System Design Practice* (U), May, 1980. For an unclassified assessment see *Soviet Military Power*, DOD, September 1981. These studies demonstrate that the dismissive attitude taken toward the scientific and technical revolution by sundry commentators is unwarranted.

12. Developments in the accuracy of Soviet strategic missiles, MIRV capabilities, and the Alpha submarine are indicative. Professors William Reese and Donald Daniels, specialists in Soviet weapons technology at the U.S. Naval Postgraduate School, were generous enough to explain these matters to me at great length.

13. Leonard Sullivan, assistant secretary of defense for program analysis and evaluation, testimony to the House Armed Services Committee, in *Military Posture* (1975a), pp. 1817–60. See appendix 1.

14. William Reese, professor of Physics at the U.S. Naval Postgraduate School in a letter dated November 21, 1980, informed me that he "had occasion to look at the constant dollar costs of several series of U.S. weapons systems over the period late 40s to early 70s, and found that in comparing series of successor systems that constant dollar costs increased at about 3% per annum. I call this 'technical inflation' and claim that it captures the U.S. trend in costs for enhanced capability. I could well believe the Soviet rate of technical inflation in the 65–80 period would be higher because the rate at which they introduced new systems was so high. Comparing the Soviet new system time with U.S. new system times (about a factor of 2–3) one might impute a 7–12% rate for Soviet technical inflation under the assumption that the added costs of more sophisticated systems be a function of vintage and not time."

15. Soviet and American technologies are supposedly commensurated through the ruble-dollar ratios. This assumption is probably workable for 1970 since the true ruble values are known from covert sources.

16. The ruble prices used by the agency to compute its Laspeyres index nominally refer to 1955. A large proportion of these ruble prices, however, were actually collected in the early sixties. They are therefore best perceived as prices prevailing circa 1960. Both for this reason and expository purposes as well, the current value of Soviet procurement is expressed in the text as $\Sigma r_i^{60} q_i^{60}$ instead of $\Sigma r_i^{55} q_i^{60}$. $\Sigma r_i^{60} q_i^{60}$ and $\Sigma r_i^{70} q_i^{70}$ are unbiased by construction because their underlying dollar values are computed from ex-post cost observations and the ruble prices are confirmed by both open and secret Soviet data.

17. The term in the numerator does not capture improvements in automated subsystems, the weapons suit, navigation, guidance, and design because the

cost estimating equations underlying R_i^{70} are based on 1970 vintage technology.

18. This axiom assumes that the production cost of the rapidly growing components of output fall faster than the slower growing components. The axiom depends solely on the behavior of relative prices and thus is not affected by inflation. The empirical validity of the axiom is well established, especially with regard to the Soviet economy. Western studies of Soviet industrial growth have never uncovered a single case that falsified this axiom.

19. The agency's best postrevision estimate of Soviet procurement in 1970, $\Sigma r_i^{70} q_i^{70}$ is 17 billion rubles. For diverse reasons I believe its 18.5 billion ruble estimate derived with the residual method is more correct. The argument advanced in the text is unaffected by the choice of either alternative estimate.

20. The CIA's estimate of the current value of Soviet procurement in 1960 valued in nominal 1955 prices, $\Sigma r_i^{60} q_i^{60}$ is 5.5 billion rubles. See chapter 2, note 2.

21. The agency estimate of real Soviet procurement in 1970, valued in early year prices, $\Sigma r_i^{60} q_i^{70}$ is approximately 5.5 billion rubles. See Swain, op. cit. Also see note 11. The invalidation of inequality 9 could also be imputed to hidden inflation, but on this point see note 26 and part II.

22. The CIA estimate of Soviet procurement growth valued in postrevision 1970 rubles is 4 percent annum. Swain, op. cit. The agency's direct cost estimate of Soviet procurement for 1970 in postrevision 1970 prices is 17 billion rubles. The value $\Sigma r_i^{70} q_i^{60}$ is estimated from these figures:

$$\Sigma r_i^{70} q_i^{60} = \Sigma r_i^{70} q_i^{70} \div \frac{\Sigma r_i^{70} q_i^{70}}{\Sigma r_i^{70} q_i^{60}}$$
$$= 17 \div (1.04)^{10}$$
$$= 11.48 \text{ billion rubles.}$$

23. The data used to perform these tests were taken from DOD worksheets. The exact values of some physical parameters contained on these worksheets were classified. Although these parameters were not used directly in my calculations, reporting exact values would nonetheless be imprudent.

24. Leonard Sullivan, testimony in *Military Posture*, House Armed Services Committee, Washington, 1975, pp. 1817–60. See appendix 1.

25. The CIA may make some allowance for retrofitting, but this seems unlikely to me because its parametric cost estimating equations tacitly assume that weapons that are externally unchanged have not been qualitatively improved. Leonard Sullivan believes that retrofitting could be an important factor in explaining why the "new information" suggests that Soviet intervintage technological progress has increased more rapidly than American intervintage technological change. (Private discussion March 11, 1981.) See chapter 2, note 15.

26. The issue of hidden inflation merits, and will be given, a fuller treatment in part II. A few preliminary observations, however, are required to complete the argument developed in the text. According to the CIA, the new information received in 1975 did not alter its estimates of the size or capabilities of Soviet military forces. If this statement is interpreted literally it implies that the discrepancy between the agency's pre- and postrevision

estimates of Soviet procurement, 5.5 and 18.5 billion rubles, is attributable completely to inflation. A portion of this price change was across the boards, but another part must have been concentrated in the fast growing component of Soviet weaponry (excluding for argument sake parametric cost estimating bias) because the agency's postrevision procurement growth rate, 4 percent, exceeded its prerevision rate.

The CIA could thus argue that the Laspeyres-Paasche order reversal identified in chapter 2 was caused by spurious innovation, unjustified price increases concentrated in serially produced weapons including surface ships, submarines, missiles, aircraft, and tanks. Such an argument suffers, however, from three fatal flaws. First, it implies an average compound rate of hidden inflation of 12.9 percent from 1960 to 1970, and a still higher rate for the fast growing components of the arsenal. Inflation rates of this magnitude can hardly be viewed as hidden, and it seems implausible in the extreme to believe that procurement officers from the Soviet Ministry of Defense would willingly pay drastically higher prices for serially produced weapons that were merely superficially ("spuriously") improved. Second, if the military procurement officers had actually sanctioned price gouging by civilian enterprise managers the effects of this action should be evident in machine-building and metalworking profit data. In chapter 10 it will be demonstrated that this is not the case. Third, if the price increases in the rapidly growing component of Soviet procurement are really bogus, due to hidden inflation, then the agency's postrevision estimates of real Soviet procurement growth from 1960 to 1979 are also bogus because they do not reflect average factor costs. To be consistent the CIA must conclude that real Soviet growth from 1960 to 1975 adjusted for unwarranted increases in serially produced weapons is not 4 percent, but .6 percent, its prerevision–preinflation estimate.

The agency can, of course, avoid this horn of its dilemma by disputing my literal interpretation of its assertion that the new information did not alter its perception of the size and capabilities of Soviet forces, contending instead that the price changes that drive its postrevision estimates of Soviet procurement growth do represent average factor cost, and implying that hidden price inflation was proportional. While this approach rescues the CIA's real procurement growth estimates, it undercuts its hidden inflation hypothesis. If hidden inflation is proportional as asserted, then no grounds exist for the Laspeyres-Paasche order reversal. Such a phenomenon implies that the average factor cost of serially produced weapons was *rising* down the learning curve, behavior that cannot be credenced without the strongest possible empirical justification.

27. See chapter 1, note 28. The magnitude of the disparity implied for 1980 is less than for 1970 because the agency's postrevision Laspeyres growth rate 1960–80 exceeds its prerevision rate: 4 versus 0 percent per annum.

CHAPTER 5

The Significance of the "New Information"

Resolving the riddle posed by the agency's concealment of the inconsistencies in Colby's testimony has revealed that the CIA's direct costing practices inherently understate real Soviet procurement growth. This finding implies that Soviet military capabilities have increased much more rapidly during the past two decades than the agency's procurement estimates suggest. However, determining the direction of the bias is a great deal simpler than ascertaining its exact magnitude. Uncertainties of two sorts frustrate precise quantification. First, the "new information" obtained from the books of the Soviet Ministry of Defense is inexact. Second, some small portion of the increase may be attributable to ruble price inflation, even though as was demonstrated in the preceding chapter intervintage technological progress explains most of the discrepancy between the agency's pre- and postrevision procurement estimates for 1970.

The degree to which these factors may distort our perception of real Soviet procurement growth is shown in Table 5.1. Panel A, line 1, reports three estimates of Soviet procurement expenditures valued at prevailing ruble prices, derived from the "new information." The entry in column 2, 17 billion rubles, represents the agency's best estimate using American definitions of defense expenditure and corresponds with an 18.5 billion ruble estimate computed with the residual methodology. The entries in columns 1 and 3, 15.3 and 18.7 billion rubles, constitute lower and upper limits within which the agency feels confident the true figure falls. The range of uncertainty exhibited by these estimates and implicit in the "new information," while not insignificant, is still sufficiently precise to form a workable impression of the magnitude of the Soviet procurement effort.

The growth rate of nominal Soviet procurement expenditures implied by these estimates is shown in panel A, line 3. All exceed 10 percent

TABLE 5.1
Real and Nominal Rate of Soviet Procurement Growth, 1960–70

	(1)	(2)	(3)
A. Nominal Growth			
1. Estimated nominal procurement 1970	15.3	17	18.7
2. Estimated Soviet procurement in 1960, valued in 1955 prices	5.5	5.5	5.5
3. Implied rate of procurement growth	10.8%	11.9%	13.0%
B. Real Paasche Growth			
1. Estimated nominal procurement 1970	15.3	17	18.7
2. Soviet industrial price deflator $\frac{\Sigma r^{70}q^{60}}{\Sigma r^{55}q^{60}}$	1.12	1.12	1.12
3. Estimated real procurement row 1 ÷ row 2	13.7	15.2	16.7
4. Estimated Soviet procurement in 1960 valued in 1955 prices	5.5	5.5	5.5
5. Implied rate of procurement growth	9.6%	10.2%	11.2%
C. Real Paasche Growth			
1. Estimated nominal procurement 1970	15.3	17	18.7
2. Soviet machine-building and metal-working price deflator $\Sigma r^{70}q^{60}/\Sigma r^{55}q^{60}$	.71	.71	.71
3. Estimated real procurement (row 1 ÷ row 2)	21.6	24.0	26.4
4. Estimated Soviet procurement in 1960 valued in 1955 prices	5.5	5.5	5.5
5. Implied rate of procurement growth	14.7%	15.9%	17.0%

Sources:

A1: *USSR: Toward a Reconciliation of Marxist and Western Measures of National Income,* ER 78–10505, CIA, October 1978, 14. The agency's "best estimate" is 17 billion rubles. Allowing for a 10 percent error range (the usual claim) produces 15.3 and 18.7 billion rubles as lower and upper bounds. The CIA's best residual estimate is 18.5 billion rubles.

A2: See chapter 2, note 2.

A3: $100[(r^{70}q^{70}/r^{55}q^{60})^{1/10} - 1]\%$

B2: Industrial enterprise wholesale prices net of turnover taxes are used as the deflator. See *Narodnoe Khoziaistvo SSSR*, 1972, p. 197. On the quantity weights see Steiner, *Inflation in Soviet Industry and Machine-Building and Metalworking (MBMW) 1960–1975.*

C2: Machine-building metalworking enterprise wholesale prices net of turnover tax are used as the deflator. See *Narodnoe Khoziaistvo SSSR*, 1972, p. 197.

per annum, indicating that if there were no ruble price inflation in the Soviet military machine-building sector real procurement would have grown 2.6 to 3.3 times faster than the postrevision CIA estimate suggests, and of course infinitely faster than its prerevision estimate (0 percent).

The assumption that there was no ruble price inflation in the Soviet military machine-building sector during the sixties is probably not very wide of the mark. As will be demonstrated in part II, no credible evidence exists supporting a hidden inflation rate in excess of 2 percent per annum, and even this upper bound must be considered problematically high. Bearing this in mind, the Soviet industrial price index can be taken as a rough indicator of the effect price inflation may have had on the real growth of Soviet procurement. This value is reported in panel B, line 2. When applied as a deflator to the procurement expenditure values derived from the new information, real Soviet procurement growth during the sixties is diversely estimated between 9.6 and 11.2 percent per annum.

Other estimates of real Soviet procurement growth are feasible. Panel C shows the effect of substituting the official Soviet machine-building and metalworking price deflator for the industrial index. Real Soviet procurement increases between 14.7 and 17 percent annually on this measure, reflecting the fact that official Soviet machinery prices fell sharply during this period.

Doubts can and have been raised about the accuracy of this index. It can also be argued that the real rates of Soviet procurement growth reported in Table 5.1 are exaggerated because the agency's 1960 procurement estimate is too low. Higher figures, between 6 and 6.4 billion rubles, have sometimes been suggested. But these adjustments and others of their kind do not alter the basic picture. Although estimated magnitudes are inexact, real Soviet procurement appears to have grown at least 2.5 times faster than the agency's postrevision estimates warrant.

The significance of the "new information" thus is clear. It tells us that sometime during the late fifties or early sixties the Soviet Union embarked upon a massive program of military modernization that profoundly affected the balance of power. This shift was broadly recognized in the Defense Department, where the qualitative improvement in Soviet weaponry was a constant source of concern, but had little impact on civilian students of national security affairs because the defects of direct costing made it appear as if real Soviet defense expenditures were growing at a negligible pace. This appearance of restraint was a mirage, however. Real procurement was growing faster than almost anyone imagined.

CHAPTER 6

Underestimating Soviet Procurement Expenditures Under Conditions of Rapid Technical Progress

The discovery that embodied Soviet military technology has been growing far more rapidly than most analysts anticipated not only demonstrates that the agency's procurement estimates have been too low, but indicates that the theoretical norms employed in the scholarly community to evaluate these estimates have been deficient, and need to be modified to explicitly take intervintage technological progress into account. More specifically, the conventional rule invariably invoked to place the CIA's procurement series in proper perspective, which postulates that dollar estimates significantly understate both the comparative size of American procurement expenditures and the rate of Soviet weapons growth, needs to be carefully reassessed.

Both propositions are derived from index number theory which suggests that if as a first approximation the effects of technological progress are ignored:

1. For purposes of static international comparison of American and Soviet procurement, ruble prices understate the relative magnitude of Soviet military expenditure because advanced American weapons, which bulk large in our arsenal, are valued at high Soviet production cost prices. Likewise dollar price comparisons overstate the relative magnitude of Soviet military expenditures because lower technology weapons which dominate the Soviet arsenal are valued at higher American production cost prices.

2. For purposes of computing rates of military expenditure growth, base year prices overstate the growth rate (Laspeyres indices) and final

year prices understate the growth rate (Paasche indices) given the reasonable assumption that prices and quantities are inversely correlated.

These propositions are basically correct, given the premise that other things are equal, but when technological progress is taken explicitly in consideration it is easily demonstrated that they need to be strongly qualified and may even be reversed:

> *Counter-Proposition 1:* As the technological level of Soviet weapons rises, ceteris paribus, the size of the dollar estimate bias must decline.

Proof: The dollar estimate bias is based on the assumption that the price of conventional weapons is relatively high in the United States, and that the share of conventional weapons in the Soviet arsenal is relatively large. Even if Soviet prices remained unchanged, the distortionary effect of high conventional weapons prices must be reduced as the composition of Soviet weapons divided between advanced and conventional weapons comes more and more to approximate the U.S. mix. If, as is likely, relative Soviet prices on average approach U.S. relatives as the weapons mix changes, then the bias must diminish further. As to the possibility of bias reversal, all that would be required is that the share of advanced weapons in the Soviet arsenal exceed that of the United States, while the relative price of advanced armament remained lower in the United States because America was further down its advanced technology learning curve. Under these circumstances, an index formed with high domestic Soviet advanced weapons prices used to weight the relatively abundant supply of advanced weapons would yield a higher index value than if American price weights were employed. This reversal of the traditional direction of the bias is due to the fact that prices and quantities would be directly instead of inversely correlated.[1]

Under present circumstances, therefore, where the share of advanced Soviet weapons is rising and their *average* is converging toward ours, it follows that dollar estimates do not significantly overstate and may actually understate the magnitude of Soviet procurement expenditures, without taking the further issue of misspecification bias into account.[2]

Another hoary artifact of index theory is the inference that the rate of Soviet procurement growth evaluated in dollars is downward biased.

Proper account of quality change does not reverse this effect, but it does intensify the magnitude of the downward bias.

Counter-Proposition 2: Quality-adjusted dollar indices necessarily impart a downward bias to the effect of qualitative improvement in Soviet weapons.

Proof: To form a quality-adjusted index, new and improved weapons must be expressed in terms of a numerically equivalent amount of their base year counterparts. Equivalence is determined by the marginal rate of prevailing product transformation between the old and the improved weapon. Since new technologies will lie higher on the Soviet learning curve than the American, dollar prices of advanced Soviet weapons will understate domestic Soviet production costs and thereby understate the change in Soviet production potential represented by the introduction of advanced armaments. This underestimate of the growth increment imputable to qualitative improvement is compounded by the overestimate of the magnitude of Soviet defense expenditures attributable to the dollar bias in the base year when Soviet armaments were substantially inferior to our own. The combined effect of understated increments and overstated base year defense expenditures necessarily biases our perception of Soviet qualitative weapons change downward.[3]

Counter-Proposition 3: The understatement of the qualitative improvement of Soviet weapons is further biased by the CIA method of price deflation.

Proof: To eliminate the effect of inflation on weapons which do not have a fixed vintage parametric dollar price, or for weapons added in later years to the parametric cost estimating population, a Laspeyres price index with base year quantity weights is used to deflate a value index of current procurement producing a Paasche quantity index with final year price weights. Since Paasche indices except in extraordinary circumstances understate growth by overstating the base, it follows directly that American dollar cost estimates using final year price weights bias Soviet defense expenditures even further below the levels acknowledged conventionally.[4] Propositions 1, 2, and 3 thus demonstrate that even if the agency possessed legitimate dollar prices for Soviet weapons both the level and rate of real Soviet procurement growth would tend to be misperceived because its analytic

conventions take inadequate account of the technological improvements being made in Soviet weaponry.

Rapid Technological Progress and Real Soviet Procurement Growth: A Geometric Intrepretation

Having shown that the diverse ways in which the agency underestimates the Soviet military buildup have a common origin in its misper-
ception of Soviet technological progress, the overall structure of the
costing-cum-measurement problem can be summarized with the aid of
a geometric demonstration.

Figure 6.1 depicts the production of Soviet military goods. Conventional weapons are arrayed on the abscissa, advanced weapons on the
ordinate. Point A represents the mix of Soviet arms produced in 1960,
point B the mix in 1970 unadjusted for improvements in quality. The
slope of the rays v_{1960} and v_{1970} indicate that the share of advanced
weapons in the Soviet arsenal has increased. The magnitude of this shift,
is understated, however, because no allowance has been made for technical change. The appropriate adjustment moves the real production
point upward and to the left. If dollar prices that place a lower relative
value on advanced weapons are used for this purpose, quality-adjusted
production will occur at C; if ruble prices are employed, production will
occur at D on the ray v'_{1970}. The distance B'D/OD indicates the degree
to which the American direct costing equations and quality adjustment
procedures understate the real change in Soviet procurement production
potential. According to the agency's measure Soviet weapons production
potential has risen OB'/OA', while the real change is actually OD/OA'.

Although the understatement of both the level and rate of change in
Soviet production may be quite serious as illustrated in Figure 6.1, index
number distortion further exacerbates matters. This is shown in Figure
6.2, which can be used to depict two alternative index measures of
postwar Soviet procurement growth, one with 1970 American price
weights (α 1970), the other with 1960 Soviet price weights (ρ 1960),
both using official American estimates of Soviet procurement in 1960
and 1970 (points A and B). The choice of 1970 American prices reflects
existing practice, the selection of 1960 Soviet ruble weights the fact first
demonstrated by Moorsteen that a Laspeyres index most accurately
characterizes the change in an economy's production potential during
periods of rapid structural transformation.[5]

As can be easily observed the use of American price weights indicates
that production potential has increased OB/OB', compared with the
much larger change OA/OA', obtained with Soviet base year price

FIGURE 6.1
The Effect of Quality Change on the Dollar Estimate of Soviet
Production Potential

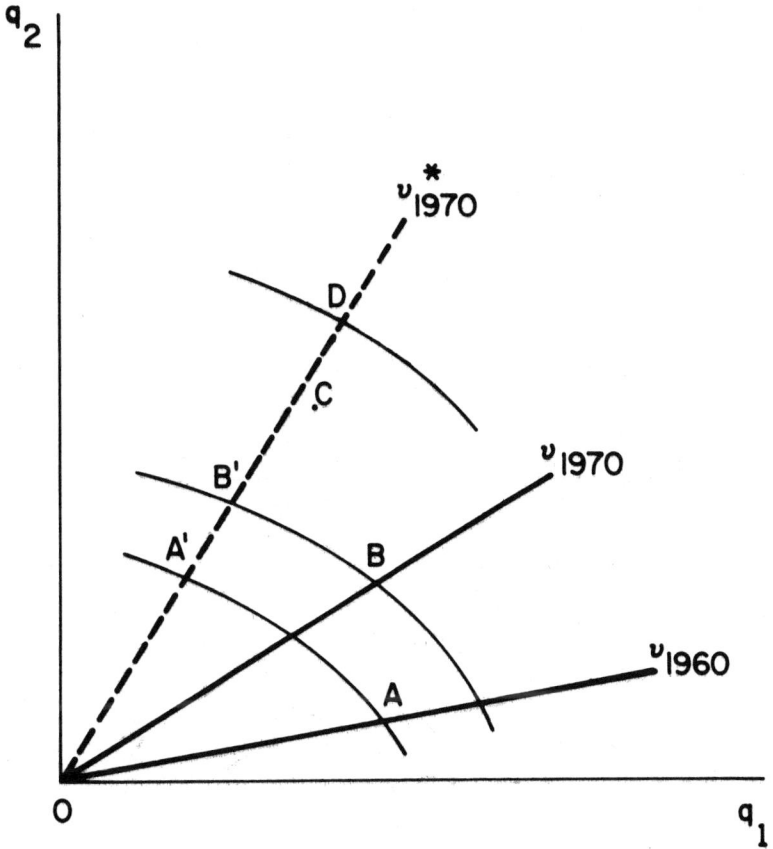

FIGURE 6.2
The Effect of Quality Change and Technical Progress on Observed
Index Bias in the Measurement of Soviet Defense Expenditures

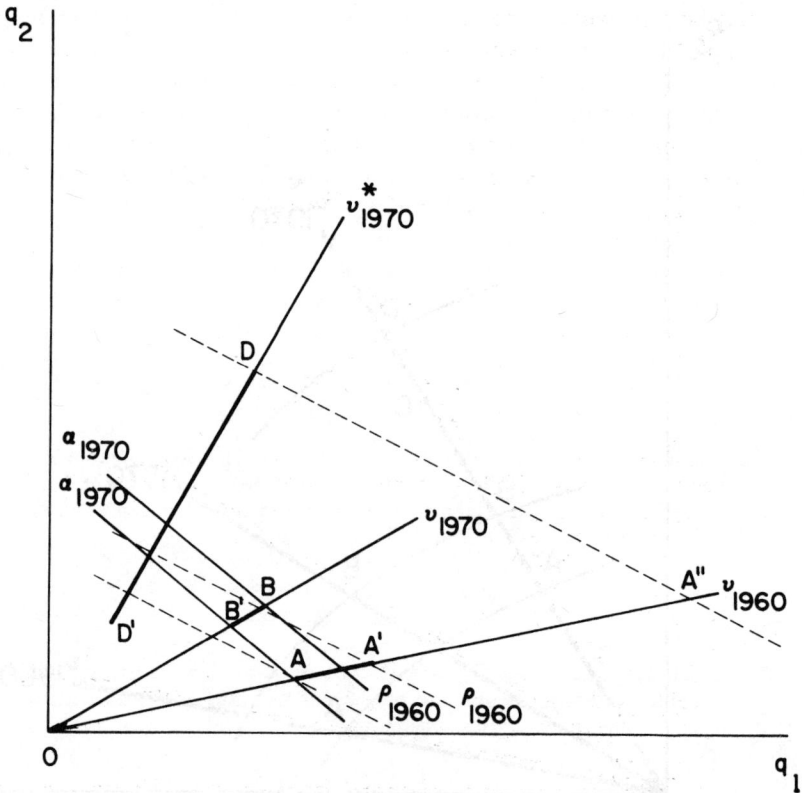

weights. Neither measure approximates, however, the real change in Soviet production potential OD/OD'. To obtain a measure of growth commensurate with the real change, Soviet base year prices would have to be applied not to the official U.S. weapons count, but to the true quality-adjusted procurement quantity at point D. This yields the estimate OA"/OA, which is similar to OD/OD'.

For those unfamiliar with index number analysis, these distinctions may be somewhat perplexing, but the important points to note are quite simple. First, the downward bias introduced into the measurement of Soviet procurement by the use of final year American prices to adjust for technical progress and quality change is compounded when American price weights are employed to compute a Paasche index of Soviet procurement growth. Second, a Laspeyres index calculated with Soviet prices produces a much greater rate of weapons growth, but the true magnitude of the change in Soviet procurement potential can only be determined if Soviet prices replace American prices in adjusting armaments for quality improvement, and all sources of technical progress are fully taken into account.[6]

Notes

1. The exact point where a positive dollar bias switches to a negative dollar bias depends on the price ratios in the United States and the Soviet Union. For example, suppose that the ratio of conventional to advanced weapons prices in the United States and the U.S.S.R. were respectively

1. $$p_{ia}/p_{ja} = 2/1; \qquad p_{ir}/p_{jr} = 1/4$$

that is $p_{ia} = 2$ dollars, $p_{ja} = 1$ dollar, $p_{ir} = 1$ ruble, $p_{jr} = 4$ rubles. The dollar-weighted index, I_a, would exceed, equal, or understate the ruble-weighted index, I_r, depending on the conventional-advanced weapon ratio, q_{ir}/q_{jr}, in the index expressions below.

1a. $$I_a \gtreqless I_r = \frac{p_{ia}^o \, q_{ir}^1 + p_{ja}^o \lambda q_{jr}^1}{p_{ia}^o q_{ir}^o + p_{ja}^o q_{jr}^o} \gtreqless \frac{p_{ir}^o q_{ir}^1 + p_{jr}^o \lambda q_{jr}^1}{p_{ir}^o q_{ir}^o + p_{jr}^o q_{jr}^o}$$

where $q_{ir}^1 = \delta q_{ir}^o; \ 0 < \delta < \infty$
$q_{jr}^1 = \rho q_{jr}^o; \ 0 < \rho < \infty$

λ is a measure of how much slower or faster advanced weapons have increased or decreased in the final compared to the base period.

Let $p_{ia}^o q_{ir}^o + p_{ja}^o q_{jr}^o = V$
$p_{ir}^o q_{ir}^o + p_{jr}^o q_{jr}^o = \theta V; \ 0 < \theta < \infty$

Then 1a becomes

1b.
$$\frac{p_{ia}^o q_{ir}^1 + p_{ja}^o \lambda q_{jr}^1}{V} \gtrless \frac{p_{ir}^o q_{ir}^1 + p_{jr}^o \lambda q_{jr}^1}{\theta V}$$

1c.
$$\frac{2q_{ir}^1 + 1\lambda q_{jr}^1}{V} \gtrless \frac{1q_{ir}^1 + 4\lambda q_{jr}^1}{\theta V}$$

multiply both sides by V

1d.
$$2q_{ir}^1 + \lambda q_{ir}^1 \gtrless \frac{q_{ir}^1 + 4\lambda q_{jr}^1}{\theta}.$$

If $q_{ir}^1/\lambda q_{jr}^1 = 3/1$ and $\theta = 1$, then

1e. $I_a = I_r$, (substituting 1 into 1d).

If $\theta \neq 1, I_a$ could be made equal to I_r by changing the ratio $q_{ir}^1/\lambda q_{jr}^1$. As $q_{ir}^1/\lambda q_{jr}^1$ declines, the dollar index monotonically falls faster than the ruble index. Thus if $\theta > 1$, a point where $I_a = I_r$ can always be found by decreasing $q_{ir}^1/\lambda q_{jr}^1$ below 3/1, and vice versa if $\theta < 1$.

It may be concluded then that for any set of ratios $p_{ia}^o/p_{ja}^o = n/1$, $p_{ir}^o/p_{jr}^o = 1/m$ bias is a monotonic function of the quantity ratio $q_{ir}^1/\lambda q_{jr}^1$ and the scalar, θ, and a point of index neutrality will always exist. In the example above, if the American conventional-advanced weapons ratio, q_{ia}^1/q_{ja}^1, were 1:1 and $\theta = 1$, index number bias reversal would occur long before the Soviet and American weapons mix converged. For less divergent price ratios, index number bias reversal would be deferred until the US-USSR arsenals were more alike. It should however be clear that as the Soviets have modernized their weapons systems, the standard assumptions concerning index number bias have become progressively more tenuous.

2. For an econometric analysis of the rate of aggregate technical progress in the Soviet Union see Desai (1976), Gomulka (1976), Rosefielde and Lovell (1977),and Weitzman (1970). On sectoral productivity see Rosefielde (1979b, 1981a). For a study of the quality of Soviet output see Spechler (1970, 1975). On the general issue of technology in the USSR see Berliner (1976), Granick (1975). An impression of the pace of improvement in Soviet arms can be effectively obtained from Lee (1978), Luttwak (1977), Nitze (1977), Parker (1978), Pipes (1977), Polmar (1977) and Wohlstetter (1977). More technical evaluations appear in Parker (1978).

In appraising the welter of evidence supporting the view that the Soviets have achieved rapid technical progress and qualitative advance in the production of civilian and military goods, it should be recognized that the index number analysis carried out here depends only on absolute technical progress, not technical progress relative to the United States.

3. From note 1 we saw that $I_a > I_r$ if the composition of Soviet weapons q_{ir}/q_{jr} is somewhat greater than the US mix, and $p_{ia}/p_{ja} > p_{ir}/p_{jr}$. To transform improved weapons into their base year analogues, old weapons are multiplied by prices representing prevailing marginal rates of transformation:

1.
$$q_{jr}^* = p_j^*/p_j \, q_{jr}$$

where the asterisk signifies the new model. Since America is undoubtedly further along its technology learning curve, the quality-improved weapon q_{jr}^* will probably be relatively cheaper in dollar than ruble prices so that

2.
$$p_{ja}^*/p_{ja} \, q_{jr} < p_{jr}^*/p_{jr} \, q_{jr}$$

and therefore the dollar quality-improved growth index must understate both the ruble-adjusted growth index where all other goods are weighted in dollars and the pure ruble-adjusted index.

3.
$$\frac{p_{ja}^*/p_{ja} \, dq_{jr}}{I_a} < \frac{p_{jr}^*/p_{jr} \, dq_{jr}}{I_a} < \frac{p_{jr}^*/p_{jr} \, dq_{jr}}{I_r}$$

4. Consider a simple two good index valued in money prices. The money price level in the base year is 1 and μ in the final year. Assume moreover that relative prices also change between the two periods. Measured in current values growth is

1.
$$I_c = \mu p_{11} q_{11} + \mu p_{12} q_{12}/p_{01} q_{01} + p_{02} q_{02}$$

where the first subscript indicates the year, the second the product.

To adjust for money inflation I_c must be deflated with a price index, conventionally with base year quantity weights

2.
$$I_p = p_{11} q_{01} + p_{12} q_{02}/p_{01} q_{01} + p_{02} q_{02}$$

which yields a Paasche quantity index with final year price weights

3.
$$\begin{aligned} I_q &= I_c/I_p \\ &= p_{11} q_{11} + p_{12} q_{12}/p_{11} q_{01} + p_{12} q_{02} \\ &= p_1 q_1/p_1 q_0 \end{aligned}$$

On current agency practice with regard to quantity weights see James Steiner (1978b) and "Price Index Methodology Used For the 1978 Dollar Cost Comparison of U.S. and Soviet Defense Activities" (1978).

5. Moorsteen (1961).
6. Other exotic biases caused by the misapplication of learning curves are discussed in Rosefielde (1982c).

Part II

HIDDEN INFLATION

CHAPTER 7

CIA Estimates of Hidden Soviet Military Machine-Building Inflation

The finding in the first part of this book that the direct costing methodology has an Achilles heel, that fixed vintage parametric cost estimation has biased the agency's estimates of Soviet procurement growth sharply downward, disproves the CIA's contention that its revised estimates of 1976 are almost entirely explained by hidden inflation. This demonstration, however, does not necessarily disconfirm the hypothesis that a substantial portion of the discrepancy between the agency's pre- and postrevision estimates of Soviet military procurement for 1970, and more recently the 140 percent discrepancy between the agency's residual and direct cost estimates of Soviet procurement for 1980 are attributable to hidden inflation. If compelling evidence exists demonstrating that hidden inflation in the Soviet military machine-building sector is significant then the explanatory power of intervintage technological change must be qualified, and its comparative importance determined.

To assess whether a cogent case can be made in favor of the proposition that hidden inflation explains the agency's 236 percent ruble procurement cost estimating error for 1970, it is instructive to begin by reviewing the methodology the CIA employs to measure unjustified increases in Soviet weapons prices.

The total change in the price level of the Soviet military machine-building sector is calculated with a Laspeyres price index computed from information contained in the agency's direct cost data bank. Since the data supporting these estimates are in every way identical with the information used to derive its estimates of real procurement, computing the total change in Soviet weapons prices is trivial. The Laspeyres rate is calculated merely by dividing the agency's best postrevision procurement estimate for 1960 by its best prerevision estimate[1]

1.
$$\frac{\Sigma r_{70}q_{60}}{\Sigma r_{55}q_{60}} = \frac{12.5}{5.5} = 2.27$$

2.
$$\dot{\mathrm{i}} = 100\,[(2.27)^{1/10} - 1] = 8.6 \text{ percent.}$$

Conceptually, the total price change measured in this way encompasses hidden inflation narrowly construed and any overt inflation detected by the Soviets with their unpublished military machine-building price indices. Presumably the agency believes that the data at its disposal matches the secret data held by the State Price Committee with sufficient precision that they can not only replicate the official price index,[2] but can calculate hidden inflation as well.[3]

Needless to say, these assumptions place a substantial burden on the CIA's limited ruble price data. The full extent of this burden, however, is concealed by the simple scalar estimate computed in equation 2. This "best" estimate in actuality constitutes only one of a large number of feasible and/or alternative "best" estimates that can be derived from agency data on current procurement costs and real procurement growth using the algebraic relationship.

3.
$$\frac{\Sigma r_{70}q_{60}}{\Sigma r_{55}q_{60}} = \frac{\Sigma r_{70}q_{70}}{\Sigma r_{55}q_{60}} \div \frac{\Sigma r_{70}q_{70}}{\Sigma r_{70}q_{60}}$$

The procurement data required to compute these alternative rates are provided in Table 7.1. Agency estimates of Soviet procurement expenditure in 1970 range from 13 to 21 billion rubles. The direct costing mean is 17 billion rubles, the best residual estimate is 18.5 billion rubles. For 1960 two alternative procurement figures are presented, the mean 5.5 billion rubles and an upper bound of 6.4 billion rubles. These estimates, taken in conjunction with the agency's postrevision real procurement growth index produce the hidden inflation rates shown in columns 4-6, for the specified periods during which inflation is thought to have occurred.[4]

They range between 2 and 20.9 percent. The upper limit presumes that Soviet procurement expenditures rose from 5.5 to 21 billion rubles from 1960 to 1970 and that the inflation process was confined to the subperiod 1966–70 when covert sources indicate Soviet weapon prices first started to increase. The lower limit assumes a significantly reduced level of procurement expenditure in 1970, 13 million rubles; a slightly increased level in 1960, 6.4 million rubles; and a greatly extended inflationary time span, the latter loosely justified by the fact that many

TABLE 7.1

Implied CIA Laspeyres Estimates of Hidden Soviet Procurement Price Inflation

Estimate	Cost of Soviet Weapons (billions of current rubles)		Duration of Hidden Inflation		
	1960	1970	15 years	10 years	5 years
1.	5.5	21	6.5%	9.9%	20.0%
2.	5.5	18.5	5.6%	8.6%	17.8%
3.	5.5	17	5%	7.6%	15.9%
4.	5.5	13	3.2%	4.8%	9.8%
5.	6.4	21	5.5%	8.3%	17.3%
6.	6.4	18.5	4.6%	6.9%	14.3%
7.	6.4	17	4.0%	6.0%	12.4%
8.	6.4	13	2%	3.2%	6.5%

Sources:
Column 1: William Colby, Director, CIA, *Allocation of Resources in the Soviet Union and China*, Joint Economic Committee of Congress, Washington, D.C., 1974, 68–69. For an analysis of Colby's chart see chapter 1.

The 6.4 billion ruble estimate is obtained by allowing a 10 percent range of error and correcting for the 6 percent rate of open inflation 1960–70 estimated by the CIA.

Column 2: Central Intelligence Agency, *USSR: Toward a Reconciliation of Marxist and Western Measures of National Income*, ER78–10505, October 1978, 14.

Column 3: The formula used to compute these rates is:

$$I = 100[((v_{70}/v_{60})/g)^{1/15} - 1]$$

where v_{70} is procurement cost in 1970, $\Sigma r_{70}q_{70}$ valued in 1970 ruble prices
v_{60} is procurement cost in 1960, $\Sigma r_{55}q_{60}$ valued in 1955 ruble prices
g is the CIA's estimate of real Soviet procurement growth
1960–1970 valued in constant postrevision 1970 prices, 1.48.

Column 4: $I = 100[((v_{70}/v_{60})/g)^{1/10} - 1]$
Column 5: $I = 100[((v_{70}/v_{60})/g)^{1/5} - 1]$

of the prices used by the agency in the early years of its direct costing effort refer to 1955.

The dispersion exhibited by these estimates is very wide and seriously undermines the credibility of the agency's contention that its estimates approximate the secret price statistics on the books of the State Price Committee, or measure hidden inflation. Some of this dispersion can, of course, be reduced by ignoring the variance of the procurement expenditure estimates for 1960 and 1970. These "best" estimates which are reported in rows 2 and 3 restrict hidden inflation to a range between

TABLE 7.2
Implied CIA Paasche Estimates of Hidden Soviet Procurement Price Inflation

Estimate	Cost of Soviet Weapons (billions of current rubles)		Duration of Hidden Inflation		
	1960	1970	15 years	10 years	5 years
1.	5.5	21	9.3%	14.3%	30.7%
2.	5.5	18.5	8.4%	12.9%	27.5%
3.	5.5	17	7.8%	11.9%	25.3%
4.	5.5	13	5.9%	9.0%	18.7%
5.	6.4	21	8.2%	12.6%	26.8%
6.	6.4	18.5	7.3%	11.2%	23.7%
7.	6.4	17	6.7%	10.3%	21.6%
8.	6.4	13	4.8%	7.3%	15.2%

Sources: Same as Table 7.1. The real Laspeyres procurement growth rate used in computing the inflation rates above is zero. See Donald Swain, Deputy Chief, Military-Economic Analysis Center, OSR, letter dated 9 August 1979.

5 and 17.8 percent. This domain can be narrowed further by excluding the estimates in column 4 on the grounds that most of the agency's procurement prices were collected in 1960, rather than 1955.

While these adjustments diminish some uncertainties, they raise other important problems. All "best" hidden inflation rates, for example, greatly exceed the rates observed in the civilian machine-building sector before and after Stalin's reign.[5] This suggests that if the agency's hidden inflation estimates are accurate, prices in the military machine-building sector have been rising at historically unprecedented rates. Although inflationary behavior of this sort cannot be ruled out, it is so implausible that the CIA itself has refrained from accepting its own "best" estimates.

Instead of fixing its estimate of hidden inflation in a range between 7.6 and 17.8 percent, the agency actually asserts that procurement prices have risen somewhat less than 4 percent per annum.[6] In circumventing the implications of its own "best" hidden inflation estimates in this way, the CIA is forced into the awkward position of preferring an outlier to its mean value estimates—an expedient that not only increases the burden of proof required to substantiate its claim, but undermines the credibility of its contention that its estimates accurately reflect the behavior of Soviet weapon prices.

This impasse may have an obvious solution, however. Since the Laspeyres rate of inflation should exceed the Paasche, perhaps more plausible "best" hidden inflation estimates could be derived using final year quantity weights that exhibit a narrow dispersion and low rates of increase. Table 7.2 reports the agency's Paasche rates of hidden inflation computed with equations 4 and 5:

4.
$$\frac{\Sigma r_{70}q_{70}}{\Sigma r_{55}q_{70}} = \frac{\Sigma r_{70}q_{70}}{\Sigma r_{55}q_{60}} \div \frac{\Sigma r_{55}q_{70}}{\Sigma r_{55}q_{60}}$$

5.
$$\dot{p} = [(\Sigma r_{70}q_{70}/\Sigma r_{55}q_{70})^{1/t} - 1].$$

As is easily seen they do not provide the desired solution. The Paasche rates not only exceed the Laspeyres rates of hidden procurement inflation and exhibit a wide dispersion, they all surpass the 4 percent annual rate favored by the agency.[7]

Notes

1. $\Sigma r_{70}q_{60} = \Sigma r_{70}q_{70} \div \dfrac{\Sigma r_{70}q_{70}}{\Sigma r_{70}q_{60}}$

   $= 18.5 \div 1.48$

   $= 12.5$

   This figure is derived from the agency's best residual procurement estimate for 1970. Its best direct cost estimate is

   $$\Sigma r_{70}q_{60} = 17 \div 1.48$$
   $$= 11.5$$

2. If the secret military machine building price indices do show high rates of inflation, the willingness of the Soviet leadership to accept this loss in the real purchasing power of the defense ruble must be explained.
3. If the agency can so easily detect the hidden inflation caused by spurious innovation with its sparse data, the inability of the State Price Committee to perform the same calculations needs to be explained as does the perverse willingness of Soviet procurement officers to acquiesce to this fraud. Why should these experts agree to pay extortive prices for "new products which are no more than slight variations of goods already being produced or even purely nominal name (designator) changes" when they are in a position to know better and cannot possibly justify their actions to their superiors, who are keenly aware of the low rates of inflation which officially prevail in the civilian sector? Indeed given the direct links that exist between military purchasers and enterprise managers, one would normally suppose that the Ministry of Defense would exert pressure to have its goods subsidized through the allocation of overhead costs to civilian goods, rather than being the object of monopolistic price discrimination. See James Steiner (1978a), p. 14. Cf. *An Analysis of the Behavior of Soviet Machinery Prices 1960–1973* (1979), pp. vi–vii.
4. $\Sigma r_{70}\, q_{70}/\Sigma r_{70}q_{60} = (1.04)^{10} = 1.48.$

5. Soviet economic arrangements do not as is sometimes supposed preclude inflation. The early years of Soviet power were characterized by monetary chaos and hyperinflation. A semblance of stability was achieved after 1926, only to give way again under the pressures of the Soviet industrialization drive. An impression of Soviet inflationary behavior in the ensuing years is provided in Table 7.1n. As is easily seen prices rose sharply from 1928 to 1950 despite the replacement of the NEP market system with comprehensive administrative price determination. Moorsteen and Powell's data show that inflation in the machinery and retail consumer goods sector during this period grew at very high rates, 4.8 and 14.1 percent per annum.

As in so many areas, Stalin's death seems to have marked the end of an epoch. Official Soviet data indicate that price stability was finally achieved under Khrushchev and his successors. From 1955 to 1978 retail consumer good prices were virtually unchanged and machinery prices reportedly declined 2.3 percent annually.

6. Donald Burton, letter dated February 21, 1979.
7. *An Analysis of the Behavior of Soviet Machinery Prices, 1960–1973*, p. vi. ". . . official indexes are clearly biased downward, most likely because of a failure to account for the discussed price inflation accompanying the introduction of new products."

TABLE 7.1 n
Soviet Machinery and Retail Consumer Goods Prices 1928–1978
(1937 = 100)

	Machinery	Retail Consumer Goods
1928	70	13.5
1930	70	
1935	93	
1940	103	103
1945	115	150
1950	196	244
1955	165	173
1960	140	173
1965	130	174
1970	124	173
1975	105	173
1978	98	174
Compound Inflation Rates		
1928–1950	4.8%	14.1%
1955–1978	−2.3%	0%

Sources: Richard Moorsteen and Raymond Powell, *The Soviet Capital Stock 1928–1962*, Table L-2, and Table L-3, pp. 558, 564. *Narodnoe Khoziaistvo 1978*, 138, 447. Moorsteen and Powell's series are used until 1955. They are linked to the Soviet series thereafter.

James Barry, chief, Economic Implications Branch, OSR, CIA, argued before the House Select Committee on Intelligence (September 3, 1980, p. 78) that the agency's best estimate of hidden inflation is 4 to 5 percent per annum, 1960–70 (cf. Table 7.1), and contends that my estimates are wrong because my 1960 values, 5.5–6.4, are too low and 1970 values, 17–18.5 billion rubles, are too high. In taking this position Barry is following Donald Swain in supposing that the 1960 value is approximately 11.5 billion rubles (see note 1); computing inflation as the line segment DE in Figure 2.1.

$$\dot{p}^* = 100[(11.5/6.4)^{1/15} - 1] = 4.0 \text{ percent per annum}$$
$$\dot{i}^* = 100[(18.5/5.5)^{1/15} - 1] = 5.6 \text{ percent per annum.}$$

This explanation however runs afoul all of the contradictions raised in chapter 2. See chapter 3, notes 2 and 3.

CHAPTER 8

CIA Estimates of Hidden Soviet Civilian Industrial Price Inflation

Although more than five years have passed since the CIA first announced its discovery that hidden inflation was rife in the Soviet military machine-building sector, no material to date has been published explaining how this conclusion was reached. The agency has preferred instead to address the issue indirectly by trying to demonstrate that hidden inflation is occurring in the Soviet civilian machine-building sector at roughly 4 percent per annum, the same rate it purports prevails in the defense sector.

This coincidence, as demonstrated in chapter 7, hardly confirms the agency's view about the existence of hidden inflation in the Soviet military machine-building sector. The CIA's direct cost data produce hidden procurement estimates from 2 to 30.7 percent per annum, which correspond with almost any external hidden inflation rate imaginable. Nonetheless, while estimates of hidden Soviet civilian machine-building inflation bear only obliquely on defense production, they may provide valuable insights into the general problem of Soviet price behavior, and therefore merit careful consideration.

I. Hidden Inflation and Real Soviet Industrial Growth

The most comprehensive exposition of the hypothesis that real Soviet industrial production is significantly exaggerated by hidden inflation is advanced by James Steiner. In his monograph, *Inflation in Soviet Industry and Machine-Building and Metalworking (MBMW) 1960–1975*, after a very long and closely argued analysis of the pertinent evidence, it is concluded that:[1]

Because official Soviet data do not reflect disguised inflation, they present an overly favorable view of Soviet economic performance,

which

- "overstates real growth *in toto*"
- "overstates to an even greater extent growth in such sectors as MBMW"
- "overstates to an increasing degree the share of such sectors as MBMW in total output"
- "overstates real growth in labor productivity throughout the economy"
- "overstates labor productivity and its growth in industry, and especially MBMW, vis-à-vis agriculture"
- "overstates the size and growth in investment (composed primarily of construction and MBMW output) relative to consumption."[2]

To sustain these conclusions Steiner advances two types of evidence: a theoretical model describing how hidden inflation is generated and a set of empirical calculations intended to validate the behavior his model predicts. The theoretical model itself is built around the principle of "profit-pull."[3] Under the prevailing system of enterprise management Steiner argues that the directors of Soviet firms are rewarded for fulfilling and overfulfilling a set of targets expressed in monetary units, foremost of which is profit.[4] As a consequence managers seeking to maximize their personal bonuses focus most of their attention on discovering and implementing policies that maximize the net revenue of the firm. Unlike the period before the 1965 economic reform when managerial bonuses depended on satisfying physical targets, principally the physical volume of output, in the postreform era bonuses are influenced both by prices and physical productivity. Other things equal the higher the level of prices the greater the profit. It follows, Steiner contends, that managers have an enormous incentive to violate price discipline and charge prices that are higher than can be justified on the basis of real production costs.

Charging prices that exceed those set by the State Price Committee, of course, is strictly illegal and cannot be accomplished with impunity because the state bank scrutinizes the terms of all interenterprise transactions to insure they occur at officially mandated prices. Steiner maintains, however, that this safeguard can be easily evaded in two instances: new products and special order goods for which established prices do not exist by definition. In both of these cases instead of prices being imposed from above they are set by the enterprises themselves, in isolation or on a negotiated basis with the purchaser, subject to final approval by the State Price Committee. While the approval of the State Price Committee might appear superficially to assure that prices for new products and special order items are set honestly, Steiner argues that the intricacies of the rules governing price formation, the complexity of enterprise financial accounts, and the cumbersomeness of Soviet price administration all combine to make it relatively easy for clever managers to deceive their superiors.[5] Even assuming that the pricing authorities were diligent and incorruptible, he believes the efforts of the price regulators cannot countervail the stratagems of managers zealously striving to maximize their personal income.[6]

Steiner recognizes, of course, that the principle of "profit pull" is not inviolable. He accepts without dispute, for example, the substantial evidence compiled by Joseph Berliner that indicates that rather than being too high, new product prices are actually too low and constitute a significant disincentive to technological innovation.[7] Steiner argues that these low prices, and the low profits they entail, only apply in the relatively unimportant case of "authentic" new products.[8] Most Soviet products, he contends, are spurious, superficially altered variants of conventional goods reclassified for the sole purpose of evading price discipline.[9] The concept of "profit-pull," properly qualified therefore in Steiner's view, remains the principal explanation of why hidden inflation exists, as well as why its impact goes undetected in the official index of Soviet industrial wholesale prices.[10]

II. The Empirical Verification of Steiner's Hidden Inflation Theory

Hidden inflation, taking Soviet accounting conventions as the standard, is the difference between the prices actually charged for goods, and the prices that should have been levied if the prevailing rules of cost-plus price formation had been applied. To empirically verify Steiner's specification of hidden inflation, two types of information are required: (1) the set of official prices actually charged for new goods and special order products, and (2) data on the real production cost of these goods including profits and turnover tax which should have been used in computing the official prices of new goods.

Neither series is readily available in the usual statistical compendia, nor does Steiner attempt to develop them directly since his principal concern is not verification per se, but the estimation of total Soviet industrial price inflation. These data, however, are necessarily embedded in his calculations and can be evaluated by carefully scrutinizing their implicit derivation. Steiner's *implicit price estimates* for new goods and special order products are contained in his aggregate industrial price series which includes both standard and nonstandard goods. These prices should be considered acceptable if it can be shown that they are validly derived from official data. This is easily accomplished by replicating Steiner's derivation of his aggregate industrial price series.

Invoking the well-known index number theorem that the ratio of any production series valued alternatively in current and constant prices yields an implicit Paasche price index with final year quantity weights, Steiner computes his total industrial price index simply by dividing the official Soviet industrial output series valued in current rubles by the same series valued in constant prices.[11]

1.
$$\frac{\Sigma p_1 q_1}{\Sigma p_o q_1} = \frac{\Sigma p_1 q_1}{\Sigma p_o q_o} \div \frac{\Sigma p_o q_1}{\Sigma p_o q_o}$$

Since it is widely believed that Soviet industrial output data, unlike Soviet industrial price data,[12] are comprehensive and include new goods and special order items, Steiner's implicit Paasche price series should capture the actual prices employed by the Soviets in valuing new products and special order goods. His implicit new goods price estimates therefore are wholly consistent with the requirements of his hidden inflation theory.

Steiner's implicit derivation of the *real production cost* of new Soviet goods is another matter, however. The principal obstacle impeding the measurement of hidden inflation in the Soviet Union is the lack of reliable data on the true accounting cost of new goods and special order items, where the official price of these products systematically exceeds the limits set by the rules of Soviet price formation. Various methods for circumventing this problem exist, short of obtaining the desired data by covert means, although their accuracy is open to considerable dispute. The most obvious of these expedients is to apply the direct cost estimating methodology used by the Central Intelligence Agency for the calculation of Soviet procurement costs.[13] The value of new Soviet goods could be computed in dollars based on conventional engineering norms and converted to rubles using ruble-dollar ratios for similar products. These estimates could then be compared with official Soviet prices for these new products, where available, to determine whether a systematic bias exists between official Soviet prices and prices estimated by the direct costing methodology. To evaluate the significance of any bias that might be detected in this way, a set of cost estimates could be made for a group of standard goods which were close substitutes for the new products being studied. If no bias were found between these estimates and official prices a compelling argument could be made in favor of the hypothesis that new Soviet product prices were indeed distorted by hidden inflation.

Although as a staff member of the Military-Economic Analysis Center of the Central Intelligence Agency[14] Steiner should have been in a position to undertake the task of direct cost estimating new Soviet goods, he adopted an entirely different methodology. Instead of calculating the real production cost of new industrial products either directly or indirectly as a component of the aggregate cost of industrial goods, he chose to employ data computed by others which he believed represented real production costs. Two alternative data series were selected, one an index of Soviet industrial production developed by the Office of Economic Research of the Central Intelligence Agency, the other by "Treml and Gallik in their work on ruble-dollar parity ratios."[15]

The former is clearly inappropriate for testing his theory since it explicitly *excludes* the new goods and special order items that he hypothesizes to be the cause of hidden inflation.[16] It follows therefore by the process of elimination that the scientific merit of Steiner's hidden inflation theory rests entirely on whether the Treml-Gallik source he employs in his alternative calculations adequately measures the real production cost of new goods and special order products.

The nature of the real production cost data embodied in the Treml-Gallik ruble-dollar parity series is clearly revealed in the derivation of Steiner's "total industrial price inflation" index.[17] Steiner develops this indicator by taking a series of industrial ruble-dollar ratios computed by "Treml-Gallik."[18]

2.
$$\frac{\sum_{i=1}^{s} r_i^t q_i^t}{\sum_{i=1}^{s} p_i^t q_i^t}$$

(where r represents ruble prices, p dollars prices), which utilizes Soviet quantity weights instead of U.S. quantity weights and multiplies it by an "updated" U.S. dollar price index of Soviet industrial output[19]

3.
$$\frac{\sum_{i=1}^{s} p_i^t q_i^{1970}}{\sum_{i=1}^{s} p_i^{1970} q_i^{1970}}$$

to obtain what he incorrectly believes is ". . . a series of current ruble to constant 1970 dollar ratios."[20]

4.
$$\frac{\sum_{i=1}^{s} r_i^t q_i^t}{\sum_{i=1}^{s} p_i^{1970} q_i^{1970}} \neq \frac{\sum_{i=1}^{s} r_i^t q_i^t}{\sum_{i=1}^{s} p_i^t q_i^t} \cdot \frac{\sum_{i=1}^{s} p_i^t q_i^{1970}}{\sum_{i=1}^{s} p_i^{1970} q_i^{1970}}$$

He then divides equation 4 by "the 1970 ruble to 1970 dollar ratio (.711)" and ignoring the small error in the preceding step obtains[21]

5.
$$\frac{\sum_{i=1}^{s} r_i^t q_i^t}{\sum_{i=1}^{s} r_i^{1970} q_i^{1970}} = \frac{\sum_{i=1}^{s} r_i^t q_i^t}{\sum_{i=1}^{s} p_i^{1970} q_i^{1970}} \bigg/ \frac{\sum_{i=1}^{s} r_i^{1970} q_i^{1970}}{\sum_{i=1}^{s} p_i^{1970} q_i^{1970}}$$

which produces an implicit ruble price index he contends accurately measures "total Soviet industrial price inflation."

The numerator of this ruble price index, which is intended to capture official transactions prices including new goods, is the official Soviet industrial output series valued in current rubles taken directly from the Soviet statistical handbook *Narodnoe Khoziaistvo SSSR*.[22] Astonishingly, the denominator derived from the Treml-Gallik ruble-dollar ratios—which is supposed to represent the real production cost of Soviet industrial goods when traced to its source—turns out to be the very same Soviet industrial output series employed in the numerator! It is obtained from the same statistical handbook, *Narodnoe Khoziaistvo SSSR*,[23] differing only to the extent that it has been distorted by the erroneous index operation performed in equation 4. (See appendix 2.)

Steiner's real production cost data therefore are not real production cost data at all in the sense required for the verification of his hidden inflation theory. It is the official Soviet industrial output series valued in prices which, according to Steiner's hypothesis, vastly exceed their real production cost. Why Steiner failed to recognize this fact is difficult to perceive. The industrial output series valued in 1970 rubles he uses as a proxy for real production cost is reported in the very same table from which he obtained his "Treml-Gallik" ruble-dollar ratios.[24] Whatever the explanation, one point is clear: his empirical calculations do not contain the real production cost data necessary to validate his theory of hidden inflation. His hypothesis therefore remains an unproven conjecture.

III. Steiner's Empirical Estimates of Hidden Inflation

Although the data Steiner employs to calculate hidden Soviet industrial inflation are inconsistent with his own specification of the hidden inflation generation process, they might be consistent with other inflation mechanisms. Do his calculations validly measure disguised inflation in some alternative sense?

Steiner's estimates derived from equation 5 can be dismissed as clearly invalid because they contain no independent information on real production cost.[25] Equation 5 merely constitutes a normalized version of the official Soviet industrial production series. His calculations based on Central Intelligence data do, however, illuminate a point of longstanding controversy in a revealing way.

The Central Intelligence Agency began publishing sample indices of Soviet industrial production in 1962.[26] These indices differed from the official Soviet GVO indices in "coverage, weighting, classification, concept of quantity, algebraic formula and purpose."[27] Although the data in both series originate ultimately from Soviet sources, the official GVO industrial series, and most especially the MBMW subsector, have consistently exhibited rates of real growth substantially higher than those displayed by the agency's sample indices.[28] Many conjectures have been advanced to explain the discrepancy.[29] The most interesting of these have focused on the data omitted from the CIA's sample, new goods and weapons.[30] Some have argued that these undetected product groups grew faster than the average in the CIA sample and account for the more rapid growth of the official industrial index.[31] Others maintained on the contrary that it was precisely these subgroups where hidden inflation was rife. The faster growth of the official series therefore was attributable not to the rapid growth of military goods, but to rapid hidden inflation.[32]

The cleavage between these two positions is especially interesting because it indicates that the explanation of the discrepant behavior exhibited by the official Soviet industrial output index and the sample index developed by the CIA has long been a subject of considerable controversy within the intelligence bureaucracy. Did the agency's series err because it understated real Soviet industrial performance, or did the official Soviet industrial series err because it was distorted by hidden inflation?

In forming his own estimates of total Soviet industrial inflation Steiner deals with this controversy in a decisive but inadmissible way. He implicitly defines total industrial inflation as the disparity between the official Soviet industrial rate of growth, and the agency's estimate of the

Soviet industrial rate of growth.[33] This is tantamount to proof by imputation and of course does not resolve the fundamental issue of whether the discrepancy between the agency's and the Soviet industrial production series is attributable to real industrial growth or inflation.[34]

It does follow, however, from the ambiguities latent in Steiner's measure of hidden inflation that his estimates cannot be considered reliable. If they capture hidden inflation at all, they do so in a manner which cannot be scientifically evaluated.

IV. Hidden Inflation: A Partial Disconfirmation

Bad empiricism cannot invalidate good theory. Despite the gross deficiencies of Steiner's quantitative analysis, his contention that Soviet industrial statistics are seriously distorted by hidden inflation may still be correct. However, in the course of his computations, he himself uncovered some important evidence that partially disconfirmed the hypothesis that new goods are the basic cause of hidden Soviet industrial inflation.

Proponents of the hidden inflation school almost invariably support their views, at least in part, on the perception that the official Soviet index of industrial prices underrepresents new goods and excludes special order products.[35] This lacuna is perceived to be the mechanism used by the Soviets to conceal the inflationary consequences of spurious innovation believed to be rampant in the industrial sector.

If this line of reasoning is correct it follows that a true comprehensive index of Soviet industrial prices that includes all new products and special order goods should exhibit a faster rate of inflation than an index that primarily measures the price behavior of standard outputs. Steiner himself has computed precisely such an index—it is the implicit Paasche industrial price series discussed previously. This index is derived from data on the current and constant value of Soviet industrial output which includes new products and special order items. For the period 1960–75, Steiner's implicit industrial price index indicates that inflation occurred at an average annual rate of two hundreths of one percent (0.02 percent).[36] Instead of registering a higher inflation rate, as some disguised-inflation theorists had conjectured, the comprehensive measure turns out to be significantly lower than the official rate, 0.58 percent—despite the fact that the latter index underrepresents new products and excludes special order goods.[37]

This evidence suggests that the official Soviet industrial price index is not significantly distorted by the omission of new goods and special order products. Although the limited nature of this test makes it impossible to deduce that Soviet industrial prices are not inflated, Steiner's own implicit Paasche price index clearly, even if only partially, disconfirms his assault on the credibility of Soviet industrial production statistics.[38]

V. Deficiencies of the "Profit-Pull" Theory of Disguised Soviet Industrial Price Inflation

Attention thus far has been focused on the empirical standing of Steiner's hidden inflation theory. But what about the "profit-pull" theory itself? Is the a priori appeal of this concept sufficiently strong to offset its empirical shortcomings?

Steiner's "profit-pull" theory rests on a variety of dubious assumptions regarding bonus maximization and price control. It is certainly true that managers in the Soviet Union are rewarded for achieving high profits. However, this perception neither implies that managers blindly strive to maximize profits oblivious of other constraints governing their bonuses, nor that they are driven to the illegal expedient of violating price discipline to achieve their ends. Insofar as profits do significantly influence managerial bonuses, their effect is limited by the size of the bonus fund, and the negative consequences entailed by too visibly exceeding conventional profit norms. The bonus fund is not unbounded. Maximum rewards do not spectacularly increase managerial incomes, especially if the maximum bonus is evaluated not with reference to managers' base salary but to their normal income, which includes average achieved profit rewards.[39] It is debatable therefore whether the incremental income that might be gained warrants the risks incurred by illegally violating price discipline, especially when it is recognized that managers operate with many degrees of freedom. They can enhance their profits by adjusting the quality, assortment, and cost of goods they produce—doing far less violence to the law using these stratagems than by following the course Steiner infers of grossly padding the production costs of spurious new goods in order to justify a massive increase in product prices.

This appraisal of the factors constraining price fraud is strengthened moreover by the fact that conspicuous success in the Soviet Union invites external scrutiny and ratcheted norms. Enterprises whose profits either equal or exceed levels that exhaust the bonus fund will find that in subsequent years their targets will be increased. If despite these adjustments management continuously fulfills and overfulfills its profit target to the limit of the bonus fund the authorities will become exceedingly suspicious and conduct an on the spot investigation.

It might be supposed that managers would run little risk in this regard because the true value of any product change is open to considerable dispute. However, this point of view confounds value theory with the rules of Soviet price formation. Despite the introduction of some aspects of hedonic pricing, Soviet prices are still governed for the most part by documentable prime production costs.[40] Even in the case of hedonic pricing the range of discretion is constrained by the prime costs of analogous products. As a consequence should the suspicions of the price inspectorate be raised by the persistent and extraordinary growth of enterprise profits (which is readily observable), verification of whether managers have violated the rules governing new price formation is a relatively straightforward and simple procedure.

Several distinguished scholars including Gregory Grossman and Morris Bornstein have suggested that Soviet authorities are indifferent to violations of price discipline and have been lax in the area of price enforcement.[41] However, the evidence they have advanced to support their position is slender and until more solid proof is forthcoming it seems prudent to conclude that Steiner's "profit-pull" theory of disguised price inflation falls more in the category of a weak conjecture than a fully articulated and compelling a priori hypothesis. From this perspective, given the deficiencies of his empirical research, Steiner's contention that Soviet real industrial production statistics are significantly distorted by hidden inflation must be regarded more as speculation than as an inference deduced from a carefully elaborated, logically consistent, empirically verified scientific theory.

Notes

1. The special attention accorded Steiner's monograph in this essay is not only merited because his analysis is the most exhaustive and ambitious to date, but also because as a document published by the Central Intelligence Agency it serves as an indication of the theories shaping the agency's perception of Soviet economic performance. Steiner has drafted a rejoinder to my critique, and I have written a reply. See Rosefielde (1982b) and Steiner (1982).
2. Steiner (1978a), pp. 57–58.
3. Ibid., pp. 10–13. "In market economies, the primary causes of inflation are generally defined as demand pull, cost push or monetary. In Soviet industry, however, the key causal factor appears to be the enterprise incentive system" (p. 10). "The key indicator of the new incentive system is profit . . ." (p. 12).
4. Ibid.
5. This statement holds for the short run. Persistently high rates of enterprise profits in the long run, however, will invite external scrutiny. A comprehensive audit should easily suffice to determine whether production costs attributed to new products are excessive within the prevailing system of cost

accounts. Total enterprise costs are finite and measurable. They cannot be misallocated to one category without affecting the cost profile of other categories. Therefore, gross violations can be easily exposed with the aid of existing accounting norms. It should also be noted that the further difficulties raised by hedonic indices do not seriously obscure the underlying prime cost basis on which all Soviet industrial products are based either directly or derivatively.

6. Ibid., p. 15. "The weakness of the state pricing organs and the vagueness of the price determination regulations, and the self-interest of the enterprise managers ensure that the resulting prices for new products—and particularly products which are only nominally new—are unduly high." Also see ibid., p. 16.

7. Ibid., p. 14. See Berliner (1975, 1976).

8. Ibid., "The arguments are valid with respect to the production of truly new products. . . . The arguments are not valid, however, with respect to the vast majority of new products which are no more than slight variations of goods already being produced or even purely nominal name (designator) changes."

   Steiner presents no evidence to support his judgment that the "vast majority" of new product innovation in the Soviet Union is spurious.

9. Ibid.

10. Ibid., pp. 28–33.

11. Ibid., pp. 33–37.

12. Bornstein (1972), pp. 358–62.

13. This methodology is fraught with problems and is probably worse than useless if it cannot be validated with direct observations on the relevant set of ruble prices. The procedure suggested in the text provides such a check.

14. Steiner (1978a), p. 1.

15. Ibid., pp. 38–46. Steiner does not explicitly assert that these series represent real production cost. However, since both are used as the denominator of his total inflation estimates, with the official Soviet industrial output series serving as the numerator, it is difficult to see how they could be interpreted in any other manner.

16. That new products, quality improved goods, and special order items are excluded from the CIA series is easily seen from the fixed composition of the sample which ". . . contains 350 commodity series of civilian production weighted by 1955 prices for products within branches, and the branches are weighted by 1955 value added weights" (Greenslade, 1972, p. 157). Cf. Greenslade (1976).

17. Steiner (1978a), Statistical Appendix, 66–74. See also Vladimir Treml and Dmitri Gallik (1973), pp. 13–14.

18. Ibid., pp. 66 and 71. The result of this calculation is reported in Table 6 and comes directly from Treml and Gallik (1973), Table 4, p. 14.

19. The ratio in expression 2 is ". . . deflated by the dollar price index (Soviet sector share weights). See Table A-7 to calculate a series of current ruble to constant 1970 dollar ratios" (Ibid., p. 71). This statement is somewhat vague. I tried interpreting it as

$$\sum_{i=1}^{s} p_i^t q_i^t \Big/ \sum_{i=1}^{s} p_i^{1970} q_i^{1970}$$

which would have eliminated the error in equation 4, but this interpretation was incompatible with the behavior of the dollar price index Steiner reports in Table A-7, p. 73. The exact form of equation 3 is provided in appendix 2, equation 14.
20. Ibid., p. 71.
21. Ibid.
22. Ibid., pp. 38–39, 71, and Table A-1, line 5.
23. Treml and Gallik (1973), Table 4, p. 14.
24. Ibid.
25. The numerator and denominator both pertain to the same official Soviet industrial output series. The prices used to value physical outputs are conceptually identical differing only in terms of the years they designate.
26. Greenslade and Wallace (1962).
27. Greenslade (1972), p. 156. The updated version of the CIA industrial production index used by Steiner is valued in 1970 prices. See Greenslade (1976), p. 270. For a discussion of these prices see *USSR: Gross National Product Accounts, 1970, Research Aid* (1975), pp. 75–76.
28. Greenslade's industrial output series grows 6.2 percent and his MBMW series 7.9 percent per annum 1960–1975. During the same period the official series grow 8.2 and 11.9 percent respectively. See Greenslade (1976) p. 271; *Narodnoe Khoziaistvo* 1969, 144–46, and *Narodnoe Khoziaistvo* 1975, 190–95.
29. The principal sources of this discrepancy identified by Rush Greenslade, the former chief of the Office of Economic Research of the CIA are examined in Greenslade (1972), pp. 174–86. They include the following explanations:

   1. GVO price weights give higher weight to the faster growing output series both between and within sectors (p. 174).
   2. "Potentially more distorting than the size of gross weights is the change in an industry's gross value as a result of a changing degree of specialization" (p. 174). Specialization here refers to secularly increasing vertical integration which has the effect of increasing intermediate stages of production, hence double counting and GVO.
   3. Differences in the definition of industrial activities. "The overall effect is hard to assess but is probably not large" (p. 179).
   4. Inventory accounting. "Increases in inventories probably have not influenced overall industry or banch of industry trends. . . ." (p. 179).
   5. "The inclusion of 'mastering new products,' the research and development expenditures, in the GVO of many enterprises of machine building raises the question of how the activities are measured" (p. 179).
   6. "More serious is the inclusion of repair activities as industrial output" (p. 180).
   7. Hidden inflation (pp. 181–86). "These considerations suggest that the investment equipment index as well as the GVO-MBMW index is overstated significantly on account of prices" (p. 186).

Other factors discussed by Greenslade, but omitted from the discussion above include:

   1. The GVO index uses a different set of price weights (1955 prices from 1960 to 1967, and 1967 prices thereafter) than the Greenslade index

which in its revised form employs 1970 prices. It should be added that these 1970 prices make no special allowance for hidden inflation as do subsequent 1970 prices employed for valuing Soviet weapons. Steiner of course attempts to offset the fact that the price weights differ between the series by normalizing his data to a 1970 base. (On the 1970 CIA price weights see *USSR; Gross National Product Accounts.*, 1970–75.)
2. Differences in coverage (p. 156).
3. Algebraic formula? (p. 156)

In Greenslade's view the most important explanation of the ten causes listed above is number two "specialization." Why he made this judgment is difficult to assess because the ratio of net output to gross output changes very slowly over time as his own citation from Eidelman indicates (p. 176).

Although hidden inflation comes seventh on Greenslade's list in my judgment he considered it the primary explanation in MBMW.

Before jumping to the conclusion that Steiner has merely validated Greenslade's second explanatory choice, however, it must be noted that many other alternatives exist. Of these the two most likely candidates are:

1. The omission of new products, and improved goods from Greenslade's index.
2. The omission of military and space hardware from Greenslade's index (p. 157).
30. Greenslade (1972), pp. 157–58.
31. Lee (1977a).
32. Greenslade (1972), pp. 166–68, 181–86. Becker has argued that the MMW index may well exclude the defense industry which would eliminate rapid weapons growth as an explanation of the disparity between the agency's and the Soviet industrial indices (Becker, 1974, p. 366). This view no longer seems to be held in the intelligence community.
33. Steiner (1978a), pp. 40–41, 75–76. All the rigmarole about I-0 weights which Steiner uses to convert the official Soviet GVO industrial output series to a final output basis probably blinds him to the real meaning of his computations.
34. Note also that the sample coverage of Steiner's ratio is inconsistent. The numerator includes all industrial output, the denominator only products included in Greenslade's commodity sample. "The GVO and sample indexes are different in algebraic formula, and purpose. There is no reason for the two to resemble each other closely either in the totals or in the parts" (Greenslade, 1972, p. 156).
35. See, for example, Becker (1974), p. 368. "If machinery prices have in fact risen on average, why does the MMW index show an almost monotonic decline? Because, say Kvasha and Krasovsky, "in calculating the index, no account was taken not only of new products but also of price changes on many old products with insignificant alterations, which were introduced chiefly in order to break away from the fixed handbook prices." The treatment of new commodities is the heart of the problem of MMW price inflation and the failure of the index to reflect that trend."
36. Steiner (1978a), p. 37.

37. Ibid.
38. Although it is often argued that the omission of new products is the basic reason the official MBMW price index understates the real inflation rate, it must be recognized that even if new products were included in the index, inflation might still be understated. The actual effect of including new products would depend on the procedures adopted for establishing appropriate base year prices. The possibility that the constant prices employed to compute the real rate of machinery growth might still conceal hidden inflation therefore cannot be disregarded.
39. Berliner (1976), pp. 431–33, 477–87. Cf. Grossman (1977), p. 148.
40. Berliner (1976), pp. 308, 311, 325.
41. Bornstein (1978), Grossman (1977), p. 140.

CHAPTER 9

CIA Hedonic Estimates of Hidden Soviet Machinery Price Inflation

The agency's determination to prove the validity of its hidden weapons price inflation hypothesis with roundabout means did not end with Steiner's treatise. In the fall of 1979 another attempt was made to demonstrate that the official Soviet civilian machine-building and metalworking price index understates the real inflation rate.

Like Steiner, Robert Leggett, the author of *An Analysis of the Behavior of Soviet Machinery Prices 1960–1973* begins with the assumption that Soviet civilian machine prices are biased upward by spurious innovation which he then attempts to measure with CIA data collected from a "large volume of Soviet technical-economic textbooks, magazines and other monographs."[1] These data are 855 price observations for several hundred related machines in the construction, automobile, machine tool and hoisting/transportation sectors. The machines studied, principally scrapers, bulldozers, rollers, graders, excavators, trucks, machine tools and cranes comprise only a small sample of the products of their respective sectors. The four sectors themselves "represent, at most, about 16 percent of the value of total machinery output."[2]

Although Leggett at times expresses his uneasiness about drawing inferences from this slender sample,[3] he nonetheless asserts that these data more reliably describe Soviet machine price behavior than the official indices.[4] The basis for this judgment is not entirely clear. No direct evidence is provided and the indirect proofs suggested illogically depend on correspondences between the behavior of the sample data and published Soviet series.[5]

The judgment that the CIA's price data are more representative of price changes in the machinery sector than the data employed by the Soviet Central Statistical Agency decisively affects the conclusions ultimately drawn from the econometric portion of the study. Table 9.1, derived from information provided in *An Analysis of the Behavior of Soviet Machinery Prices 1960–1973*, demonstrates that the price changes manifested by the sample data are strikingly inconsistent with, and greatly exceed those officially reported for the construction, automobile, machine tool and hoisting/transportation machinery sectors in 1967.[6] According to the agency's unadjusted data the 1967 economic reform increased prices 31 percent, a figure completely incommensurate with the official estimate of 5 percent for these subsectors, and the 0 percent aggregate rate recorded for all branches of machine building and metal-working.[7] The uncritical presumption that the agency's data are more reliable than those used by TsSU thus predetermines the conclusion that the real rate of Soviet inflation exceeds the reported rate. Any econometric study based on the sample data will reveal rates of machinery inflation substantially higher than the official rate simply because the sample data display greater upward price change than the data employed by TsSU.

Acceptance of the superior representativeness of the sample data also has another surprising implication. It suggests that inflation in the Soviet civilian machine building sector is not concealed by disguising price increases as legitimate quality surcharges, but by the deliberate falsification of TsSU's price statistics. The price increases displayed by the sample data are entirely unconcealed, and should be reflected in the

TABLE 9.1
The Effect of the 1967 Soviet Price Reform on the Construction, Automobile, Machine Tool, and Hoisting/Transportation Sectors

	Total		Construction		Automobile		Machine Tool		Hoisting/ Transportation	
	CIA	Official	CIA	Official	CIA	Official	CIA	Official	CIA	Official
1965	100	100	100	100	100	100	100	100	100	100
1967	131	105	118	100	133	105	131	106	120	107

Source: An Analysis of the Behavior of Soviet Machinery Prices 1960–73
CIA: Table 7. This estimate was calculated by comparing price changes for identical machines. It was not computed hedonically. The same weights used to compute the author's composite hedonic index are employed to calculate the composite "link" index shown above under the heading "Total."
Official: Figure 1. These official Soviet price changes were compiled by the CIA. I assume here that these statistics refer to the entire reform which was implemented in two phases, one effective October 1, 1966, the second January 1, 1967. This is the reason 1965 is used as the base in the table rather than 1966.

official data base. Since they are not, it follows either that the sample data are unrepresentative, or TsSU falsified its published series.

It is not clear precisely why Leggett study does not recognize this, or why he refrained from claiming that the inflation the agency hypothesizes in the military machine building sector was confirmed by the unconcealed inflation manifested in the sample data. For the period 1960 to 1967 the sample data indicate that Soviet civilian machine-building prices were rising 3.9 percent per annum, compared with the 1.3 percent annual rate of decline shown by the official MBMW price index.[8] The rate exhibited by the sample data could easily have been interpreted as confirming the 4 percent rate conjectured for military procurement inflation.

Perhaps Leggett was skittish about pressing the argument that the Soviets deliberately falsify their published civilian machinery price statistics because this would focus attention on the representativeness of the CIA's sample data.[9] Or perhaps the agency's commitment to the concept of hidden inflation prompted him to disregard the ostensible meaning of the sample data. Whatever the motive, however, Leggett does not dwell on the significance of the sample data.[10] He focuses instead on using them to estimate the hidden inflation latent in the dataset and to prove "that the practice of pricing 'new' products excessively high does exist in the Soviet Union and does contribute to inflation in machinery prices."[11]

The hidden inflation Leggett desires to estimate is additional to, and not part of, the overt inflation already computed from the sample data. It eludes the usual methods of detection because it is disguised by spurious product differentiation. Instead of simply raising the prices of established goods, Leggett conjectures the Soviets replace older machines with new superficially improved models at sharply higher prices. Because these machines technically have different nomenclature numbers de facto price increases go unrecorded. Prices of older products remain fixed while the authorities pretend high new model prices are fully justified by their spurious improvements.

The method chosen in Leggett's study to calculate the hidden inflationary consequences of these fraudulent new product innovations utilizes a semilogarithmic hedonic price estimating equation developed for other purposes by Zvi Griliches:[12]

1. $\ln P_{it} = \alpha + \beta_1 X_{1it} + \beta_2 X_{2it} \ldots \beta_n X_{nit}$
$$+ \ldots \beta_{d_1} D_1 \ldots \beta_{d_n} D_n + \mu_{it}$$

which specifies that Soviet machinery prices, P_{it} are determined by quality variables X_{jit}, a set of dummy variables D_j, and a normally distributed stochastic error term μ_{it}. The specification implies that the formation of Soviet machinery prices can be explained by a few technical characteristics such as horsepower and weight "determined by Soviet machinery specialists to be the most important characteristics of each type machine—subject to the availability of data," and dummy variables that capture the price changes concentrated in years of general price revision.[13]

Machine characteristics can therefore be thought of as determining the proper prices for new products compared with older models, subject to adjustment for changes in the price level picked up by the price reform dummy variables. The difference between observed prices and estimated prices computed from the quality characteristics and dummy variables is an unexplained residual that may contain hidden inflation. To test for the presence of hidden inflation and to estimate its magnitude a trend term should be introduced into equation 1:

2. $\ln P_{it} = \alpha + \beta_1 X_{1t} + \beta_2 X_{2it} \ldots \beta_n X_{nit}$

$$+ \ldots \beta_{d_1} D_1 \ldots \beta_{d_n} D_n + T + \mu_{it}$$

which discriminates price changes associated with price reforms from the continuous process of new product innovation.[14]

This direct method of estimating hidden inflation is not used in Leggett's study, perhaps because it posed serious problems of multicollinearity.[15] The presence and magnitude of hidden inflation is inferred instead from the fact that the rate of machinery price change estimated by the dummy variable exceeds the rate directly computed from the sample data with index methods.[16] This approach is suspect because the very fact that hidden inflation is correlated with price reforms and is not a continuous process neither conforms with the underlying pattern of new product innovation, nor the mechanics of new product price formation as they are usually understood.[17]

However, even if this logical incongruity in Leggett's method of estimating hidden inflation is ignored, the magnitude of the new product price inflation uncovered is not very significant. Table 9.2 presents his estimates of Soviet machinery inflation, computed both hedonically and with his unweighted index method. The table shows that for the entire period 1960–73 the annual hedonic rate of inflation for all machinery in the sample was 2.6 percent, compared with the direct unweighted index rate of 2 percent. The difference between these rates constitutes the agency's summary estimate of new product hidden price inflation—.6 percent per annum!

TABLE 9.2

CIA and Official Soviet Estimates of Machinery Price Trends, 1960–73

(Construction, Automobile, Machine Tool, Hoisting/Transportation Machinery only)

	All Machinery			Construction			Trucks			Machine Tools			Cranes		
	H	S	O	H	S	O	H	S	O	H	S	O	H	S	O
1960	100	100	—	100	100	—	100	100	—	100	100	—	100	100	—
1965	—	101	100	100	102	100	100	103	100	100	100	100	100	91	100
1967	145	132	105	131	120	100	149	138	105	129	131	106	140	110	107
1971	144	132	—	133	120	—	149	138	—	—	—	—	132	107	—
1973	139	129	—	132	114	—	141	139	—	—	—	—	135	97	—
Compound Annual Rates of Inflation															
1960–67	5.5%	4.0%		3.9%	2.6%		5.9%	4.7%		3.7%		3.9%	4.9%	1.4%	
1960–73	2.6%	2.0%		2.2%	1.0%		2.7%	2.6%					2.3%	.2%	

Sources: An Analysis of the Behavior of Soviet Machinery Prices 1960–73.
Hedonic Indices (H): Table 15, p. 23, Table 10, p. 17.
Sample Indices (S): Table 7, p. 10. The aggregate all machinery index was computed with the weights reported in Table 15, p. 23.
Official Soviet Indices (O): Figure 1, p. 12.

Table 9.3 provides a finer breakdown of the magnitude and sectoral incidence of hidden Soviet machinery inflation. It reveals that new product price inflation is most intense in the crane subsector and least severe in machine tools where new goods are purportedly *under*priced. It also suggests that hidden inflation was concentrated in 1967 and was slowly reversed thereafter causing the long term rate to decline. These findings are not very convincing. More than anything else they suggest that the "dummy" variable for 1967 is picking up some unexplained part of the residual variance associated with the price reform instituted in that year.

Leggett's estimates of hidden new product inflation thus appear to be no better founded than his estimates of open Soviet civilian machine-building inflation. The hidden inflation estimates in addition to being quantitatively small, are difficult to interpret, are inconsistent with the underlying pattern of product innovation, display puzzling sectoral anomalies, are potentially sensitive to omitted quality variables and may well be affected both by the weighting scheme used to compute the price-relative index and the specification of the hedonic price estimating equation.

These hidden inflation estimates suffer moreover because the scanty sample data from which they are derived are inconsistent with official price statistics. This is a fatal defect. Although the agency may genuinely believe that its sample data are more reliable than those employed by the Soviet Central Statistical Agency in their published machinery price series, this judgment is unlikely to be widely shared unless it is corroborated with strong proofs that the CIA has thus far failed to provide. Without these proofs, the agency's conjectures about civilian machinery price inflation come down to a judgment about whose data are more creditable, the CIA's or TsSU's.[18] This is a test the sample data cannot pass and it follows directly that the evidence put forward in *An Analysis of the Behavior of Soviet Machinery Prices 1960–1973* neither confirms

TABLE 9.3
CIA Estimates of Hidden New Product Price Inflation, 1960–73
(Compound Annual Rates)

	All Machinery	Construction	Trucks	Machine Tools	Cranes
1960–67	1.5	1.3	1.2	– .2	3.5
1960–73	.6	1.2	.1	—	2.5

Source: See Table 9.2. Note: trucks constitute 69 percent of the total gross value of output of these subsectors. The truck estimate therefore dominates the aggregate hidden inflation rate.

the existence of open nor hidden new production inflation in the Soviet civilian machine-building sector.

Leggett of course does not concur. His study of Soviet machinery price behavior concludes:

> Price inflation did occur in the machine-building sector during the period 1960–73, according to our analysis. Furthermore, this inflation was the result of the setting of prices for new or improved products at higher levels than warranted by the improvement in the technical characteristics of the new products as well as of the upward revision of machinery prices in 1967.[19]

> Our analysis indicates that prices, once established, remained constant . . . except when major reforms or revisions were carried out. For products in our sample that did change, however, the average rate of price inflation was found to be about 4 percent per year during 1961–73.[20] The impact of inflation in machinery prices, however, might be thought to be most severe in the production of military hardware. . . . On the other hand, it can be countered that defense industries are subject to more effective quality control than other sectors of industry. . . . On balance, however, the more rapid pace of innovation, product obsolescence, and technological change in the military sector probably means that the new product pricing effect outweighs other considerations.[21]

Notes

1. CIA, *An Analysis of the Behavior of Soviet Machinery Prices, 1960–1973*, National Foreign Assessment Center, ER 79-10631, December 1979, p. 8. A truncated version of this anonymous study has recently been published under the author's name. See Robert E. Leggett, "Measuring Inflation in the Soviet Machinebuilding Sector, 1960–1973," *Journal of Comparative Economics*, vol. 5, no. 2, June 1981, pp. 169–84. The new variant introduces a few changes and many evasions, but does not obviate the critique set forth in this chapter. Leggett's revised study is analyzed in Rosefielde (1982a).
2. Ibid., p. 10.
3. Ibid., pp. 8, 10. Various sources place the total number of Soviet prices between 10 and 15 million. Although several hundred machinery prices might seem to be a large sample it is unlikely that these prices weighted by physical output volumes represent more than a few tenths of one percent of total Soviet machinery value.
4. "Thus the findings should be both a fairly accurate reflection of the behavior of prices of established products in the four branches and generally indicative of revisions in prices of established products in other machine building products. . . . Overall, a combination of the differences noted in 1967 and the unusual nature of Soviet indexes in the late 1960s and early 1970s increases our skepticism regarding the official data." Ibid., p. 11.
5. Ibid., pp. 10–11.

6. The raw rate of inflation implicit in the agency's sample is measured by its "link" index. Price quotations for identical products are paired, formed into price-relatives and indexed on an unweighted basis. See Ibid., p. 8.
7. Ibid., pp. 1, 12.
8. Ibid., Table 7, p. 10, and p. 1. I have weighted the subsectors to obtain an aggregate index using the weights employed by the CIA study to compute the hedonic index. See Table 15, p. 23.
9. The agency historically has taken the position that Soviet civilian statistics are broadly reliable if careful attention is paid to the definition of the series. Until recently, it has accepted the accuracy of the official MBMW price index, subject to two qualifications: (1) military hardware might not be included in the index; (2) the index might understate new product price inflation. The agency's sample data now add a third source of misrepresentation: the deliberate exclusion of machinery sectors experiencing high rates of price inflation, which implies that the MBMW price index is completely fraudulent. The possibility that the agency's historical position is wrong, that officially published Soviet data on the civilian economy is "freely invented" of course cannot be ruled out on logical grounds, but its implications for the credibility of all Soviet data are so great that its assertion cannot sensibly be accepted without very strong proof.
10. "Nonetheless, these findings must be considered in the light of the weaknesses inherent in the indexes constructed here. . . . The most serious shortcoming of these indexes, however, is that they do not measure hidden inflation caused by enterprises which "simulate innovation" (Ibid., p. 11).
11. Ibid., p. 19.
12. Ibid., p. 13.
13. Ibid. Notice that the variables used are similar in type to those employed in the CIA's direct cost estimating relationships. They are very aggregative and are unlikely to really capture the magnitude of qualitative improvements in new Soviet machinery. For example, if the Soviets reduced the weight of new model machines to save fuel this could well show up as a deterioration in quality.
14. $P = e^{\alpha} \cdot e^{\beta_1 X_{1it}} \cdot e^{\beta_2 X_{2it}} \cdot \ldots \cdot e^{\beta_n X_{nit}} \cdot e^{\beta d_1 D1} \cdot \ldots \cdot e^{\beta d_n D_n} \cdot e^{T} \cdot e^{\mu}_{it}$
15. Ibid., pp. 14–15.
16. "Since the hedonic indexes cover established machines as well as the relationship between price and quality of new products, a comparison of the hedonic indexes with the price-relative indexes provides some additional insights into price behavior during the reform period. For example, the hedonic indexes exceed the price-relative indexes for cranes, excavators, trucks, and scrapers in 1967. This suggests that in these sectors, prices for products with changing characteristics were increased more than quality improvements would justify in terms of implied price-setting formulas" (Ibid., p. 17).
17. Occasional remarks indicate that Leggett is sensitive to this problem, "Because dummy variables could not be used for all years between 1960 and 1967, however, the timing has to be inferred" (Ibid., p. 16).
18. Some specialists have suggested that the official machine-building and metalworking index is falsified by the omission of military hardware. If the sample data on construction machinery, trucks, machine tools, and cranes are also omitted along with other sectors that exhibit positive rates of inflation then the published statistics have almost no rationale at all. Of course,

this possibility cannot be disproved, but the consensus of the profession does not support the view that contemporary official Soviet data on the civilian economy are intentionally and systematically faked. See note 9.

19. Ibid., p. 23.
20. Ibid., p. 24.
21. Ibid.

CHAPTER 10

Becker's Estimates of Hidden Soviet Machine-Building Inflation

Neither of the agency studies analyzed in the preceding chapters rely entirely on direct quantitative proofs to sustain the hypothesis that hidden inflation is rampant in the Soviet civilian machine-building sector. Both copiously cite the writings of Western scholars to suggest that the quantitative research of numerous independent specialists confirms the existence of a 4 percent rate of hidden Soviet machinery inflation. The impression conveyed by these references is misleading, however. Numerous studies of hidden inflation have indeed been written, but only two have seriously attempted to quantify its magnitude: Abraham Becker's monograph on the machine-building sector and David Howard's essay on Soviet retail market.

Becker's study is especially pertinent to the controversy under discussion. It not only appears to have been animated by the classified data on Soviet procurement prices collected in the late sixties and early seventies that showed Soviet weapons were more expensive than previously thought,[1] but it laid the foundation for the CIA's subsequent efforts to prove that inflation in the civilian machine-building sector was high enough to explain the discrepancy between its pre- and postrevision estimates of Soviet procurement for 1970.

Table 10.1 summarizes Becker's empirical findings and compares them with the official series. It indicates that instead of declining 1.4 percent per annum, Soviet machine-building and metalworking prices crept upwards at an annual rate of 1.4 percent, or about one-third the rate subsequently claimed by the agency.

Becker's series is derived inferentially from scattered evidence in the Soviet literature:

1. From 1960 to 1966 the average rate of increase is taken to be 2 percent.[2]

TABLE 10.1
Soviet Machine-Building and Metalworking Industrial Wholesale Price Indices 1960–70

	Becker	Official
1960	100	100
1961	102	96.1
1962	104	96.6
1963	106	96.6
1964	108	93.3
1965	110	93.3
1966	113	90.1
1967	113	89
1968	113	89
1969	114	87
1970	115	85
Compound Annual Inflation Rate 1960–70	1.4%	−1.4%

Source: Abraham Becker, "The Price Level of Soviet Machinery in the 1960s," *Soviet Studies*, Vol. XXVI, No. 3, July 1974, pp. 365, 378.

2. "No change is assumed in 1967 compared with the 1966 level—that is, the trend of the 1960s is believed to be neutralized by once-for-all reductions in 1967."[3]
3. "The rate of increase of prices after 1968 is assumed to have been halved to 1 percent per year. According to one source, scattered cuts in 1968 reduced the machinery price level by 5 percent compared with the level of 1 July 1967 (Kuznetsov and Koshuta, 'Novyi etap sovershenstvovaniya sistemy tsen na produktsiyu mashinostroeniya,' *Voprosy ekonomiki,* 1971, No. 5, pp. 71–72). On the basis of the evidence supplied above, this seems doubtful, especially as the official MMW index registers no change at all in that year."[4]

Of the three criteria listed, only points one and three entail judgments that depart significantly from the trend exhibited by the official series. The evidence cited to support point one—the assumption that machinery prices rose two percent annually from 1960 to 1966—is obtained from N. T. Chertko who declared that the 'cost of equipment rose 5 percent annually' in the period 1959–1967."[5] Noting that "Chertko's explanation raises so many questions as to defy comprehension," Becker and Treml converted the 5 percent estimate to 2 percent by assuming that Chertko was so befuddled that in carrying out his calculations he mistook the current series for the constant one and subtracted where he should have divided.[6] This inference is supported by D. Palterovich's suggestive, but obscure, statement that " 'by our approximate calculation the value of production equipment increased by 2 percent annually on account of price increases. . . .' "[7] The rationale for the assumed 1 percent rate of inflation from 1968 to 1970 is confined to the remarks quoted in point three.

Needless to say, this evidence can hardly be taken seriously as a basis for rejecting either the direction or magnitude of the official price series. As Becker himself put it, "I have been bold enough to attempt to estimate an actual index of machinery prices, but no one should view these numbers as more than crude inferences drawn from incomplete evidence."[8]

Despite the evident merit of this candid disclaimer, Becker's estimates have gained wide currency because they suited the needs of the CIA, confirmed old suspicions, were concordant with the emerging theory of the Second Economy, and appeared to be institutionally plausible. In marshalling the available evidence, to make his estimates as cogent as possible, Becker meticulously inventoried all the usual arguments motivating Soviet managers to introduce spurious new products,[9] explained the administrative factors encouraging the violation of price discipline,[10] and demonstrated why the official machine-building and metalworking price index failed to adequately measure hidden new product price inflation.[11] These theoretical propositions led him to deduce that hidden new product price inflation existed in the machine-building sector, that the rate of inflation was significant and virtually impervious to external scrutiny because of the deficiencies of the MBMW price index. Thus, while Becker did not place great confidence in his own quantitative estimates, he succeeded nonetheless in persuading himself and others that his series was reasonably consistent with the theory and practice of Soviet price formation.

In drawing this conclusion, however, Becker failed to perform a variety of tests which reveal that the new product pricing mechanism he envisages is incompatible with the behavior of the official MBMW price index, plausible rates of price fraud, and historical trends in machine-building profits. Let us consider each of these issues in turn.

The first test compares the pattern of price reductions in the machine-building and metalworking sector implied by Becker's analysis with the pattern reported in the official statistical record. According to Becker no new products were introduced into the sample used to compute the MBMW index between 1961 and 1970, leading to its rapid obsolescence.[12]

If this supposition is true, it should be anticipated that with a fixed sample of standard goods, MBMW prices should decline most rapidly from 1961 to 1965, diminishing asymptotically thereafter, as productivity gains decline down the learning curve.

Table 10.2 reports the actual behavior of the official MBMW price series.[13] From 1961 to 1970 prices fall somewhat erratically at a mean rate of 1.7 percent. In some years no price change occurs, in others the rate is substantial probably indicating a lagged, bunched, bureaucratic response to declining production costs. Most importantly, however, instead of cost savings declining asymptotically as Becker's characterization of the commodity sample implies, the average price decline during the second quinquennium 1966–70, 2 percent, actually exceeds that of the first quinquennium 1961–65, 1.4 percent.

The salience of this contrafactual evidence is vivified by comparing the behavior of the official MBMW price index with a composite MBMW learning curve derived from Soviet sources,[14] with explicit allowance made for overhead costs. Based on the behavior of the composite MBMW learning curve, costs and hence prices should have declined 4.5 percent during the first quinquennium and 0.3 percent thereafter, assuming goods in the 1961 sample were all new, or 1.2 and .06 percent on a vintage-weighted basis, just the reverse of what actually occurred. Whatever the explanation, it seems clear that the behavior of the official index is inconsistent with Becker's description of this aspect of the hidden inflation issue.

The second test evaluates whether the rates of hidden new product inflation implied by Chertko's and Palterovich's estimates appear reasonable in terms of the risks of detection and prosecution, which confront Soviet enterprise managers.

It is beyond dispute that managers possess some latitude in manipulating cost data to justify the prices they set (or request be set) for nonstandard goods.[15] The allocation of enterprise production costs to different purposes is always somewhat arbitrary and clever managers can be expected to exploit these ambiguities to their maximum advantage. Within this gray area the risk-reward ratio clearly inclines toward deception. Beyond a certain point, however, creative cost accounting takes on the appearance of overt fraud and the risks of criminal sanctions loom larger and larger compared with the marginal benefit.

Although it is impossible to assess a priori where the frontier of the gray area might lie, it is probably safe to presume that the risks of detection are positively and monotonically correlated with the hidden inflation rate on nonstandard goods (new products, improved products, and special order items). As a consequence, while analysts will surely

TABLE 10.2
Annual Percentage Change in Soviet Unit Machinery Costs

Year[1]	Official MMW Price Index[2]	Learning Curve[3]	Sample Weighted Learning Curve[4]
1961	− 3.9	− 7.6	− 2.4
1962	+ 0.5	− 6.8	− 1.7
1963	0	− 4.2	− 1.0
1964	− 3.4	− 2.6	− .6
1965	0	− 1.5	− .3
1966	− 3.4	− 0.8	− .15
1967	− 2.3	− 0.4	− .07
1968	0	− 0.2	− .03
1969	− 2.2	− 0.07	− .03
1970	− 2.3	− 0.02	− .02
1961–1965	− 1.4	− 4.5	− 1.2
1966–1970	− 2.0	− 0.3	− .06
Mean	− 1.7	− 2.4	− .6

[1] Each date refers to the period of time between the given and the preceding year.

[2] The official machine building-metalworking price index reported here is valued in industrial wholesale prices. See Abraham Becker, *Ruble Price Levels and Dollar Ruble Ratios of Soviet Machinery in the 1960s* (R-1063-DDRE), Rand Corporation, January 1973, p. 4.

[3] The learning curve describes the average behavior of technical instruments, radio receivers, turbogenerators, steam generators and steam engines. It is not inclusive and is reported here only as an indication of the behavior of Soviet learning curves. The curve was pieced together by averaging the behavior of eight nonagricultural machine products published in Joseph Berliner, *The Innovation Decision in Soviet Industry* (Cambridge, MIT Press, 1976), 267, and extrapolating on the assumption that later year costs fell according to the formula $\dot{g}_t = (\dot{g}_{t-1})^{1.15}$ where $\dot{g}$ is the rate of cost reduction and t is a time subscript. For example, if $\dot{g}_{1964} = .026$, then $\dot{g}_{1965} = (.026)^{1.15} = .015$. The exponent used here for purposes of extrapolation is arbitrary and was chosen to provide an example of a function where the rate of change diminishes in a regular fashion. The cost saving rates reported above are 40 percent below Berliner's statistics to allow for the effect overhead costs would have on moderating price reductions attributable to production costs savings narrowly construed. The unadjusted rates are provided in footnote 14.

[4] The sample weighted learning curve assumes that the 1961 sample consisted of machinery from ten different vintages, each accounting for ten percent of the total number of machines surveyed. This assumption is based on Soviet estimates which indicate that new machines comprise ten percent of machinery production in any given year.

disagree about the precise point at which the Chertko-Palterovich MBMW inflation estimates should be rejected, it can be asserted with some confidence that their general plausibility will diminish with the magnitude of hidden inflation on nonstandard goods required to bring the aggregate rate about.

Table 10.3 provides some insight into how the hidden inflation rate on nonstandard goods and the rate of change in the MBMW price level

TABLE 10.3
Determinants of the Behavior of Soviet Machine-Building and Metalworking Prices

Rates of Nonstandard Good Hidden Price Inflation (Percent) (1)	The Aggregate Inflation Rate (Percent) (2)	
	a	b
− 10	− 4.05	− 4.55
− 5	− 3.55	− 3.80
0	− 3.05	− 3.05
5	− 2.55	− 2.30
10	− 2.05	− 1.55
15	− 1.55	− .80
20	− 1.05	− .05
25	− .55	.70
50	1.95	4.45
75	4.45	8.20

Notes: Column 1 represents hypothetical rates of hidden inflation. Column 2a is calculated from the equation $\dot{p} = .1\dot{p}_n - 3.05$; column 2b from the equation $\dot{p} = .15\dot{p}_n - 3.05$. For a fuller description see the text above.

are related. Column 1 presents a range of hypothetical hidden price inflation rates for new products, qualitatively improved goods, and special order items. Columns 2a and 2b are computed as follows. First it is assumed that changes in the aggregate MBMW price level are a function of hidden inflation p_n^t/p_n^o (where the ratio measures only illicit deviations from initially established prices) which occurs because nonstandard goods are priced higher than they should be according to prevailing rules of price formation; wage increases w^t/w^o which affect prime cost (sebestoimost'), and technical progress k^t/k^o which reduces unit production costs:

1.
$$\frac{p^t}{p^o} = \phi\left(\frac{p_n^t}{p_n^o}, \frac{w^t}{w^o}, \frac{k^t}{k^o}\right)$$

where p^t/p^o = the aggregate price level at time t compared with some initial level

p_n^t/p_n^o = the comparative price level for nonstandard goods in two time periods. By definition the physical characteristics of nonstandard goods differ at times t and o.[16]

w^t/w^o = the ratio of money wage rates in both periods

k^t/k^o = the ratio of unit production costs at t and o; that is the change in unit costs attributed to technical progress[17]

Given base year quantity weights, changes in the aggregate price level are specified to depend on the net effect of increased money wages, cost decreases attributed broadly to technical progress, and the establishment of unwarrantedly high prices for nonstandard goods.

Second, for simplicity it is assumed that the share of nonstandard output in total MBMW production is constant over the period in question,[18] as are the rates of price fraud $\dot{p}_n$, wage increase $\dot{w}$, and technical progress $\dot{k}$. The aggregate MBMW inflation rate for a single year or the entire period can then be expressed as

2.
$$\dot{p} = \alpha_1 \dot{p}_n + \alpha_2 \dot{w} - \alpha_3 \dot{k}$$

where α_1, α_2, and α_3 are coefficients that measure the contribution each variable makes to the change in the MBMW price level.

Values for the parameters and the independent variables of equation 2 can be obtained from the specialized literature, Soviet statistical compendia, and by econometric estimation. The first coefficient, α_1, is set equal to .1 in approximate conformity with estimates provided by Becker's sources, V. Senchagov, A. Tolkachev, and D. Palterovich, for the share new types of equipment comprise of total machinery production.[19] Presumably these estimates include improved variants of standard products but the sources are not entirely clear on this point. They appear however to exclude special order items, which according to Kvasha and Krasovsky comprise almost 50 percent of all machinery in the *construction* sector.[20] Allowances have been made for this in Table 10.3, column 2b by assuming alternatively that $\alpha_1 = .15$. It needs to be emphasized, however, that special order goods play a decidedly subordinate role in Becker's theory of hidden inflation because although following Kvasha and Krasovsky these goods may be overpriced by 30–40 percent,[21] it is not asserted either that the degree of overpricing, or their share in total machinery production is increasing. Since the hidden inflation rate depends on the change in some initial price level, and not the relationship of the level to "true" cost, special order items cannot be considered an important element in the hidden inflation mechanism.[22]

The wage coefficient α_2 is set at 0.375, which represents the share of the total value of machine-building and metalworking output directly imputable to wages.[23] This formulation implies that all wage increases are fully passed through to product prices in every sector. Since wages constitute only one component of cost, unlike price fraud, or technological progress where growth is defined as a share of total cost, the degree to which wage increases augment prices depends on the wage share of value added. The value added standard as opposed to the gross cost norm that encompasses intermediate inputs is employed here to insure definitional consistency with the price fraud and technological progress variables, which abstract from intermediate goods. The average annual increase in MBMW money wages cited by Becker for the period 1955–66 is 2 percent.[24]

Technical progress is defined as the annual percentage reduction in the primary factor cost of production attributed to improved technique and is assumed to occur at a uniform rate for all machinery production. Since technical progress affects the total primary cost of production, α_3 is set equal to one. The uniform rate at which technical progress takes place is treated as an average rate for any given year and for the period as a whole in conformity with our prior assumption that the ratio of nonstandard to standard machine types is constant. The rate of technical progress itself has been estimated using CES production function techniques for the MBMW sector.[25] Other estimates are, of course, tenable, especially since hidden inflation may impart an upward bias to measured productivity. The figure used here, however, does not differ too greatly from the economy-wide rate of neutral technical progress so that if hidden inflation is restricted to the MBMW sector, our estimate of technical progress should not be too far off on this score.

Inserting the parameter and independent variable values derived above into equation 2

3.
$$\dot{p} = 1.\dot{p}_n + .375\,(2) - 3.8$$
$$= .1\dot{p}_n - 3.05.$$

The figures reported in Table 10.3, column 2a are computed from this relationship. Column 2b is calculated on the alternative assumption that $\alpha_1 = .15$.

As is readily discernible whether reference is to a theory of inflation driven primarily by spurious innovation and quality change (column 2a) or to one which also allows for the exponential divergence of prices from production costs for special order items (column 2b), aggregate MBMW price inflation at rates close to the one estimated by Becker requires a very high hidden inflation rate on nonstandard goods. In the case which appears to correspond most closely with Becker's interpretation of the aggregate inflation process (column 2a, and equation 3) a 1.95 percent annual rate of aggregate MBMW price inflation necessitates a 50 percent annual increase in the rate at which current new product prices p_n^t exceed the new product price level of the preceding year p_n^o. The corresponding rate for an expanded interpretation of Becker's theory (column 2b) is 33 percent.

Fraud of these proportions is hardly nontrivial and would entail risk-taking behavior on the part of Soviet managers, which seems inconsistent with the risk adverse propensities usually thought to describe Soviet management. This impression is reinforced moreover when it is recognized that we are dealing with average rates of price fraud. If a normal distribution is assumed, then a substantial proportion of Soviet managers in the MBMW sector must be willing to bear what would seem to be an incredible amount of risk, while the authorities must be presumed to be staggeringly inept and/or indifferent to this sort of crime.

The force of these inferences can, of course, be called into question by challenging the rate of technical progress econometrically estimated for k, or by disputing the α_1 coefficient suggested by the Soviet sources Becker cites. Since k is a constant the reader can easily substitute alternative estimates derived econometrically or via the Solow-Abramovitz method in equation 3.[26] Such estimates may vary considerably, but it is unlikely that they will be less than 2 percent, the critical value at which managerial risk-taking begins to lie within the bounds of reason.

While some portion of this growth is attributable to increased investment, unless the output elasticity of Soviet capital is far higher than most analysts suppose technical progress (the residual) should substantially exceed 2 percent, confirming our conclusion that Becker's hidden inflation estimate implies an improbably high degree of Soviet managerial risk-taking.[27]

Challenging the validity of α_1 is likely to be even less fruitful. To push α_1 much beyond .1, special order items must be included in the hidden inflation generation mechanism. Since the special order share of total machinery remained more or less constant during the 1960s, this implies increasing special order price premiums, and a growing divergence between unit cost and sales price. Even Kvasha and Krasovsky refrain from making such a claim for it is easily seen that if the hidden inflation rate were merely 12.5 percent per annum (the rate required to generate aggregate MBMW at 1.95% annually, α_1 = .4),[28] the divergence between unit cost and price would grow from 35 percent (the mean of Krasovsky's range) to 338 percent in 10 years, rising exponentially thereafter.[29]

The implausibility of such manifest fraud need not be belabored. It is, however, revealing to recognize that a similar debility affects Becker's preferred hidden inflation mechanism, which stresses the primacy of spurious innovation and quality change. To see why this is, suppose that in 1960 all new products were priced at cost, but thereafter prices diverged from costs at a fixed annual rate reflecting Becker's fundamental premise that the price of last year's spurious innovations are used as a benchmark for further increasing the prices of this year's vintage of spurious new machinery.[30] Let us moreover use the lowest of the two hidden inflation rates, p_n = 33 percent, shown earlier to be sufficient for the generation of a 1.95 percent aggregate MBMW inflation rate. After 10 years, given these assumptions the divergence between the unit cost of production of new machines and their sales prices would reach 1632 percent![31]

As before other rates of increase could be assumed, but by now it should be clear that Becker's explanation of hidden inflation is untenable as he has formulated it. Managers could not assume the risks, and bureaucrats could not tolerate the gross abuse that his theory entails.

Before terminating this evaluation of the plausibility of Becker's MBMW hidden inflation estimates, one last test must be considered. It follows necessarily from the fact that p_n^t/p_n^o must be nonnegative for hidden inflation to exist at all (regardless of how much price exceeds unit cost initially), that if hidden inflation is a real phenomenon profit margins must expand as prices diverge exponentially from unit costs at a rate in excess of what can be accounted for by official productivity and price data. The expected trend in the rate of MBMW profit can be calculated from information provided in equation 3. In the absence of hidden inflation the net effect of technical progress k, changes in the money wage rate $\dot{w}$, and the officially reported reduction in the price level $\dot{p}$ should have increased MBMW profits 1.4 percent annually from 1960 to 1970 and −1.08 percent from 1970 to 1976.[32]

Any hidden inflation that took place in MBMW would have constituted an additional source of profit growth. To compute the effect hidden inflation should have had on the MBMW profit rate, given Becker's estimated aggregate MBMW inflation rate of 1.9 percent, equation 3 can be rearranged and solved for $\alpha_1\dot{p}_n$:

$$\alpha_1\dot{p}_n = \dot{p} - \alpha_2\dot{w} + \alpha_3 k$$
$$= 1.9 - .75 + 3.8$$
4.
$$= 4.95$$

This effect added to the other factors determining the profit rate (technical progress, wages, and officially acknowledged changes in the money price level, 1.4 percent, 1960–70) implies that if Becker's hypothesis is correct MBMW profits should have risen 6.4 percent per annum during the sixties and 3.9 percent annually in the seventies.

Table 10.4 presents data on MBMW profits that can be used to disconfirm this supposition. The data, taken from official sources, show that the trend in the MBMW profit rate divides into three distinct ep-

TABLE 10.4
Profit Rates in the Soviet Machine-Building and Metalworking Sector, 1960–76

Year	Official	Becker (implied)
1960	19.8	19.8
1961		26.2
1962	21.7	22.6
1963	21.9	39
1964	22.1	45.4
1965	21.9	51.8
1966	24.9	58.7
1967	25.5	64.6
1968	26.8	71.0
1969	26.7	77.4
1970	27.5	83.8
1971	23.2	87.7
1972	24.2	91.6
1973	19.1	95.5
1974	20.0	99.4
1975	20.7	103.3
1976	17.6	107.2
dπ/dt 1960–1965	2.0%	6.4%
dπ/dt 1966–1970	2.5%	6.4%
dπ/dt 1971–1976	−4.4%	3.9%

Source: Narkhoz, various years.
Method: The profit rate is computed by dividing total MBMW annual profit by the gross MBMW capital stock. This measure excludes working capital (material'nye oborotnye sredstva).

Becker's implied rates are calculated by adding the annual rates of growth computed in the text for the designated periods to the profit rate prevailing in the previous year, beginning initially with the official rate 19.8 in 1960.

ochs. Between 1960 and 1965 the profit rate drifts up modestly at approximately 2 percent per annum. A sharp discontinuity occurs in 1966, presumably for reasons related to the overall price reform of 1967,[33] after which the profit rate resumes its gradual ascent now at 2.5 percent per annum. In 1971 another sharp discontinuity is observed, this time in the reverse direction, with the profit rate declining 4.4 percent from 1971 to 1977.

These rates are drastically lower than those implied by Becker's hidden inflation hypothesis, whether evaluated annually or on a cumulative basis. The cumulative effect is vividly illustrated in column 3 of Table 10.4. If Becker were correct not only should the MBMW profit rate have risen secularly, it should have grown to a level in excess of 100 percent per annum. Instead the MBMW profit rate peaks in 1970 at 27.5 percent and declines to 17.6 by 1976. Here as with the other tests performed in part II, the evidence very strongly disconfirms the hypothesis that the Soviet MBMW sector is riven with hidden inflation, and suggests that Becker's disclaimer was more justified than he himself understood.

Notes

1. Abraham Becker is a well known authority on Soviet defense expenditures at the Rand Corporation. He served as the American member of the United Nations' Expert Group on the Reduction of Military Budgets, the U.N. Expert Group on the Measurement of Military Expenditure and wrote the book *Military Expenditure Limitation for Arms Control* for ACDA in 1977. A long time consultant to the air force with close links to the Military Economic Advisory Panel, which supervises the work of the Military Economic Analysis Center, OSR, CIA, it seems highly unlikely that Becker could have been unaware of the covert procurement price information obtained in the late sixties and early seventies when he wrote his Rand monograph on hidden inflation. According to Steiner, Becker worked closely with him in preparing his monograph, *Inflation in Soviet Industry and Machine-Building and Metalworking (MBMW) 1960–1975*, analyzed in chapter 8.
2. Becker (1974), p. 377.
3. Ibid.
4. Ibid.
5. Ibid., note 64.
6. Ibid.
7. Ibid., p. 378, note 68. No information is provided explaining how Palterovich's "approximations" were calculated.
8. Ibid., p. 363.
9. Ibid. Becker's source is the deputy chairman of the State Price Committee, A.N. Komin, who he quotes as saying: "High prices on obsolete machinery led to increased prices on new machinery" (p. 370); and the gap between estimated planned cost and actual expenditures "has been increasing from year to year and has turned into a distinctive chronic deficiency of investment planning" (p. 374).
10. Gregory Grossman (1977); Morris Bornstein (1978).
11. Becker (1974), pp. 363–67.
12. Ibid., p. 369. This argument is probably fallacious. Soviet real output data which includes all industrial output is published in real and nominal terms. Dividing these series, which differ only by their prices, provides no evidence of the hidden inflation Becker anticipates based on the assumption that hidden inflation is concentrated in goods omitted from the industrial price index, but included in the real output series. See *Narodnoe Khoziaistvo SSSR (1975)*, p. 191, Becker (1974), pp. 364–67. Cf. Steiner (1978a), 33–37.
13. The period rates 1961–65 and 1966–70 are simple averages of the annual rates. If enterprise wholesale prices were used instead of industrial wholesale prices the rate at which MBMW prices decline would be slightly altered.

In principle, enterprise wholesale prices that reflect official factor cost more accurately than industrial wholesale prices should be used for comparison with cost savings along the learning curve. However, since Becker used industrial wholesale prices in his essay, they are reported here to avoid unnecessary confusion.

14. See Table 1, note 3. The unadjusted cost savings (in percent) are:

1961	− 12.6	1966	− 1.
1962	− 11.3	1967	− 0.9
1963	− 7.0	1968	− 0.5
1964	− 4.7	1969	− 0.2
1965	− 2.9	1970	− 0.08
1961–65	− 7.5	1966–70	− 0.5

15. Bergson (1947), pp. 222–25.
16. The heterogeneity of nonstandard goods blurs the entire conception of hidden inflation because legitimate differences in quality may easily be misinterpreted as unwarranted price increases. In forming the price ratio p_n^t/p_n^o, however, it is implicitly assumed that the products in question have somehow been adjusted to a standardized basis.
17. In the simple model used here technical progress is determined on the assumption that the marginal productivities of capital and labor are constant, as is the elasticity of factor substitution. In the calculations reported below derived econometrically using a CES production function the elasticity of factor substitution is substantially less than 1. Other specifications of course can be employed. The analysis performed here, however, should not be greatly modified because what counts for our purposes is not how cost savings are imputed, but the rate at which total costs decline annually from all sources.
18. I have experimented with elaborate models that relax this assumption. For any plausible range over which the new goods ratio might vary, the basic conclusions derived below are not significantly altered.
19. Becker (1974), p. 368, notes 17–19. James Steiner (1978a, p. 52) accepts this estimate and misuses it to perform an incorrectly specified test of the type carried out above.
20. Ibid., p. 373.
21. Ibid.
22. Ibid., p. 368. "The treatment of new commodities is the heart of the problem of MMW price inflation and of the failure of the index to reflect that trend."
23. Wages and value added in the MBMW sector were computed from input-output data for 1966. See Treml (1972), pp. 435–47. MBMW is defined here as sectors 12–36, excluding repairs. Value added was derived by adding depreciation to national income produced in MBMW. The aggregate wage was 8,648,987 thousand rubles, value added 23,047,800.
24. The choice of the value added convention is unlikely to significantly affect the results reported in Table 2. The use of money wages as opposed to the "social" wage which includes wages (*zarabotnaia plata*) plus other payments in money and kind for housing, education, welfare, etc., was dictated by the fact that many forms of supplementary income are not borne directly by the enterprise and therefore do not function as a cost internal to firms which must be taken into account in setting product prices. For a discussion

of this distinction and the reliability of Soviet wage statistics see Schroeder (1972), 287–96.

The 2 percent annual rate of money wage growth cited by Becker may appear low in light of recent Soviet experience. From 1965 to 1976, for example, industrial wages grew at a compound annual rate of 4.5 percent (*Narodnoe Khoziaistvo za 60 Let*, p. 472). Industrial wages, however, rose much more slowly from 1958 to 1966, 2.5 percent per annum, for the period in which Becker has MBMW wage data obtained from *Trud SSSR*. The MBMW rate reported by Becker therefore is not anomalous. See *Narodnoe Khoziaistvo SSSR (1970)*, p. 657.

25. Steven Rosefielde (1979).
26. Steven Rosefielde (1979, 1980c). Also see Martin Weitzman (1970), Padma Desai (1976), Stanislaw Gomulka (1976), Rosefielde and Lovell (1977).
27. Steven Rosefielde (1976). It should also be noted that industrial worker productivity valued in constant prices rose 5.2 percent annually from 1960 to 1970. Productivity per worker rose 7.4 percent per annum in the MBMW sector. Any reasonable allowance made for the growth of capital and its output elasticity could not drive residual productivity below 2 percent per annum.
28. The value $\alpha_1 = .4$ represents a subjective upper-bound estimate of the nonstandard goods' share of MBMW production. It assumes that the construction sector purchases more nonstandard products than other users of MBMW goods.
29. The CIA study, *An Analysis of the Behavior of Soviet Machinery Prices, 1960–75*, is also suspicious of Krasovsky's calculations. See p. 20.
30. See note 8.
31. $p_n^{1970}/p_n^{1960} = 1732$
32. For the period 1970–76 MBMW prices fell more rapidly than during the sixties, and wages rose more rapidly. Prices declined at a 3.35% annual rate (*Narodnoe Khoziaistvo SSSR*, 1977, p. 197), while wages in industry rose 4.1% annually. Adjusting for the wage share of value added (see equation 3), the expected profit trend for the period 1970–76 can be estimated as follows:

$$\pi = \dot{k} - \dot{p} - \alpha_2\dot{w}$$
$$= 3.8 - 3.35 - 1.53$$
$$= -1.08$$

33. Becker notes that profit margins on military procurement may have been substantially increased in 1967. Perhaps the jump in MBMW profits reported in Table 10.4 is due in part to an early transition to higher procurement prices. But this, of course, is ajar with Becker's guess that procurement is omitted from MMW production and price series (Abraham Becker, 1974, 336 and 379, esp. notes 70–71).

Becker makes several other remarks on profits which indicate that he believes MBMW profit rates fell immediately after 1967, instead of rising as indicated by the *Narodnoe Khoziaistvo* data. The reason for this discrepancy is not apparent (ibid., p. 379).

CHAPTER 11

Howard's Estimates of Hidden Soviet Retail Price Inflation

The only other "independent" quantitative study ostensibly support-ing the agency's hidden military procurement inflation hypothesis is David Howard's monograph, *The Disequilibrium Model in a Controlled Economy*, in which an attempt is made to demonstrate that repressed inflation in the Soviet state retail market has caused collective farm sales and savings to increase and reduced voluntary employment.[1] To properly test this theory, Howard develops price indices for Soviet retail sales that purport to measure hidden inflation.[2] Minimum and maximum es-timates of hidden inflation computed from his price indices are reported in Table 11.1. They indicate that the annual rate of hidden retail price inflation from 1955 to 1972 was between .8 and 1.2 percent, rates roughly in line with Becker's estimate for the civilian machine-building sector.[3]

Hidden inflation, as defined by Howard, represents the degree to which prices charged in the state retail sector (excluding the collective farm market) exceed those entered in the official Soviet retail price index.[4] This is a narrow definition that excludes the phenomenon of spurious new products, or the effects of repressed inflation.[5] Although these are important omissions, especially the failure to take explicit account of quality adulteration and spurious technical change, the def-inition is nonetheless serviceable.

Ideally, hidden inflation in Howard's sense should be estimated as the difference between two Laspeyres price indices, the first measuring all relevant prices and quantities, the second the selected sample of these values used in the official index.[6]

TABLE 11.1
David Howard's Estimates of Hidden Soviet Retail Price Inflation
(1955 = 100)

Year	Minimum	Maximum
1955	100.0	100.0
1956	101.9	102.5
1957	104.8	108.7
1958	104.5	105.6
1959	104.7	105.9
1960	105.3	107.3
1961	104.5	105.7
1962	105.8	106.6
1963	106.5	106.7
1964	106.1	106.7
1965	108.2	110.2
1966	108.0	109.7
1967	108.8	111.5
1968	109.4	112.8
1969	110.6	114.6
1970	111.6	116.6
1971	113.4	119.4
1972	114.4	121.9
Compound Annual Rate of Hidden Inflation 1955–72	.8%	1.2%

Source: David Howard, "A Note on Hidden Inflation in the Soviet Union," *Soviet Studies* XXVIII, no. 4, October 1976, Table 6, p. 607. The figures shown above are obtained by subtracting open official inflation in the state retail sector from Howard's minimum and maximum estimates.

1.

$$H = \frac{\sum_{i=1}^{n} p_i^t q_i^o}{\sum_{i=1}^{n} p_i^o q_i^o} - \frac{\sum_{i=1}^{m} p_i^{*t} q_i^o}{\sum_{i=1}^{m} p_i^o q_i^o}$$

Equation 1 expresses this relationship by suggesting that the set of prices (p_i) and quantities (q_i) needed to measure the full impact of inflation is larger than the set employed by the Central Statistical Administration ($n > m$). Presumably, goods experiencing especially high rates of inflation would be omitted from the official index if the state desired to conceal the true rate of inflation. In addition, the official index may understate the true price level because the prices at which goods are actually transacted exceed those established by the State Price Committee, and utilized by TsSU in forming the official price index. This potential source of bias is indicated above by the term $p_i^{*'}$, which distinguishes recorded prices from actual transactions prices.

Calculating equation 1 is a trivial exercise provided the necessary data are available. The Soviets no doubt possess much of the requisite information, but Western analysts do not. To estimate H foreign specialists must find an alternative measure for the "true" retail price index (the fir . term on the right).

One well known and obvious method for accomplishing this objective is to compute a Paasche retail price index from available data on real consumers' goods production (and/or sales), and data on the current value of retail sales.

2.
$$\hat{I} = \frac{\sum_{i=1}^{r} p_i^t q_i^t}{\sum_{i=1}^{r} p_i^o q_i^o} \Bigg/ \frac{\sum_{i=1}^{r} p_i^o q_i^t}{\sum_{i=1}^{r} p_i^o q_i^o} = \frac{\sum_{i=1}^{r} p_i^t q_i^t}{\sum_{i=1}^{r} p_i^o q_i^t}$$

and substitute this estimate into equation 1:

3.
$$\hat{H} = \frac{\sum_{i=1}^{r} p_i^t q_i^t}{\sum_{i=1}^{r} p_i^o q_i^t} - \frac{\sum_{i=1}^{m} p_i^{*t} q_i^o}{\sum_{i=1}^{m} p_i^o q_i^o}$$

The merit of this procedure depends on the accuracy and comprehensiveness of the real consumer's good production index used to derive the Paasche price index, the conformability of the prices and quantities employed in forming the underlying production index and the official Laspeyres price index;[7] and the structural characteristics of the quantity weights q_i^t and q_i^o.[8]

Accuracy, conformability, and structure all pose serious problems. The Soviets do not publish real consumers' goods production indices that are definitionally consistent with the official retail price index. As a consequence the production index itself must be estimated by Western specialists as best they can, largely from diverse official sources. The resulting calculations are subject to a wide margin of error. Gertrude Schroeder's discussion of the Bronson-Severin consumers' goods production index, which was used by Howard in forming his hidden inflation estimates, makes this abundantly clear.[9] Likewise, the coverage (conformability) of the relevant data sets leaves a great deal to be desired;

the Bronson-Severin index being far less comprehensive than the official index.[10]

Even if these deficiencies were somehow alleviated, equation 3 would still suffer from index number "ambiguity." The quantity weights in the official price index pertain to the bundle of goods prevailing in the base year. However, the quantity weights in the derived Paasche price index refer to the commodity bundle of the current year. If these weights differ significantly then the resulting estimate of hidden inflation $\hat{H}$ could diverge substantially from "true" hidden inflation H solely because of the use of inconsistent quantity weights. Whether index number "ambiguity" will in fact seriously distort any given measure of hidden inflation cannot be determined a priori. However, and this is the crucial point, the possibility that $\hat{H}$ will diverge significantly from H for all three reasons identified above is very great, so that most specialists would place little confidence in an hidden inflation estimate of the form $\hat{H}$, unless it were confirmed by other evidence.

Perhaps for this reason Howard has adopted a different method for estimating $\hat{H}$. Instead of employing equation 3, his hidden inflation estimate is expressed as

4.
$$\overline{H} = p_t^*(100\Delta)/X_t$$

where p_t^* is the official Laspeyres retail price index, Δ is the difference between an index of official sales deflated by the official retail sales index and the Bronson-Severin index of real consumer goods production; X_t also pertains to the Bronson-Severin index.[11] Expressed in index form equation 4 can be rewritten as follows:

5.
$$\overline{H} = \frac{\sum_{i=1}^{m} p_i^{*t}q_i^{o}}{\sum_{i=1}^{m} p_i^{o}q_i^{o}} \left[\frac{\sum_{i=1}^{n} p_i^{t}q_i^{t} \sum_{i=1}^{m} p_i^{o}q_i^{o}}{\sum_{i=1}^{n} p_i^{o}q_i^{o} \sum_{i=1}^{m} p_i^{*t}q_i^{o}} - \frac{\sum_{i=1}^{r} p_i^{o}q_i^{t}}{\sum_{i=1}^{r} p_i^{o}q_i^{o}} \right] / \frac{\sum_{i=1}^{r} p_i^{o}q_i^{t}}{\sum_{i=1}^{r} p_i^{o}q_i^{o}}$$

The second term on the right is composed of two subindices: nominal official retail sales, $\sum_{i=1}^{n} p_i^{t}q_i^{t}/\sum_{i=1}^{n} p_i^{o}q_i^{o}$; and the official retail sales price deflator $\sum_{i=1}^{m} p_i^{*t}q_i^{o}/\sum_{i=1}^{m} p_i^{o}q_i^{o}$.

If the subset of products in the official price deflator is unbiased, (invoking the standard null hypothesis when the issue of bias is in question), then the deflated nominal retail sales index simplifies to a Paasche index of real sales:

6.
$$\frac{\sum_{i=1}^{n} p_i^t q_i^t}{\sum_{i=1}^{n} p_i^t q_i^o} = \frac{\sum_{i=1}^{n} p_i^t q_i^t \sum_{i=1}^{m} p_i^o q_i^o}{\sum_{i=1}^{n} p_i^o q_i^o \sum_{i=1}^{m} p_i^{*t} q_i^o}$$

because via the null hypothesis

7.
$$\frac{\sum_{i=1}^{m} p_i^o q_i^o}{\sum_{i=1}^{m} p_i^{*t} q_i^o} = \frac{\sum_{i=1}^{n} p_i^o q_i^o}{\sum_{i=1}^{n} p_i^t q_i^o}$$

Inserting this expression into equation 5 yields:

8.
$$\overline{H} = \frac{\sum_{i=1}^{m} p_i^{*t} q_i^o}{\sum_{i=1}^{m} p_i^o q_i^o} \left[\frac{\sum_{i=1}^{n} p_i^t q_i^t}{\sum_{i=1}^{n} p_i^t q_i^o} - \frac{\sum_{i=1}^{r} p_i^o q_i^t}{\sum_{i=1}^{n} p_i^o q_i^o} \right] \Bigg/ \frac{\sum_{i=1}^{r} p_i^o q_i^t}{\sum_{i=1}^{r} p_i^o q_i^o}$$

which contains the difference term

9.
$$\frac{\sum_{i=1}^{n} p_i^t q_i^t}{\sum_{i=1}^{n} p_i^t q_i^o} - \frac{\sum_{i=1}^{r} p_i^o q_i^t}{\sum_{i=1}^{r} p_i^o q_i^o}$$

computed by subtracting the Bronson-Severin Laspeyres index of real consumer good production from the estimated Paasche index of real official retail sales. This operation which is the key step in Howard's estimation procedure however is invalid because the indices involved are formally inconsistent, one Paasche the other Laspeyres, and because they are derived from alien population sets.

These deficiencies moreover cannot be eliminated by simplifying equation 8

10.
$$\overline{H} = \frac{\sum_{i=1}^{m} p_i^{*t} q_i^o \sum_{i=1}^{n} p_i^t q_i^t \sum_{i=1}^{r} p_i^o q_i^o}{\sum_{i=1}^{m} p_i^o q_i^o \sum_{i=1}^{n} p_i^t q_i^o \sum_{i=1}^{r} p_i^o q_i^t} - \frac{\sum_{i=1}^{m} p_i^{*t} q_i^o}{\sum_{i=1}^{m} p_i^o q_i^o}$$

because the first term on the right which is supposed to constitute a legitimate Lespeyres index of actual retail sales cannot be validly reduced to the desired form. Equation 10 can be simplified to

$$
11. \qquad \overline{H} = \frac{\displaystyle\sum_{i=1}^{n} p_i^t q_i^t \; \sum_{i=1}^{r} p_i^o q_i^o}{\displaystyle\sum_{i=1}^{n} p_i^o q_i^o \; \sum_{i=1}^{r} p_i^o q_i^t} - \frac{\displaystyle\sum_{i=1}^{n} p_i^t q_i^o}{\displaystyle\sum_{i=1}^{n} p_i^o q_i^o}
$$

by properly assuming that the official retail price index is unbiased (equation 7), but if an attempt is made to further rationalize this expression by assuming that the Bronson-Severin real consumer good production index and the unpublished official real retail sales index, calculated from alien populations are fortuitously coincident:

$$
12. \qquad \frac{\displaystyle\sum_{i=1}^{n} p_i^o q_i^t}{\displaystyle\sum_{i=1}^{n} p_i^o q_i^o} = \frac{\displaystyle\sum_{i=1}^{r} p_i^o q_i^t}{\displaystyle\sum_{i=1}^{r} p_i^o q_i^o}
$$

equation 11 reduces to a measure of index number price disparity (where $\overline{H}$ is the difference between the true Paasche and the true Laspeyres retail price index)

$$
13. \qquad \overline{H} = \frac{\displaystyle\sum_{i=1}^{n} p_i^t q_i^t}{\displaystyle\sum_{i=1}^{n} p_i^o q_i^t} - \frac{\displaystyle\sum_{i=1}^{n} p_i^t q_i^o}{\displaystyle\sum_{i=1}^{n} p_i^o q_i^o}
$$

because by assumption (equation 7), the official retail price index is unbiased.[12]

This revealing outcome moreover cannot be circumvented by substituting a Laspeyres index of actual retail sales for the Paasche index contained in equation 8 to assure conformability with the Bronson-Severin index:

$$
14. \qquad \overline{H} = \frac{\displaystyle\sum_{i=1}^{m} p_i^{*t} q_i^o}{\displaystyle\sum_{i=1}^{m} p_i^o q_i^o} \left[\frac{\displaystyle\sum_{i=1}^{n} p_i^o q_i^t}{\displaystyle\sum_{i=1}^{n} p_i^o q_i^o} - \frac{\displaystyle\sum_{i=1}^{r} p_i^o q_i^t}{\displaystyle\sum_{i=1}^{r} p_i^o q_i^o} \right] \Bigg/ \frac{\displaystyle\sum_{i=1}^{r} p_i^o q_i^t}{\displaystyle\sum_{i=1}^{r} p_i^o q_i^o}
$$

which simplifies to:

15.
$$\overline{H} = \frac{\sum\limits_{i=1}^{m} p_i^{*t}q_i^o \sum\limits_{i=1}^{n} p_i^o q_i^o \sum\limits_{i=1}^{r} p_i^o q_i^o}{\sum\limits_{i=1}^{m} p_i^o q_i^o \sum\limits_{i=1}^{n} p_i^o q_i^o \sum\limits_{i=1}^{r} p_i^o q_i^t} - \frac{\sum\limits_{i=1}^{m} p_i^{*t}q_i^o}{\sum\limits_{i=1}^{m} p_i^o q_i^o}$$

because equation 12 cannot be further reduced to a valid Laspeyres index of actual Soviet retail prices.[13]

Howard has recently argued that these inferences are erroneous.[14] He contends that the "deflated nominal retail sales index" he uses should not be simplified to either a Paasche or a Laspeyres "real retail sales index." To assess whether this assertion saves his calculation, equation 5, which already contains his "deflated index of nominal retail sales" can be simplified to:

16.
$$\overline{H} = \frac{\sum\limits_{i=1}^{n} p_i^t q_i^t \sum\limits_{i=1}^{r} p_i^o q_i^o}{\sum\limits_{i=1}^{n} p_i^o q_i^o \sum\limits_{i=1}^{r} p_i^o q_i^t} - \frac{\sum\limits_{i=1}^{m} p_i^{*t}q_i^o}{\sum\limits_{i=1}^{m} p_i^o q_i^o}$$

This expression is virtually identical to equation 11, differing only insofar as Howard begs the question by assuming that the official retail price index is biased (see equation 12). As before, equation 15 can be transformed into an ambiguous estimate of H, calculated as the difference between a Paasche and a Laspeyres price index,[15]

17.
$$\overline{H} = \frac{\sum\limits_{i=1}^{n} p_i^t q_i^t}{\sum\limits_{i=1}^{n} p_i^o q_i^t} - \frac{\sum\limits_{i=1}^{m} p_i^{*t}q_i^o}{\sum\limits_{i=1}^{m} p_i^o q_i^o}$$

but only by tendentiously assuming that the Bronson-Severin consumer good production index is fortuitously an unbiased estimator of the unpublished official real retail sales index (equation 12).[16]

Such an estimate, which in effect assumes that hidden inflation can be directly measured by subtracting the official retail price index from the Bronson-Severin index of consumer good prices:

18.
$$\overline{H} = \frac{\sum\limits_{i=1}^{r} p_i^t q_i^t \sum\limits_{i=1}^{r} p_i^o q_i^o}{\sum\limits_{i=1}^{r} p_i^o q_i^o \sum\limits_{i=1}^{r} p_i^o q_i^t} - \frac{\sum\limits_{i=1}^{m} p_i^{*t}q_i^o}{\sum\limits_{i=1}^{m} p_i^o q_i^o}$$

has no objective scientific merit, however. The critical assumptions on which it rests are not determined by sampling the true population of Soviet retail prices, but merely by untenably assuming on a priori grounds that a Western index computed from an alien population coincides with the true index; that the official retail price index is *biased*; and that the true Paasche price index equals the true Laspeyres price index. A priori assumptions of this sort cannot suffice to establish or disestablish the existence of hidden inflation in the Soviet retail sector, and it can thus be concluded that insofar as Howard's estimates of hidden retail price inflation are meaningful, and do not degenerate into an irrelevant measure of index number price disparity, they are the consequence of the implausible a priori assumptions that govern his calculations.[17]

Notes

1. Howard's analysis of repressed inflation and his empirical tests are defective. See Rosefielde (1980a). Also see Katz (1979), Nissanke (1979).
2. Howard (1979), p. 69, and Howard (1976), p. 607.
3. Howard (1976), p. 607.
4. As the title of Howard's essay suggests, his principal concern is to measure *hidden* inflation in Soviet retail sales sector, not *open* inflation outside the state sector. For this reason he does not employ data on collective farm market prices in estimating hidden inflation in state retail food prices. Instead, Howard assumes ". . . that the hidden inflation in food is equal to that in durables and soft goods . . ." (Howard, 1976, p. 604). At the very end of his article, for the sake of completeness, Howard does compute an estimate of total retail price inflation which includes the collective farm market. In computing this measure he purportedly relies on the official collective farm market price index. The reader, however, should note that because Howard's estimate of hidden inflation exceeds the officially acknowledged rate of inflation on the collective farm market, his general consumer price index is actually lower than his state retail price index. See Howard (1976), pp. 605–08, esp. Table 5, columns 1 and 2, and Table A1, column 4.
5. Howard's narrative sometimes gives the impression that his technique does capture the influence of these factors. For example, he writes, "However, this estimate of the overall state retail price index probably overstates the total hidden inflation rate since it is easier to invent 'new' or improved products in the durables and soft goods sector than in the food sector" (Howard, 1976, p. 604). The technique he employs, however, cannot discriminate these phenomena. He neither computes hedonic indices of qualitative changes, nor product innovation, and the Bronson-Severin real consumers' good production index on which he relies makes no adjustment for spurious new products introduced at unjustifiably high prices.

   For a fuller discussion of the mechanics of hidden inflation see Bornstein (1972, 1976, 1978), Berliner (1975), Becker (1974), and Grossman (1977).

6. The official price index may understate inflation as defined above either because goods exhibiting high rates of increase are omitted, or because recorded prices understate actual transactions prices.
7. The estimated Paasche price index unlike the ideal Laspeyres measure will typically be based on a smaller and often less accurate data set than the one employed for computing the official price index.
8. The mix of consumer goods produced varies from year to year. Since the mix in any two years is unlikely to be identical, measured price change will differ depending on the quantity weights chosen.
9. Gertrude Schroeder and Barbara Severin (1976), pp. 644–45.
10. Ibid.
11. "Still another way is to estimate the actual price level and hence the amount of hidden inflation. In the rest of this article such a method is used." The reader should carefully observe that the method Howard employs is not formally equivalent to computing a retail price index. This is explicitly acknowledged by the author, "There is no good way to construct an independent index of state retail prices by obtaining price quotations for recent years, as Janet Chapman did for the prewar period . . ." (Howard, 1976, p. 608).
12. The official retail price index is derived from detailed TsSU retail price data which other things equal should constitute a statistically valid sample of retail prices. Howard of course presumes otherwise, but it is invalid scientific method to assume the truth of a relationship that one is trying to empirically prove.
13. For a more detailed proof of this assertion see Steven Rosefielde (1980h), pp. 425–26.
14. David Howard (1980), pp. 580–82.
15. Note that the first term on the right in equation 3 is derived from equation 2 where all indices are computed from the same sample population. Howard's derivation does not satisfy this criterion.
16. Howard has attempted to demonstrate that his method does yield a valid Paasche index of actual Soviet retail prices by arguing that his penultimate equation

1. $$p_t^a = 100 \left(\sum_{}^{n} p_i^{at} q_i^t \sum_{}^{n} p_i^o q_i^o \right) / \sum_{}^{n} p_i^{ao} q_i^o \sum_{}^{n} p_i^o q_i^t$$

simplifies to

2. $$p_t^a = 100 \sum_{}^{n} p_i^{at} q_i^t / \sum_{}^{n} p_i^{ao} q_i^t$$

if it is assumed that "$p_i^o = p_i^{ao}$, that is, if Bronson's and Severin's series reflects actual prices" (see Howard, 1980, p. 581). The merit of this assertion can be evaluated by reconstructing Howard's derivation. Equation 1 expressed in our notation is:

1a. $$p_t^a = 100 \left(\sum_{i=1}^{n} p_i^t q_i^t \sum_{i=1}^{r} p_i^o q_i^o \right) / \left(\sum_{i=1}^{n} p_i^o q_i^o \sum_{i=1}^{r} p_i^o q_i^t \right)$$

The assumption that $p_i^o = p_i^{ao}$ implies that the prices in the terms $\sum_{i=1}^{r} p_i^o q_i^o$, $\sum_{i=1}^{n} p_i^o q_i^o$ and $\sum_{i=1}^{n} p_i^o q_i^t$ are interchangeable, but of course does not mean that

3. $$\sum_{i=1}^{r} p_i^o q_i^o = \sum_{i=1}^{n} p_i^o q_i^o$$

because the quantities, q_i subsumed under each summation are obtained from different population sets. Howard ignores this obstacle, however, treating equation 3 as a valid equality, deriving the intermediate form:

4. $$p_t^a = 100 \sum_{i=1}^{n} p_i^t q_i^t / \sum_{i=1}^{r} p_i^o q_i^t$$

which is a synthetic Paasche price index with alien value components. He then inadmissibly transforms equation 4 to a legitimate index of actual retail prices:

2a. $$p_i^a = 100 \sum_{i=1}^{n} p_i^t q_i^t / \sum_{i=1}^{n} p_i^o q_i^t$$

by tacitly but incorrectly assuming that if $p_i^o = p_i^{ao}$, then

5. $$\sum_{i=1}^{n} p_i^o q_i^t = \sum_{i=1}^{r} p_i^o q_i^t;$$

or in other words, that the Bronson-Severin estimate of real consumer good production in year t, valued in base year prices corresponds exactly with real Soviet retail sales in year t, valued in base year prices. Such a proof, which involves picking apart the elements of the products subsumed under the summation signs and rearranging them at will, is nonsense.

17. This conclusion, needless to say, does not prove that Soviet retail sales have been free from hidden inflation. Soviet retail prices for many goods (coffee, gold, higher quality consumer goods) have risen and the possibility that these increases are not completely reflected in the official price indices cannot be categorically rejected.

Part III

THE SOVIET ARMS BUILDUP

CHAPTER 12

Extrapolating Soviet Procurement Trends into the Seventies

I. The Resolution of the CIA's 236 Percent Procurement Cost Estimating Error

Only one conclusion can be reasonably drawn from the foregoing analysis. The entire 236 percent discrepancy between the CIA's pre- and postrevision procurement estimates for 1970 should be imputed to real increases in the quantity and quality of Soviet military equipment achieved during the sixties. This judgment, of course, was already foreshadowed by the tests performed in chapter 4 which showed that the agency's fixed vintage parametric dollar and ruble estimates made no allowance for intervintage technological progress and therefore were greatly downward biased. The evidence, however, did not preclude the possibility that some significant part of the cost estimating discrepancy might still be explained by hidden inflation. This line of reasoning has now been foreclosed. The analysis conducted in part II has demonstrated that the agency's hidden inflation hypothesis is supported by little more than the cryptic testimony of a few Soviet scholars, Stalinist precedent, and an appeal to dubitable theories of new product fraud (see appendix 5).

II. Real Soviet Procurement Growth

The closing of this lacuna makes it possible to assess the magnitude of the Soviet arms buildup in a relatively unambiguous way. This appraisal is carried out in the ensuing chapters in two steps. First, inferences drawn in parts I and II for the sixties are extended to the seventies.

TABLE 12.1
William Lee's Residual Ruble Estimates of Soviet Military
Procurement, 1960–80

Year	Procurement	Growth Rate (percent)
1960	5.5	
1970	18.8	
1971	20.7	
1972	23.8	
1973	26.6	
1974	29.3	
1975	33.4	
1976	36	
1977	42	
1978	48	
1979	56	
1980	66	
1970–75		12.1
1975–80 (planned)		14.5
1970–80		13.4

Sources: William Lee, *The Estimation of Soviet Defense Expenditures 1955–75*, Table 4.1, p. 56.
1975–80: William Lee, "USSR Gross National Product in Established Prices," *Jahrbuch der Wirtschaft Osteuropas*, Band 8, Table 14, p. 429.
Estimates 1976–80 derived with data obtained from the 10th Five-Year Plan. All values are expressed in constant 1970 rubles.

Then a procurement series adjusted for intervintage technological change is constructed for the full period 1960–79 which serves both as a measure of objective Soviet military capabilities and as the basis for evaluating the burden of Soviet defense.

The best estimate of real Soviet procurement growth during the sixties, subject to the margin of error discussed in chapter 5 and the analysis of hidden inflation carried out in part II, is 12.9 percent per annum. This growth rate is calculated from the CIA's best procurement estimate for 1960, 5.5 billion rubles;[1] and its best estimate for 1970, 18.5 billion rubles,[2] assuming as the disconfirmation of the agency's hidden inflation hypothesis suggests that military machine-building prices were stable throughout the decade.[3] Estimates in a range between 11 and 15 percent per annum are also tenable,[4] in line with the real annual rate of machine-building growth, 13.3 percent, achieved during the decade.[5]

Calculating real Soviet procurement growth for the seventies is a more troublesome matter because the agency has been unable to obtain additional data on Soviet arms expenditures directly from the books of the Ministry of Defense,[6] and has failed to rectify the deficiencies of its direct costing method. As a consequence, CIA procurement estimates for the seventies severely understate the real growth of Soviet armaments. The magnitude of this understatement can be estimated by assuming that the correspondence between the agency's postrevision direct cost procurement growth rate (4 percent per annum) and the real rate (12.9 percent) can be extrapolated into the seventies. According to the agency, Soviet procurement grew at an annual rate of 4 percent from 1967 to 1977,[7] just as it had during the sixties,[8] suggesting that the quality-adjusted rate grew pari passu at 12.9 percent per annum.

The validity of this procedure can be confirmed by adjusting the CIA's fixed vintage parametric cost growth estimates for intervintage technological progress to determine whether the extrapolated growth rates are supported by the CIA's weapons counts. This is accomplished by calculating either of the following equations:

1.
$$\dot{g}_1^* = \dot{g} + \left[\left(\frac{\sum_{i=1}^{k} D_i^{*79,79} (\beta_{i1}^{79}, \beta_{i2}^{79}, \ldots, \beta_{is}^{79})}{\sum_{i=1}^{k} D_i^{79,70} (\beta_{i1}^{79}, \beta_{i2}^{79}, \ldots, \beta_{is}^{79})} \right)^{1/9} - 1 \right]$$

where the numerator of the ratio is the DOD's "Sovietized" variable vintage procurement estimate for 1979, the denominator is the CIA's fixed vintage estimate (see chapter 4, section VI), and $\dot{g}$ is the agency's official estimate of Soviet procurement growth, 1970–1979 or

2.
$$\dot{g}_2^* = \dot{g} + \left[\left(\frac{\sum_{i=1}^{k} D_i^{*79,79} (b_{i1}^{79}, b_{i2}^{79}, \ldots, b_{is}^{79})}{\sum_{i=1}^{k} D_i^{79,70} (b_{i1}^{79}, b_{i2}^{79}, \ldots, b_{is}^{79})} \right)^{1/9} - 1 \right]$$

where the numerator and denominator represent pre-"Sovietized" estimates of American procurement cost (see chapter 4, section VI). The exact values of these adjusted growth rates cannot be reported, but they are consistent with the rate shown in equation 3:

3.
$$\dot{g}_3^* = \dot{g} + \left[\left(\frac{\sum_{i=1}^{n} D_i^{74,79} (b_{i1}^{79}, b_{i2}^{79}, \ldots, b_{is}^{79})}{\sum_{i=1}^{n} D_i^{74,70} (b_{i1}^{70}, b_{i2}^{70}, \ldots, b_{is}^{70})} \right)^{1/9} - 1 \right]$$

$$= 9.3 \text{ percent}$$

where the bracketed term represents American intervintage technological progress from 1970 to 1979 derived from Leonard Sullivan's (assistant secretary of defense for program analysis and evaluation) estimate of "technical growth" (see chapter 4, section VI and appendix 1). This dollar cost estimate of Soviet procurement growth is only 1.3 percentage points below the extrapolated dollar rate (see chapter 13, Table 13.2, column 5) and a few percentage points below the ruble rate. It demonstrates that the Department of Defense's variable vintage parametric dollar estimates grew nearly as rapidly as the extrapolated Soviet rate and that our estimates are strongly consistent with variable vintage American parametric cost estimates adjusted for Soviet retrofitting, the comparatively high rate of Soviet military RDT&E, and the usual index number effects.[9]

The merit of this inference is buttressed by the residual method which attempts to estimate Soviet procurement expenditures as the difference between total machinery production and civilian use. Although the technique is not foolproof, it was applied successfully by William Lee, who predicted before the new information was acquired that Soviet procurement expenditures in 1970 were 18.5 billion rubles.[10] The CIA subsequently carried out an independent recalculation of the 1970 estimate using the residual method and replicated Lee's finding.[11]

For the decade of the sixties, Lee's residual estimates correspond almost exactly with the agency's.[12] They differ insignificantly from the CIA's best procurement estimates: 5.5 billion rubles in 1960, 18.5 billion rubles in 1970. CIA residual estimates for the seventies have just been disclosed, and correspond with the figures Lee presented to the Senate Armed Services Committee.[13] These figures, which are derived from ex-post data through 1975 and planning data thereafter, are reported in Table 12.1. They reveal that for the first half of the seventies realized Soviet procurement growth was 12.1 percent per annum, and that the planned rate for 1975 to 1980 is 14.5 percent.

These estimates do not differ substantially from the trend of the sixties, and are supported by Defense Intelligence Agency estimates of Soviet military machine-building production, 12 percent per annum 1965–78, recently reported by its director, Lt. General Eugene Tighe, Jr.[14] Taken in conjunction with the stability of the CIA's direct cost procurement growth series, they strongly suggest that the pattern of the sixties can be prudently extrapolated to the seventies, even though the covert data needed to conclusively confirm this deduction have not yet been procured.

Notes

1. This estimate is supported both by the direct cost and residual methods. CIA data suggest the upper bound of uncertainty for the 1960 procurement estimate is 6.4 billion rubles. This upper bound is calculated by assuming that the true value is 10 percent higher than 5.5 billion rubles, or 6.05 billion rubles. For the sake of comparability this estimate is then adjusted for the 6 percent open change in the MBMW price level caused by the price reform of 1967. The open change was calculated from newspaper data (according to Don Burton) but is not corroborated by the official MBMW price index. Judging from internal CIA data made available to me in unclassified form, the agency made a strong effort to acquire data pertaining to the 1967 price reform but was not particularly successful. See Andrew Sheren, "The Soviet Price Reform of 1967," Internal CIA Memorandum, July 14, 1972 and Barbara S. Minnich, "Selected Materials on the Soviet Price Reform of July, 1967," Internal CIA Memorandum, USSR/EE Division, USSR Branch, January 1968.

   This upper bound is confirmed by applying William Lee's (1977a) 1970 procurement (NSE durables)/machine-building gross value of output (MMW GVO) ratio, 19.1 percent to 1960 Soviet MMW GVO, 34 billion rubles. See Lee (1977a),pp. 56, 61. Since Lee's 1970 NSE durables/MMW GVO was subsequently confirmed by covert data, the 6.4 billion ruble upper bound suggests that the rapid rate of growth reported in the text is not explained by the underestimation of Soviet procurement expenditures in the base year 1960.

   Note also that the 5.5 billion ruble estimate is consistent with the high rates of intervintage technological progress exhibited by U.S. weapons. If it is assumed that the CIA has correctly calculated the rate of quantitative Soviet procurement growth (4 percent per annum), and that qualitative improvements increased at the U.S. rate (6 percent per annum), then Soviet procurement in 1960 can be estimated as:

$$r_{70}q_{60} = \Sigma r_{70}q_{70}/(1.10)^{10}$$

1.
$$= 17/2.59$$
$$= 6.6$$

2. See chapter 1, note 1. The precise definitional differences between the residual and direct cost procurement nomenclature are unclear. The components of the residual category are spelled out in Lee (1977a). Although I have chosen to use the 18.5 billion ruble estimate for the purposes at hand, the lower estimate could easily be employed instead without significantly altering the conclusions drawn in the text. Soviet procurement during the sixties using the lower rate grew 11.9 percent per annum. I personally prefer the higher estimate because I suspect that the assumptions used by the agency in computing procurement from the new information err on the side of caution, that is, understate the true value. Cf. William Lee (n.d.), p. 423.

3. The fact that our analysis disconfirms the hidden inflation hypothesis implies that the official price indices are not biased on this score. This suggests that the price decline exhibited by the official MBMW index may be legitimate

and that real procurement instead of being 18.5 billion rubles could be as high as 26.4 billion rubles in 1955 prices. See Table 5.1, panel C, row 3, column 3. I have chosen not to use this higher estimate primarily because the civilian machine-building price series may not be a very good surrogate for the military machine-building series. Since industrial wholesale prices rose 1 percent per annum and MBMW prices declined 1.3 percent per annum from 1960 to 1970, the most neutral assumption one can make under these circumstances is to postulate that military MBMW prices were stable throughout the sixties.

4. See Table 5.1.
5. *Narkhoz 1972*, p. 166.
6. Statements attributed to Brezhnev indicate that total Soviet defense expenditures rose from 50 billion rubles in 1970 to 58 billion rubles in 1972, or roughly 8 percent per year. See William Lee (1979), p. 21. This rate is somewhat slower than the rate for the sixties, 11.5 percent. See William Lee, "USSR Gross National Product in Established Prices, 1955–1975," *Jahrbuch der Wirtschaft Osteuropas*, Band 8, p. 429.
7. CIA, *Estimated Soviet Defense Spending: Trends and Prospects*, National Foreign Assessment Center, SR 78–10121, June 1978, p. 2. This assumption ignores the issue of learning curve bias. See Rosefielde (1982c).
8. Donald Swain, private letter 9 August 1979. "Third, it should be noted we have no official estimates of procurement growth in the 60s but the roughly 4 percent figure (closer to 4.5 percent by current definitions) applies since 1965. We think this will probably hold up for the early 60s as well."
9. *Soviet and U.S. Defense Activities, 1970–1979: A Dollar Comparison*, SR 80–10005, January 1980, p. 4. William Lee (1977a), pp. 281–95. See chapter 4, note 25.
10. Lee, Ibid.
11. CIA, *USSR: Toward a Reconciliation of Marxist and Western Measures of National Income*, National Foreign Assessment Center, ER 78–10505, October 1978, p. 14.
12. Lee reports his estimates in bands. His mean values differ slightly from 5.5 and 18.5 billion rubles.
13. Lee (1979). The data themselves are derived in Lee (n.d.), p. 429. See chapter 1, note 28. The agency's data for the late seventies, unlike Lee's are based on ex-post, rather than plan statistics. Also the CIA has acknowledged that it has failed to acquire any Soviet weapons prices since the early seventies and therefore has no grounds for imputing the discrepancy between its direct cost and residual estimates for 1980 to hidden inflation. See Rosefielde (1982d).
14. Lt. General Eugene Tighe, Jr. (1979), p. 99. Also see Norbert Michaud (1980).

CHAPTER 13

Real Soviet Procurement Growth, 1960–79

I. Ruble Estimates of Real Soviet Procurement Growth, 1960–79

Real Soviet procurement growth and the downward bias displayed by the CIA's direct cost estimating methodology can now be assessed for the entire period from 1960 to 1979. Table 13.1 and Figure 13.1 restate the results of the preceding chapter in serial form. Column 1 presents the agency's original prerevision series valued in 1955/60 prices extrapolated to 1979 at the average growth rate prevailing for 1970 to 1975. It indicates that real Soviet procurement increased from 5.5 to 6.2 billion rubles from 1960 to 1979, resulting in the cumulative expenditure of 115 billion rubles.[1]

Columns 2 and 3 represent the CIA's revised perception of Soviet arms growth. These series are extrapolated from its best direct cost and best residual procurement estimates for 1970 using the agency's best direct cost estimate of Soviet procurement growth, 4 percent per annum. Cumulative Soviet procurement expenditures for 1960 to 1979 for the former measure computed on the revised basis are 371.9 billion rubles— 223 percent higher than its prerevision figure.[2]

Columns 5–7 contain the author's Soviet procurement expenditure series extrapolated from the CIA's procurement estimate for 1960, 5.5 billion rubles, and the diverse rates of real growth, 11 to 15 percent (as discussed in chapter 12). The cumulative magnitude of these expenditures for 1960 to 1979 is 440 billion rubles—283 percent higher than the agency's original total, but only 18 percent higher than its revised estimate. The broad consistency between this latter estimate and the author's is explained by the fact that the low rate of growth calculated by

TABLE 13.1
Soviet Military Procurement, 1960–79 (Billions of Rubles)

	CIA				Rosefielde			CIA	Rosefielde
	(1)	(2)	(3)	(4)	(5)	(6)	(7)	(8)	(9)
1960	5.5	11.5	12.5	5.5	5.5	5.5	5.5	100	100
1961	5.6	12	13	5.7	6.1	6.2	6.3	104	112
1962	5.6	12.4	13.5	5.9	6.8	7	7.3	108	127
1963	5.7	12.9	14.1	6.2	7.5	7.9	8.4	113	144
1964	5.8	13.5	14.6	6.4	8.3	8.9	9.6	117	162
1965	5.8	14	15.2	6.7	9.3	10.1	11.1	122	184
1966	5.8	14.6	15.8	7	10.3	11.4	12.7	126	207
1967	5.7	15.1	16.4	7.2	11.4	12.9	14.6	131	235
1968	5.6	15.7	17.1	7.5	12.7	14.5	16.8	137	264
1969	5.6	16.4	17.8	7.8	14.1	16.4	19.3	142	298
1970	5.5	17	18.5	8.1	15.6	18.5	22.3	148	336
1971	5.6	17.7	19.2	8.5	17.3	20.9	25.6	154	380
1972	5.6	18.4	20	8.8	19.2	23.6	29.4	160	429
1973	5.7	19.1	20.8	9.2	21.4	26.6	33.8	166	483
1974	(5.8)	19.9	21.6	9.5	23.7	30.1	38.9	173	547
1975	(5.9)	20.7	22.5	9.9	26.7	33.9	44.8	180	616
1976	(5.9)	21.5	23.4	10.3	29.2	38.3	51.5	187	696
1977	(6.0)	22.4	24.3	10.7	32.4	43.3	59.2	194	787
1978	(6.1)	23.3	25.3	11.1	36	48.8	68.1	202	887
1979	(6.2)	24.2	26.3	11.6	39.9	55.2	78.3	210	1004
1960–69	57.2		150	65.9		100.8			
1970–79	58.3		221.9	97.7		339.2			
1960–79	115		371.9	163.6		440			

Compound annual rate of growth (percent) 1960–79						
.6	4	4	4	11	12.9	15

Sources: CIA, *Estimated Soviet Defense Spending*, National Foreign Assessment Center, SR-78–10121, June 1978, p. 2. Donald Swain, Deputy Chief, Military-Economic Analysis Center, OSR, CIA, private letter, August 9, 1977. See chapter 2.

Method: Column 1: CIA prerevision 1955/60 ruble series computed with the direct cost method. This series grew zero percent per annum 1960–70 and 1.2 percent until 1975. See notes to Table 2.1. According to Swain, the prerevision series grew on an intra period basis at the long term rate 1960–75. This phenomenon has been taken into account by assuming that Soviet procurement grew 1.2 percent per annum 1960–1965, and fell at the same rate thereafter 1965–70. The cumulative figures for 1970–79 assume that the growth observed for the early seventies would have persisted throughout the decade. See chapter 2. If 1970 prerevision rubles were employed the series should be uniformly increased by 6 percent.

Column 2: This series is computed from the CIA's best direct cost procurement estimate for 1970, 17 billion rubles and the agency's postrevision annual ruble procurement growth rate 1960–1979, 4 percent.

Column 3: Same as column 2 except the CIA's best residual method procurement estimate for 1970, 18.5 billion rubles is used in place of the direct cost estimate. If, as appears likely, the official Paasche ruble series is adjusted for learning as the dollar series is (see chapter 4, section IX and chapter 13, notes), column 3 overstates the growth rate and understates cumulative outlays before allowance is made for intervintage technological progress.

Column 4: Same as column 1, except the agency's 4 percent postrevision average annual growth rate is used to extrapolate the series.

Column 5: The lower bound adjusted ruble procurement growth rate discussed in chapter 12, 11 percent, is used to extrapolate Soviet arms growth 1960–79. The base year estimate for 1960, 5.5 billion rubles, is the agency's and has been confirmed with the residual method.

Column 6: Same as column 5, except the "best" adjusted procurement growth rate 12.9 percent is used instead of the lower bound rate.

Column 7: Same as column 6, except the upper bound adjusted ruble procurement rate, 15 percent, is used instead of the lower bound rate.

Column 8: Index of either CIA series reported in columns 2 and 3.

Column 9: Index of the "best" adjusted ruble procurement growth series, column 6.

N.B. Since the analysis carried out in part II failed to uncover any significant hidden inflation the prices employed in Table 13.1 pertain more or less interchangeably to 1955 or 1970.

FIGURE 13.1

Soviet Military Procurement, 1960–79 (Billions of Rubles)

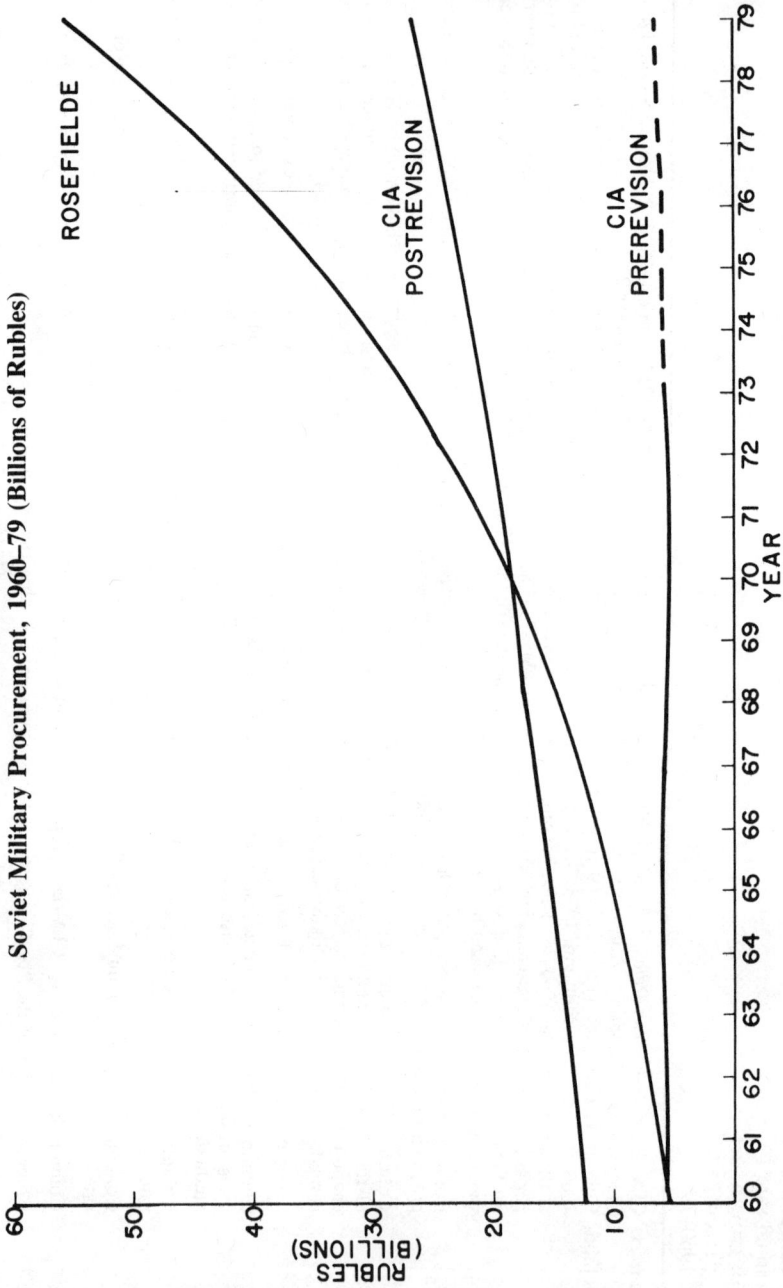

the CIA applied to its postrevision procurement estimate for 1970, 18.5 billion rubles, overstates the level of Soviet arms spending by 50 percent for 1960 to 1970 (extrapolated retrospectively from 1970) and understates it by 50 percent for 1970 to 1979, producing a relatively small net cumulative underestimate.

The consistency of the author's and the CIA's cumulative measures does not mitigate the enormous discrepancy between the agency's prerevision cumulative procurement expenditure figure and its postrevision estimate. The threefold increase attributable to the new information should have suggested that Soviet military capabilities were greater than previously supposed. But as was shown in chapter 1, the agency chose to deny that its postrevision estimates modified its understanding of the real magnitude of Soviet defense expenditures.[3] The high cumulative procurement expenditure total for the sixties that emerged from postrevision calculations was disregarded, and has never been explicitly reconciled with its prerevision estimate.

The CIA has instead taken the position that the long-term growth trend constitutes the best indicator of Soviet procurement effort. Table 13.1, column 8, quantifies this interpretation. The series indicates that Soviet procurement expenditures barely doubled from 1960 to 1979. Unlike the cumulative figures, this characterization is sharply at variance with the quality-adjusted index reported in column 9, which shows a tenfold increase during the past two decades and implies that real Soviet procurement expenditures in absolute terms grew five times more than the agency's postrevision series indicate. Cumulative expenditures consistent with this disparity are easily derived by applying the CIA's 4 percent postrevision annual rate of real weapons growth to its official 1960 procurement estimate of 5.5 billion rubles, instead of its 1970 figure. This cumulative expenditure series, reported in Table 13.1, column 4, reveals that when the same base is used cumulative procurement spending adjusted for intervintage technological progress exceeds the agency's estimate not by 18 percent, as shown in column 3, but by 167 percent. This divergence—440 versus 163.6 billion rubles—constitutes the best summary measure of the cumulative bias caused by fixed vintage parametric cost estimating, and indicates just how far afield the CIA's perceptions of Soviet military capability would have been in the absence of the "new information."

II. Dollar Estimates of U.S. and Soviet Real Procurement Growth, 1960–79

The ruble estimates reported in Table 13.1 have one important drawback, however. They cannot be directly compared with American pro-

TABLE 13.2
U.S. and Soviet Defense Procurement (Billions of 1978 Dollars)

	Soviet						US	Index		
		CIA		Rosefielde				Soviet		US
								CIA	Rosefielde	
	(1)	(2)	(3)	(4)	(5)	(6)	(7)	(8)	(9)	(10)
1960	30.6	23.4	13.3		13.3		27.8	76	43	89
1961	31	24	13.6		14.5		28.7	78	47	88
1962	31.4	24.6	13.6		15.7		33	80	51	101
1963	31.9	25.3	13.8		17.1		36.2	83	56	111
1964	32.3	26	13.9		18.6		29.7	85	61	91
1965	32.8	26.7	14.1		20.2		23.6	87	66	72
1966	32.4	27.5	13.9		21.9		30.8	90	72	94
1967	32.1	28.2	13.8		23.8		38.6	92	78	118
1968	31.6	29	13.6		25.9		42.8	95	85	131
1969	31.3	30	13.5		28.2		40.1	98	92	123
1970	30.4	30.6	13.3		30.6		32.7	100	100	100
1971	31	31.4	13.5		34.1		27.7	103	111	85
1972	31.1	31.6	13.6		37.2		24.5	103	122	75
1973	31.1	34.5	13.8		43.3		22.7	113	142	69
1974	31.2	35.5	(14)		47.8		20.9	116	156	63
1975	31.2	36.4	(14.1)		52.5		20	119	172	61
1976	31.3	37.3	(14.3)		57.5		19.1	122	188	58
1977	31.4	37.7	(14.6)		62.3		20.9	123	204	64
1978	31.4	38.6	(14.7)		68.1		21.4	126	223	65
1979	(31.5)	41	(14.9)	66.7	75.8	87.4	23.6	134	248	72

1960–69	317.3	264.5	137	199.2	331.3
1970–79	311.9	354.6	140.8	509.2	233.5
1960–79	629.2	619.1	277.8	708.4	564.8
Compound annual rate of growth (percent)					
1960–70	.2	2.7	0	8.7	1.2
1970–79	.2	3.3	1.2	10.6	−2.8
1960–79	.2	3.0	.6	9.6	−.7

Source: CIA, *Soviet Defense Procurement Trends and Prospects*, Testimony of Donald F. Burton, Chief, Military-Economic Analysis Center, Office of Strategic Research, National Foreign Assessment Center, before Subcommittee on General Procurement, Committee on Armed Forces, United States Senate, November 1, 1979.

Column 1: Hypothetical CIA Paasche dollar arms series computed during the sixties by deflating current values with DOD procurement deflators. See chapter 4, section IX and chapter 13, note 5. The series is expressed in 1978 dollars. The same series expressed in 1960 prices is presented in Table 13.1n, column 3

Column 2: Value for 1960 computed by discounting the agency's 1970 ruble value 30.6 billion rubles (in 1978 prices) by 2.7 percent per annum, the mean weighted Paasche rate 1960–70. See Table 2.1. The remaining estimates are taken from Burton's testimony, p. 7.

Column 3: Hypothetical CIA Laspeyres procurement series, computed by assuming that without adjustment for intervintage technological progress the agency's Laspeyres dollar series would have exhibited the same growth pattern as its ruble Laspeyres estimates. See Table 13.1, column 1. The base year dollar estimate for 1960 is calculated by discounting the CIA's published procurement value for 1970 expressed in 1978 prices with the compound rate of procurement growth 1960–70, 8.7 percent, estimated on the assumption that the dollar Laspeyres rate of growth ℓ_d is related to the Paasche rate, as the ruble Laspeyres rate ℓ_r is to the ruble Paasche P_d:

$$\ell_d = P_d \cdot \frac{\ell_r}{P_r};$$

$$p_{78}q_{60} = \frac{p_{78}q_{70}}{(1+\ell_d)^{10}} = \frac{30.6}{(1.087)^{10}} = 13.3.$$

TABLE 13.2 (Continued)

Column 4:   Adjusted dollar estimates of Soviet procurement are computed as follows: First, the adjusted aggregate dollar rate of growth is calculated by forming a ratio of the CIA's dollar and ruble rates. The dollar rates are: 1960–70, 2.7 percent per annum; 1970–79, 3.3 percent per annum. See Table 2.1; Burton, p. 7. The ruble rate is 4 percent per annum, 1960–79. These ratios are then used to proportionally discount the adjusted ruble growth rate. The lower bound adjusted ruble rate reported in Chapter 12, 11 percent per annum, is used in column 4. The proportionally adjusted dollar rates are assumed to be separable into a detectable component calculated by the agency and a qualitative component including some undetected weapons not measured by the direct cost method. The agency's numbers are accepted for the detectable component. The rate of qualitative improvement is determined by computing the total adjusted dollar increase, subtracting the CIA's growth increment, and calculating the pure rate of qualitative growth from this residual. These annual rates are 5.7 percent 1960–70 and 7 percent 1970–79. They are used to calculate the dollar value of qualitative improvements made year by year. These improvements are added to the agency's estimate to compute the values shown in the table. See footnote 8.

Column 5:   Same as column 4 except the best adjusted annual ruble procurement growth rate 12.9 percent is used instead of the lower bound 11 percent. The mean annual adjusted dollar rates are 7.2 percent 1960–70 and 8.8 1970–79. The value for 1960 was computed by discounting the 1970 value with the adjusted annual aggregate dollar procurement growth 8.7 percent.

Column 6:   Same as column 4 except the upper bound adjusted annual ruble procurement growth rate 15 percent is used instead of the lower bound 11 percent. The upper bound annual adjusted dollar rates are 8.8 percent 1960–70, and 10.8 percent 1970–79.

Column 7:   U.S. procurement expenditures in 1978 prices. Values 1960–69 are official U.S. DOD procurement outlays in constant prices provided by Colonel USAF Frederick Giessler, Assistant Director OSD/Net Assessment, adjusted to a calendar year basis to conform with the CIA outlay series. Values 1970–79 are from Burton's testimony. Although the CIA makes other adjustments to its series, DOD and CIA series for the seventies correspond very closely with one another.

Column 8:   Index of column 2, 1970 = 100. CIA cost estimating relationships use 1970 as a base.

Column 9:   Index of column 5, 1970 = 100.

Column 10: Index of column 7, 1970 = 100.

N.B.   The values listed in this table have been read from CIA charts. The cumulative statistics differ by 1–3 percent from those reported by the agency. The official cumulative estimates 1970–79 are: Soviet 360 billion dollars, U.S. 240 billion dollars.

curcment expenditures because the CIA does not publish a ruble valued series of U.S. weapons, with U.S. procurement weights. Although this debility is not insuperable (see Table 16.1 and Figures 16.1 16.2), to compare Soviet and American procurement trends as effectively as possible, dollar estimates need to be employed.

The CIA publishes most of the requisite dollar statistics in accordance with the January 1979 version of the defense planning categories (DPPC) of the U.S. Defense Department.[4] These estimates correspond with the agency's postrevision ruble series and are computed from the same physical output series, using the same methodology as its direct ruble cost estimates. They are reported in Table 13.2, column 2 and indicate that Soviet procurement grew 3 percent annually from 1960 to 1979, at a cumulative cost of 619.1 billion dollars.

Dollar estimates analogous to the agency's prerevision ruble series are unavailable. The CIA does not calculate Laspeyres dollar estimates, and denies having computed a Paasche series during the sixties by deflating its current value estimates. Nonetheless, for comparative purposes some impression of the CIA's implicit Paasche series can be obtained by backcasting the agency's official 1970 dollar estimate with the growth rate calculated by deflation from the official Paasche dollar series 1970–78,[5] adjusted for the intraperiod growth cycle exhibited by the prerevision Laspeyres ruble series. This series, presented in column 1, suggests that Soviet weapons spending grew .2 percent annually 1960–79, resulting in a total cumulative outlay of 629.2 billion dollars; a figure 2 percent higher than the agency's published estimate.

A hypothetical Laspeyres dollar series computed with a 1960 base, estimated by assuming that the dollar Laspeyres procurement growth rate bears a fixed relationship to the true ruble Laspeyres rate, extrapolated by analogy with the CIA's prerevision ruble Laspeyres procurement growth rates, zero percent 1960–70 and 1.2 percent 1970–79 is presented in column 3. Its cumulative magnitude is 227.8 billion dollars.

The author's quality series adjusted for intervintage technological progress are reported in columns 4–6. They are computed in three steps. First the total quality adjusted change in Soviet procurement expenditures from 1960 to 1979 is calculated by assuming that the true, unbiased dollar rate of growth bears the same relationship to the unbiased ruble rate as the agency's official Paasche dollar rate bears to its postrevision (Paasche) ruble rate.[6] The validity of this procedure is confirmed by adjusting the CIA's fixed vintage procurement estimates with the DOD's estimate of American intervintage technological progress (see chapter 12, equation 3). For the subperiods 1960–69 and 1970–79 these unbiased rates are 8.7 and 10.6 percent.[7] The total change calculated in this manner is next subdivided into detected and undetected components. The agency's official Paasche dollar series is accepted as an adequate measure of the quantitative growth of Soviet weaponry. Undetected qualitative growth is computed as a residual by subtracting the detectable change from total estimated unbiased growth.[8] This complex procedure is adopted in order to avoid losing valuable information regarding the behavior of individual observations that deviate from the trend extrapolated between the initial and final years of the series.[9]

The results of these computations reveal that real Soviet procurement from 1960 to 1979, measured in constant 1978 dollars, grew between 8.9 and 10.4 percent per annum, depending on the adjusted ruble rate used to estimate the dollar rate.[10] The mean cumulative value of these series, shown in column 5, is 708.4 billion dollars—a figure that is 14 percent greater than the agency's published estimate, 13 percent higher than the hypothetical Paasche estimate and 155 percent greater than the hypothetical Laspeyres estimate. This pattern parallels the cumulative ruble findings previously analyzed in Table 13.1, and provides a variety of standpoints for evaluating comparative Soviet and American procurement expenditures.

U.S. procurement expenditures are presented in Table 13.2, column 7. They display a great deal more variability than the Soviet series, rising at an average annual rate of 1.2 percent from 1960 to 1970. For the entire period 1960–79 real American procurement expenditures fall .7 percent per annum while adjusted real Soviet procurement expenditures rise 9.6 percent and the agency's Paasche estimates increase 3 percent annually.

Cumulative U.S. procurement expenditures also exhibit a distinctive pattern. During the sixties real American weapons expenditures totaled 331.3 billion dollars—66 percent greater than the quality-adjusted Soviet measure, and 25 percent greater than the upward-biased, published CIA Paasche estimate. However, cumulative U.S. procurement expenditures during the seventies declined 26 percent to 233.5 billion dollars. As a consequence both the agency's Paasche figure and the author's estimate of Soviet procurement expenditures exceed American outlays: the former by 52 percent, the latter by 118 percent. These correspondences also characterize the full period relationships for 1960 to 1979. Cumulative, Soviet procurement expenditures adjusted for intervintage technological progress exceed real American outlays by 25 percent, while the official CIA Paasche measure exceeds it by 10 percent. Only the hypothetical Laspeyres series indicates that cumulative Soviet procurement expenditures were lower than the United States' throughout the sixties and seventies.

FIGURE 13.2
U.S. and Soviet Military Procurement, 1960–79 (Billions of 1978 Dollars)

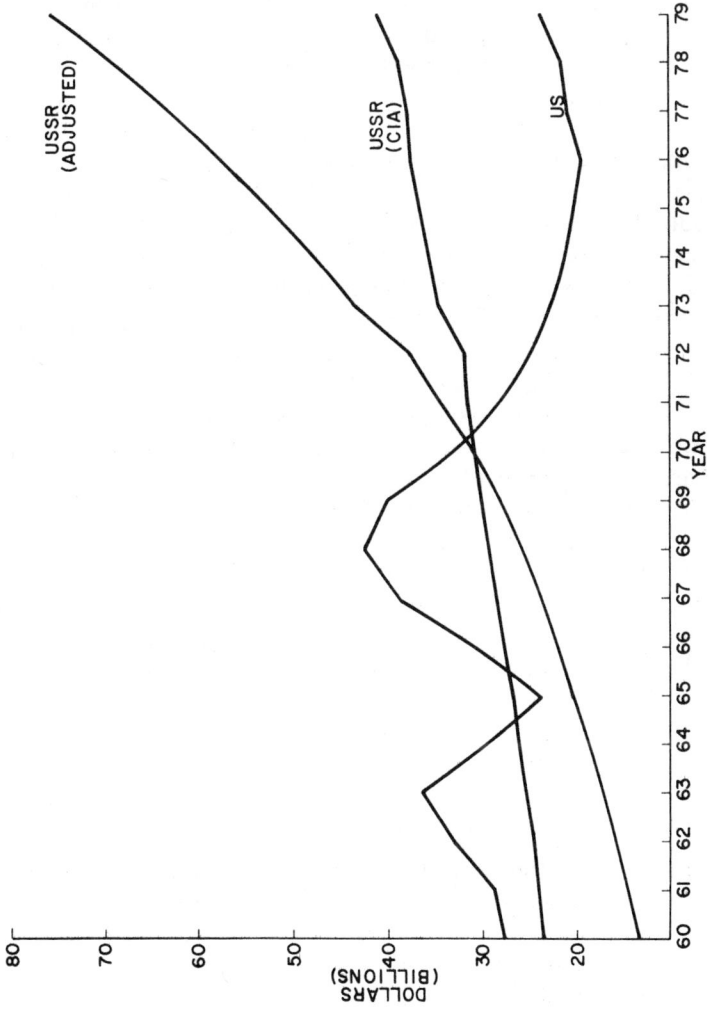

The perception of Soviet procurement expenditures conveyed by the CIA's dollar estimates significantly understates the Soviet military capabilities in much the same manner as its ruble estimates do. All the agency's series exhibit low rates of growth, and underestimate real cumulative outlays during the seventies. While it is true that this downward bias is partly offset in the case of the agency's official Paasche series by the upward bias from 1960 to 1969, suggesting that the comparatively high level of U.S. procurement outlays expended during the Vietnam War were largely offset by the equally high level of comparative Soviet procurement expenditures during the seventies,[11] the quality-adjusted series illustrated in Figure 13.2 (see also Figures 16.3 and 16.4) tells a very different story. It demonstrates that while American procurement expenditures associated with the Vietnam War did indeed raise U.S. outlays far above those of the Soviets, the extraordinary magnitude of real Soviet expenditures from 1970 to 1979 more than compensated for this imbalance.[12] The growth trend established in the sixties (8.7 percent per annum) and accelerated in the seventies (10.6 percent per annum) propelled cumulative Soviet expenditures in the latter subperiod ahead of American expenditures by 118 percent,[13] creating an asymmetry that is likely to widen rapidly if past trends are any guide to the future. This conclusion is confirmed by the data presented in Table 13.3 which compare the Department of Defense's U.S. procurement series with the CIA's Soviet series, adjusted for Leonard Sullivan's estimate of American intervintage technological progress (see chapter 4, equation 15 and appendix 1). Table 13.3 and Figure 13.3 demonstrate that if the CIA's fixed vintage parametric estimates (column 1) which are derived from DOD weapon cost data are properly adjusted for DOD documented intervintage technological change, cumulative Soviet expenditures during the seventies exceed those of the United States by 103 percent, before making allowance for the possibility that military intervintage technological progress was higher in the Soviet Union than the U.S.[14]

III. Dollar Estimates of Real U.S. and Soviet Strategic, Land, Tactical Air Force and General Purpose Naval Procurements, 1970–79

A fuller appreciation of the implications of this reversal of comparative U.S.-Soviet military capabilities is provided by disaggregating total procurement into various mission-specific categories in order to determine whether strengths in some areas compensate for deficiencies elsewhere. The relevant data are reported in Tables 13.4–9 and illustrated in Figures 13.4–9.

TABLE 13.3
Soviet and American Procurement Growth, 1970–79 (Variable Vintage Parametric Estimates)

	Soviet	U.S.
1970	30.6	32.7
1971	33.3	27.7
1972	35.5	24.5
1973	41.1	22.7
1974	44.8	20.9
1975	48.7	20
1976	52.9	19.1
1977	56.7	20.9
1978	61.5	21.4
1979	69.3	23.6
1970–79	474.4	233.5
Compound annual rate of growth (percent) 1970–79	9.3	−2.8

Sources: The Soviet series is computed by adjusting the CIA's fixed vintage dollar estimates in Table 13.2, column 2, with American intervintage technological progress derived from Leonard Sullivan's estimates of U.S. "technical growth," 1970–79:

$y_t = y_t^{CIA} (1.06)^{t-1}$. The cumulative total is

$$\sum_{t=1}^{9} y_t = \sum_{t=1}^{9} y_t^{CIA} (1.06)^{t-1}.$$

The U.S. series is taken from Table 13.2, column 7. Sullivan's estimate is discussed in appendix 1.

Table 13.4 compares U.S. and Soviet strategic forces procurement including intercontinental ballistic missile forces, submarine-launched ballistic missiles and their associated submarines, intercontinental bombers, medium and intermediate range missiles, and bombers. According to the CIA if Soviet strategic forces procurement had been built in the United States to Soviet performance specifications, using American production techniques the dollar value of these weapons in 1970 would have been 10.3 billion dollars (in 1978 prices), or slightly double the comparable U.S. figure. Making no allowance for intervintage technological progress, CIA data indicate that annual Soviet strategic forces procurement expenditures rose slowly during the seventies at 2.4 percent per annum, while U.S. outlays declined reciprocally. As a consequence of

FIGURE 13.3
Soviet and American Procurement Activities, 1970–79 (Variable
Vintage Parametric Estimates)

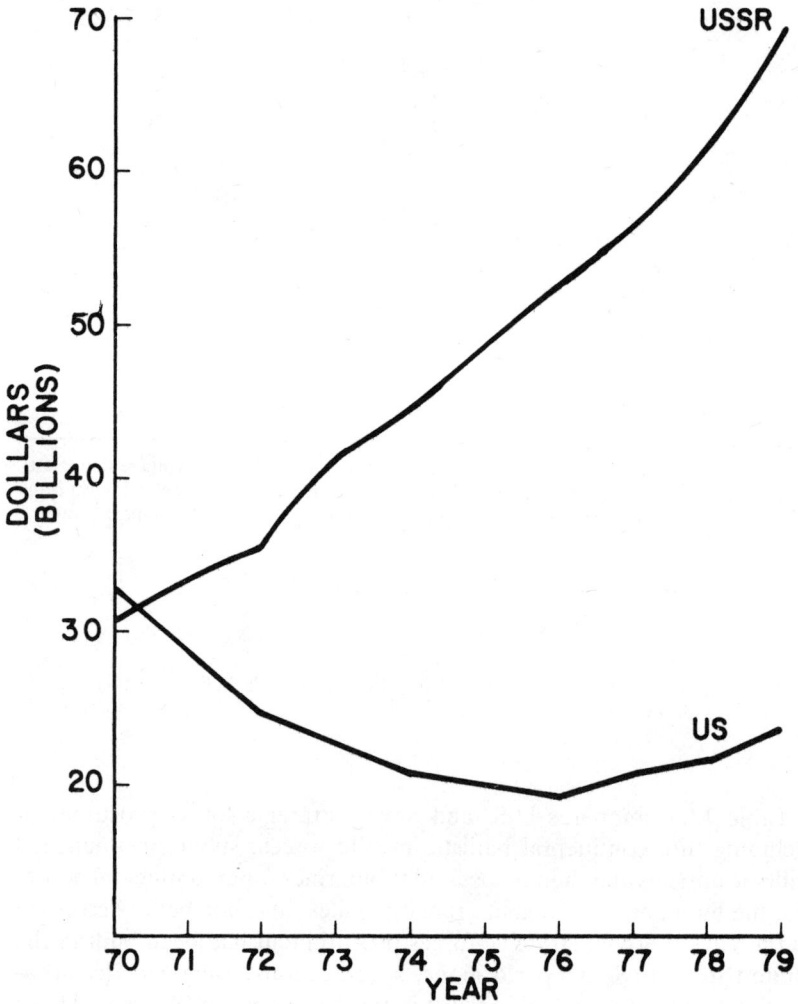

TABLE 13.4
U.S. and Soviet Strategic Forces Procurement
(Billions of 1978 Dollars)

| | Soviet | | US | Soviet | | US |
	CIA	Rosefielde		CIA	Rosefielde	Index
1970	10.3	10.3	5.5	100	100	100
1971	9.3	10.2	5.3	90	99	96
1972	8.5	10.4	5.1	83	101	93
1973	10	13	4.9	97	126	89
1974	11.9	16	4.3	116	155	78
1975	12	17.4	3.5	117	165	64
1976	12.3	19.1	3.4	119	185	62
1977	12.7	21	3.8	123	204	69
1978	12.4	22.3	4.0	120	217	73
1979	12.8	24.5	4.3	124	238	78
1970–79	112.2	164.2	44.1			
Compound annual rate of growth (percent) 1970–79)	2.4	10.1	−2.2			

Source: See Table 13.2
Column 1: Burton, p. 9
Column 2: Same method used in Table 13.2, column 5.
Definition: Strategic force procurement includes intercontinental ballistic missile forces, submarine launched ballistic missiles and their associated submarines, intercontinental bombers, medium and intermediate range missiles and bombers.
N.B. The values listed in this table have been read from CIA charts. The cumulative statistics differ several percent from those reported by the agency. The official cumulative estimates 1970–79 are: Soviet 110 billion dollars, U.S. 40 billion dollars.

these trends the agency calculates that cumulative Soviet strategic forces procurement from 1970 to 1979 exceeded U.S. procurements by a factor of 2.5, a disparity that is significantly increased when intervintage technological progress is taken into account. Column 2 reveals that the value of Soviet strategic forces procurement in 1979, adjusted for fixed vintage parametric cost estimating bias, is approximately 24.5 billion dollars—nearly twice the agency's estimate. Adjusted cumulative Soviet strategic forces procurement exceed U.S. outlays by a factor of 3.7.

A similar pattern is exhibited by comparative U.S. and Soviet intercontinental attack procurement expenditures, which exclude medium and intermediate range missiles and bombers from the category of stra-

FIGURE 13.4
U.S. and Soviet Strategic Forces Procurement

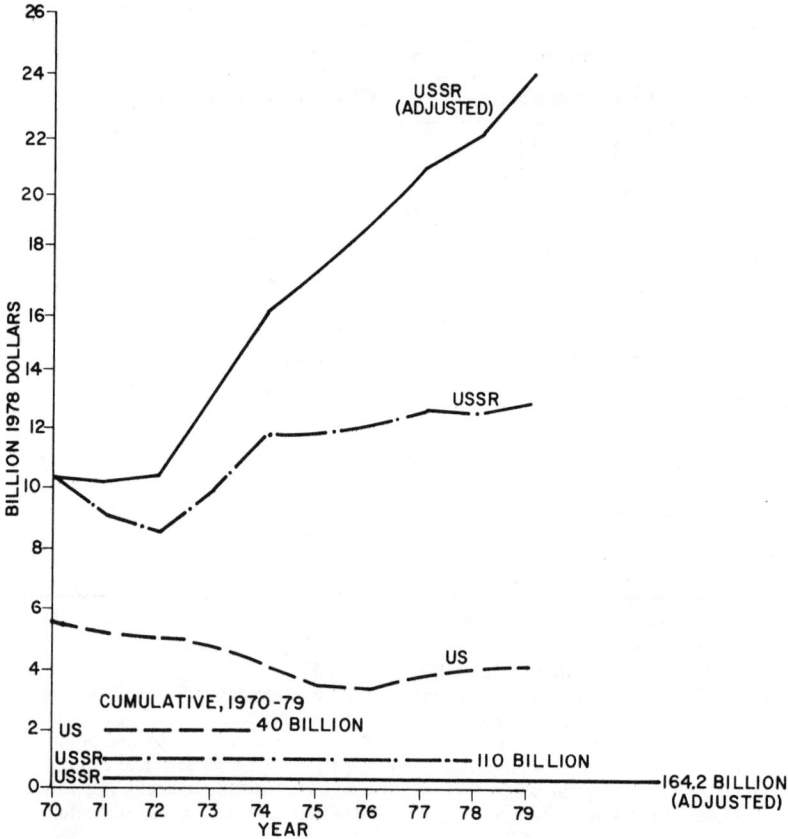

tegic forces procurement. Table 13.5 and Figure 13.5 show Soviet intercontinental attack procurement rising during the seventies as U.S. outlays fall and indicate a comparative cumulative Soviet advantage of 190 percent excluding, and 275 percent including, intervintage technological change.

The asymmetries that characterize the strategic arena are also evident in comparative general purpose forces procurement trends (Table 13.6, Figure 13.6). According to the CIA's fixed vintage parametric cost estimates Soviet general purpose forces procurement including ground and tactical air forces would have cost 17.7 billion dollars to produce

TABLE 13.5
U.S. and Soviet Intercontinental Attack Procurement
(Billions of 1978 Dollars)

| | Soviet | | US | Soviet | | Index US |
	CIA	Rosefielde		CIA	Rosefielde	
1970	4.9	4.9	3.6	100	100	100
1971	3.9	4.3	3.2	80	88	89
1972	3.9	4.8	3.1	80	98	86
1973	5.1	6.5	2.9	104	133	81
1974	6.2	8.2	2.6	127	167	72
1975	6.3	8.9	2.3	129	182	64
1976	6.1	9.3	2.2	124	190	61
1977	5.5	9.4	2.6	112	192	72
1978	5.1	9.8	2.8	104	200	78
1979	5.3	10.9	2.7	108	222	75
1970–79	52.3	77	28			
Compound annual rate of growth (percent) 1970–79	.9	9.3	−2.5			

Source: See Table 13.2
Column 1: Burton, p. 11.
Column 2: Same method used in Table 13.2, column 5.
Definition: Intercontinental attack procurement includes intercontinental ballistic missile forces, submarine launched ballistic missiles and their associated submarines, and intercontinental bombers.
N.B. The values listed in this table have been read from CIA charts. The cumulative statistics differ several percent from those reported by the agency. The official cumulative estimates 1970–79 are: Soviet 50 billion, U.S. 30 billion dollars.

in 1970 valued in 1978 prices. U.S. expenditures in the same year were 20.7 billion dollars. During the seventies the Soviets continually increased their general purpose programs at an average compound rate of 3.7 percent per annum, while U.S. outlays once again declined reciprocally. By the end of the decade the Soviets were significantly outproducing the United States. In 1979 their general purpose forces procurement reached 24.5 billion dollars without adjusting for intervintage technological progress. Including qualitative change the figure increases to 44.6 billion dollars, compared with 14.3 billion for the United States. For the decade as a whole CIA estimates put Soviet general purpose ground forces procurement at 205.9 billion dollars. The quality-adjusted

FIGURE 13.5
U.S. and Soviet Intercontinental Attack Procurement

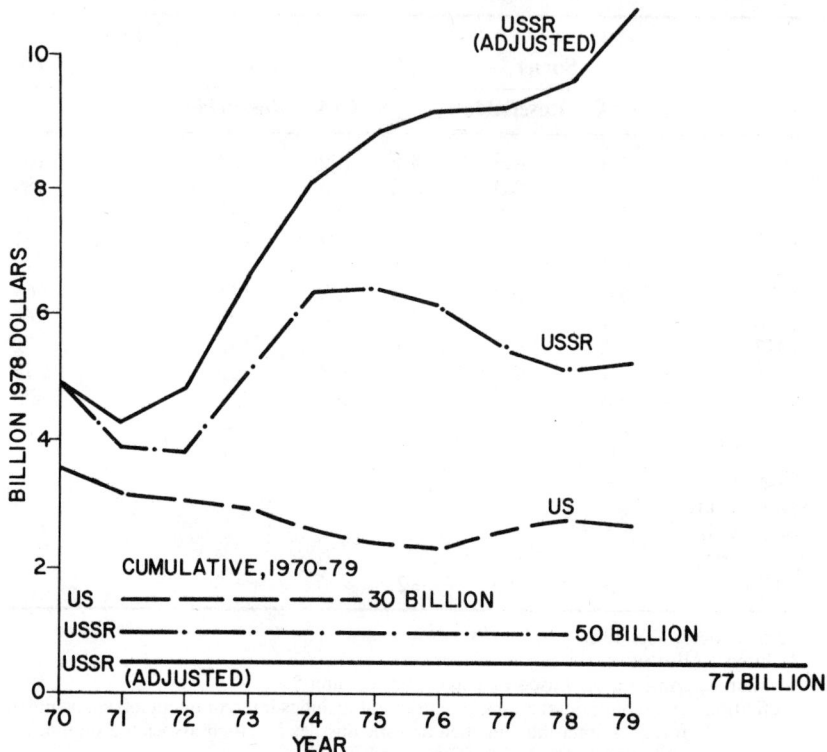

value is 295.4 billion dollars—211 percent higher than U.S. general purpose grounds forces expenditures.

These aggregate trends mask important differences between the behavior of land forces procurement and tactical air forces (all land- and seabased fixed wing aircraft that are used in a combat role and, on the U.S. side, multipurpose aircraft carriers. Helicopters used for ground attack are not included, nor are those aircraft and aircraft carriers which have an ASW mission). Tables 13.6 and 13.7 reveal that whereas the Soviets held a substantial edge in land forces procurement in 1970 (7.7 versus 5.7 billion dollars), American tactical air force procurements exceeded those of the Soviets in the same year by 5.6 billion dollars (8.6 versus 3 billion dollars). This disparity has often been cited to suggest that although the United States was outmatched in some areas, these deficiencies were compensated by American air superiority. Judg-

TABLE 13.6
U.S. and Soviet General Purpose Forces Procurement
(Billions of 1978 Dollars)

	Soviet		US		Index Soviet		US
	CIA	Rosefielde			CIA	Rosefielde	
1970	17.7	17.7	20.7	100	100		100
1971	18.8	20.4	16.8	106	115		81
1972	19.5	22.8	13.9	110	129		67
1973	20.7	25.8	12.7	117	146		61
1974	20	27.1	12.3	113	153		59
1975	20.5	29.8	11.8	116	168		57
1976	21.1	32.8	11.8	119	185		57
1977	21.1	35.3	12.5	119	199		60
1978	22	39.1	13.2	124	221		64
1979	24.5	44.6	14.3	138	251		69
1970–79	205.9	295.4	140				
Compound annual rate of growth (percent) 1970–79	3.7	10.8	−3.0				

Source: See Table 13.2.
Column 1: Burton, p. 12.
Column 2: Same method used in Table 13.2, column 5.
Definition: General purpose forces procurement includes ground and tactical air forces.
N.B. The values listed in this table have been read from CIA charts. The cumulative
   statistics differ 0–2 percent from those reported by the agency. The official cumu-
   lative estimates 1970–79 are: Soviet 210 billion, U.S. 140 billion dollars.

ing by the pattern of tactical air force procurements during the seventies, the Soviets concurred with this assessment. The CIA's estimates indicate that Soviet tactical air force procurement grew 7.2 percent per annum from 1970 to 1979—more than twice as fast as any other category. However, despite this effort, if intervintage technological progress is ignored, the agency's statistics still show the United States holding a small advantage both in annual and cumulative expenditures, despite the decline displayed by the U.S. series. American deficiencies in overall procurement expenditures thus appear to be partially offset in one important category. When intervintage technological progress is taken into account, however, this conclusion is unfortunately invalidated. Instead of Soviet tactical air force procurement in 1979 being 5.6 billion dollars

FIGURE 13.6
U.S. and Soviet General Purpose Forces Procurement

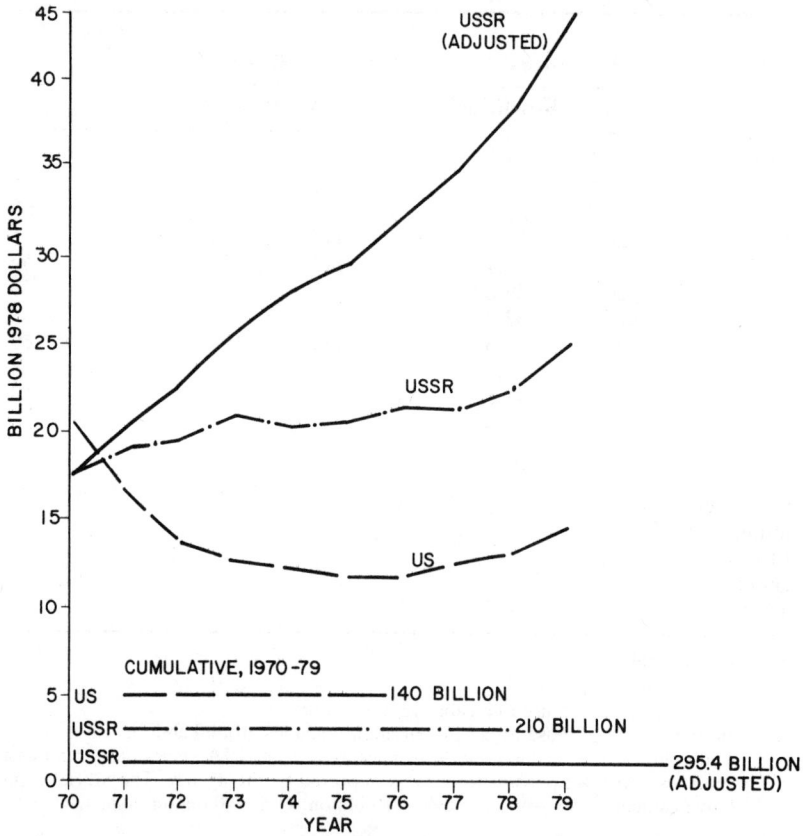

as the agency estimates, it is 9 billion dollars—41 percent higher than the equivalent U.S. figure. This surprising reversal is not confined to 1979. When qualitative improvements are properly taken into consideration, cumulative Soviet tactical air force procurements exceed those of the United States by a small margin, 63.8 to 61.5 billion dollars. Thus even in tactical air force procurements—the last bastion of U.S. superiority—the Soviets have forged ahead.

General purpose naval procurements including major surface combatants over 1,000 tons, minor surface combatants, attack submarines, ASW aircraft carriers, carriers, amphibious warfare ships, and naval forces directly supporting the fleet have also historically been an area

TABLE 13.7
U.S. and Soviet Land Forces Procurement (Billions of 1978 Dollars)

	Soviet		US	Index Soviet		US
	CIA	Rosefielde		CIA	Rosefielde	
1970	7.7	7.7	5.7	100	100	100
1971	8.7	8.7	3.8	103	113	67
1972	8.4	9.8	2.5	109	127	44
1973	8.3	10.5	2.2	108	136	39
1974	8.3	11.4	2.2	108	148	39
1975	8.5	12.5	1.7	110	162	30
1976	9	14.1	1.5	117	183	26
1977	9.1	15.3	2.6	118	199	46
1978	9.1	16.5	2.9	118	214	51
1979	9.8	18.5	3.5	127	240	61
1970–79	86.2	125	28.6			
Compound annual rate of growth (percent) 1970–79	2.7	10.2	−3.7			

Source: See Table 13.2.
Column 1: Burton, p. 13.
Column 2: Same method used in Table 13.2, column 5.
N.B. The values listed in this table have been read from CIA charts. The cumulative statistics differ 4–5 percent from those reported by the agency. The official cumulative estimates 1970–79 are: Soviet 90 billion, U.S. 30 billion dollars.

of American strength. Table 13.9 and Figure 13.9 nonetheless reveal that Soviet programs eclipsed those of the United States in the seventies. The now familiar pattern emerges once again. According to the agency Soviet general purpose naval procurement grew 3.1 percent per annum while U.S. outlay fell 1.5 percent annually 1970–1979. Taking intervintage technological progress into account, the rate of Soviet general naval procurement growth rises to 10.5 percent over the decade. Due to these disparities Soviet naval programs cumulatively exceeded those of the United States by 36 percent according to the CIA's estimates and by 106 percent adjusted for qualitative change.

The mission by mission comparisons surveyed above all convey the same impression. During the decade of the seventies the Soviets have devoted enormous resources to outproducing the United States in all weapon categories, with priority accorded to tactical air force and general purpose naval procurements. Their efforts have been successful in

TABLE 13.8
U.S. and Soviet Tactical Air Procurement (Billions of 1978 Dollars)

	Soviet		US	Soviet		Index US
	CIA	Rosefielde		CIA	Rosefielde	
1970	3	3	8.6	100	100	100
1971	4	4.3	6.9	133	143	80
1972	4.8	5.4	6.0	160	180	70
1973	5	5.9	5.6	166	197	65
1974	5.6	6.8	5,3	187	227	62
1975	5.4	7	5.4	180	233	63
1976	5.3	7.3	5.7	177	243	66
1977	4.5	6.9	5.7	150	230	66
1978	5.3	8.2	5.9	177	273	69
1979	5.6	9	6.4	187	300	74
1970–79	48.5	63.8	61.5			
Compound annual rate of growth (percent) 1970–79	7.2	13	−2.6			

Source: See Table 13.2
Column 1: Burton, p. 13.
Column 2: Same method used in Table 13.2, column 5.
Definition: Tactical air force procurement consists of all land- and sea-based fixed wing aircraft that are used in a combat role and, on the U.S. side, multipurpose aircraft carriers. Helicopters used for ground attack are not included, nor are those aircraft and aircraft carriers which have an ASW mission.
N.B. The values listed in this table have been read from CIA charts. The cumulative statistics differ 1–3 percent from those reported by the agency. The official cumulative estimates 1970–79 are: Soviet 50 billion, U.S., 60 billion dollars.

all areas judged either with the CIA's fixed vintage parametric cost estimates, or after adjustment for intervintage technological change.[15]

IV. Total Soviet Defense Expenditures

The dimensions of the Soviet military buildup can also be illuminated by correcting the CIA's dollar and ruble estimates of total defense spending for its underestimation of Soviet procurement growth. Table 13.10 and Figure 13.10 show that when total defense expenditures are adjusted for intervintage technological progress the long run dollar rate of growth rises from 2–2.4 percent to 4.5 percent per annum. This causes total

FIGURE 13.7
U.S. and Soviet Land Forces Procurement

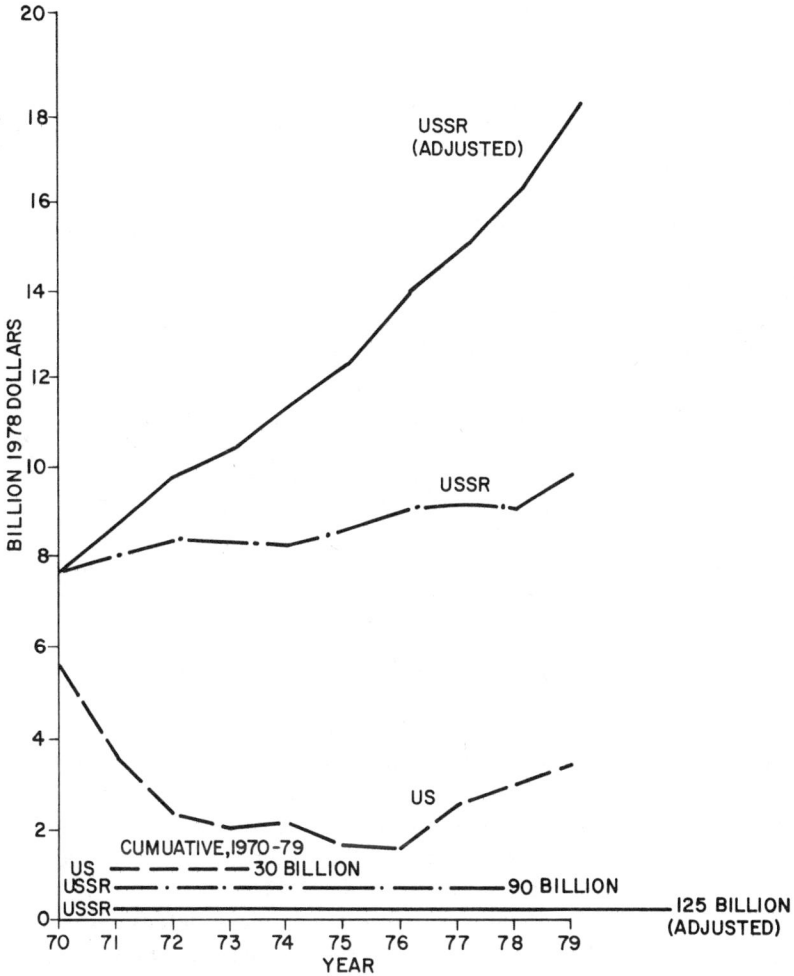

Soviet defense expenditures to exceed U.S. expenditures by a much wider margin during the seventies than the CIA's published series suggests, and raises cumulative defense expenditure by 25 percent from 1.72 to 2.15 trillion dollars compared with the agency's hypothetical Laspeyres defense spending series, and 4 percent compared with the published series. The higher cumulative value of the published series,

FIGURE 13.8
U.S. and Soviet Tactical Air Procurement

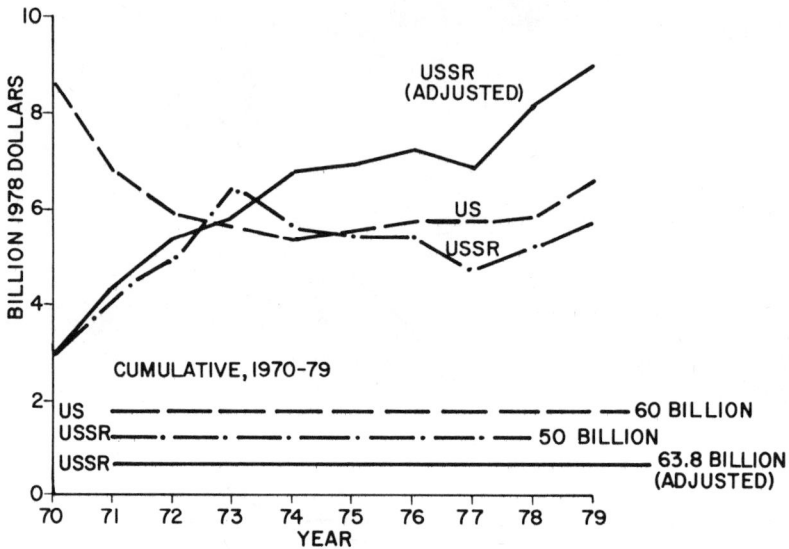

as before, is explained by the overvaluation of pre-1970 procurement estimates (see chapter 13, section II and chapter 4, section VIII).

Table 13.11 and Figure 13.11 restate total defense expenditures in rubles. As might be anticipated the adjusted ruble rate of growth exceeds the dollar rate causing a comparatively large disparity between U.S. and Soviet ruble defense activities. Otherwise, however, the pattern exhibited by the ruble series parallels the dollar findings with a few specific exceptions discussed in the notes to Table 13.11.

The main trends in comparative Soviet-American defense spending implicit in these alternative dollar and ruble series are summarized in Figures 13.12 and 13.13. They reveal that Soviet defense activities exceeded American activities in 1979 by 79 percent and 172 percent respectively. Contrary to the assertion recently advanced by one prominent American scholar that Soviet defense spending in 1977 was only slightly higher than the American military outlays valued in dollars and was lower valued in rubles, the figures disclose that this interpretation, although compatible with the agency's hypothetical Laspeyres series, is very wide of the mark (compare Tables 16.1–16.2, and Figures 16.1–16.4).

TABLE 13.9
U.S. and Soviet General Purpose Naval Procurement
(Billions of 1978 Dollars)

	Soviet		US	Index Soviet		US
	CIA	Rosefielde		CIA	Rosefielde	
1970	6	6	4.8	100	100	100
1971	5.9	6.4	4.6	98	107	96
1972	5.2	6.3	4.5	87	105	94
1973	4.9	6.6	4.4	81	110	92
1974	5.1	7.5	4.3	85	125	90
1975	5.3	8.4	4.2	88	140	88
1976	5.4	9.3	4.1	90	155	85
1977	6	10.8	4	100	180	83
1978	6.6	12.4	4	110	207	93
1979	7.9	14.7	4.1	132	245	85
1970–79	58.3	88.4	43			
Compound annual rate of growth (percent) 1970–79	3.1	10.5	−1.5			

Source: See Table 13.2.

Column 1: Burton, p. 16.

Column 2: Same method used in Table 13.2, column 5.

Definition: General purpose naval procurement includes major surface combatants over 1,000 tons, minor surface combatants, attack submarines, ASW aircraft carriers, carriers, amphibious warfare ships, and naval forces directly supporting the fleet.

N.B. The values listed in this table have been read from CIA charts. The cumulative statistics differ 3–4 percent from those reported by the agency. The official cumulative estimates 1970–79 are: Soviet 60 billion, U.S. 45 billion dollars.

FIGURE 13.9
U.S. and Soviet General Purpose Naval Procurement

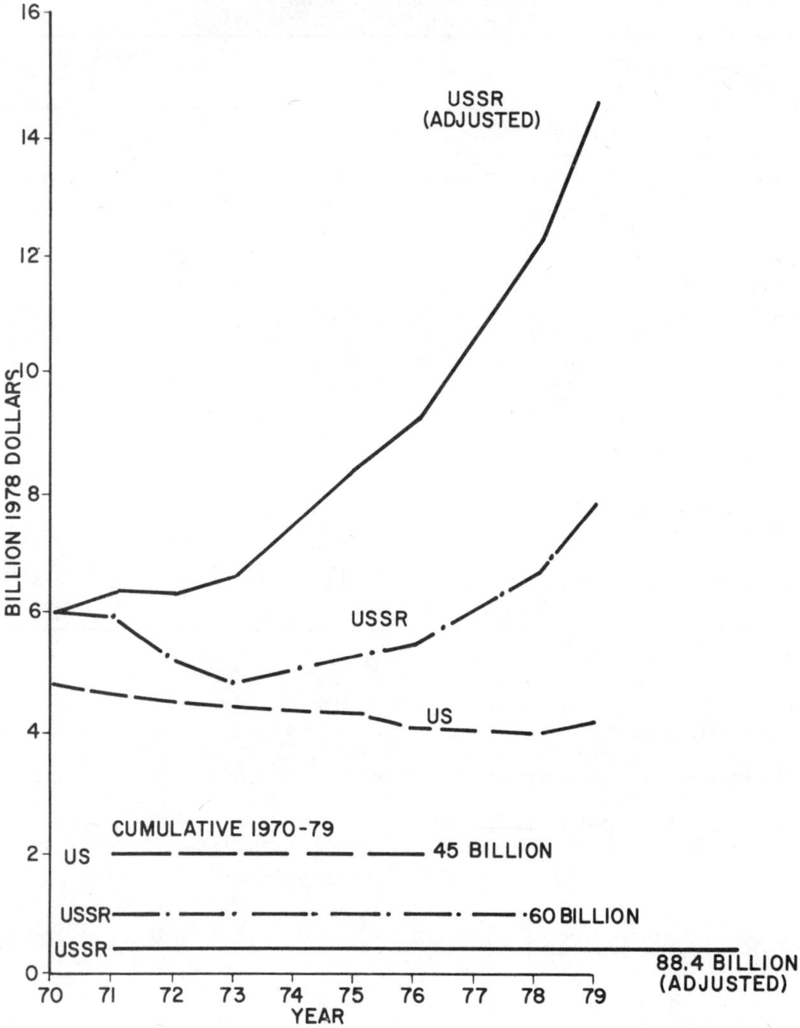

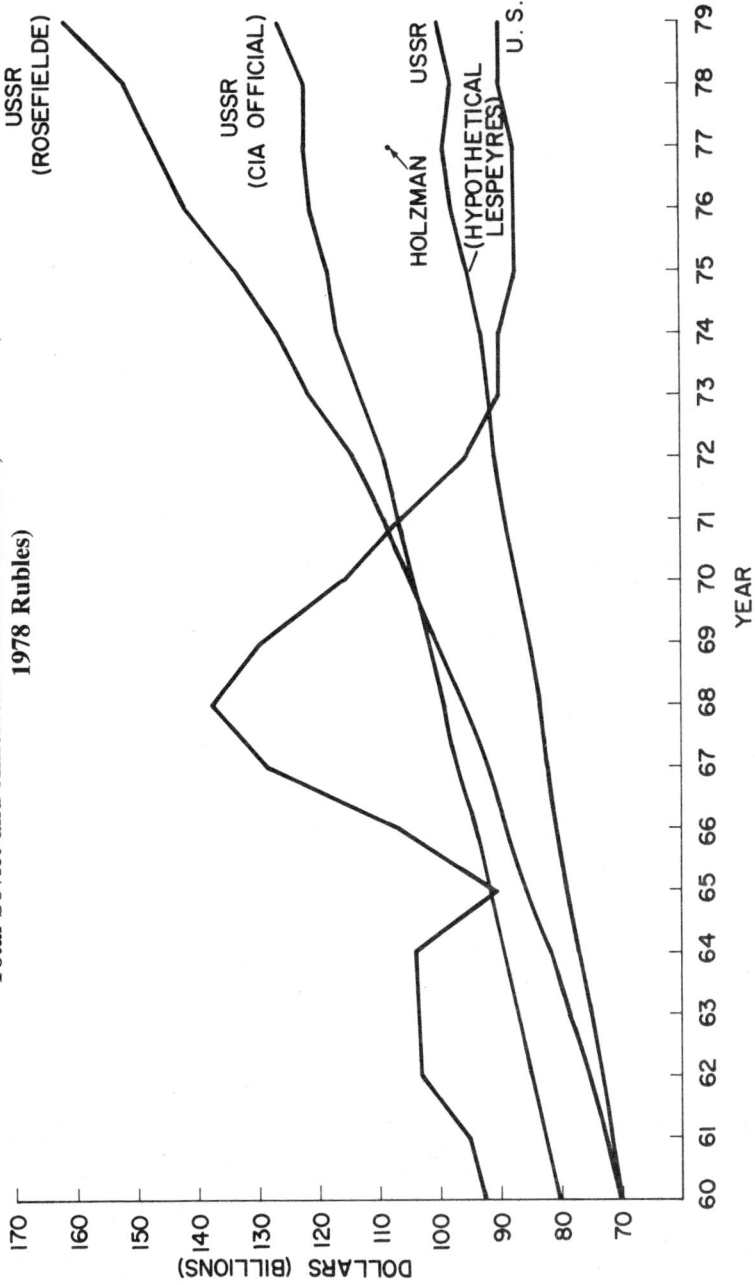

FIGURE 13.10
Total Soviet and American Defense Activities, 1960–79 (Billions of 1978 Rubles)

TABLE 13.10
Total Soviet and American Defense Activities, 1960–79 (Excluding Military Pensions and RDT&E Valued in Billions of Constant 1978 Dollars)

	Soviet			US		Soviet/US		Holzman
	Official CIA (1)	Hypothetical CIA (2)	Rosefielde (3)	(4)	Column 1÷4 (5)	Column 2÷4 (6)	Column 3÷4 (7)	(8)
1960	80	69.9	69.9	92.6	.86	.75	.75	
1961	82.1	71.6	72.5	95	.86	.75	.76	
1962	84.6	73.1	75	102.9	.82	.71	.73	
1963	86.6	75.3	78.3	103.5	.84	.73	.76	
1964	88.9	77.2	81.4	103.9	.86	.74	.73	
1965	91.3	79.2	84.7	90.9	1.00	.87	.93	
1966	93.8	80.7	88.2	106.5	.87	.76	.82	
1967	96.8	82.2	91.9	128.2	.75	.64	.72	
1968	98.9	83.7	95.8	137.6	.72	.61	.70	
1969	101.6	85.4	100	129.6	.78	.66	.77	
1970	104.5	87.2	104.5	116	.90	.75	.9	
1971	106.6	88.4	109	106.6	1.00	.83	1.02	
1972	108.8	90.5	114.1	95.2	1.14	.95	1.20	
1973	113.6	91.7	121.2	89.8	1.27	1.02	1.35	
1974	116	92.4	126.3	89.4	1.30	1.03	1.41	
1975	117.8	(94.7)	133.1	87.4	1.35	(1.08)	1.52	
1976	120.8	(97.7)	141	87.4	1.38	(1.12)	1.61	
1977	121.6	(98.4)	146.2	87.5	1.39	(1.12)	1.67	1.18
1978	121.6	(97.7)	151.2	89.8	1.35	(1.09)	1.68	
1979	126.1	(99.9)	160.9	89.8	1.40	(1.11)	1.79	

Annual Compound Rate of Growth (Percent)	2.4	2.0	4.5	-.2	.85	1.06
Cumulative 1960-79	2061.	1716.9	2145.2	2030.3	1.02	

Sources:

Column 1: Values 1970–78 are taken from *A Dollar Cost Comparison of Soviet and U.S. Defense Activities*, CIA, SR79–10004, January 1979, p. 4. The value for 1979 is obtained from *Soviet and U.S. Defense Activities, 1970–1979: A Dollar Cost Comparison*, CIA, SR80–10005, January 1980, p. 4. A 9 percent deflator was employed to adjust this value to a 1978 price standard (see p. 11). Values 1960–69 were computed by discounting the 1970 figure at a compound rate of 2.7 percent per annum. Cf. the chart shown in *A Dollar Cost Comparison of Soviet and U.S. Defense Activities 1966–1976*, SR–10001U, January 1977, p. 8 and Figure 14, *Allocation of Resources in the Soviet Union and China-1975*, p. 28. According to Donald Burton and Donald Swain, Chief and Deputy Chief, Military-Economic Analysis Center, OSR, CIA, the proportions of Soviet defense spending remained unchanged 1960–70. Cf. William Colby, *Allocation of Resources in the Soviet Union and China (1974)*, pp. 65–70.

Column 2: Computed by subtracting the CIA's postrevision procurement series 1960–79 (Table 16.2, column 2) from total official CIA defense expenditures (Table 13.10, column 1), and adding back the CIA's hypothetical Laspeyres dollar procurement series extrapolated from 1975–79 (Table 16.2, column 1 and Table 13.2, column 3).

Column 3: Computed by subtracting the CIA's postrevision procurement series 1960–79 (Table 16.2, column 2) from total official CIA defense procurement series (Table 16.2, column 4).

Column 4: U.S. defense expenditures 1966–76 are taken from CIA sources: *A Dollar Cost Comparison of Soviet and U.S. Defense Activities, 1966–76*, CIA, SR–10001U, January 1977; *A Dollar Cost Comparison of Soviet and U.S. Defense Activities, 1968–78*, CIA, SR–10004, January 1979; *Soviet and U.S. Defense Activities, 1970–79: A Dollar Cost Comparison*, CIA, SR80–10005, January 1980. These figures differ from the conventional U.S. defense budgetary statistics because they have been adjusted to conform with the agency's Soviet estimates. The CIA's series is defined for the calendar year instead of the fiscal year. Military pensions, RDT&E expenditures, NASA space activities, civil defense, foreign military sales, military assistance programs, and veterans' programs are excluded from the agency's estimates; defense related nuclear programs funded by the DOE, selective service activities and defense related activities of the U.S. Coast Guard are included.

For the period 1960–65 I have used the same DOD outlay data as the agency (excluding defense related DOE, Coast Guard and selective service expenditures) kindly provided by colonel USAF Frederick Giessler, Assistant Director OSD/Net Assessment, and Major Lance Lord, Military Assistant OSD/Net Assessment. These data have been adjusted to a calendar year basis by prorating expenditures intertemporally, and adjusted with DOD deflators. Since my DOD based series follows the agency's closely 1966–1979, the values estimated 1960–65 should be consistent with the CIA's unpublished estimates for these years.

Column 8: Holzman, "Are the Soviets Really Outspending the U.S. in Defense?" *International Security*, Spring 1980, Vol. 4, No. 4, p. 99. Holzman's best revised dollar valued ratio of Soviet-American defense spending including RDT&E is 1.18–1.27. Deleting RDT&E reduces the CIA's estimate from 1.4 to 1.35 (See *Allocation of Resources in the Soviet Union and China-1978*, JEC, p. 52). Discounting the mean value of Holzman's range proportionally for this effect yields a best estimate of 1.18.

TABLE 13.11
Total Soviet and American Defense Activities, 1960–79 (Including Military Pensions and RDT&E Valued in Billions of Constant 1970 Rubles)

| | Soviet | | | US | | Soviet/US | | Holzman |
| | Postrevision CIA | Prerevision CIA | Rosefielde | | Column 1÷4 | Column 2÷4 | Column 3÷4 | |
	(1)	(2)	(3)	(4)	(5)	(6)	(7)	(8)
1960	28.5	14.3	14.3 (22.5)	37.7	.76	.38	.38	
1961	29.7	14.9	15.5	39.1	.76	.38	.40	
1962	30.9	15.5	16.9	41.9	.74	.37	.40	
1963	32.1	16.1	18.3	42.4	.76	.38	.43	
1964	33.3	16.7	19.8	42.9	.78	.39	.46	
1965	34.7	17.4	21.7	37.6	.92	.46	.58	
1966	36.1	18.1	23.7	43.9	.82	.41	.54	
1967	37.5	18.8	26	52.3	.71	.36	.50	
1968	39.5	19.8	28.7	55.8	.71	.35	.51	
1969	41.5	20.8	31.6	52.5	.79	.40	.60	
1970	42	21	43.5	47.5	.80	.44	.92	
1971	43.5	21.8	46.7	44.3	.98	.49	1.05	
1972	43	22.5	50.2	40.6	1.11	.55	1.24	
1973	47.5	23.8	55	38.8	1.22	.61	1.42	
1974	49.5	24.8	59.7	33	1.50	.75	1.81	
1975	51.5	(25.8)	64.7	32.2	1.60	(.80)	2.01	
1976	53.3	(26.8)	70.3	32.3	1.66	(.83)	2.18	
1977	54.5	(27.3)	75.4	32.6	1.67	(.84)	2.31	.70–.97
1978	(57)	(28.5)	82.5	33.4	(1.71)	(.91)	2.47	
1979	(60)	(30)	91	33.5	(1.79)	(.90)	2.72	

Annual Compound Rate of Growth (Percent) 1960–75			
4	4	10.2 (7.6)	–.6

Cumulative 1960–79						
847.8	424.7	855.5	814.3	1.04	.52	1.05

Sources:

Column 1: The official CIA postrevision series of estimated Soviet defense expenditures 1967–77 in 1970 rubles is taken from *Estimated Soviet Defense Spending: Trends and Prospects*, CIA, SR78–10121, June 1978, p. 2. Values for 1978–79 are extrapolated at 4.5 percent per annum, the average rate 1967–1977 (see p. 2). Estimates for the period 1960–66 are calculated by discounting the agency's 1967 figure at a compound rate of 4 percent per annum (see William Colby's testimony in *Allocation of Resources in the Soviet Union and China–1974*, pp. 65–70.

The CIA's ruble series is defined differently than its dollar series. Two variants are estimated, one using Soviet definitions, the other U.S. definitions. The latter unlike the dollar series includes RDT&E, and military pensions, and is reported as a range. The estimate used in column 1 is the midpoint of the range. The U.S. definition has been selected here to facilitate comparison with U.S. defense expenditures.

Column 2: The CIA's prerevision ruble defense expenditure series is computed by reducing its postrevision series by half. According to *Estimated Soviet Defense Spending in Rubles, 1970–1975*, CIA, SR76–10121U, May 1976, p. 1 the CIA's postrevision estimate for 1975 "is about twice the previous estimate." Since the agency's pre and postrevision series both grow at 4 percent per annum 1960–79, the new evidence implies that the prerevision series was 50 percent less than the postrevision series throughout this period.

Column 3: The author's estimate of total Soviet defense expenditures is calculated by subtracting the CIA's prerevision unpublished ruble procurement series 1970–79 (Table 16.1, column 1) from its unpublished prerevision total defense expenditures series 1960–69 (Table 13.11, column 2) and its postrevision series 1970–79 (Table 13.11, column 1), and then adding back the author's estimates of Soviet procurement 1960–79 (Table 13.1, column 5).

While this procedure is logically consistent, it is affected by a deep contradiction in the CIA's characterization of its pre and postrevision series. On one hand, the agency contends that the growth rate for both series is the same. On the other hand, it asserts that its prerevision estimate for 1960 and its postrevision estimate for 1970 are correct. But if the latter is true then the implied rate of nonprocurement growth 1960–70 is 11 percent per annum, not 4 percent per annum. And if the former is true, then the latter cannot be correct. The bracketed term makes allowance for this contradiction by assuming that the nonprocurement component of Soviet defense expenditures in 1960 can be estimated by discounting the CIA's postrevision nonprocurement estimate for 1970 at a compound rate of 4 percent per annum. The resulting long term growth rate of total defense spending 1960–79 on this measure

TABLE 13.11 (Continued)

is 7.6 percent per annum; and the rate 1960–70 is 6.8 percent per annum, the precise figure shown in the official Soviet defense budget.

Column 4: Total American defense expenditures in rubles are calculated in three steps. First, the dollar series reported in Table 13.10, column 4 is adjusted to conform with the agency's ruble definition of Soviet defense spending by adding RDT&E and pension expenditures to the total. These data are obtained from the Office of Net Assessment, and have been converted to a calendar year basis. Defense related activities of the DOE, the Coast Guard and the selective service have been omitted; with the result that my U.S. series is slightly underestimated.

Second, this series is deflated to a 1970 price base.

Third, the 1970 series is then converted to rubles with the agency's implicit 1970 defense ruble-dollar ratio. This ratio is computed by dividing the CIA's 1970 dollar estimate of Soviet procurement, adjusted to include RDT&E, pensions and other expenditures (2 billion dollars were allotted for the latter two categories) by its 1970 ruble estimate:

1.

$$\frac{r^{70}}{p^{70}} = \frac{\Sigma r_i^{70} q_i^{70}}{\Sigma p_i^{70} q_i^{70}} = .64$$

where q_i represents Soviet quantity weights. For a discussion of the effect of Soviet quantity weights see chapter 16.

Column 8: Holzman, "Are the Soviets Really Outspending the U.S. on Defense?" *International Security*, Spring 1980, Vol. 4, No. 4, p. 99.

Note: A reconciliation of the CIA's 50-billion-ruble postrevision defense spending estimate with its Soviet national product accounts for 1970 is provided in appendix 5.

FIGURE 13.11

Total Soviet and American Defense Activities, 1960–79 (Billions of 1970 Rubles)

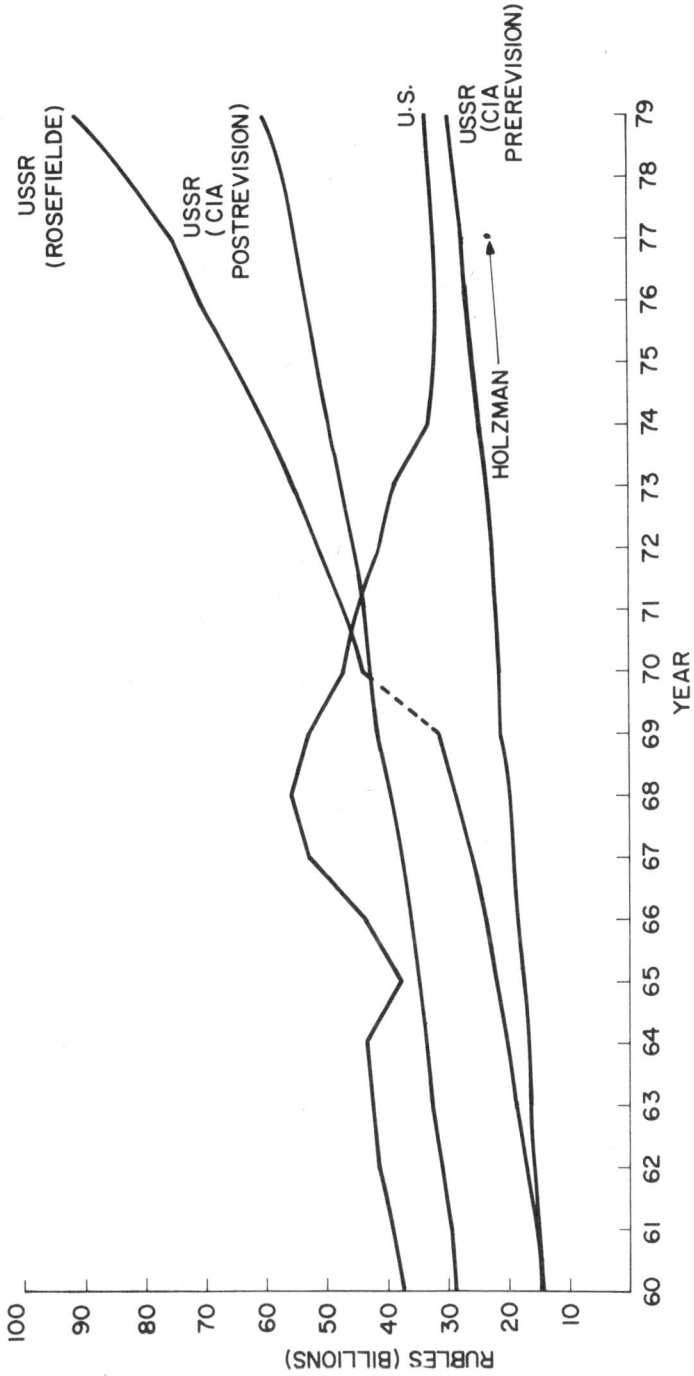

FIGURE 13.12

Soviet-American Total Defense Activities Ratios (Dollar Trends 1960–79)

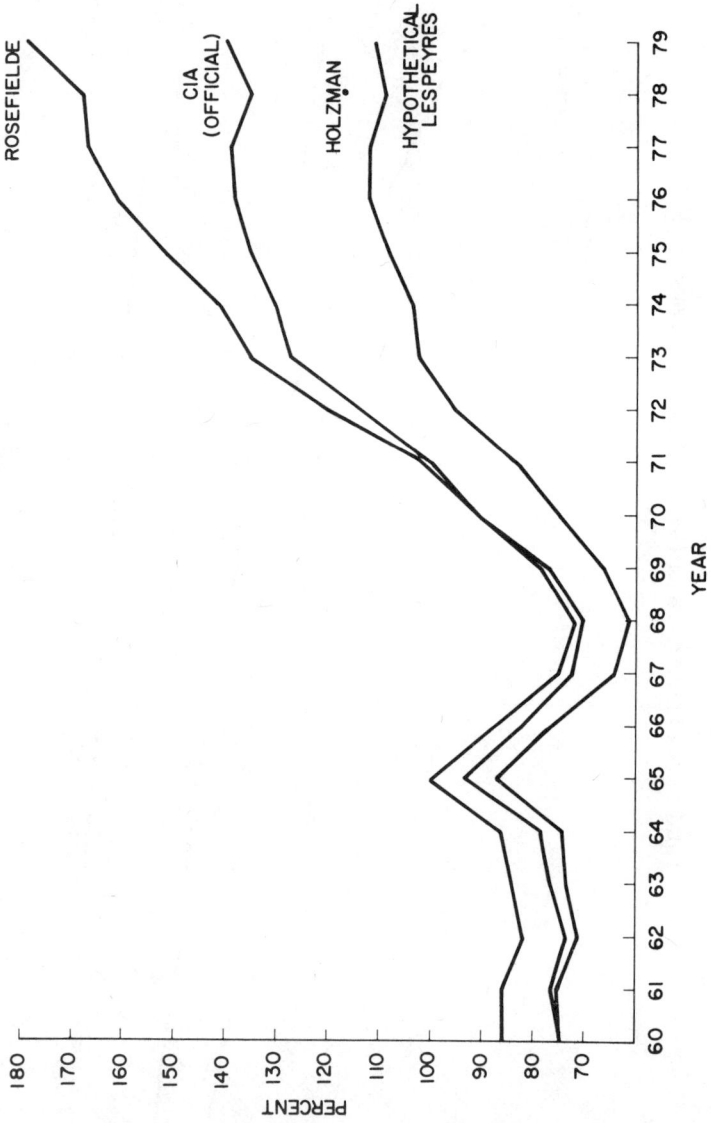

FIGURE 13.13
Soviet-American Total Defense Activities Ratios (Ruble Trends 1960–79)

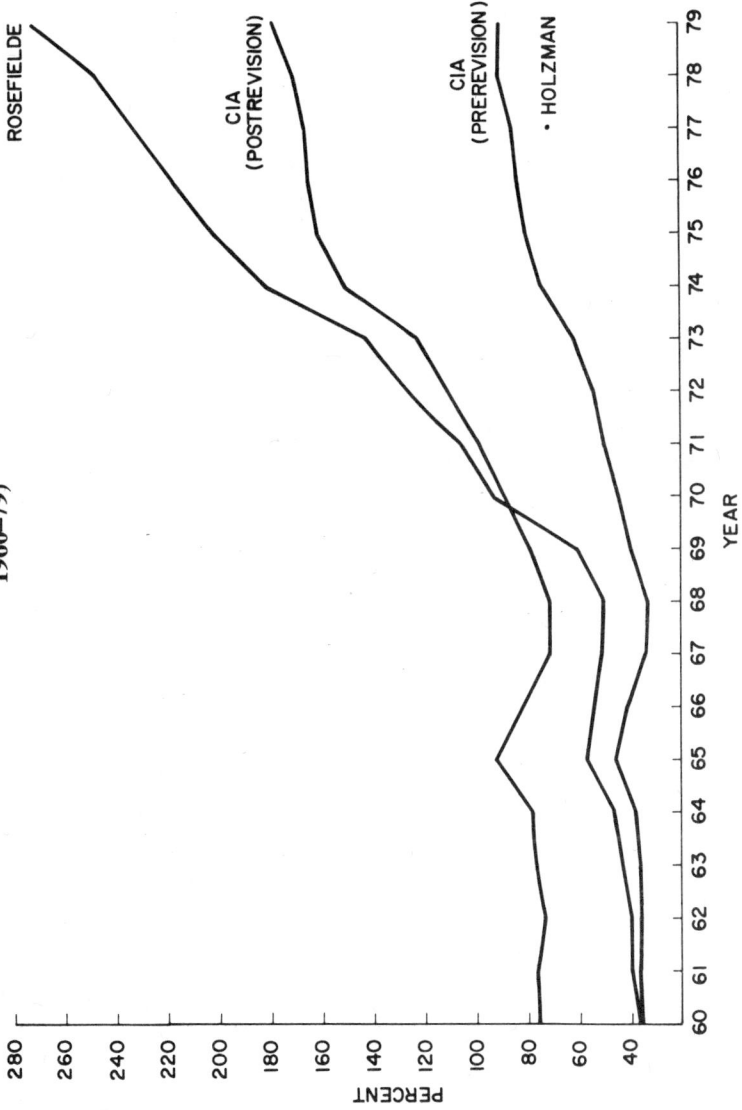

Notes

1. If prerevision 1970 prices were employed, the values reported in column 1 would be uniformly 6 percent higher.
2. If 1970 prerevision prices are used the cumulative total exceeds the agency's by 210 percent.
3. See chapter 1. Cf. Becker (1980).
4. Donald Burton (1979), p. 8.
5. Learning curves have an exotic effect on the CIA's Paasche dollar indices. Table 13.1n demonstrates that the agency's dollar estimates of Soviet procurement valued in 1978 dollars decline when allowance is made for learning in the years after 1975. The CIA's 1970 estimate of Soviet procurement for example made in 1975 and expressed in 1978 dollars is 37.5 billion dollars, only .6 billion dollars less than estimated weapon expenditures in 1978, allowing for learning through 1979. If the exotic learning effects which produced these results were at work before 1970, the rate of growth 1970–78, .2 percent per annum, may be taken as a proxy for the Paasche dollar series 1960–70 the agency disclaims informally computing during the sixties. See Rosefielde (1982c).
6. The ruble growth rates are given in Table 13.1, column 1. The 1960 procurement expenditure base valued in 1960 dollar prices, adjusted to the 1978 price level, is computed by extrapolation. It is assumed that the real quality-adjusted dollar rate of growth bears the same relationship to the real quality-adjusted ruble rate as the agency's Paasche dollar rate bears to its postrevision ruble rate:

$$\dot{g}_{1960-70} = \frac{2.7}{4}\,(12.9) = 8.7 \text{ percent}$$

This rate is then applied to the agency's 1970 dollar estimate (adjusted to the 1978 price level) to calculate the 1960 value:

$$y^{60} = 30.6 \div (1.087)^{10} = 13.3 \text{ billion dollars.}$$

This figure implies a ruble-dollar procurement ratio in 1960, measured in 1960 prices of .9, a ratio that corresponds almost exactly with the official Soviet exchange rate which Franklyn Holzman, Abraham Becker, and Treml-Gallik all consider accurate. See Franklyn Holzman, *Foreign Trade under Central Planning*, pp. 258–66; Abraham Becker, "National Income Accounting in the USSR." In Treml and Hardt (eds.), *Soviet Economic Statistics*, pp. 109–10; and Vladimir Treml and Dimitri Gallik, *Soviet Studies on Ruble/Dollar Parity Ratios*, Foreign Economic Reports, no. 4, November 1973, p. 10. It is also equivalent to the implicit ruble-dollar ratio I estimate for 1970 and the CIA's postrevision 1970 ruble-dollar ratio. These correspondences suggest either that the machine-building-metalworking ruble-dollar ratio reported by Treml and Gallik, .50–.54 in 1960 prices, which builds on prior calculations by Becker is too low, or that their machine-building parities are not good surrogates for weapons. See Treml and Gallik, p. 21. Implicit CIA ruble-dollar procurement ratios 1960–70 are reported in Table 13.2n.

TABLE 13.1n

Successive Paasche Estimates of Soviet Procurement (Selected Years Expressed in Billions of 1978 Dollars)

Observation		Price Set			
		1975	1977	1978	1979
	A. All Procurement				
1970		37.5	31.3	31.5	31
1975		44.9	35.0	36	37.3
1978				37	38.1
	B. General Purpose Naval Procurement				
1970			10.8	9.9	8.6
1975			10.8	9.9	8.6
1978				11.3	10.8

Interpretation: Procurement estimates arrayed along each row represent dollar values expressed in constant 1978 dollars for the year specified in the row heading. These estimates which all pertain in principle to the same physical set of weapons differ from one another because unit CIA weapons costs in constant 1978 dollars decline over time, most likely reflecting the learning curve adjustments built into computerized costing routines. The column headings represent the current prices used by the CIA to value the weapons produced in the year specified by the row heading. Current value estimates have all been reduced to a consistent 1978 price base with DOD procurement deflators.

Method: Each entry has been read from official CIA charts. These observations are valued in current dollars, $\Sigma p_i^{t+j} q_i^t$. All current value estimates are deflated to a 1978 price base with DOD procurement deflators: $\Sigma p_i^{t+j} q_i^t / \Sigma p_i^t q_i^t$.

Sources: *A Dollar Cost Comparison of Soviet and U.S. Defense Activities, 1966–1976; A Dollar Cost Comparison of Soviet and U.S. Defense Activities, 1967–77; A Dollar Cost Comparison of Soviet and U.S. Defense Activities, 1968–78, Soviet and U.S. Defense Activities, 1970–79: A Dollar Cost Comparison.*

Comments: The agency revises its estimates from time to time to reflect new information on Soviet programs. These adjustments may to some extent blur the annual comparisons reported above. Definitional and data problems preclude extending our comparisons to current value series computed in pre-1975 prices. CIA investment estimates were raised across the board in 1981 by 2 billion dollars (valued in 1979 prices) due to its improved estimate of construction costs. Since construction is excluded from procurement, this revision has no effect on the estimates contained in Table 4.1. See *Soviet and U.S. Defense Activities, 1971–80: A Dollar Cost Comparison,* p. 9.

7. See chapters 2 and 4. Most of the discrepancy between the agency's pre- and postrevision ruble procurement estimates is attributable to the misspecification of qualitative improvements in its dollar parametric cost estimating relationships, not to relative prices. This justifies the assumption of proportionality.

TABLE 13.2 n
Implicit CIA Ruble-Dollar
Procurement Ratios 1960–70

	Constant Value Series			Current Value Series		
	(1) Rubles	(2) Dollars	(3) Ruble/Dollar	(4) Ruble	(5) Dollar	(6) Ruble/Dollar
1960	5.5	10.8	.51	5.5	14.1 (6.1)	.39 (.90)
1961	5.6	11.1	.50	5.6	14.6	.38
1962	5.6	11.4	.49	5.6	14.7	.37
1963	5.7	11.7	.49	5.7	14.6	.39
1964	5.8	12	.48	5.8	15.2	.38
1965	5.8	12.3	.47	5.8	15.5	.37
1966	5.8	12.7	.46	5.8	16.2	.36
1967	5.7	13	.44	5.7	16.9	.33
1968	5.6	13.4	.42	5.6	17.6	.32
1969	5.6	13.7	.41	5.6	17.9	.31
1970	5.5	14.1	.39	5.5 (17)	18.3	.3 (.93)

Sources; See Tables 13.1 and 13.2; Department of Defense procurement deflators (outlays).

Column 1: The CIA's unpublished prerevision ruble Soviet procurement series computed with early year 1960 dollar parametric cost estimating relationships, converted to rubles with 1955 MBMW ruble-dollar ratios. The cyclical trend mentioned in Swain's letter is incorporated in these estimates. It should be noted that the agency's published dollar series does not exhibit this trend. See *A Dollar Cost Comparison of Soviet and U.S. Defense Activities, 1966–1976*, p. 8.

Column 2: The CIA Paasche dollar series (Table 13.2, column 2) is computed from the Becker-Treml-Gallik 1960 machinery ruble-dollar ratio, expressed in 1960 prices. Note the discontinuity between columns 2 and 5. The base of the former may be calculated with 1960 CERs, the latter with 1970 CERs.

Column 3: Column 1 divided by column 2.

Column 4: Same as column 1. The bracketed term is the agency's best direct cost postrevision ruble procurement estimate valued in 1970 prices.

Column 5: The CIA's Paasche dollar procurement (column 2), adjusted to a current price basis with the Department of Defense procurement deflators (outlays). Almost identical results are obtained with the Commerce Department's (1972) fixed weight GNP index. See *Survey of Current Business*, vol. 60, no. 1, January 1980, p. 40.

Column 6: Column 4 divided by column 5. The bracketed term for 1960 represents the implicit Laspeyres ruble-dollar ratio valued in 1960 prices. The bracketed term for 1970 represents the CIA's best postrevision ruble-dollar ratio in 1970 prices. (The dollar component was originally computed in 1978 prices, and was then deflated to 1970 prices with DOD procurement deflators. This means that they may be biased downward by the agency's learning adjustment.) See Rosefielde (1982c) and note 6.

8. See note 2. $\dot{g}_{1970-79} = \dfrac{3.3}{4}$ (12.9) = 10.6 percent. The faster rate of growth (10.6 percent) calculated for the seventies, reflects a narrowing disparity between the agency's ruble and dollar estimates and is consistent with index number relativity theory. See chapter 6. CIA Paasche dollar weapons growth rates computed during the seventies appear to be only mildly distorted by learning curve bias. See Rosefielde (1982c). A sense of the real rate of physical weapons growth is provided by the order of battle data in *Soviet Military Power*, DOD, September 1981.

9. The undetected rates of quality growth computed in this manner are shown in the table below.

TABLE 13.3 n
Estimates of the Dollar Rates of Quality Growth
in Soviet Procurement

	(1)	(2)	(3)
1960–70	5.7	7.2	8.8
1970–79	7	8.8	10.8

column 1: Rosefielde's quality-adjusted series assuming real ruble procurement growth of 11 percent per annum.
column 2: same, assuming 12.9 percent annual growth.
column 3: same, assuming 15 percent annual growth.

10. The CIA published detailed annual Soviet procurement estimates which deviated significantly from the underlying trend for the first time in November 1979. See Burton (1979). These deviations affect the cumulative measure of real Soviet defense expenditure.

11. "The trends in the cost of military investment—the procurement of weapons and equipment (exclusive of RDT & E costs) and the construction of facilities—follow closely those for total defense costs in both countries." "For the 1966–1976 period as a whole, cumulative estimated dollar costs of Soviet defense activities and U.S. defense outlay are about the same." CIA, *A Dollar Cost Comparison of Soviet and U.S. Defense Activities, 1966–1976*, SR 77–10001U, January 1977, pp. 5–7.

12. It should also be recognized that much of America's procurement expenditures in the sixties went for weapons and ordnance used up during the Vietnam war. This should not be counted in any calculation of the present Soviet-American arms balance.

13. The ruble Laspeyres rate of growth is calculated by discounting the ratio of the CIA's postrevision 1970 value to its 1960 estimate:

$$1. \qquad \dot{i}_r = 100 \ (r_{55}q_{70}^{*}/r_{55}q_{60})^{1/10}$$
$$= 12.9$$

where q_{70}^{*} is interpreted as realized quality-adjusted procurement. Since the dollar Laspeyres rate is computed by multiplying the dollar Paasche rate by the ratio of the ruble Laspeyres to the ruble Paasche rates:

2.
$$\dot{i}_d = \dot{p}_d \cdot \frac{\dot{i}_r}{\dot{p}_r}$$

its conceptual meaning is clearly governed by the rate of Soviet, not American intervintage technological progress embodied in $\dot{i}_r$.

14. The fact that the average quality of U.S. weapons was rising during the seventies due to intervintage technological progress does not mean that the declining trend in U.S. weapons procurement was mitigated. The cost of these qualitative improvements are already included in the official series. Had the United States acquired the same number of weapons in 1979 as it did in 1970, it would have spent 55.2 billion dollars instead of 32.7 billion dollars (in constant 1978 prices) to cover the cost of qualitative improvements. However, the Defense Department purchased far fewer weapons in 1979. Although the average quality was greatly improved, the numbers of weapons purchased fell more than enough to offset the qualitative gains.

15. Burton (1979), p. 44. For direct weapon by weapon comparisons see Rosefielde (1982c).

CHAPTER 14

The Increasing Burden of Soviet Defense

The distortion of Soviet military force potential caused by the agency's fixed vintage parametric cost estimating methodology is not confined to the problem of sizing. It also affects the CIA's assessment of Soviet intentions deduced from trends exhibited by agency statistics on the Soviet burden of defense.

Table 14.1 and Figure 14.1 report these statistics for the period 1960–77. They are computed from the procurement estimates found in Table 13.1, and real Soviet net material product data, adjusted to Western GNP standards by a conversion factor derived from the agency's factor cost estimates of Soviet gross national product.[1] Columns 1–4 present CIA burden statistics calculated from its unpublished ruble procurement series, its best postrevision direct cost and residual Paasche series, and the hybrid estimates derived from its 1960 procurement figure, 5.5 billion rubles, extrapolated with the Paasche growth index. They all exhibit a similar declining pattern, reflecting the fact that the agency's real procurement growth series increase more slowly than real Soviet GNP. The CIA's highest procurement burden estimates, displayed by its best residual series, fall continuously from 7.3 percent of GNP in 1960 to 5.2 percent in 1977. Its lowest procurement burden estimates derived from its Laspeyres series decrease from 3.2 percent in 1960 to 1.3 percent in 1977.

The magnitude of the Soviet procurement burden expressed in the CIA data are all comparatively high by world standards, suggesting that caution is in order in appraising Soviet military intentions. The agency's best direct cost estimate for 1977, for example, is roughly 380 percent greater than the analogous U.S. figure.[2] The potential ominousness of this disparity is diminished by the putative trend in the procurement burden. While the social cost of Soviet procurement is incontestibly great, agency data indicate that the Soviets have systematically reduced

TABLE 14.1

Soviet and American Procurement Expenditures as a Share of GNP
(percent)

	Soviet					US
	CIA				Rosefielde	
	(1)	(2)	(3)	(4)	(5)	(6)
1960	3.2	6.7	7.3	3.2	3.2	2.4
1965	2.3	5.9	6.4	2.8	4.2	1.7
1970	1.6	5.0	5.5	2.4	5.5	2.0
1975	1.3	4.6	5.0	2.2	7.5	1.1
1977	1.2	4.5	4.9	2.2	8.7	1.0

Sources: Procurement expenditure data are taken from Table 13.1, columns 1–4, and 6.
Soviet GNP data are calculated in 1970 prices from net material product data
reported in *Narodnoe Khoziaistvo SSSR*, 1972, pp. 531, 1977, p. 404, and "za
60 let," pp. 485–6. The NMP statistics are converted to GNP using the correspondence ratio, 1.17 implied by Rush Greenslade in "The Real Gross National
Product of the USSR, 1950–1975," in *Soviet Economy in a New Perspective*,
Joint Economic Committee of Congress, 1976, p. 278. The GNP values used in
the text for the years 1960, 1965, 1970, 1975, and 1977 are 170, 234, 340, 449,
and 496 billion rubles.

U.S. procurement data in 1978 dollar prices are taken from Table 13.2, column
7. American GNP estimates in constant 1978 prices are compiled from data
provided in *Survey of Current Business*, Vol. 60, No. 1, January 1980, pp. 38–43.

Definitions:

Column 1: The CIA's Laspeyres procurement burden estimate.

Column 2: The CIA's Paasche procurement burden estimate based on its best direct cost
computation.

Column 3: The CIA's Paasche procurement burden estimate based on its best residual
calculation.

Column 4: The CIA's Paasche procurement burden estimate extrapolated from its 1960
base year figure.

Column 5: The author's quality adjusted procurement burden estimate assuming a 12.9
percent real annual rate of arms growth.

Column 6: American procurement expenditures (CIA series) as a share of GNP. The
peak U.S. procurement burden during the sixties occurred in 1968 when it
reached 2.6 percent of GNP.

Note: The Soviet burden ratios presented above measure procurement as a share of GNP,
valued at factor cost. Alternative ratios can also be calculated using GNP series
derived from the CIA's Soviet GNP estimate for 1970 valued at established prices.
These ratios will be 10.7 percent lower than the factor cost ratios. Other adjustments
discussed in appendix 5 could reduce procurement burden valued at established
prices by 2.8 percent (i.e. B/1.028).

the share of material resources they allocated to procurement throughout the sixties and seventies, a pattern hardly consistent with the view
that the Soviets might be committed to achieving their political objectives through the aggressive use of force.

FIGURE 14.1
Soviet and American Procurement Burden Trends, 1960–77

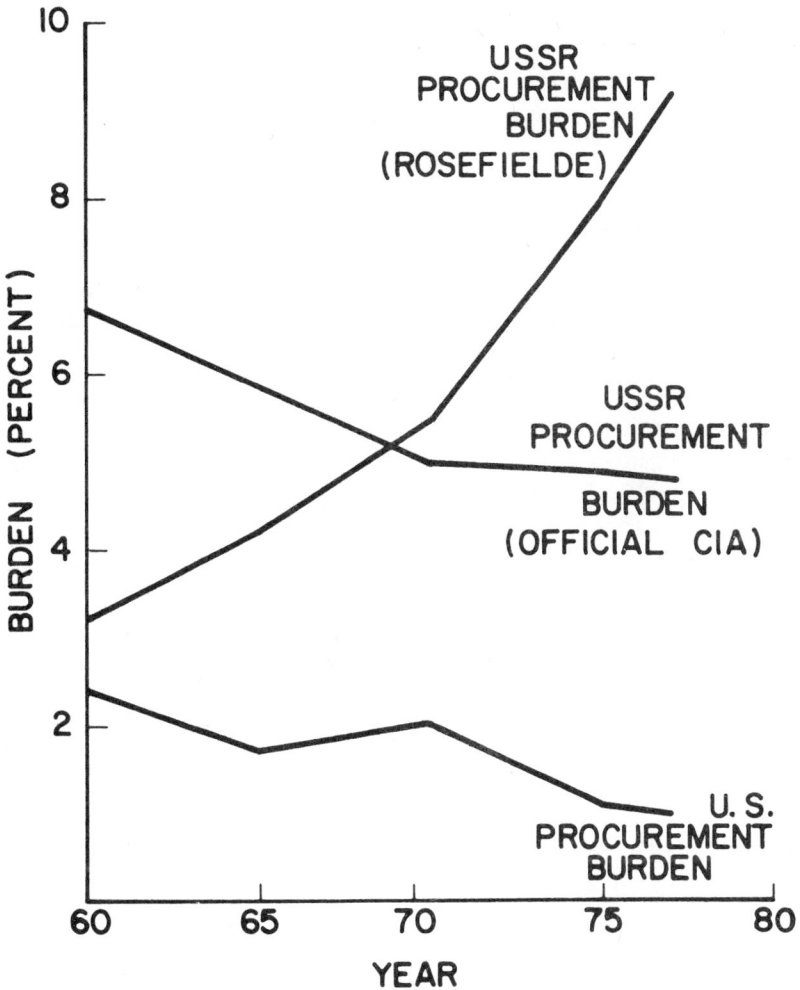

Procurement burden estimates, adjusted for intervintage technological progress presented in column 5, contradict this interpretation. Like the CIA's calculations, the quality-adjusted estimates confirm that Soviet procurement expenditures are high by international standards—820 percent greater than the correlative U.S. figure for 1977—but unlike its estimates, the procurement burden of Soviet defense rises steadily due to the effects of intervintage technological change. This suggests that the leadership has not adopted a policy of gradually demilitarizing its economy, nor has it exhibited conspicuous restraint in building up its armed forces as is often supposed.[3] Instead, the Soviets have apparently concluded that the increasing social cost of defense they have chosen to bear is at least offset by the potential utility of military force.

This impression is confirmed by the broader measure of social cost reported in Table 14.2 and Figure 14.2. Total Soviet defense expenditures including procurement, construction, manpower, RDT&E, operations, and maintenance computed by the agency and the author are all comparatively high. The CIA's best direct cost estimate for 1977, using its Soviet definition of defense expenditures,[4] is 12.7 percent— 202 percent greater than the U.S. defense burden, 4.2 percent.[5] The author's quality-adjusted defense burden estimate is higher still, 16.5 percent—four times the U.S. figure.

These extraordinary magnitudes are buttressed by the trend in the defense burden adjusted for intervintage technological progress exhibited in column 5, which shows the share of Soviet GNP devoted to military uses rising continuously at .4 percent per year from 1960 to 1979. Starting at a relatively modest level in 1960, these statistics reveal that by 1977 the social costs of Soviet defense grew to a point where it rivaled the defense burden prevailing in 1940, on the eve of the Second World War.[6] This correspondence, of course, does not mean that a third world war is imminent, but it does demonstrate that the Soviet attitude toward the potential utility of force is hardly casual.[7]

CIA defense burden trends predictably counterindicate the inferences drawn above. They display an asymptotically declining pattern from 1960 to 1977, which could easily be construed to mean that the Soviets have adopted a long term policy of gradually expanding social expenditures without compromising their fundamental national security needs. Just as the CIA's procurement growth estimates understate Soviet military capabilities, its burden data understate the sacrifices the leadership is prepared to make to support its military objectives. In this regard, the trend exhibited by the agency's defense burden estimates is only slightly less disinformative than the official Soviet series which includes some military expenditures, but excludes weapons. Indeed, if it were not for the effect of the new information, the agency burden data would not differ very greatly from official Soviet figures, especially for the seventies. The CIA's prerevision average defense burden estimate for the past decade is 6.1 percent, only 1.9 percentage points higher than the mean Soviet figure.

TABLE 14.2
Soviet and American Defense Expenditures as a Share of GNP
(percent)

	Soviet						US
	CIA				Rosefielde	Official	
	(1)	(2)	(3)	(4)	(5)	(6)	(7)
1960	10	18	18.8	10	10	5.5	8.2
1965	8.3	15.7	16.3	8.7	10.1	5.4	6.4
1970	6.6	13.6	14	10.9	14	5.3	7.0
1975	6.0	12.4	12.8	10.0	15.3	3.9	4.7
1977	5.7	12.3	12.7	9.9	16.5	3.5	4.2

Sources: Procurement expenditure data are taken from Table 13.1 columns 1–4, and 6. CIA mean estimates of total Soviet defense expenditures (Soviet definition) are obtained from *Allocations of Resources in the Soviet Union and China*, Joint Economic Committee of Congress, Washington, 1974, pp. 68–69; CIA, *Estimated Soviet Defense Spending in Rubles, 1970–75*, SR 76–10121U, May, 1976, p. 1 and CIA, *Estimated Soviet Defense Spending: Trends and Prospects*, SR 78–10121, June 1978, p. 1. These mean estimates for 1960, 1970, 1975, and 1977 are 17, 47.5, 57.5 and 63 billion rubles valued in 1970 prices. Cf. Table 13.11, column 1 which reports alternative CIA estimates based on U.S. definitions. Official Soviet defense expenditure data in current prices are obtained from various editions of *Narodnoe Khoziaistvo SSSR*. The values for 1960, 1970, 1975 and 1977 are 9.3, 17.9, 17.4 and 17 billion rubles. Soviet GNP data are reported in the "Sources" section of Table 14.1.

U.S. defense expenditure data are taken from Table 13.10, column 4. American GNP estimates in 1978 prices are computed from data provided in *Survey of Current Business*, Vol. 60, No. 1, January 1980, pp. 38–43.

Method: Official CIA burden estimates are reported in column 3, based on Soviet definitions of defense expenditure. Alternative estimates are computed by subtracting the procurement series in Table 13.1, column 3 for the years 1970, 1975, and 1977 from the official estimates in Table 14.2, column 3, and adding back the diverse procurement figures in Table 13.1, columns 2, 4, and 6.

Soviet defense spending in 1960 is estimated in two different ways. Prerevision estimates are employed in columns 1, 4 and 5. Postrevision estimates are used in columns 2 and 3. The value used in column 3 is calculated by discounting the postrevision estimate for 1970 by the CIA's long term estimate of total Soviet defense expenditure growth: $y_{60} = 47.5/(1.04)^{10} = 32.1$. The figure employed in column 2 is 1.5 billion rubles less, 30.6 billion rubles, reflecting the difference between the agency's best direct cost and best residual estimates of Soviet procurement spending.

Total Soviet defense spending in 1965 is also computed in two different ways. Columns 1, 4 and 5 are calculated by adding *non*procurement expenditures, 14 billion rubles ($y_{65}^n = 11.5 (1.04)^5$), to the procurement estimates reported in Table 13.1, columns 1, 4 and 6. The resulting total procurement values are 19.8, 20.7 and 24.1. Columns 2 and 3 are computed as before by discounting: $y_{65} = 47.5/(1.04)^5 = 39$ billion rubles (column 3: $y_{65}^* = y_{65} - 1.5 = 37.5$).

Definitions:

Column 1: The CIA's Laspeyres defense burden estimate.

TABLE 14.2 (Continued)

Column 2: The CIA's Paasche defense burden estimate based on its best direct cost computation.

Column 3: The CIA's Paasche defense burden estimate based on the agency's best residual calculation.

Column 4: The CIA's Paasche defense burden estimates extrapolated from its 1960 base year figure.

Column 5: The author's quality adjusted estimate assuming a 12.9 percent real annual rate of growth.

Column 6: The official, published Soviet defense budget as a share of GNP in current prices.

Column 7: U.S. defense expenditures as a share of GNP. The peak U.S. burden during the sixties occurred in 1968 when it reached 8.5 percent of GNP.

Note: The Soviet burden ratios presented above measure defense as a share of GNP, valued at factor cost. Alternative ratios can also be calculated using a GNP series derived from the CIA's Soviet GNP estimate for 1970 valued at established prices. These ratios will be 10.7 percent lower than the factor cost ratios. Other adjustments discussed in appendix 5 could reduce the defense burden valued at established prices by 2.8 percent (i.e. B/1.028).

Burden estimates of these magnitudes were given credence as late as 1976 and are still believed in some quarters today despite their manifest incongruity with the scale of Soviet defense programs and the long-term pattern of Soviet military expenditure. Table 14.3, which juxtaposes the author's burden statistics for the sixties and seventies with Abram Bergson's calculations for the years 1937–55, reveals that the social costs of defense throughout the entire 1937–77 period have never fallen below 10 percent of the Soviet gross national product. After reaching a wartime high of 39.8 percent in 1944, the defense burden did return to the prewar level where it remained during the post-Stalin consolidation period. However, this interlude did not last much beyond the precarious years following Khrushchev's famous secret speech delivered to the 20th Party Congress in 1956 denouncing the crimes of the Stalin era. By 1960, Soviet military spending reverted to its historical pattern. Although the hopes spawned by Khrushchev's doctrine of peaceful coexistence, transmuted later into the doctrine of detente, may have persuaded the agency that the declining trend in the Soviet defense burden exhibited both by its direct cost estimates and official Soviet budgetary statistics was reasonable, in the final analysis it is now clear that this interpretation was premised on faulty calculation.

FIGURE 14.2
Soviet and American Defense Burden Trends, 1960–77

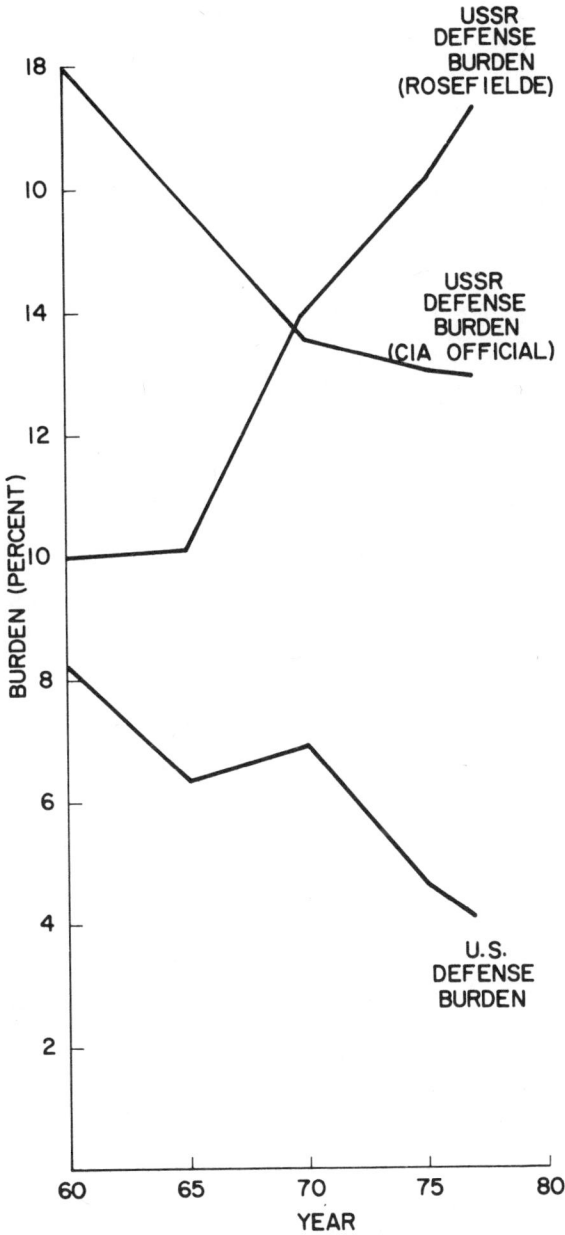

TABLE 14.3
The Soviet Defense Burden, 1937–77

	Bergson	Rosefielde
1937	10.5	
1940	17.3	
1944	39.8	
1950	10.9	
1955	10.7	
1960		10
1970		14
1975		15.3
1977		16.5

Sources: Abram Bergson, *The Real National Income of Soviet Russia Since 1928*, Harvard University Press, Cambridge, 1963, p. 237. Table 14.2, column 5. Bergson's estimates are valued at ruble factor cost for diverse years.

Notes

1. See the sources listed in Table 14.1.
2. U.S. procurement defined on the same basis as Soviet procurement in 1977 (in 1978 prices)was 20.9 billion dollars. See Table 13.2, column 7. American GNP in 1977 in 1978 prices was 2.027 trillion dollars, implying a procurement burden of 1 percent. The ratio of the CIA's best direct cost burden estimate to the American estimate is 4.8/1.
3. See Abraham Becker (1979), pp. 360–61.
4. The Soviet definition of defense expenditures according to agency calculations is roughly 12 percent larger than the figure based on U.S. definitions. See CIA, *Estimated Soviet Defense Spending in Rubles, 1970–1975*, SR-76-10121U, May 1976, pp. 1–2.
5. American GNP in 1977 valued in 1979 prices was 2.274 trillion dollars. American defense expenditures (U.S. definition) were 95 billion dollars, implying a burden of 4.2 percent. If Soviet expenditures are recalculated on an American definitional basis, the disparity reported in the text declines to 180 percent (11.9 ÷ 4.2). See *Soviet and U.S. Defense Activities, 1970–1979: A Dollar Cost Comparison*. SR80–10005, 1980, p. 4.
6. Compare entries in Table 14.2, column 5, and Table 14.3, column 1.
7. In December 1981 the agency acknowledged that its residual method burden estimated for 1980 corresponds closely with Lee's: 20 percent measured at established ruble prices.

CHAPTER 15

The Widening Procurement Gap

The misreading of Soviet national priorities fostered by the agency's flawed calculations is not restricted to its assessment of the past. During the eighties, despite a worsening economic outlook, the CIA forecasts that real Soviet military spending will increase 4–5 percent per annum measured in rubles and 3–4 percent per annum calculated in dollars, more or less in line with its understanding of the long-term trend.[1] Taken at face value, this scenario suggests that the Soviets will not endeavor to capitalize on the advantage they gained during the seventies by increasing their rate of arms accumulation above 3–4 percent per annum (measured in dollars). It also implies that the United States will not encounter any serious difficulties keeping pace with the Soviets, and reversing the asymmetries that arose during the preceding decade. If the agency's fixed vintage parametric cost estimates were correct, and its trend evaluation on target, simple arithmetic indicates that the United States could offset the Soviet military buildup by increasing its real procurement expenditures 4–6 percent per annum. Such a rate of expenditure growth while constituting a decisive break with the negative growth trend of the recent past would not be especially onerous, and even if applied to all defense spending would cause only a modest rise in the economic burden of defense spread out comfortably over the decade.

This comparatively roseate outlook is inconsistent with the facts, however. Real Soviet procurement did not grow 3–4 percent during the seventies, it increased at a double digit rate. The continuation of this trend in the eighties, therefore does not imply that the Soviets will be content to gradually augment their recent gains as the agency infers, but means that the Soviets are driving to achieve a substantial degree of military superiority over the United States. Procurement estimates adjusted for intervintage technological progress reveal this objective is not frivolous. The gap between Soviet and American procurement is already very large, 218 percent in 1979 alone, and cannot be easily rectified without entailing an extraordinary increase in the American economic burden of defense. If the United States chooses it can technically maintain cumulative arms parity with the Soviets in the eighties, but contrary to the agency's perception this objective cannot be accomplished without significant national sacrifice.

This assertion is supported by the data presented in Table 15.1. The first two columns derived from the CIA's 1979 dollar estimate of Soviet procurement adjusted for intervintage technological progress, project Soviet arms production forward from 1980 to 1990 assuming alternatively that procurement is fixed at the present level, or continues growing at 10.6 percent per annum as it did in the seventies. Columns 3 and 4 provide analogous estimates for the United States, except that the rate of growth envisaged in 1980 by Congress, 4 percent per annum, is substituted for the -2.8 percent rate experienced from 1970 to 1979.

Cumulative estimates for each series subject to the assumptions discussed in chapter 12 are reported in the appropriate columns. They soberingly reveal that if the policies of the recent past, or those currently under consideration, are adhered to new additions to the Soviet arsenal during the eighties will exceed those of the United States by a margin between 167 and 517 percent. In absolute terms, the Soviets will spend between 553 billion and 1.345 trillion dollars more than the United States.

These are enormous sums. Should the United States allow the Soviets to achieve the advantage indicated, the Soviets could conceivably attain a dangerous degree of military superiority over the United States and its allies. Forestalling such a destabilizing arms imbalance, however, may be very costly. Even assuming the best plausible case in which the level of Soviet procurement expenditures remain unchanged, American weapons outlays would have to increase just over 20 percent annually from 1980 to 1990 to achieve cumulative parity. On a less optimistic set of assumptions, extrapolating Soviet arms growth at the rates observed in the seventies, American weapons outlays would have to increase 29 percent annually. Such a rate of growth implies that real American procurement expenditures in 1990 would be 16 times greater than they were in 1979.

The levels of economic burden entailed by the rates of procurement growth are shown in Table 15.2, columns 5 and 6. Assuming that American GNP grows 3.4 percent annually in the eighties, the rate observed from 1947 to 1979, and that nonprocurement defense expenditures are restrained to the 4 percent figure envisaged by Congress, the

TABLE 15.1

Projected U.S. and Soviet Defense Procurement Expenditures, 1980–90
(Billions of 1978 Dollars)

	Soviet		U.S.	
	(1)	**(2)**	**(3)**	**(4)**
1980	75.8	83.8	23.6	24.5
1981	75.8	92.7	23.6	25.5
1982	75.8	102.5	23.6	26.5
1983	75.8	113.4	23.6	27.6
1984	75.8	125.4	23.6	28.8
1985	75.8	138.7	23.6	29.9
1986	75.8	153.4	23.6	31.1
1987	75.8	169.7	23.6	32.3
1988	75.8	187.7	23.6	33.6
1989	75.8	207.6	23.6	35.0
1990	75.8	229.6	23.6	36.4
1980–90	883.8	1604.5	259.6	331.2
Compound annual rate of growth 1980–90	0	10.6	0	4

Sources: Columns 1 and 2 are derived from Table 13.2, column 5. Columns 3 and 4 are derived from Table 13.2, column 7.
The alternative rates of growth used to project these series are shown in the table. The 10.6 percent rate of Soviet procurement growth represents the observed rate reported by the author. The zero rates are hypothesized, while the 4 percent rate corresponds with 1980 Congressional projections.

U.S. burden of defense in 1990 will rise to a level between 9.1 and 15.9 percent. These magnitudes are double and treble those prevailing today or anticipated at the end of the decade (Table 15.3, column 4).

The social cost of such an augmented burden will be very severe. Table 15.3, columns 7 and 9 reveal that the cumulative loss in foregone social expenditures caused by the diversion of resources to defense, assuming that the federal budget grows proportionally with GNP, will be between 607.1 billion and 1.322 trillion dollars, 12 to 26 times the sacrifice currently foreseen (Table 15.3, column 6). On the most favorable set of assumptions real social expenditures in 1990 will be nearly the same as 1980; on less favorable premises they may be more than 50 percent below current levels, declining from 374 billion to 176.8 billion dollars measured in constant 1978 prices.

TABLE 15.2
Projected U.S. Defense Expenditures 1980–90 (Constant 1978 Dollars) and the Implied Burden of Defense (Percent)

	Defense Expenditures			Defense Burden		
	(1)	(2)	(3)	(4)	(5)	(6)
1980	103.5	107.1	109.3	4.6	4.8	4.3
1981	107.6	115.9	121.3	4.6	5.0	5.2
1982	111.9	125.8	135.8	4.7	5.2	5.6
1983	116.4	137.2	153.8	4.7	5.5	6.2
1984	121.1	150.1	176	4.7	5.8	6.9
1985	125.9	165.1	203.7	4.7	6.2	7.7
1986	130.9	182.5	238.7	4.8	6.6	8.7
1987	136.2	202.7	282.6	4.8	7.1	9.9
1988	141.6	226.1	338.2	4.8	7.7	11.5
1989	147.3	253.7	408.9	4.8	8.3	13.5
1990	153.2	285.8	493.7	4.9	9.1	15.9

Sources: Table 13.2; column 7 and the *Survey of Current Business*, Vol. 60, No. 1, January 1980, and Vol. 66, No. 5, May 1980.

Method:

Column 1: Defense expenditures are projected at 4 percent per annum in accordance with 1980 Congressional budgetary allocations.

Column 2: Nonprocurement is extrapolated at 4 percent per annum rate. Procurement is projected 19.6 per annum, the rate required to achieve cumulative parity, assuming no growth in the present level of Soviet procurement expenditures.

Column 3: Same as column 2, except Soviet procurement is assumed to grow 10.6 percent annually requiring a U.S. rate of procurement growth of 28.8 per annum.

Column 4: The defense burden associated with column 1. GNP is extrapolated at 3.4 percent annually, the rate prevailing 1947–79.

Column 5: Same as 4, except column 2 is used in the numerator.

Column 6: Same as 4, except column 3 is used in the numerator.

While it would be a great exaggeration to suggest that the United States could not meet the challenge indicated by these simple extrapolations, if it chose to, it would be equally wrong to suppose that the burden would be borne with equanimity. Meeting the burgeoning Soviet military challenge could prove more difficult than appraising its true dimensions, even if the CIA is correct in forecasting a drastic slowdown in the rate of aggregate Soviet economic growth during the eighties. Whether GNP grows 1–3 percent annually as the agency has recently conjectured,[2] at the 5.5 percent rate that officially prevailed from 1970 to 1978, or somewhere in between, the Soviets should easily be able to devote enough resources to procurement to impose a double digit burden of defense on the United States, assuming the United States chooses to prevent any further decline in its relative military power.

TABLE 15.3
The Social Cost of Defense, 1980–90
(Constant 1978 Dollars)

						Foregone Social Expenditures		
	(1)	(2)	(3)	(4)	(5)	(6)	(7)	(8)
1980	483.5	380	376.4	374	380.7	.7	4.3	6.7
1981	500	392.4	384.1	378.7	393.6	1.2	9.5	14.9
1982	517	405.1	391.2	381.2	407	1.9	15.8	25.8
1983	534.6	418.2	397.4	380.8	420.8	2.6	23.4	40
1984	552.7	431.6	402.6	376.7	435.1	3.5	32.5	58.4
1985	571.5	445.6	406.4	367.8	450	4.4	43.6	82.2
1986	590.9	460	408.4	352.2	465.2	5.2	50.8	113
1987	611.1	474.5	408.4	328.5	481.1	6.6	72.7	152.6
1988	631.8	490.2	405.7	293.6	497.4	7.2	91.7	203.8
1989	653.3	506	399.6	244.4	514.3	8.3	114.7	269.9
1990	675.5	522.3	389.7	176.8	531.8	9.5	142.1	355
Cumulative Undiscounted Social Cost of Defense						51.1	607.1	1322.3

Source: Table 15.2
Method:
Column 1: U.S. government expenditures in constant 1978 prices extrapolated to 1990 at the 1947–79 annual rate of aggregate growth, 3.4 percent.
Column 2: Funds available for social expenditures assuming a 4 percent annual rate of defense expenditure growth.
Column 3: Funds available for social expenditures assuming annual procurement growth of 19.6 percent and nonprocurement defense spending of 4 percent.
Column 4: Funds available for social expenditures assuming annual procurement growth of 28.8 percent and nonprocurement defense spending of 4 percent.
Column 5: Projected social expenditures assuming 3.4 percent annual rate of growth.
Columns 6–8: Foregone social expenditures after allowance for the increase in federal resources attributable to the growth of GNP at a rate of 3.4 percent per annum. Columns 6–8 are calculated by subtracting social expenditures reduced by increased defense outlays (columns 2–4) from forecasted unreduced social spending (column 5).

Notes

1. *Estimated Soviet Defense Spending: Trends and Prospects, 1978,* pp. ii–iii, 9–11. See also *Allocation of Resources in the Soviet Union and China—1979,* JEC, June 26, 1979, pp. 16–24.
2. *Allocations of Resources in the Soviet Union and China—1979,* p. 16. According to Stanfield Turner, former director of the CIA, "We now expect Soviet GNP to grow at somewhat less than 3 percent annually over the next few years (down from our earlier estimate of about 4 percent) and then fall gradually. If oil production declines to 10 mb/d by 1985, growth in GNP would be perhaps 2% in the mid-1980s. On the other hand, a sharper fall in oil production, say to 2 mb/d in 1985 could well push growth in GNP to

less than 1 percent in the mid 1980s." The growth rate forecast in *Estimated Soviet Defense Spending: Trends and Prospects, 1978*, p. 9 was 3–3.5 percent per annum. The figure 2 mb/d is almost certainly a misprint. Before its recent volte-face the agency's lower bound estimate of Soviet oil production was 6–8 mb/d. The current official Soviet production rate (October 1981) is in excess of 12.5 mb/d.

Part IV

ARMS SUPERIORITY

CHAPTER 16

Dollar Estimates, Ordinality, and the Potential Military Utility of Soviet Arms

It is tempting to directly infer from the evidence compiled in chapters 13–15 that the Soviets have achieved arms superiority by assuming that a dollar's worth of "Sovietized" American equipment, adjusted for intervintage technological progress, has the same potential military utility as a dollar's worth of American equipment. Although this assumption is entirely reasonable, the required correspondence is not necessarily implied by theory or construction. Therefore, before concluding that the Soviets have indeed achieved arms superiority over the United States in the late 1970s, it needs to be shown that direct dollar cost estimates, "Sovietized" and adjusted for intervintage technological progress, are reliable ordinal indicators of comparative military utility. A strong case for this proposition can be formally elaborated as follows with the aid of modern economic utility theory.

The potential military utility of an average dollar's worth of procurement, issues of doctrine, combat scenario, élan aside, is determined by the potential military utility of diverse weapons weighted by their procurement shares. This relationship can be expressed algebraically as the linear sum of a series of n utility values, u_i, and their corresponding procurement shares λ_i,

1. $$U = \lambda_1 u_1 + \lambda_2 u_2 \ldots, + \lambda_n u_n$$

where the utility of each weapon is a function of its performance characteristics:

2. $$u_i = \phi_i(v_1, v_2, \ldots, v_m).$$

Utility functions of the form ϕ generally are not unique.[1] Evaluating the potential combat utility of a vector of performance characteristics depends on sundry subjective and objective criteria. Different weapons experts will usually assign different utility values to the same bundle of performance characteristics and disagree about the relative utility of individual weapons. As a consequence, while it is broadly recognized that potential military utility indicators can be calculated, and that they are positive functions of performance capability, unambiguous best indicators of potential military utility cannot be found.

This impediment is not fatal, however. Meaningful statements about potential military utility can be made by relaxing the implicit assumption of cardinality. This is easily accomplished by rewriting equations 1 and 2, not as absolute utility measures, but as ordinal indicators where the judgment of individual experts determine the ordinal utility rank accorded to each weapon:

3.
$$W_i^j = \lambda_1 w_1^j + \lambda_2 w_2^j, \ldots + \lambda_n w_n^j$$

and

4.
$$w_i^j = \phi_i^j(\alpha_1, \alpha_2, \ldots, \alpha_m)$$

Indicators of the form W^j provide numerical assessments of the potential military utility of a dollar's worth of procurement, given the subjective and objective criteria applied by individual weapons analysts in determining the functions ϕ_i^j.

The utility value w_i of any weapon, for the entire class of utility estimates w_i^j will be a positive function of its corresponding dollar value,

5.
$$w_i^j = \theta(p_i \, q_i)$$

if the performance characteristics which determine utility are positive, monotonic ordinal functions of production cost:

6.
$$\alpha_i = g(\sum_{h=1}^{s} p_h \, q_h)$$

so that

7.
$$w_i^j = G[\phi_i^j(\alpha_1, \alpha_2, \ldots, \alpha_m)]$$

where G is a function transforming performance characteristics into dollar values. This assumption is not particularly stringent since it merely implies that the cost of better quality goods is greater than the cost of lower quality goods, but it has a powerful implication. If the price of the weapons q_i in arsenal A exceeds the price of the same weapons in arsenal B:

8. $$p_i^A > p_i^B \text{ because } \frac{G^A(\alpha_1, \alpha_2, \ldots, \alpha_s) >}{G^B(\alpha_1, \alpha_2, \ldots, \alpha_m),}$$

then the potential military utility of the weapons (q_i) in arsenal A will unambiguously exceed the potential military utility of the same weapons in B:

9. $$w_i^{jA} > w_i^{jB}$$

regardless of the exact ordinal value assigned to weapon q_i by the jth weapons expert. Since this correspondence will hold for all weapons systems satisfying equation 8, it follows directly that if the number of weapons in each class q_i in arsenal A exceeds those in arsenal B:

10. $$p_1^A q_1^A + p_2^A q_2^A \ldots + p_k^A q_k^A > p_1^B q_1^B + p_2^B q_2^B \ldots + p_k^B q_k^B$$

then the aggregate utility of arsenal A will exceed the aggregate utility of arsenal B for these classes of arms:

11. $$\sum_{i=1}^{k} w_i^{jA} > \sum_{i=1}^{k} w_i^{jB}.$$

If in any binary comparison of potential military utility it should turn out that the k weapon systems in the class q_i exhaust the entire set of weapons in both arsenals, then the potential military utility of arsenal A will unequivocally exceed arsenal B. However, in most binary comparisons although equations 10 and 11 may hold for weapons systems 1, . . . ,k, the reverse relationship may apply for weapons $k+1$, . . . ,n:

12. $$\sum_{i=k+1}^{n} p_i^B q_i^B > \sum_{i=k+1}^{n} p_i^A q_i^A$$

and

13. $$\sum_{i=k+1}^{n} w_i^{jB} > \sum_{i=k+1}^{n} w_i^{jA}$$

To obtain a class of ordinal values W^j which establishes for all j experts that the potential military utility of a dollar's worth of weapons 1, . . . ,n, in arsenal A (or the total utility of that arsenal) exceeds the utility of arsenal B, it must be assumed that the production cost of all weapons corresponds with the ordinal utility rank assigned by all j experts:

14. $w_1^j > w_2^j \ldots > w_n^j = \psi(p_1q_1) > \psi(p_2q_2) \ldots > \psi(p_nq_n).$

If the ordinal transitivity ordering shown in equation 14 holds, then the judgment:

15. $W^{jA} > W^{jB}$

will follow directly from the dollar relationship:

16. $\displaystyle\sum_{i=1}^{n} p_i \, q_i^A > \sum_{i=1}^{n} p_i \, q_i^B$ (for homogeneously defined q_i: $q_i^A = q_i^B$).

The assumption that the production cost of all weapons corresponds with the ordinal utility rank assigned by all j experts for the arsenal of a specific country may not be too wide of the mark if production costs are market-determined and the composition of the arsenal reflects the priorities of the military leadership. A similar inference may be drawn where the composition of the arsenals of two countries are broadly similar. However, in instances where force structures are noticeably dissimilar, the ordinal correspondence between production cost and utilities may be weak. The assertion that dollar values provide a workable indicator of potential military utility in such cases may therefore be extremely tenuous.

   This implies that while dollar values may be good ordinal indicators of potential military utility, they may not always be so. More specifically, dollar values will be reliable ordinal indicators of potential utility for the entire class of j expert appraisals preserving inequalities 15 and 16 if, and only if:

A. the production cost of weapons in the set $k+1, \ldots, n$ does not understate utilities $u_{k+1} \ldots, u_n$ drastically enough to cause aggregate potential military utility to be inversely related to production cost; that is, if

17. $\displaystyle\sum_{i=1}^{k} p_i \, q_i^A - p_i \, q_i^B - \sum_{i=k+1}^{n} p_i \, q_i^B - p_i \, q_i^A > 0$

does not imply

18. $$\sum_{i=1}^{k} w_i^{jA} - w_i^{jB} - \sum_{i=k+1}^{n} w_i^{jB} - w_i^{jA} < 0$$

B. dollar prices do not systematically overstate the quality of weapons set A, that is,

19. $$G^A[\phi_i^j(\alpha_1, \alpha_2, \ldots, \alpha_m)] \not\prec G^B[\phi_i^j(\alpha_1, \alpha_2, \ldots, \alpha_m)] = p_i$$

Proponents of the view that dollar estimates of Soviet procurement greatly overstate the potential military utility of the Soviet arsenal must therefore believe that direct dollar cost estimates violate either condition A or B. The evidence in favor of the first proposition is not especially compelling. As was demonstrated in chapter 13, the dollar value of Soviet procurement adjusted for intervintage technological progress exceeds that of the United States by a wide margin in every major weapons category: strategic forces, intercontinental attack, general purpose forces, land forces, tactical air forces, and naval forces. This suggests that the set $k+1, \ldots, n$ is null, and that the potential military superiority of Soviet weapons is virtually assured on the weak ordinal transitivity conditions embodied in equations 10 and 11. Of course, the set $k+1, \ldots, n$ is not really null. A finer breakdown reveals that the cumulative value of some American weapons systems such as helicopters and aircraft carriers exceeds those of the Soviet Union. This class of weapons is relatively small, however.[2] The likelihood that their utility is so disproportionally great that it reverses the direction of advantage shown by the dollar indicator cannot be very high.

The contention that the potential military utility of Soviet weapons does not exceed the utility of American arms for all practical purposes therefore rests on the premise that dollar estimates overstate the real dollar value of Soviet weapons. This proposition ordinarily takes two forms. First, it is deduced from index number theory that dollar estimates overstate the value of Soviet weapons. Second, it is surmised that the adjustments made by the Central Intelligence Agency for the size, weight, habitability, and performance characteristics of Soviet weapons do not take their inferior quality adequately into account.

Strictly speaking, the first argument is irrelevant. Dollar estimates may well overstate the ruble factor cost of producing Soviet arms (although as we have already seen in chapter 6 even this proposition is dubitable), but this disparity in no way indicates that the potential military utility of a dollar's worth of Soviet equipment computed with the direct cost method is incommensurate with a dollar's worth of U.S. arms. Nonetheless, Franklyn Holzman has recently argued that comparisons of Soviet and American weapons in dollars and rubles could cause the paradoxical result that the value of Soviet weapons exceeded those of the United States in dollars;

20.
$$\sum_{i=1}^{n} p_i \, q_i^S > \sum_{i=1}^{n} p_i \, q_i^A$$

but not in rubles;[3]

21.
$$\sum_{i=1}^{n} r_i \, q_i^A > \sum_{i=1}^{n} r_i \, q_i^S.[3]$$

Such an outcome would not necessarily violate equation 10, but it would indicate that some or all of the ordinal transitivity assumptions underlying inequalities 15 and 16 were invalid.

The existence of a Holzman paradox with the assumption that utilities are ordinally proportional to production costs leads to the conclusion that the potential military utility of Soviet weapons is simultaneously higher and lower than that of the United States. This can be tested by revaluing American arms outlays in rubles, which is accomplished by multiplying annual American procurement in constant dollars by the CIA's ruble-dollar ratios:

22.
$$r_t \, q_t^A = \sum_{i=1}^{n} p_{it} \, q_{it}^A \, (r_{it}/p_{it}),$$

an operation producing values that are directly comparable with the CIA's ruble estimates of Soviet procurement. The agency itself employs this procedure to calculate the ruble value of American procurement, but its estimates, and the weapon-specific ruble-dollar ratios r_{it}/p_{it} used to form them are classified.[4]

The classified series can be closely approximated by performing the same operation specified in equation 22,

23.
$$r_t \, q_t^A = p_t \, q_t^A \, (r_t/p_t)$$

with the CIA's implicit aggregate ruble-dollar procurement ratio r_t/p_t:

24.
$$\frac{r_t}{p_t} = \frac{\sum_{i=1}^{n} r_{it} \, q_{it}^S}{\sum_{i=1}^{n} p_{it} \, q_{it}^S}$$

where q_{it}^S represents Soviet procurement quantity weights. Estimates derived from equation 23 will differ from equation 22 only to the extent that the aggregate ruble-dollar ratio employing Soviet weights diverges from the aggregate ratio using American weights:

25.
$$D = \frac{r_t^A}{p_t^A} \Big/ \frac{r_t^S}{p_t^S} \geq 1.$$

It is impossible to ascertain a priori just how important this effect might be, but related evidence suggests that it is not very great. Ruble-dollar ratios for all machine-building and metalworking computed by Treml and Gallik using Soviet and American quantity weights were respectively .50 and .54 in 1960, and .572 and .666 in 1963.[5]

American procurement outlays valued in rubles, computed in accordance with equation 23 and employing the CIA's aggregate implicit ruble-dollar ratios, are reported in Table 16.1. Subject to the limitations stipulated in equation 24, they shed considerable light on Holzman's hypothesis that Soviet weapons superiority may be the fictitious consequence of dollar valuation.[6] Two alternative sets of ruble estimates are provided. The first, presented in column 3, employs the CIA's 1960 implicit aggregate ruble-dollar procurement ratio, .39, adjusted for U.S. inflation (see Table 13.2n). This series shows American procurement rising from 6.2 billion rubles in 1960 to a peak of 9.5 billion rubles in 1968, falling thereafter to 5.2 billion rubles in 1979. The second series listed in column 4 is derived with the agency's implicit aggregate ruble-dollar ratio for 1970, .93.[7] It displays the same pattern as the first set of estimates, but begins and ends at a much higher absolute ruble value level, 14.7 and 12.5 billion rubles respectively. Compared with the CIA's and the author's ruble estimates of Soviet procurement presented in Table 16.1, columns 1 and 2, both U.S. series tell a now familiar story. Figure 16.1 indicates that Soviet procurement, adjusted for intervintage technological progress, exceeds American ruble expenditures as early as 1964 using the prerevision ruble-dollar parity (corrected for inflation), and surpasses it by 1970, using the postrevision parity. Moreover, Soviet procurement expenditures exceed both U.S. ruble series throughout the seventies, pointedly falsifying Holzman's hypothesis.

TABLE 16.1
Soviet and American Military Procurement, 1960–79
(Billions of 1970 Rubles)

	Soviet		American	
	CIA (1)	Rosefielde (2)	Prerevision (3)	Postrevision (4)
1960	5.5	5.5	6.2	14.7
1961	5.6	6.2	6.4	15.2
1962	5.6	7	7.4	17.4
1963	5.7	7.9	8.1	19.2
1964	5.8	8.9	7.2	10.9
1965	5.8	10.1	5.3	12.5
1966	5.8	11.4	6.8	16.3
1967	5.7	12.9	8.5	20.5
1968	5.6	14.5	9.5	22.7
1969	5.6	16.4	8.9	21.1
1970	17	18.5	7.3	17.3
1971	17.7	20.9	6.2	14.7
1972	18.4	23.6	5.4	12.9
1973	19.1	26.6	5.0	12
1974	19.9	30.1	4.7	11.1
1975	20.7	33.9	4.4	10.6
1976	21.5	38.3	4.3	10.1
1977	22.4	43.3	4.7	11.1
1978	23.3	48.8	4.8	11.3
1979	24.2	55.2	5.2	12.5

Sources:
Column 1: Values for 1960–69 are taken from Table 13.1, column 1. They are adjusted by assuming that the CIA's series 1960–65 grew at 1.2 percent per annum; then declined at the same rate 1965–69 as suggested by Donald Swain's letter August 9, 1979. Values for 1970–79 are taken from Table 13.1, column 2. The data for the sixties are based on early vintage cost estimating relationships. Estimates for the seventies are derived from 1970 fixed vintage parametric cost estimating relationships converted to rubles with diverse ruble-dollar ratios.
Column 2: Table 13.1, column 6.
Column 3: Underlying values 1960–69 are official U.S. DOD outlays in constant 1970 prices provided by Colonel USAF Frederick Giessler, Assistant Director, OSD/NET Assessment, adjusted to a calendar basis to conform with the CIA outlay series. Underlying values 1970–79 are CIA statistics from Table 13.2, deflated to a 1970 price base with the DOD procurement deflator. The ruble series 1960–79 is computed by multiplying every element of the dollar series by the ruble-dollar ratio for 1960 implied by the agency's official Paasche dollar series, adjusted for U.S. inflation, .39. See Table 13.2n, column 6.
Column 4: Same as column 3 except the ex-post 1970 ruble dollar ratio .93 is used to transform the dollar values. See Table 13.2n, column 6.

FIGURE 16.1
Soviet and American Military Procurement, 1960–79 (Valued in 1970
Rubles: Adjusted for Intervintage Technological Progress)

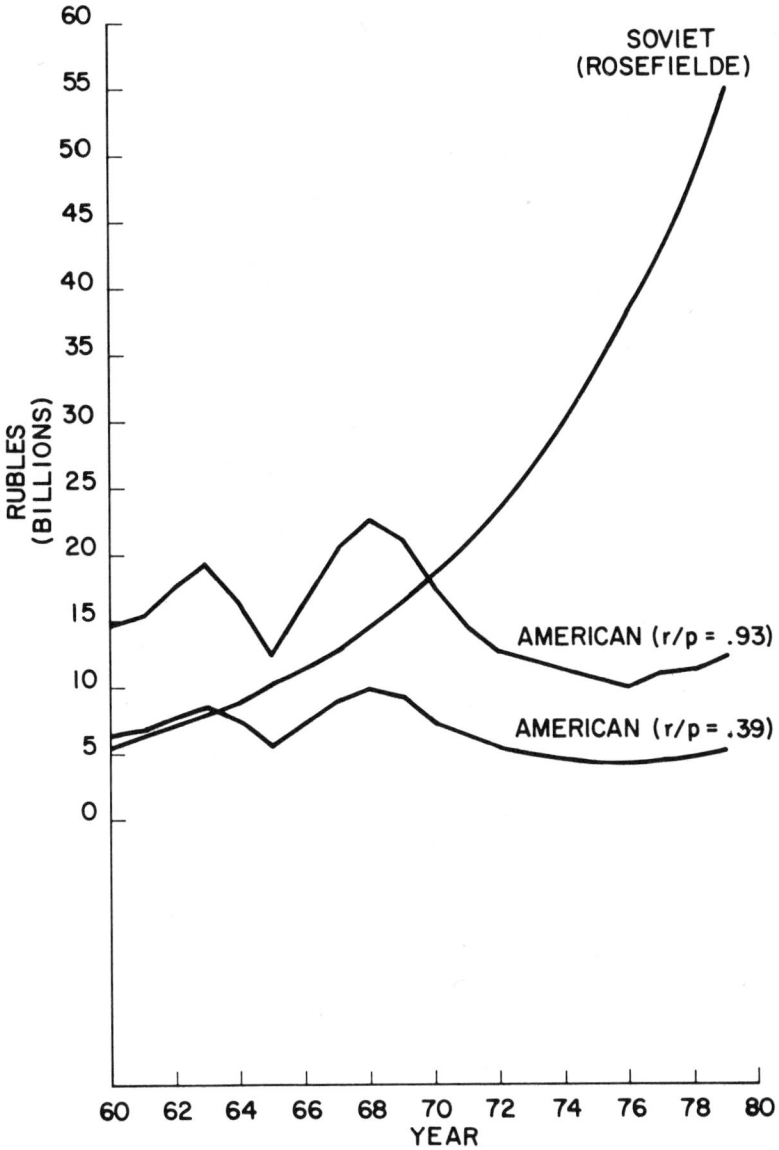

FIGURE 16.2
Soviet and American Military Procurement, 1960–79 (Valued in 1970
Rubles)

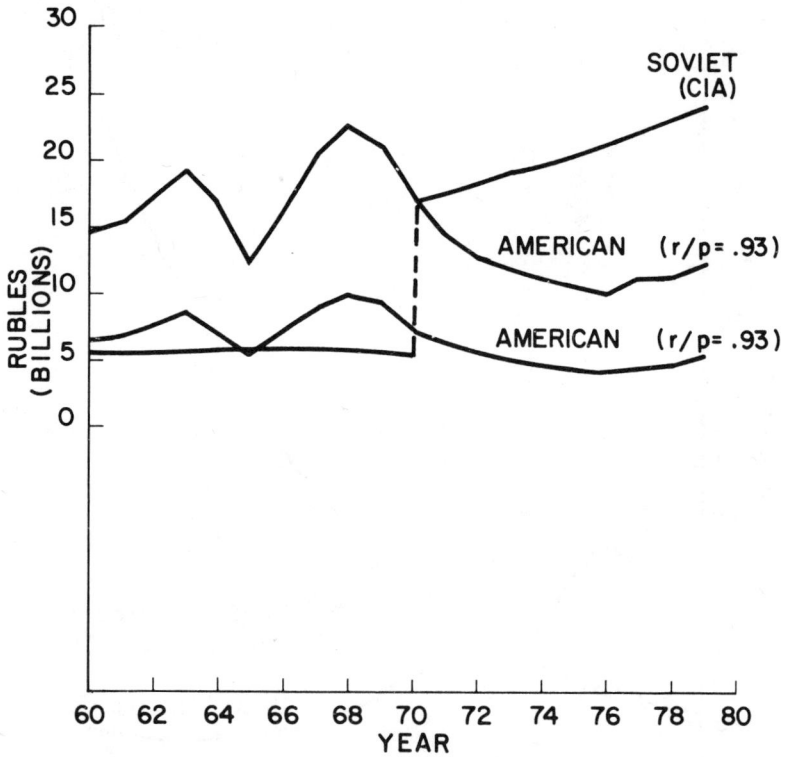

This conclusion is reinforced in Table 16.1 and Figure 16.2 which demonstrate that even if no account is taken of intervintage technological progress, the agency's ruble estimates of Soviet procurement exceed its ruble estimates of American procurement for most of the seventies. It follows directly therefore that unless the CIA's aggregate ruble-dollar procurement ratio for 1970—calculated from a large number of component ratios (see appendix 4) and confirmed by the new information— is substantially understated, the potential military utility of Soviet weapons exceeds that of the United States measured both in dollars and rubles. (Cf. Tables 13.10–13.11 and figures 13.12–13.13.)

The second form of the proposition that dollar cost estimates overstate the real dollar value of Soviet weapons because the qualitative adjustments made by the CIA for the size, weight, habitability, and performance characteristics of Soviet arms are inadequate, likewise, cannot be sustained. As has already been demonstrated in chapter 4, the agency's fixed vintage parametric costing methodology substantially understates the real value of American weapons produced after 1970,

26. $$\hat{p}_i^{70} \, q_i^{80} < p_i^{70} \, q_i^{80}$$

where $\hat{p}_i^{70}$ are the CIA's fixed vintage direct dollar cost price estimates for 1970 and p_i^{70} are the actual prices which reflect the cost of intervintage qualitative progress. This implies ceteris paribus, that the agency's dollar estimates of Soviet weapons derived from the same fixed vintage parametric costing relationships understate the true, quality-adjusted value of Soviet procurement:

27. $$\hat{p}_i \, q_i^S < p_i \, q_i^S,$$

and suggests further that the real value of any weapon q_i in the Soviet arsenal measured with the agency's prices $\hat{p}_i$ will be understated compared with the same weapon in the U.S. arsenal measured in constant ex-post prices, p_i:

28. $$\hat{p}_i \, q_i^S < p_i q_i^A$$

For the direction of the inequality in equation 28 to be reversed, the adjustments made by the CIA, "Sovietizing" its fixed vintage parametric estimates of American weapons into their Soviet equivalents, must systematically overstate the value of Soviet procurement. The "Sovietizing" procedures employed by the agency make this outcome very unlikely, however. Gross differences in size, weight, habitability, structural specifications, and propulsion systems are readily taken in account by the CIA's fixed vintage costing equations. Less visible attributes such as the quantity of subsystems and ordnance are estimated conservatively, and are sharply discounted for their presumed qualitative inferiority.[8] As a consequence, the agency's estimates account reasonably well for some differences between Soviet and American equipment and conservatively discount others.

These adjustments appear to be excessive from the standpoint of potential military utility. According to a comprehensive, six-volume DIA study on comparative Soviet-American weapon quality, it was concluded that while the potential combat performance and technology of most Soviet weapons were still marginally inferior to the United States, utility per dollar was far higher because the Soviets sacrificed comfort for fire power, and were exceedingly cost efficient in optimizing their technological options.[9] It thus appears that the agency's fixed vintage dollar cost estimates of Soviet procurement are unlikely to overstate quality in the base year and may well understate potential military utility. Likewise, my own dollar estimates which are derived directly from the agency's should not overstate the dollar value of Soviet procurement, and may well understate potential military utility, if my estimates for intervintage technological progress are not wide of the mark.

These inferences not only satisfy condition B, they obviate the last serious objection that can be raised against the proposition that my dollar estimates of Soviet procurement are valid ordinal indicators of the relative potential military utility of Soviet and American weapons. It can of course still be argued that potential military utility is not the same thing as actual military utility. In any given combat scenario, a variety of factors such as doctrine, skill, élan, command control, and locale might allow U.S. forces to triumph over Soviets, even though the potential military utility of Soviet weapons exceeded that of the U.S. If a cogent case can be made for supposing that American skill, élan, doctrine, command control, and logistic capabilities offset the superior potential military utility of Soviet weapons, then the supposition that dollar estimates are valid indicators of both potential and actual military utility may ultimately have to be rejected. Until such a demonstration is made, it needs to be clearly understood that dollar cost estimates of Soviet procurement are not meaningless indicators of comparative Soviet and American military potential. Given reasonable and general assumptions about the relationship between value measures and utility, the dollar series calculated in this volume and summarized in Table 16.2 and Figures 16.3–4 indicate that the potential military utility of Soviet arms is superior to that of the United States.[10]

TABLE 16.2
Soviet and American Military Procurement, 1960–79
(Billions of 1978 Dollars)

		Soviet			American
		CIA		Rosefielde	
	(1)	(2)	(3)	(4)	(5)
1960	13.3	23.4	23.4	13.3	27.8
1961	13.5	24	23.9	14.5	28.7
1962	13.6	24.6	24.3	15.7	33.0
1963	13.8	25.3	24.8	17.1	36.2
1964	13.9	26	25.3	18.6	29.7
1965	14.1	26.7	25.8	20.2	23.6
1966	13.9	27.5	25.3	21.9	30.8
1967	13.8	28.2	24.8	23.8	38.6
1968	13.6	29	24.3	25.9	42.8
1969	13.5	30	23.9	28.2	40.1
1970		30.6		30.6	32.7
1971		31.4		34.1	27.7
1972		31.6		37.2	24.5
1973		34.5		43.3	22.7
1974		35.5		47.8	20.9
1975		36.4		52.5	20
1976		37.3		57.5	19.1
1977		37.7		62.3	20.9
1978		38.6		68.1	21.4
1979		41		75.8	23.6

Sources:

Column 1: Table 13.2, column 3. The estimates reported here have been adjusted by assuming that the CIA's series 1960–65 grew at 1.2 percent per annum; then declined at the same rate 1965–69 as suggested by Donald Swain's letter August 9, 1979.

Column 2: Table 13.2, column 2.

Column 3: The growth pattern displayed in column 2 is superimposed on the agency's Paasche 1960 estimate 23.4 billion dollars. This value also can be interpreted as the Laspeyres base if the ruble-dollar ratio in 1960 used by the agency was .51. See chapter 13, note 6.

Column 4: Table 13.2, column 5.

Column 5: Values 1960–69 are official U.S. DOD procurement outlays in constant prices provided by Colonel USAF Frederick Giessler, Assistant Director, OSD/Net Assessment, adjusted to a calendar year basis to conform with the CIA outlays series. Values 1970–79 are CIA statistics from Table 13.2, column 7. Although the CIA makes other adjustments to its series, and has developed its own procurement deflators, the DOD and CIA series for the seventies correspond very closely with one another. N.B. The charts which appear in the CIA's dollar cost reports (i.e., Figure 1, *A Dollar Cost Comparison of Soviet and U.S. Defense Activities, 1966–76*, p. 6) imply that the agency uses TOA data for its U.S. estimates. This apparently had been the practice before 1976, but not thereafter when outlay data replaced TOA estimates. See *A Dollar Cost Comparison of Soviet and U.S. Defense Activities, 1966–76*, p. 13–14.

FIGURE 16.3
Soviet and American Military Procurement, 1960–79 (Valued in 1978
Dollars: Adjusted for Intervintage Technological Progress)

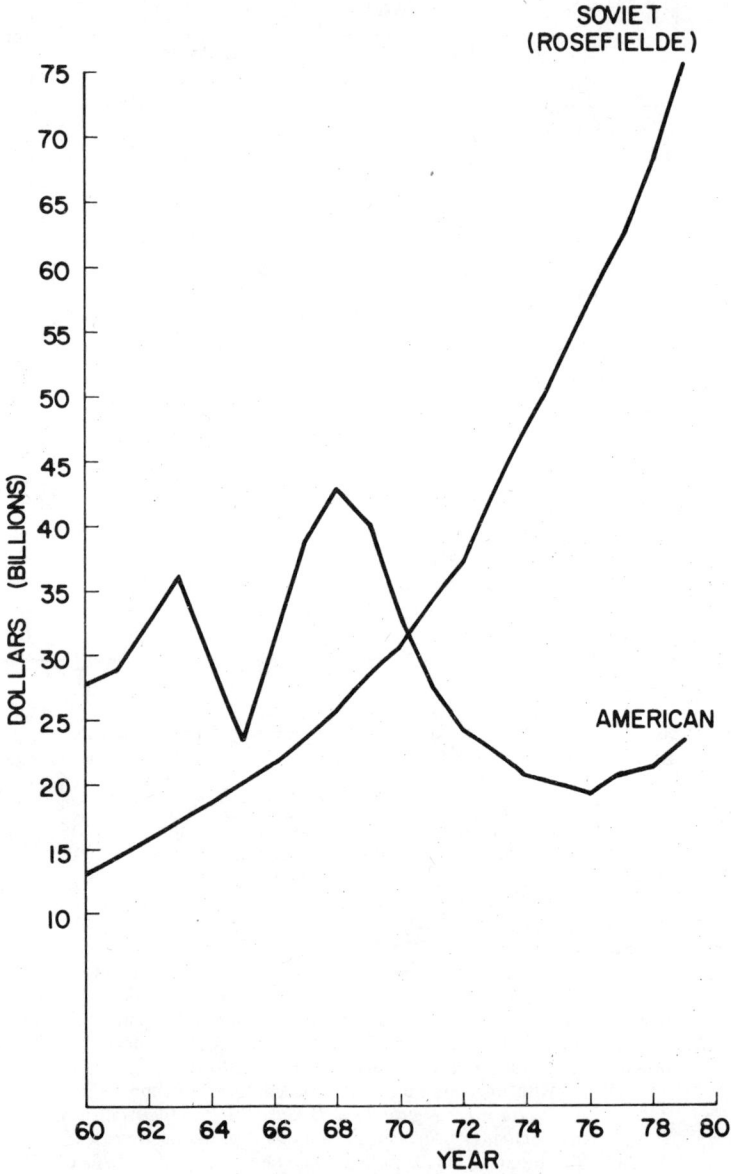

FIGURE 16.4

Soviet and American Military Procurement, 1960–79 (Valued in 1978 Dollars)

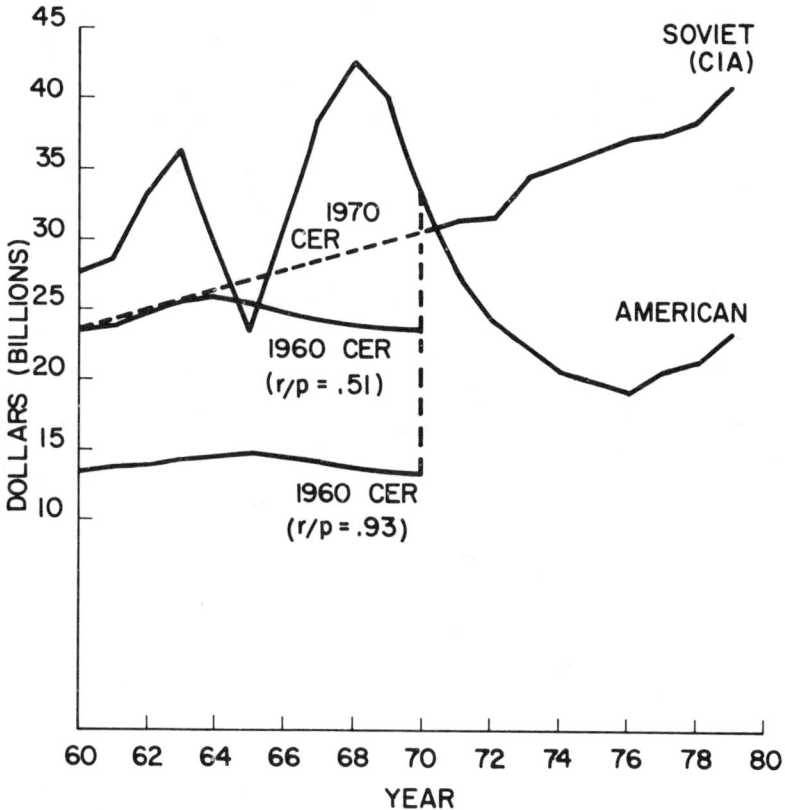

Notes

1. The utility theory developed in this chapter is drawn from the standard literature on economic welfare functions including Abraham Bergson (1938), pp. 318–34; Jan van de Graaf (1957); Paul Samuelson, "Bergsonian Welfare Economics" in Rosefielde, ed. (1981a).
2. See John Collins and Anthony Cordesman (1978); Royal United Services Institute and Brassey's (1981); Patrick Parker (1980), pp. 9–35.
3. Franklyn Holzman (1980a), pp. 91–99.
4. The agency only reports ruble estimates of comparative Soviet-American expenditures for total defense outlays. See *A Dollar Cost Comparison of Soviet and U.S. Defense Activities, 1968–1978*, January 1979, p. 5.

5. Vladimir Treml and Dimitri Gallik (1973), Table 9, p. 21, Table 10, p. 23.
6. Holzman (1980a), pp. 98–102.
7. See the bracketed term in Table 13.2n, column 6. Although the dollar component of the ruble-dollar ratio is expressed in 1970 dollars, it was estimated by deflation from the official CIA series in 1978 prices and therefore may be biased downward by the agency's learning curve adjustment. See Rosefielde (1982c).
8. Cf. Holzman, ibid., pp. 95–97.
9. This conclusion is culled from the unclassified portion of a classified document. See DIA, *U.S. and Soviet Weapon System Design Practice (U)*, May, 1980.
10. The CIA learning curve adjustments also understate its dollar and ruble estimates of Soviet procurement. See Rosefielde (1982c).

Part V

NATIONAL SECURITY
IMPLICATIONS

CHAPTER 17

The Illusion of Soviet Arms Restraint

The conclusion that the Soviets have achieved arms superiority in the late seventies, taken together with the supporting information provided in part IV on the size, growth, and momentum of the Soviet arms buildup, has a number of far-reaching implications for the assessment of postwar American national security policy analysis. First, it demonstrates that the agency's twenty-five-year experiment with fixed vintage parametric cost estimation has been a failure. Second, it shows that data critical to the formulation of rational American defense policy during the sixties and seventies were profoundly biased. Third, it disconfirms the widely held view that annual and cumulative Soviet procurement outlays are still less than those of the United States.[1] Fourth, it contradicts the twin suppositions that the Soviets would not seek, and/or could not achieve cumulative weapons superiority by the late seventies. Fifth, it invalidates all theories of the arms race casting the United States in the role of perpetual leader and the Soviet Union in the role of perpetual follower. Sixth, it falsifies the hypothesis that the Soviets will curtail their procurement programs if the United States restrains its own outlays. Seventh, it reveals that the Soviets preferred to let a golden opportunity for general disarmament negotiations pass, when it attained de facto cumulative procurement superiority while the agency's estimates showed they were far behind. Eighth, it demonstrates that the Soviets do not believe that their defense interests are better served by mutually balanced forced reductions from a position of near cumulative parity than by achieving a comfortable margin of arms superiority. Finally, it suggests that the Soviets are pursuing a policy of arms supremacy that will allow them to achieve a strong defense, police their empire, expand, attain a preemptive first strike capacity, or disarm from strength, whichever objective and/or objectives prove to be most desirable.

These implications do not unequivocally explain why the Soviets have chosen to adopt an arms procurement strategy that has given them cumulative superiority, nor do they indicate how the United States should have structured its national security policy to have countered the Soviet challenge. The conjoint issues of intentions and optimal national security policy are highly complex and cannot be adequately addressed within the confines of the present volume. However, the estimates of Soviet procurement adjusted for intervintage technological progress do enable us to reject some widely held theories about past Soviet defense expenditures and to identify a few key characteristics that appear to be determining their future course. These theories can be broadly divided into two classes, one which stipulates that the Soviet Union would not, or could not, overtake the United States militarily by the late seventies; the other that if the Soviets did attempt to achieve military parity with America, or even sought a margin of superiority it was only because they were reacting to the imperatives of the arms race.

The first class of theories which deny that the Soviets would or could seek military supremacy in a nuclear age are predicated on diverse assessments of Soviet economic capabilities, national priorities, foreign-cum-defense-cum-military objectives, official Soviet defense budgetary statistics, and alternative military expenditure data compiled by SIPRI and the CIA. This class of theories and the estimates that support them are falsified by the revised estimates that take intervintage technological progress into account. The adjusted estimates reported in Table 13.2 demonstrate that Soviet procurement expenditures were not stagnant during the sixties, at one-third the U.S. level as the agency's early vintage series suggest.[2] They are inconsistent with the hypothesis that the pace of Soviet procurement growth has been restrained,[3] and disconfirm Holzman's assertion that Soviet defense expenditures are currently less than U.S. expenditures valued in rubles and perhaps even measured in dollars as well.[4] The adjusted data indicate that Soviet procurement policy during the sixties and seventies was precisely the reverse of what the first class of theories suppose. The Soviets not only chose to catch up with, overtake, and surpass the United States militarily in the shortest possible time, but they succeeded, expanding their procurement outlays at double digit rates from 1960 to the present.

The second class of theories falsified by the estimates derived in this study portray the United States as the principal cause of the Soviet-American arms race. These theories do not dispute the contention that the Soviets have sought to attain cumulative arms parity, or may have achieved some degree of military superiority over the United States. Instead, they attempt to explain the behavior of Soviet procurement expenditures in terms of prior U.S. outlays.[5] It is argued that the Soviet arms program is determined by the direction and rate of U.S. military spending. When American outlays rise, Soviet procurement expenditures follow suit. When they decline, so do the Soviet expenditures.

This causal specification has encouraged some arms control advocates to suppose that the arms spiral between the Soviet Union and the United States could be terminated if America, in its role as leader, unilaterally restrained its arms expenditures. The data presented in Table 13.2 and the projections illustrated in Table 15.1 indicate that this supposition is disconfirmed by the facts. American procurement outlays have been in a downward trend since 1968, while Soviet arms production has risen steadily at more than 10 percent per annum. The data provide no indication whatsoever that the United States "caused" the Soviets to continue expanding their procurement programs during the seventies, or that the Soviets have mechanically followed the U.S. lead by reducing their procurement outlays as some arms race theorists hypothesized.

It could be counterargued that Soviet procurement did not actually surpass U.S. outlays until the late seventies, and therefore it would be premature to expect them to follow the American lead until the early eighties. This sophisticated version of the theory cannot be summarily dismissed, but it should be noted that CIA assessments of Soviet procurement programs currently in progress do not support this surmise.[6]

Indeed, the evidence at hand points to precisely the opposite conclusion. The Soviets appear to have had a golden opportunity during the first two years of the Carter administration to negotiate a general arms control agreement advantageous to their side. CIA procurement estimates for 1975 and 1976 misleadingly suggested that the United States still enjoyed a substantial cumulative procurement advantage, when the Soviets had already virtually eliminated the cumulative procurement gap.[7] President Carter proposed significant bilateral reductions in American and Soviet intercontinental ballistic forces in March and April 1977.[8] American public opinion in the wake of the Vietnam War was favorably inclined toward disarmament initiatives and the CIA had inadvertently granted the Soviets several years grace by misattributing the "new information" on Soviet procurement expenditures to hidden inflation.

If the Soviets believed their long-term national security interests were best served by mutually balanced force reductions, they clearly should have seized the initiative. The fact that they did not reveals a great deal about Soviet defense policy preferences. It indicates that if the Soviets are prepared to limit their arms expenditures they prefer to do so from a position of strength rather than one of parity. It can also be inferred that because the prospects for disarmament are likely to be inversely correlated with the magnitude of the disparity between Soviet and American procurement outlays, that in deciding against a major disarmament initiative from 1976 to 1978, the Soviets revealed that they were seeking superiority for other purposes. Their motives may have been diverse. They may have wanted to enhance their power to police their empire (Poland) to expand their boundaries (Afghanistan), to Finlandize Western Europe, to wield increased influence in the Third World, to launch a preemptive first-strike with their strategic nuclear forces, or as some still believe they may have been driven by defensive paranoia, Kremlin fears, and complexes.

The data derived in this study cannot be used to discriminate the relative plausibility of these motives. They do suggest, however, that the Soviets are seeking to increase their arms superiority for some or all the reasons enumerated above, and that any American national security policy that presumes otherwise will be seriously misguided.[9]

Notes

1. Franklyn Holzman has recently argued that if adjustments were made for the CIA's overstatement of embodied Soviet weapons technology, and allowances were made for aggregation bias, annual Soviet *defense* expenditures valued in dollars might be lower than those of the United States. Holzman also asserts that if U.S. and Soviet defense expenditures were compared in rubles U.S. outlays would far exceed those of the Soviets. See Holzman (1980a), pp. 86–104. For a critical appraisal of his analysis see appendix 4.
2. For a discussion of the CIA's unpublished early vintage dollar estimates see chapter 4, section IX and chapter 13, note 5. Cf. Wohlstetter (1975).
3. Abraham Becker (1979), pp. 360–61. Cf. Wohlstetter (1975).
4. On the issue of ruble valuation see chapter 16. See also note 2.
5. A fuller discussion of these theories is provided in Albert Wohlstetter (1977), pp. 110–168. Wohlstetter's conclusions are similar to my own.
6. "Unlike the average consumer, the defense sector was not affected by the slowdown in the rate of economic growth. During the past few years, estimated Soviet defense spending grew more rapidly than GNP. . . . This is in contrast to the 1965–1978 period, when defense absorbed a relatively constant 11–13 percent of GNP. . . . Despite the poor performance of the economy, evidence on Soviet military production and development indicates that Soviet defense spending will continue to increase at least through 1985 at or near the long-term rate of 4–5 percent. If so, the defense share of Soviet GNP could rise to about as much as 15 percent by 1985" (*The Soviet Economy in 1978–79 and Prospects for 1980*, ER80–10328, June 1980, p. 16).
7. A situation that the Soviets must have clearly understood.
8. For an illuminating explanation of why the Soviets rejected the Carter initiative see William Lee (1980a), pp. 55–88, esp. 76–79.
9. For a detailed weapon-by-weapon review of Soviet and U.S. capabilities and trends, along with a discussion of their potential use, see Royal United Services Institute and Brassey's (1981); and *Soviet Military Power*, DOD, 1981. Cf. Wohlstetter (1975).

Part VI

FALSE SCIENCE

CHAPTER 18

The Facade of Scientific Neutrality

In the preceding three parts of this monograph attention has been focused on assessing the consequences of the CIA's misestimation of Soviet procurement expenditures. It has been demonstrated that the agency's direct costing estimates prevented the national security policy-making community from recognizing that the Soviets achieved arms superiority in the late seventies and spawned a variety of erroneous theories that have seriously obfuscated the rational evaluation of Soviet intentions. These findings stand on their own and bring one major phase of this inquiry to completion.

Our analysis of effects, however, tells us nothing about their cause. Why did the agency misappraise the dimensions of the Soviet arms buildup? Is the underestimation explained by a technical flaw in its cost estimating equations? Or does the fault lie elsewhere, in the factors that impelled the agency to rationalize the manifest inconsistencies in its estimates, instead of discovering that they did not take intervintage technological progress adequately into account?

The validity of the first explanation depends on whether the agency's confidence in its direct cost methods was supported by rigorous scientific hypothesis tests. If it can be shown that the adjustments made to its prerevision series rendering them inconsistent with its postrevision series were scientifically justified (see chapter 2); that the suppression of the prerevision series was warranted (see chapter 1); that the evidence disconfirming its estimates was rejected on plausible grounds, then the hypothesis that the agency's underestimation of the Soviet arms buildup is explained by an adventitious specification error can be believed.

If on the contrary it can be demonstrated that the CIA assiduously avoided systematically testing and evaluating the theorems and subordinate hypotheses of its direct costing methodology, then the first hypothesis must be rejected, and it follows that the underestimation of the Soviet arms buildup is attributable not to flaws in the methodology per se, but to the configuration of factors preventing the CIA from properly reconciling its direct cost estimates with intelligence information obtained from other sources. Part VI demonstrates that the second explanation is the correct one. This is accomplished in Chapter 18 by formally expressing the direct costing methodology as a scientific hypothesis, and then systematically examining how the agency has gone about verifying its theorems and subordinate hypotheses. This examination reveals that the CIA relied on invalid deductive a priori methods to rationalize the inconsistencies between its direct cost estimates and the mass of evidence disconfirming them, and that it has never implemented a rigorous program to systematically test and evaluate the theorems and subordinate hypotheses that underlie its direct costing methodology.

The CIA's principal hypothesis that the value of Soviet weapons can be accurately calculated without open access to official Soviet procurement data can be formally expressed in terms of its constituent theorems and subordinate hypotheses:[1]

> *Hypothesis: Parametric cost estimating procedures will provide reliable estimates of the ruble and dollar cost of Soviet procurement, if physical weapons counts are accurate.*

Theorem 1: Accurate dollar cost estimates of Soviet weapons can be calculated by

1. counting weapons with satellite photography and other national technical means;
2. valuing weapons with fixed vintage parametric cost estimating equations derived from data on the ex-post cost of analogous American equipment; and
3. adjusting for differences in size, weight, structural design, habitability, ordnance, and other qualitative factors ("Sovietization").

Theorem 2: Accurate ruble cost estimates of Soviet weapons can be calculated by transforming dollar estimates with ruble-dollar ratios.

Theorem 3: Ruble and dollar estimates computed according to theorems 1 and 2 will behave consistently from the standpoint of index number theory.

Each of these theorems can be expressed in terms of a series of testable subordinate hypotheses:

Theorem 1: testable subordinate hypotheses:
    1. weapons counts are accurate;
    2. fixed vintage parametric cost estimates accurately measure costs in time t;
    3. fixed vintage parametric cost estimates accurately measure intervintage technological progress, adjusted for learning;
    4. adjustments made for differences in the size, weight, structural design, habitability, ordnance, and other qualitative aspects of Soviet weapons in time t are accurate; and
    5. adjustments made for differences in the size, weight, structural design, habitability, ordnance, and other qualitative aspects of Soviet weapons in time $t+i$, $i = i (1, \ldots, n)$ are accurate.

Theorem 2: testable subordinate hypotheses:
    1. theorem 1 is correct;
    2. ruble-dollar ratios for civilian machinery and equipment are reliable surrogates for ruble-dollar ratios of military procurement in time t; and
    3. in time $t + i$, $i = i (1, \ldots, n)$.

Theorem 3: testable subordinate hypotheses:
    1. theorems 1 and 2 are correct;
    2. ruble rates of Soviet procurement growth should exceed the comparably defined dollar rate, valued in prices of year t, or $t + i$;
    3. ruble rates of procurement growth valued with prices of year t, should exceed those valued with prices of the year $t + i$;
    4. dollar rates of procurement growth valued with prices of year t, should exceed those valued with prices of year $t + i$; and
    5. the ratio of U.S. to Soviet procurement valued in dollars should be lower than in rubles.

Theorems

1–3: general subordinate hypothesis:

    1. algorithms and computations are accurate.

The tests required to validate these subordinate hypotheses are:

Tests of Theorem 1:

1. corroborate that weapons counts in every year studied are accurate with multiple intelligence methods;
2. the premise that fixed vintage parametric cost estimates measure American weapon costs accurately in time t is true by construction, subject to known statistical estimating variances for each individual weapon;
3. the potential bias caused by intervintage technological progress is assessable by valuing the same set of *American* weapons with parametric costing relationships of time t and t + 1, adjusted for learning and comparing results. The cost estimating equations required are computed by the material acquisition branches of the U.S. Defense Department;
4. the accuracy of adjustments made for differences in the size, weight, structural design, habitability, ordnance, and other qualitative aspects of Soviet weapons can be corroborated with multiple national intelligence methods and by performing detailed engineering studies for weapons produced in time t; and
5. the same tests can be performed to evaluate the qualitative adjustments made for weapons produced in time t + i.

Tests of Theorem 2:

1. test Theorem 1;
2. the reliability of civilian machinery and equipment as surrogates for military MBMW ruble-dollar ratios can be verified by obtaining ruble prices for Soviet weapons by covert means; calculating ruble-dollar ratios with the appropriate parametric dollar cost estimate in time t, and comparing the results; and
3. the same test can be performed to evaluate ruble-dollar ratios for weapons produced in time t + i.

Tests of Theorem 3:

1. test Theorems 1 and 2;
2. the expectation that ruble rates of procurement growth will exceed the dollar rates can be assessed

by calculating procurement growth in dollars and rubles;
3. the expectation that ruble rates of procurement
   growth will be faster in base year than in later year
   prices can be confirmed by calculating ruble procurement growth rates in prices of year t and t + i;
4. the same test can be applied to evaluate the dollar
   rates of arms growth; and
5. the expectation that the ratio of U.S. to Soviet procurement valued in dollars should be lower than in
   rubles can be verified by calculating both ratios in
   prices of time t, and/or t + i.

Tests of the general subordinate hypothesis on accurate calculation:
1. sample computations can be employed to verify al-
   gorithms. Calculations can be replicated.

The structure of interrelationships among the theorems and subordinate hypotheses delineated above that comprise the CIA's direct costing hypothesis can be elucidated with the aid of a theory interdependence
diagram. Figure 18.1, which illustrates how the agency's dollar estimates
of Soviet procurement (Theorem 1) are linked to its ruble estimates
(Theorem 2) and how both codetermine the behavior of its procurement
growth indices (Theorem 3), indicates that the principal hypothesis is
an ordered hierarchy in which each theorem depends on the validity of
its own subordinate hypotheses (the vertical relationship between Theorem 1, and subordinate hypothesis S_{ij}); higher order theorems (the hor-
izontal relationship between Theorem 1, Theorem 2, and Theorem 3)
depend on their antecedents. This double hierarchy of theory depend-
ence implies that the principal hypothesis is weakly decomposable. If
S_1 and S_2, representing the 5 subordinate hypotheses of Theorem 1 are
empirically verified, then Theorem 1 will be confirmed regardless of
whether Theorem 2 and/or 3 are sustained. However, if S_1 and S_2 are
falsified, Theorem 2 and Theorem 3 cannot be validated because the
dollar estimates that govern the ruble estimates and the behavior of the
agency's procurement growth indices will be biased. Similarly, Theorem
1 and Theorem 2 may be empirically verified, even if S_5 and S_6 (which
represent the 5 subordinate hypotheses of Theorem 3) are falsified, but
Theorem 3 cannot be confirmed if either Theorem 1 and/or Theorem
2 is invalidated.

The 14 empirically testable subordinate hypotheses of Theorems 1–3
and the weak decomposability of the principal hypothesis provide an
objective standard for evaluating the scientific merit of the agency's

FIGURE 18.1

Experimental Design Schema for Testing and Verifying the Validity of the Hypothesis that Soviet Weapons Expenditures Can Be Reliably Calculated with Direct Costing Method

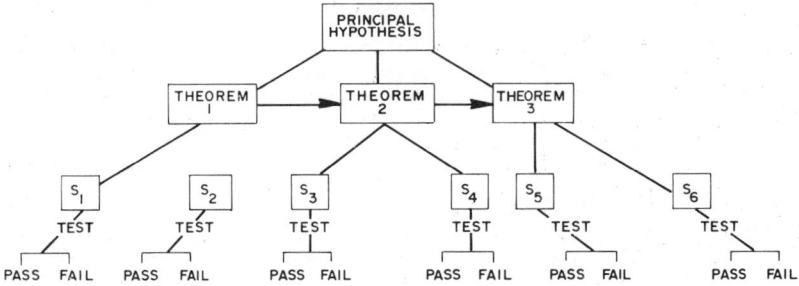

verification procedures. Since it has already been established that the direct costing method can be formulated into a series of empirically testable propositions, the merit of its verification procedures depends on whether these 14 subordinate hypotheses were thoroughly tested prior to the method's official adoption in the early sixties, and whether in the wake of subsequent disconfirming events special attention was devoted to testing Theorem 1 on which the validity of Theorem 2 and Theorem 3 largely rest.

The evidence compiled in parts I and II of this volume shows beyond any reasonable doubt that the 14 subordinate hypotheses of direct costing were not systematically and rigorously tested before the methodology was officially adopted. Had the third subordinate hypothesis of Theorem 1 been tested, for example, it would have been immediately discovered that the agency's dollar estimates of *American* weapons in time t + i did not correspond with actual cost measured in constant prices. Likewise, if subordinate hypotheses 2, 3, 4, and 5 of Theorem 3 had been tested in time t + i, all the perverse index number effects discussed in chapters 2, 3, and 4 would have emerged long before they unexpectedly manifested themselves in the early seventies.

These failures indicate either that the agency's hypothesis testing program was excessively lax, or the CIA had not formulated its method into a series of empirically testable subordinate hypotheses and as a consequence was not in a position to scientifically evaluate its properties. The agency's subsequent response to disconfirming events demonstrates that the latter alternative correctly characterizes its verification procedures. Table 18.1 lists 12 major events from 1965 to 1980 that strongly disconfirmed the accuracy of the CIA's procurement estimates along with information on the probable error source, tests performed, and the explanation offered to reconcile each discrepancy. Ten of the 12 disconfirming events point to methodological deficiencies in direct costing, 2 to nonimputable causes. In all 10 instances involving potential methodological failure, the proper scientific response, given the weak decomposability of the principal hypothesis would have been to test the subordinate hypotheses of Theorem 1.

Had the agency done so, Figure 18.2 demonstrates that all 12 disconfirming events would have been validly explained. The evaluation of Theorem 1, subordinate hypothesis 3, would have disclosed that fixed vintage parametric cost estimating equations did not take adequate account of intervintage technological progress, and the substitution of variable vintage parametric cost estimating equations would have eliminated the dollar procurement estimating discrepancies (Table 18.1, entries 3, 10, 11, 12), the ruble costing discrepancies (Table 18.1, entries 1, 2, 4, 8, 9), and the perverse index number relativity effects (Table 18.1, entries 5, 6, 7).

Instead of following this course, the CIA—relying on the unexamined proposition that if its weapons counts were accurate, its dollar estimates were correct—"explained" the 12 disconfirming events with a variety of unverified, a priori hypotheses. The sensitivity of the dollar cost estimates to the method chosen to compute real series was suppressed.[2] The ruble discrepancies it asserted were caused by hidden inflation (or hidden deflation),[3] and the inconsistencies among its dollar and ruble procurement growth series were attributed to unusual relative price effects.[4] When pressed, a variety of empirical studies were undertaken to confirm the exogenous hidden inflation hypothesis,[5] but as shown in chapters 8, 9, and appendices 2 and 3 these tests were ill-conceived. Similarly, when confronted with the DOD's variable vintage procurement estimates, the agency unsuccessfully attempted to impute the discrepancies to differences in accounting conventions, rather than concede the possibility that its methodology was flawed.[6]

In all instances, the agency's response to disconfirming events has followed a predictable pattern. Instead of formally elaborating and testing the theorems and subordinate hypotheses of its direct costing methodology, explanations are sought in weak, a priori theories of dollar and ruble price behavior. This approach, which substitutes conjecture for rigorous empiricism, is the antithesis of legitimate scientific method and reveals that at bottom the agency's procurement underestimates are not attributable to an adventitious specification error, but to its false science.

TABLE 18.1

Evidence Falsifying the Subordinate Hypotheses of the CIA's Direct Costing Methodology, 1965–80

Evidence	Probable Error Source	Test Performed	Explanation
1. CIA ruble estimates of Soviet procurement implausibly grew between zero percent and one percent per annum 1960–70, sharply departing from the long term Stalinist trend.	Method	None	The Soviet Union was in the process of changing from a revolutionary to a postrevolutionary society, instituting the rule of law, abandoning its ideological fear of capitalist encirclement, and its ideologically motivated expansionism. It was deemphasizing military concerns, and striving to reform its economy to achieve a modern mass consumption society.
2. The official Soviet defense budget grew 6.8 percent per annum 1960–69, a rate which seemed inconsistent with the agency's estimate of Soviet procurement growth, zero percent per annum.	Method	None	The official Soviet defense budget reported current expenditures, not real growth. Perhaps military procurement prices were rising, or procurement was being given a low priority.
3. Dollar estimates of Soviet procurement calculated during the sixties implausibly grew faster than the ruble series.	Method	None	These were current value estimates. Real dollar growth rates were not computed during the sixties. See chapter 4, section IX and chapter 13, note 5.
4. The official Soviet defense budget 1969–74 displayed no growth, but	Method	None	The Soviet military machine-building sector is hyperproductive. This caused

the revised 1970 fixed vintage ruble series indicated that procurement was growing 3–4 percent per annum.			prices to fall with the result that procurement measured in current prices was unchanged, while it grew in real terms.
5. Index number rank order reversals: ruble Paasche > dollar Paasche > ruble Laspeyres.	Non-Imputable	None	Exotic relative price effects (chapter 2).
6. Index number rank order reversals: dollar Paasche > hypothetical Paasche ≥ hypothetical Laspeyres.	Non-Imputable	None	Exotic relative price effects (chapter 2 and chapter 13, note 5).
7. The inconsistency between the CIA's pre and postrevision procurement estimates cannot be reconciled with any set of meaningful price relatives.	Method	None	Exotic relative price effects (chapter 4).
8. Ruble procurement outlay figure for 1970 obtained covertly from Soviet MOD was 236 percent higher than the CIA's direct cost estimate (confirming Lee) suggesting that the hidden inflation might not fully explain the initial failure of test S_4.	Method	None	Hidden inflation was severer than initially surmised (chapter 1, part II).
9. Scholarly literature on hidden inflation in the Soviet Union did not support the inflation rates implied by the agency's direct cost estimates.	Method	Three research papers written all using flawed methodologies. See chapters 8	The scholarly literature is wrong. The agency's tests prove that hidden inflation explains the ruble costing discrepancy (part II).

TABLE 18.1 (Continued)

10. Information on intervintage technological progress and fixed vintage parametric cost estimating bias demonstrated that it was highly probable that the dollar cost of American weapons were greatly understated by the agency's direct costing method.	Method	and 9 and appendix 3. None	This information does not pertain to "Sovietized" American weapons.
11. Theorem 1 implies that if the direct costing method (using fixed vintage CERs) understates the subsequent dollar cost of American weapons, it understates the derivative dollar cost of "Sovietized" American weapons.	Method	Axiom of Theorem 1	The difference between dollar estimates of American weapons computed with variable vintage CERs, properly "Sovietized," and the CIA's fixed vintage "Sovietized" estimates is small.
12. Information obtained disconfirming the assertion that the difference between American weapons computed with variable vintage CERs properly "Sovietized," and the CIA's fixed vintage "Sovietized" estimates is small.	Method	Improper accounting reconciliation	The difference is definitional. DOD estimates are based on "future technology," a distinction disputed by the DOD. No adjustments made.[1]

Note: The author has called all the evidence listed above to the agency's attention in one form or another at various times during the past five years.

1. The attribution of the discrepancy between the CIA and DOD's estimates of the current cost of one major class of weapons to "future technology" is an uninspired guess on the CIA's part. I have examined the documentation behind the costing model used by the agency and it is clear that the source of the discrepancy lies in its model, not as the DOD cost estimators have assured me in "future technology."

FIGURE 18.2

Experimental Design Schema for Testing and Verifying the Validity of the Hypothesis that Soviet Weapons Expenditures Can Be Reliably Calculated with Direct Costing Method

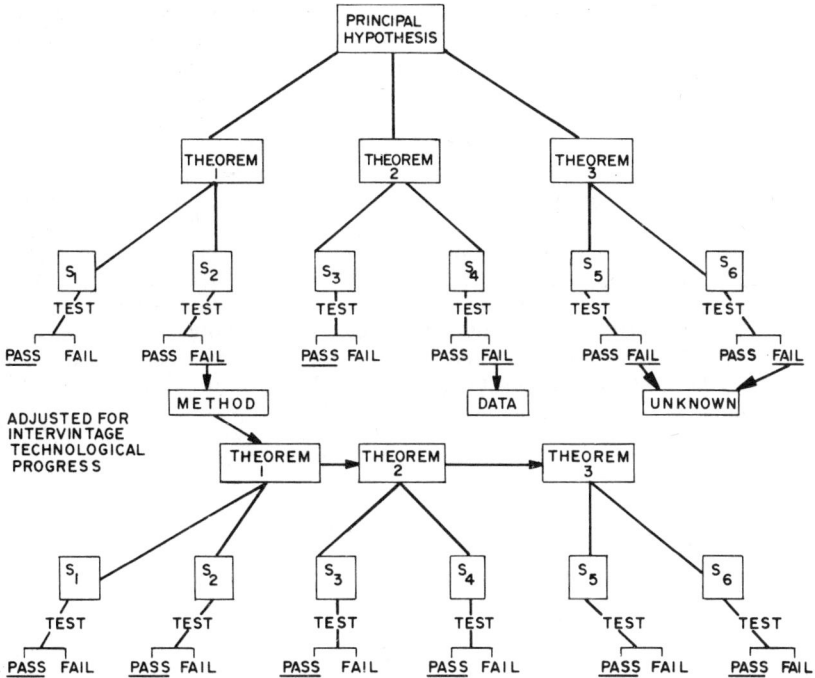

PRINCIPAL HYPOTHESIS

THEOREM 1 — THEOREM 2 — THEOREM 3

S_1 TEST — PASS FAIL
S_2 TEST — PASS FAIL
S_3 TEST — PASS FAIL
S_4 TEST — PASS FAIL
S_5 TEST — PASS FAIL
S_6 TEST — PASS FAIL

METHOD   DATA   UNKNOWN

ADJUSTED FOR INTERVINTAGE TECHNOLOGICAL PROGRESS

THEOREM 1 → THEOREM 2 → THEOREM 3

S_1 TEST — PASS FAIL
S_2 TEST — PASS FAIL
S_3 TEST — PASS FAIL
S_4 TEST — PASS FAIL
S_5 TEST — PASS FAIL
S_6 TEST — PASS FAIL

Notes

1. The standards of scientific verification developed in this chapter draw heavily on the postpositivist methodology of Romano Harré. See Harré (1970); Romano Harré and P.F. Secord (1973); Rosefielde (1979), pp. 1–9; and Rosefielde (1980d).
2. Table 13.2n demonstrates that the ruble dollar ratio computed for 1960 Soviet machinery by Becker-Treml-Gallik is inconsistent with the ruble dollar ratio calculated from the agency's official Paasche series, suggesting that the cost-estimating relationships underlying these ratios pertain to different CER vintages. Also see Table 13.1n and Rosefielde (1982c).
3. See chapter 3, note 2.
4. See chapters 2–4. Barry of course contends that all inconsistencies are explained by the "fact" that I cull my numbers from noncomparable, published CIA estimates. See chapter 3, note 2.

5. "We are convinced, and we have published a number of studies on this, that there is measurable inflation in Soviet machinery as a whole and in defense machinery in particular" (Barry, Ibid., see chapter 3, note 2).

6. In his reply to Congressman Robert McClory, Robert Huffstutler, director, OSR, CIA, states: "That is actually a significant point, and one can generalize this in the costing of Soviet naval combatants. We have been in some discussions with the Navy as to why, when they look at Soviet ships, they might get higher costs than we do, and when we actually got down to the details on it, it turns out that if you look at the actual design of most Soviet ships, that they simply do not have the compartmentation or damage control systems, the secondary safety systems and backup that United States Naval ships have. The U.S. Navy would not build ships that way. So that as you go in and examine some of those, American ships are safer. As a result, they also survive combat, certainly conventional combat situations, more readily than Soviet ships would. It is an open question, of course, what is going to happen in some sort of nuclear engagement, but U.S. ships do have redundant systems, and they are safer ships insofar as the crew is concerned. As a result, the U.S. ships cost more" (*CIA Estimates of Soviet Defense Spending*, Permanent Select Committee on Intelligence, House of Representatives, September 3, 1980, p. 82). Huffstutler discussed this matter with me on September 3, 1980. I then consulted the navy study to which he alludes, exploring the details with the authors, to verify if the OP96 estimates were "Sovietized." They were.

CHAPTER 19

Behind the Facade

I. Factors Determining the CIA's Estimates of Soviet Defense Spending

It follows directly from the formal demonstration that the CIA did not rigorously elaborate and test the theorems and subordinate hypotheses of its direct costing methodology that the underestimation of the Soviet military buildup should not be attributed to methodological deficiencies beyond the agency's control, but to the configuration of factors that prevented it from reconciling its direct cost estimates with the data falsifying them. For the purposes of this study, these factors can be classified into two broad categories: one a-rational, the other rational. The first category includes the array of psychological factors (aversions, phobias, etc.) that might explain why the CIA avoided systematic hypothesis testing. The second category includes a diverse set of causes ranging from logical inferences drawn from speculative theories of Soviet economic, political, and military behavior, to paradigms of bureaucratic action, to the exogenous imposition of external authority. Some illustrative examples of these rational factors are presented in Table 19.1.

Unlike the a-rational psychological factors, these rational causes suggest that the CIA's biased direct cost estimates were consciously fixed either by the agency itself or by some other authority. Each paradigm embodies its own rationale which departs in varying degrees from the agency's mission of providing the national security policymaking community with accurate, impartial estimates of Soviet procurement. These rationales together with the a-rational factors, form an explanatory continuum in which the values assigned to the CIA's estimates are deter-

TABLE 19.1

An Illustrative List of Extra-Scientific Factors Determining the CIA's Direct Cost Estimates

Paradigm	Directive Agency	Mechanism	Intent
I. Internal Control Models			
1. Armchair theorizing	key CIA and/or MEAP personnel	estimates arbitrarily adjusted, reconciled, and suppressed	Make published estimates conform with intuitive expectations of what Soviet procurement expenditures "should" be. Intuitive judgments are based on speculative pseudo inductive assessments of economic and political factors constraining Soviet weapons production and the advantages the Soviets might expect to accrue from arms control.
2. Bureaucratic politics	key CIA personnel	estimates arbitrarily adjusted, reconciled, and suppressed	Protect the autonomy of the CIA from being infringed by other agencies including DOD, ACDA, OMB, NSA, the State Department, Congress, and the president.
3. Public interest	key CIA and/or MEAP personnel	estimates arbitrarily adjusted, reconciled, and suppressed	Protect the public from being mislead by high DOD estimates of Soviet procurement and low ACDA estimates.
4. Social Activism	key CIA and/or MEAP personnel	estimates arbitrarily adjusted, reconciled, and suppressed	Make published estimates support arms control and disarmament policies in order to curb the arms race, reduce international tensions, reduce the risk of nuclear war, and prevent federal resources being diverted from programs serving human needs.

5. Subversion	key CIA and/or MEAP personnel	disinformation; estimates arbitrarily adjusted, reconciled, and suppressed	Disguise the Soviet arms buildup; inhibit U.S. defense expenditures.
II. External Control Models			
6. National intelligence-national security policy integration	Office of the president	Executive directives	Fashion estimates of Soviet procurement expenditures that are consistent with an integrated set of national security policies.
7. Great Society politics	Congress	Congressional directives; oversight authority; budgetary coercion	Prevent the CIA from colluding with DOD in fabricating high estimates of Soviet procurement that might unjustifiably divert resources from programs servicing human needs.
8. Disarmament coalition	ACDA and the State Department	bureaucratic politics, public pressure	Promote detente and disarmament.
9. Deception	Soviet counter-intelligence	Manipulate published Soviet defense budget	Disguise the Soviet arms buildup; deceive world opinion; inhibit U.S. defense expenditures.

mined in descending order of merit by casual theory, bureaucratic politics, obstinacy, extraneous social theory, interest group advocacy, and deception.[1]

Although the data required to discriminate the comparative merit of these alternative explanatory paradigms is not available in the public domain, the array of causes outlined above places the potential consequences of the CIA's false science in a revealing light because it suggests that in eschewing comprehensive scientific hypothesis-testing the agency not only prevented itself from correctly estimating the dimensions of the Soviet arms buildup, but provided mechanisms through which the extraneous and/or malevolent motives of others could invisibly influence its estimates and the dispassionate assessment of its methodology.

II. The Soviet Role in Shaping the CIA's Estimates of Soviet Defense Spending[2]

The possibility that alien influences could have affected the CIA's evaluation of the Soviet arms buildup raises the ultimate issue of whether Soviet counterintelligence played a role in shaping the values the agency assigned to its defense expenditure estimates. The evidence at our disposal is inadequate to prove that the Soviets influenced the CIA in this way because as Table 19.1 indicates many factors about which little is known may have determined the agency's perceptions. It can be easily shown, however, that Soviet counterintelligence may have influenced the CIA's defense expenditure estimates because recent evidence has revealed that the Soviets tried to conceal their arms buildup throughout the sixties and seventies by falsifying their published defense statistics.

This falsification took two forms. The "new information" obtained by covert means in 1975 showed that during the sixties the Soviets attempted to deceive the CIA by drastically understating the level of their official budgetary defense expenditures.[3] Judging by the Rand studies of the day derived from the official Soviet defense budget and the widely held view in academia that the Soviet defense budget was not greatly distorted, this ploy was reasonably successful.[4] Table 19.2 demonstrates moreover that in 1970 the Soviets embarked on a new course. Instead of confining their falsification to the level of Soviet defense expenditures, they began flagrantly falsifying its growth trend as well. The official series indicates that total defense spending declined .4 percent per annum from 1970 to 1979, when the calculations performed in chapter 13 show they were rising at 8.5 percent per annum. After a decade of relatively rapid growth, 6.8 percent per annum, with-

TABLE 19.2
Official Soviet Defense Expenditures
(Billions of Rubles at Current Prices)

	Total Expenditures y	Compound Annual Rate of Growth Measured from the Base Year		
		1960	1965	1970
	(1)	(2)	(3)	(4)
1960	9.3			
1961	11.6	24.7		
1962	12.6	16.4		
1963	13.9	14.3		
1964	13.3	9.4		
1965	12.8	6.6		
1966	13.4	6.3	4.7	
1967	14.5	6.6	6.4	
1968	16.7	7.6	9.3	
1969	17.7	7.4	8.4	
1970	17.9	6.8	6.9	
1971	17.9	6.1	5.7	0
1972	17.9	5.6	4.9	0
1973	17.9	5.2	4.3	0
1974	17.7	4.7	3.5	− .3
1975	17.4	4.3	3.5	− .6
1976	17.4	4.0	2.8	− .5
1977	17.2	3.7	2.5	− .5
1978	17.2	3.5	2.3	− .5
1979	17.2	3.3	2.1	− .4

Source: Narodnoe Khoziaistvo SSSR, various issues.

All entries in columns 2 and 3 are computed according to the formula:
$$\dot{g} = 100 \left[(y_{t+i}/y_t)^{1/t+i} - 1 \right]$$

The negative rates in column 4 are computed according to the formula:
$$\dot{g} = 100 \left[(1 - (y_{t+i}/y_t)^{-1} + 1))^{1/t+i} - 1 \right]$$

out so much as a word of explanation the official Soviet defense budget suddenly ceased increasing.

The abruptness with which this change was implemented indicates that Soviet counterintelligence may have obtained information from sources it considered reliable that this volte-face would not backfire by prodding the CIA to reconsider the validity of its direct cost estimates. Whether this information was acquired directly from sources inside the agency, by replicating the CIA's direct cost estimates with its own data, or from the secondary literature,[5] Table 19.2 suggests that Soviet counterintelligence may have concluded that by gradually reducing the official long-term rate of Soviet defense expenditure growth (columns 2 and 3) to a rate commensurate with the CIA's secret prevision series (column 4) it could encourage the agency to believe its own low estimates of Soviet defense expenditure growth,[6] remove an obstacle that might impede the CIA from publicly avowing its direct cost estimates,[7] and induce impartial observers to suppose that the Soviets had no intention of trying to achieve arms superiority.

Future researchers will have to determine whether this falsification of the growth of official defense budgetary expenditures enabled the Soviets to achieve these conjectured objective. Regardless of the final verdict, it is clear from the evidence that the Soviets undertook a set of the growth of official defense budgetary expenditures enabled the Soviets to achieve these conjectured objectives. Regardless of the final knowledge, ability, and determination, but because some other configuration of factors had already determined the agency's perceptions, rendering the Soviets' actions superfluous. It can thus be concluded that the CIA's false science not only caused the agency to underestimate the Soviet arms buildup, it also provided Soviet counterintelligence with an opportunity that may have been quickly exploited to "corroborate" the agency's mistaken direct cost estimates and to remove a potentially embarrassing statistical discrepancy that might have deterred the CIA from publicly disseminating its views.[8]

Notes

1. Based on my personal experiences and extensive discussions with others, it seems to me that paradigm 1, "armchair theorizing," and an a-rational aversion to systematic hypothesis testing are the best explanations of the agency's behavior. Paradigms 2 and 3 were frequently mentioned by agency personnel in my conversations with them; however, I had the distinct impression that these factors served to justify the estimates as they stood, rather than as a basis for determining their values. Paradigms 5 and 9 are discussed in section II of this chapter. Together with paradigm 4 they form a troika of factors that I believe may have had some significant but unquantifiable influence on the agency's estimates. For example, before the "new information" was officially sanctioned, it was common for agency personnel to deny that Soviet defense spending could be substantially higher than indicated in the falsified defense budget. Paradigms 6, 7, and 8 form a cluster which I believe had almost no influence on the agency's calculations, despite the judgment of one knowledgeable legislative assistant who is convinced that paradigm 6 predominates. There is no doubt that the CIA pays attention to the opinions of the president, the Congress, and the disarmament coalition, but I do not believe they dictate the agency's estimates. Cf. Wohlstetter (1975).
2. For a recent review of Soviet penetration of U.S. intelligence see Edward Jay Epstein (1980), pp. 34–108. See also the case of David Barnet, the first

CIA officer in the agency's 34-year history to be convicted of espionage (*Washington Post*, October 30, 1980, p. 1).

3. The official Soviet defense budget indicated that total Soviet defense expenditures in 1970 were 17.9 billion rubles. Based on the "new information," the CIA now estimates that the true figure was 45–50 billion rubles. See *Estimated Soviet Defense Spending in Rubles, 1970–1975*, SR76-10121, CIA, May 1976, p. 1.

4. Abraham Becker (1964); Becker (1969); Nancy Nimitz (1963); Nimitz (1974); Nimitz (n.d.); Abram Bergson (1961), p. 23, 362–63. For a later discussion of these issues see Franklyn Holzman (1975).

5. Open sources began to suggest that Soviet defense expenditure growth was very slow and might be less than the Soviets stated toward the end of the sixties. See Becker (1969), pp. 163–66.

6. On several occasions during the extended process in which it was shown that weapons were excluded from the Soviet defense budget, I observed the CIA deride the notion because they were convinced that the official defense budget was sufficiently accurate to serve as a check on their 1970 fixed vintage CER procurement series. I was also informed that this issue played an important role in the internal debate which preceded the release of the news that Soviet defense expenditures were 100 percent higher than previously supposed.

7. The CIA did not openly publish its direct cost estimates until the mid-seventies.

8. By the time Colby publicly reported the CIA's estimates of Soviet defense expenditure, growth had already fallen to a range 3.5–4.7 percent per annum, fortuitously bounding the agency's estimate of 4 percent per annum.

Conclusion

Because the CIA did not follow sound scientific practice (systematically testing the theorems and subordinate hypotheses of its direct costing methodology) and relied on false scientific procedures to determine its published estimates of Soviet procurement, it underestimated the size, growth, and momentum of the Soviet arms buildup, allowing the Soviets to achieve uncontested arms superiority in the late 1970s. All the factors that brought about this result continue in force despite the fact that the new administration has concluded on other grounds that the balance of military power has shifted in favor of the Soviets. This suggests that the development of effective national security policies which can efficiently counter the growing Soviet challenge will continue to be impeded in the eighties by the CIA's direct cost estimates. Unless this situation is rectified by substituting variable vintage cost estimating relationships for the fixed vintage CERs currently employed, rational responses to the increasing asymmetries in Soviet-American military power will ultimately be frustrated by the agency's underestimation of Soviet procurement expenditures and the false configuration of arms race, arms control, and disarmament theories it sustains.

True Science: Correct Methods of Computing and Evaluating Estimates of Soviet Procurement in Dollars and Rubles

Estimating Soviet procurement expenditures will always be an uncertain undertaking. Nonetheless, several steps can be taken by the Central Intelligence Agency to purge its estimates of their downward bias and to assure that its diverse series are legitimately consistent. The first, and most important, improvement is the replacement of the fixed vintage dollar parametric cost estimating relationships it uses to value Soviet military procurement with variable vintage, constant dollar CERs.

As explained in chapter 4, the cost estimating relationships currently employed by the CIA are derived largely from ex-post data on the production cost of American weapons built in 1970, valued in 1970 prices. These CERs embody the technology of 1970, and are not adequately adjusted for new technological innovations that occur over time. Some adjustments, of course, are made for visible improvements in the characteristics of new Soviet weapon models (no allowance is made for retrofitting), but they are for the most part calculated with the embodied technology of 1970, rather than in terms of the technology prevailing in the year the adjustment is made.

The consequence of using obsolete U.S. technology to value Soviet weaponry is most vividly revealed in comparisons of Soviet and U.S. procurement. Under existing procedures the value of Soviet and U.S. weapons are calculated according to two different conventions. U.S. weapons are valued in constant prices, with the technology of the given year, while Soviet equipment is measured in constant prices with the technology of 1970. This inconsistency means that the agency's published ratio of Soviet and U.S. procurement in effect compares Soviet procurement growth excluding most technical change, with U.S. procurement growth including embodied technological progress. Unless the qualitative improvement in Soviet military equipment is nonpositive, this dual standard necessarily implies that the CIA's comparisons understate both the absolute and comparative level of Soviet weapon production.

This understatement can only be remedied by measuring U.S. and Soviet procurement consistently. Two norms are conceivable. The agency can either recompute its U.S. procurement estimates with 1970 cost estimating relationships, or it can recalculate its Soviet series with variable, given year CERs. The first approach has the advantage that 1970 American CERs are known, and pose few computational problems. The disadvantages of utilizing the fixed vintage standard are significant, however. Fixed vintage estimates understate the rate of growth of procurement and the level of total military expenditures for both countries. This point is illustrated in Figure P1 which graphs Soviet and American procurement expenditures from 1970 to 1979 alternatively with fixed and given year technology. American procurement valued with 1970 CERs has been calculated for didactic purposes using Leonard Sullivan's estimates of U.S. intervintage technological progress. Figure P1 shows that Soviet military equipment in 1979, measured in 1970 CERs, is 28.3 billion dollars less than the quality-adjusted estimate, and American procurement valued in 1970 CERs is 9.4 billion dollars less than actual U.S. expenditures. Although Figure P2 indicates that the ratio of these fixed vintage estimates produces a reasonable impression of the change in comparative Soviet-U.S. procurement expenditures (assuming that the quality of Soviet and American equipment is growing at the same rate), this positive effect does not alter the understatement of the real level of procurement in both nations.

To eliminate the understatement in the agency's comparative measure, without biasing the level of Soviet and U.S. procurement expenditures downward, consistent variable vintage measures must be used. Ideally, this should be accomplished with annual engineering estimates of Soviet weapons continuously updated for changes in product quality.

TABLE P1
Comparative Soviet and American Dollar Procurement Activities (1978 Prices)

	Soviet Procurement		U.S. Procurement			USSR/US	
	Fixed Vintage 1970 CERs (1)	Variable Vintage CERs (2)	Fixed Vintage 1970 CERs (3)	Actual (4)	CIA (5)		Consistent Fixed or Variable Vintage CERs (6)
1970	30.6	30.6	32.7	32.7	.94		.94
1971	31.4	33.3	26.1	27.7	1.13		1.20
1972	31.6	35.5	21.8	24.5	1.29		1.45
1973	34.4	41	19.1	22.7	1.52		1.80
1974	35.5	44.8	16.6	20.9	1.70		2.14
1975	36.3	48.6	14.9	20	1.82		2.44
1976	37.3	52.9	13.5	19.1	1.95		2.76
1977	37.7	56.7	13.9	20.9	1.80		2.68
1978	38.5	61.4	13.4	21.4	1.80		2.87
1979	41	69.3	14	23.6	1.74		2.93

Sources:
1. Official CIA series of Soviet procurements, Table 13.2, column 2.
2. Author's estimated series of Soviet procurement, adjusted for American intervintage technological progress, Table 13.3, column 1.
3. CIA's estimates of U.S. procurement, adjusted for American intervintage technological progress, 6 percent per annum.
4. CIA's estimates of U.S. procurement, Table 13.2, column 7.
5. CIA's ratio of Soviet-American procurement, column 1 divided by column 4.
6. Consistently defined fixed or variable CER comparison of Soviet-American procurement, column 1 divided by column 3, or column 2 divided by column 4.

FIGURE P1
Soviet and American Procurement Valued in 1978 Dollar Prices with
Fixed and Variable Technology

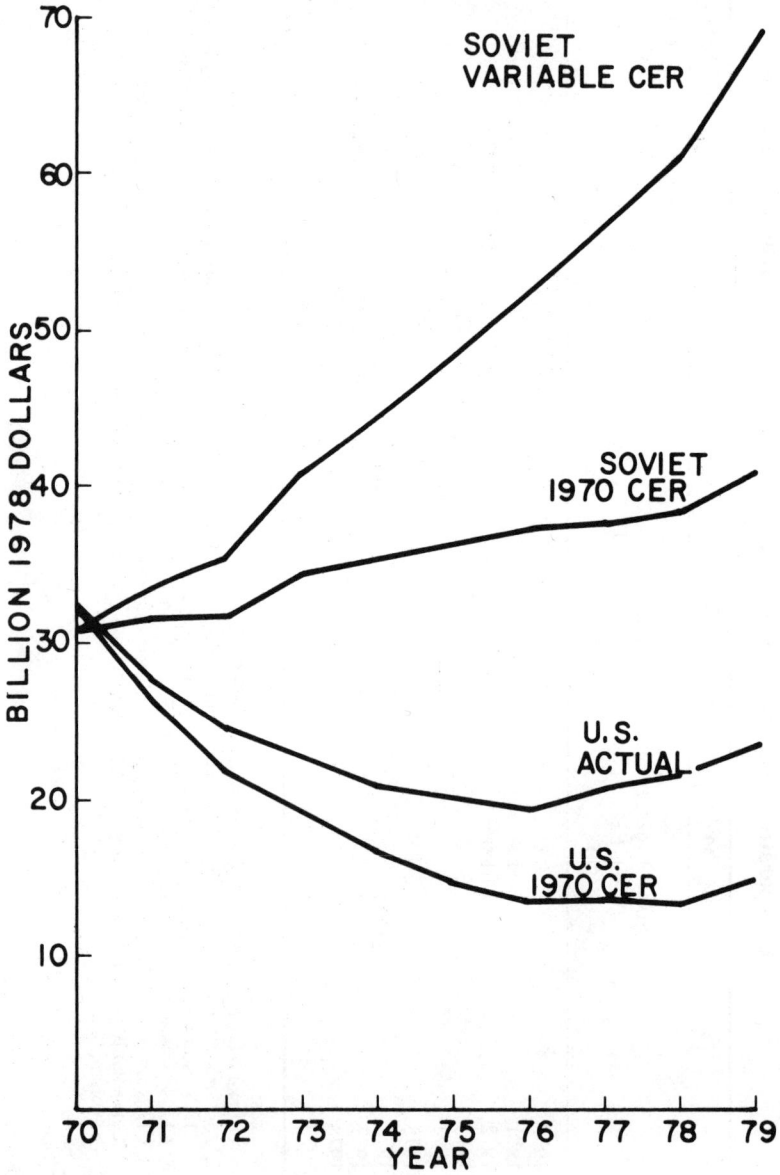

Such a procedure is, of course, impractical because of the demands it places on the acquisition of technical intelligence, and its computational requirements.

A good second best exists, however. Soviet weapons can be calculated in given year American CERs, valued in constant 1970 prices, "Sovietized," and adjusted where possible for the differential rate of Soviet-U.S. qualitative improvements estimated by other means. The resulting procurement series, reflecting the embodied qualitative improvement in U.S. equipment, is illustrated in Figure P1 (Soviet Variable CER). Unlike the fixed vintage series, these variable vintage estimates accurately reflect the trend in comparative Soviet-U.S. procurement expenditures (see Figure P2) without distorting the real quantitative and qualitative magnitude of Soviet arms production. They have the double virtue of reliably representing both the absolute and comparative level of Soviet procurement expenditures within the limits set by our knowledge of Soviet weapons technology, and therefore should be preferred over all available alternatives.

The use of variable vintage American CERs to compare Soviet and American weapons production is appealing for other reasons as well. It avoids the erroneous assumption implicit in the CIA's present method that Soviet and U.S. equipment are more comparable for the technology of 1970, than for other vintages, 1971, 1972, . . . , 1979, etc. It necessitates the annual reassessment of the coefficients employed in "Sovietizing" U.S. weapons, and it requires no additional covert information.

Variable vintage dollar cost estimating relationships are used by the procurement branches of all U.S. military services to assess the cost of purchasing new weapons systems. They are calculated from ex-post production costs, and are continuously revised. As such they should be ideal for generating estimates of Soviet procurement that are comparable with those of the United States, and should be readily accessible to the agency.

Adoption of the variable vintage standard will necessitate a variety of related changes in the valuation of Soviet procurement factor costs. Table P2 presents a sample worksheet used for calculating Soviet warships with current CERs. Panel B indicates that CERs are employed in only two-fifths of the categories subsumed under the heading of "pricing," basic construction and ordnance, which account for roughly 50 percent of total ship-building costs. The remaining 50 percent is attributable to current labor costs, profits, and change orders. Although CIA practice with regard to these latter categories is obscure, especially its handling of "change orders," it is likely that they are either valued in 1970 CERs or in the case of "change orders" omitted altogether. If

FIGURE P2
Soviet-American Procurement Ratios: CIA Versus Consistently
Defined Fixed or Variable CER Measures

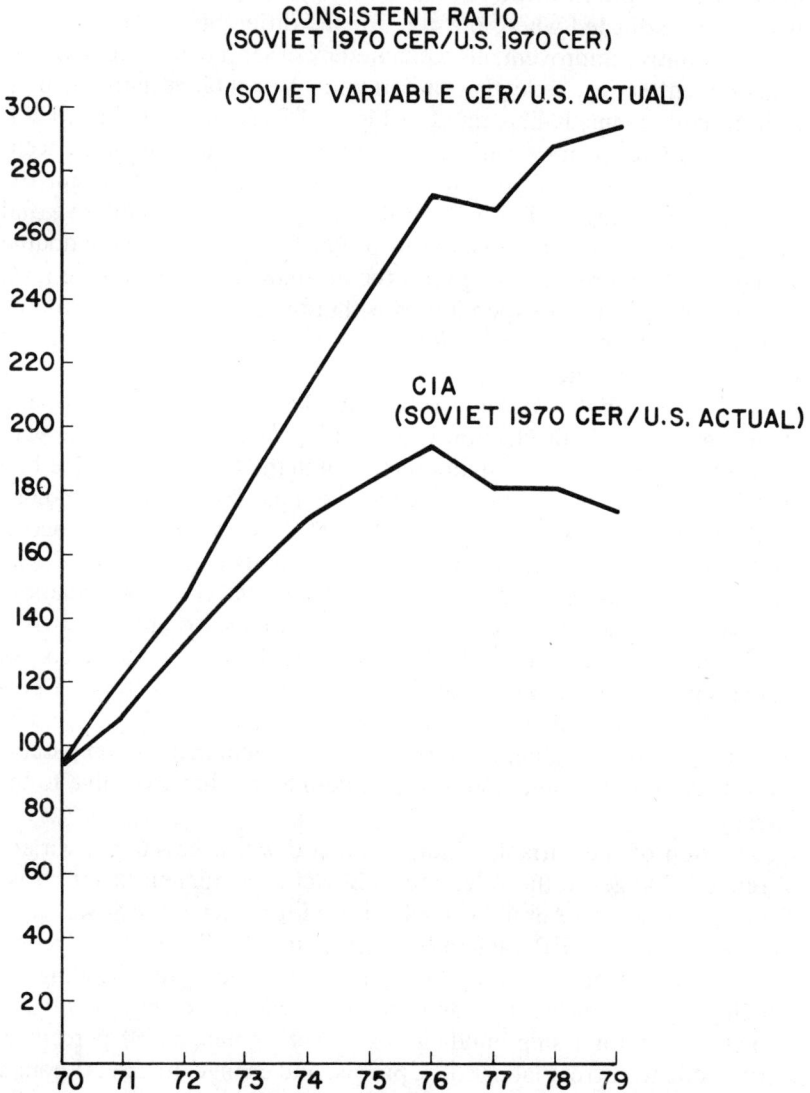

CONSISTENT RATIO
(SOVIET 1970 CER/U.S. 1970 CER)

(SOVIET VARIABLE CER/U.S. ACTUAL)

CIA
(SOVIET 1970 CER/U.S. ACTUAL)

TABLE P2
Sample Worksheet for Costing Soviet Warships

		Kara
A.	*Physical Parameters*	
	1. Ship characteristics	SEA 03D
	2. Ship weight	Classified
B.	*Pricing*	
	1. CER's	
	a. U.S. version	CSG
	b. Soviet version	
	i. Construction, HME, propulsion	-25%
	ii. Engineering services	-50%
	2. Labor cost	$18 per hour
	3. Profit	13%
	4. Change orders	14%
	5. Ordnance, special HME, electronics (GFM)	
	a. U.S. version (CERs)	CSG
	b. Soviet version	-25%

this conjecture is accurate, the agency will have to revise these procedures to assure consistency with actual U.S. weapons costs. Under the variable vintage standard, labor costs and profits must reflect current nonmaterial input shares (adjusted for inflation), and "change orders"—which may easily account for 14 percent of ex-post U.S. costs—must be included as part of the expense of building Soviet ships in the United States.

The early adoption of these recommendations should constitute an important step forward toward the achievement of a reasonably accurate, unbiased set of Soviet military procurement estimates that can support meaningful assessments of the level and growth of Soviet military procurement and the constellation of policy issues they entail. This outcome is not completely certain, but true science is a surer bet than the alternative which currently holds sway.

APPENDICES

APPENDIX 1

The "Technical Growth" of American Procurement, 1942–80

The 6 percent rate of American intervintage technological progress shown in chapter 4, equation 14, was derived in 1975 by Leonard Sullivan, assistant secretary of defense for program analysis and evaluation, and was reported to the House Armed Services Committee, April 14, 1975 (see "Five Year Defense Topline Projections," *Military Posture*, House Armed Services Committee, Washington, 1975, pp. 1817–60; and "Force-Structure and Long-Range Projections," House Budget Committee, Part 1, July 10, 1975, pp. 1–54. Mr. Sullivan also kindly provided me with the documentation supporting his calculations and discussed them with me in some detail). "Technical growth," as he refers to it, is computed from historical data from 1942 to 1980 (estimated) on the unit cost (in constant FY 74 dollars) of tanks, aircraft engines, general purpose bombs, strategic missiles, air-to-air ground missiles, air-to-air missiles, strategic bombers, cargo helicopter airframes, observation helicopter airframes, utility/attack helicopter airframes, electronic subsystems of air-to-air missiles, fighter aircraft, SLBMs, tanks, fighter aircraft, attack aircraft, submarine launched torpedoes, attack aircraft carriers, nuclear attack submarines, and destroyer escorts. Changes in unit cost reflect both product improvement and the superior technology embodied in new systems; defined for the kth weapon procured. Using linear regression techniques, Sullivan's staff estimated the compound annual rate of unit cost growth (in constant prices) for each weapon system; they then employed these growth rates to calculate the quality-improved cost in 1980 of tanks, destroyers, carriers, submarines, strategic missiles, bombers, air-to-air missiles, air-to-surface missiles, helicopters, fighters, and attack aircraft. These unit costs were aggregated and compared with the unit cost of the same systems before adjustment for qualitative change. The resulting ratio discounted t years:

1.
$$\tau = 100[(y_{80}^*/y_{80})^{1/32} - 1]$$
$$= 6 \text{ percent per annum}$$

is Sullivan's estimate of aggregate "technical growth."

This growth rate implies that during the past three decades the quality of aggregate U.S. procurement measured in terms of real unit cost rose at a compound rate of 6 percent per annum. Sullivan believes that this trend has not been significantly affected by the changing product mix and can be utilized to forecast future acquisition costs (see "Defense Economics: Modernization Through Left-Overs," paper delivered at the USAFA-RAND Conference on the Economics of National Security, U.S. Air Force Academy, August 16, 1979, p. 11; Nitze, "Correlating National Security Strategy and Defense Investment," in W. S. Thompson (ed.), *National Security in the 1980s: From Weakness to Strength*, Transaction Books–Institute for Contemporary Studies, 1980, pp. 337–74; "Strategic Top-Down Planning," Systems Planning Corporation, October 1980). This judgment implies either that over the aggregate procurement cycle "technical growth" has been increasing uniformly for new and product improved systems, or that the contribution to aggregate growth made by new and product improved systems moves reciprocally. The latter characterization most closely parallels Sullivan's view. He has argued on numerous occasions that the rate of product improvement is lower than the rate of technological growth embodied in new systems. On average he believes product improvements on a unit cost basis have risen 3 percent per annum, while the technology embodied in new systems has increased 9 percent per annum (see "Defense Economics: Modernization Through Left-Overs," pp. 11–12. Sullivan suggested the 9 percent estimate to me when we discussed these matters on March 11, 1981). To sustain the average 6 percent rate of technology growth over the procurement cycle, given these average differentials, the contribution of product improvements must decline during the expansionary phase and increase over the contractionary phase. This cyclical pattern implies that the average rate of intervintage technology progress was probably considerably higher during the seventies than the long-term average product improvement rate, perhaps in line with the long-term trend in aggregate "technological growth"—a result consistent with my own direct estimates (equations 12 and 13) of the upward shift in the average American parametric cost estimating regression line from 1970 to 1979. It also suggests that American intervintage technological progress during the sixties, which contained several intraperiod cycles, was in the neighborhood of 3 percent per annum, in line with William Reese's independent estimate (see chapter 4, note 14).

With regard to *Soviet* "technological growth" Sullivan and I examined this issue together at length. It was his judgment that the Soviet approach to technological growth stressed product improvement over new systems innovation; and that the Soviets hewed a middle course between the incrementalism adopted by Western commercial entities and the tendency exhibited in new U.S. programs to completely redesign products. As a consequence, drawing on his knowledge of Soviet and U.S. procurement development programs, and the direct evidence which I provided, Sullivan concludes that Soviet intervintage technological progress from 1960 to 1979 was probably around 6 percent per annum, slightly below my dollar estimate of 6.6 percent per annum reported in Table 13.2 (the difference between the total rate of Soviet growth from 1960 to 1979, 9.6 percent, and the rate of volume growth, 3 percent).

APPENDIX 2

Reconstruction of Steiner's Ruble Price Index for Soviet Industrial Output

Approach 1

A step-by-step description of Steiner's computational method is provided in the Statistical Appendix to his monograph, *Inflation in Soviet Industry and Machine-Building and Metalworking (MBMW) 1960–1975*, pages 66–74. The results of each step are reported in individual tables. These results can be checked by replicating his calculations. To ascertain the analytic content of Steiner's estimates, all that needs to be done is to formally restate each of his steps, verifying the correctness of this reformulation by replicating the results he reports in his tables.

Steiner's computation of his ruble price index for Soviet industrial output (Approach 1) is mechanically performed in four simple steps reconstructed below:

Step 1: "Soviet GVO industry in current dollars (Table A5) is calculated by multiplying US GVO industry (Table A4) by the announced Soviet data on their industrial product as a percent of US product (Table A3)" (p. 66).

Soviet GVO in current dollars, that is gross Soviet industrial output valued in dollars, can be expressed algebraically as

1.
$$Q_s = \sum_{i=1}^{s} p_i \, q_i$$

where p_i represents the dollar price of the ith Soviet industrial good q_i. These values were first computed by Treml and Gallik in *Soviet Studies on Ruble/Dollar Parity Ratios.* See Table A1, column 4. The derivation of these statistics is explained by Treml and Gallik on page 13.

Steiner reproduces the Treml and Gallik figures by multiplying Table A2 by Table A4.

Table A2 represents U.S. industrial output in Soviet definition (i.e., classification) taken directly from Treml and Gallik. See Table A3.

Algebraically,

2.
$$Q_A = \sum_{i=1}^{n} p_i \bar{q}_i$$

where the symbol $\bar{q}_i$ represents the ith American good valued in dollar prices, p_i. Table A4 is not one table, but two. The first is a dollar wholesale price index (*Business Statistics,* 1975, pages 48–49), the second "share structure of Soviet GVO industry" obtained from *Narodnoe Khoziaistvo SSSR* in constant 1967 prices. The wholesale price index for each industry has the form:

3.
$$P = \frac{p_i^t \bar{q}_i^{67}}{p_i^{67} \bar{q}_i^{67}}$$

The summation signs are omitted for consistency. The ith product in our notation refers to a specific industry. Since Steiner's wholesale price indices pertain to individual industries, no summation across industries is implied. The share structure of Soviet industrial GVO can be expressed for each sector as

4.
$$S = \frac{r_i^{67} q_i^t}{\sum_{i=1}^{s} r_i^{67} q_i^t}$$

TABLE A1
Ruble/Dollar Ratios for Total Industrial Product, 1960–70

Year	Soviet output, in billions of rubles (1)	U.S. output, in billions of dollars (2)	Ratio of Soviet/U.S. output (3)	Soviet output, in billions of dollars (4)	Ruble/dollar ratio (5)
1960	157.4	408.6	.600	245.2	.642
1961	172.6	410.7	.605	248.5	.695
1962	188.4	441.7	.630	278.3	.677
1963	201.0	464.7	.650	302.2	.665
1964	212.4	491.4	.655	321.9	.660
1965	229.4	539.7	.650	350.8	.654
1966	248.3	589.2	.655	385.9	.643
1967	285.9	610.2	.670	408.8	.699
1968	322.8	659.3	.700	461.5	.699
1969	345.0	702.8	.700	492.0	.701
1970	374.3	697.1	.755	526.3	.711

Table A1 corresponds with Treml and Gallik's Table A4.
The derivation of these statistics is explained by Treml and Gallik on page 13.

Treml-Gallik: Methodological Description
(page 13)

B. *Industrial Product*

Beginning in 1959, TsSU has annually published comparisons of the absolute levels of Soviet and U.S. industrial product. Unlike the similar measure for national income, no dollar totals are ever given and all the information available is that in a given year Soviet gross value of industrial output (GVO) was "about 60 percent" or "more than 75 percent" of the U.S. (see table B-1). Imperfect as this information is, it is still possible to estimate implied ruble/dollar ratios, although with a considerable degree of probable error. Using the analogy with national income comparisons, the writings of Soviet scholars, and some tests of alternative methods, it was concluded that the Soviet/U.S. industrial output ratios were probably obtained as follows:

1. U.S. output for the given year is computed on the basis of published U.S. statistics but adjusted to accord with Soviet statistical practices and definitions; this output is calculated in current wholesale prices.

2. Soviet output is in terms of current enterprise prices.

3. A sample of Soviet industrial commodities of unknown size and composition is prepared and priced in current U.S. wholesale and current Soviet enterprise prices and the ruble/dollar ratio is estimated as

$$R_s = \frac{\sum q_s P_s}{\sum q_s P_u}$$

TABLE A1 (Continued)

4. Soviet output in dollars is obtained by dividing the output in rubles by the ruble/dollar ratio derived under point 3.

5. Soviet output as a percentage of U.S. output is given as

$$C_u = \frac{\dfrac{\sum Q_s P_s}{R_s}}{\sum Q_u P_u}$$

Accordingly, the implied ruble/dollar ratio (Soviet weights) can be estimated by using three values: Soviet output, U.S. output, and the Soviet/U.S. output ratio. From the formula in point 5 it follows that

$$R_s = \frac{\sum Q_s P_s}{\sum Q_u P_u \cdot C_u}$$

The ruble/dollar ratios for total industrial product estimated by this method are shown in table 4, together with the underlying data.

---

where the output share for any year t in industry i is valued in 1967 enterprise wholesale ruble prices.

The procedure by which indices 3 and 4 are manipulated, and then multiplied by expression 2 to obtain gross Soviet industrial output valued in current dollars (equation 1), is not explained. Presumably an operation of the following sort is required:

5.
$$\sum_{i=1}^{s} p_i\, q_i = \sum_{i=1}^{n} p_i\, \bar{q}_i \cdot \frac{\sum_{i=1}^{s} p_i\, q_i}{\sum_{i=1}^{n} p_i\, \bar{q}_i}$$

This would produce the same results as those reported by Treml-Gallik. Indeed the statistics given by Steiner in Table A5 are identical with those found in Treml-Gallik. See Table A1, column 4. How Steiner achieved this with the indices reported in his Table A4, however, is obscure.

Step 2: "Dividing Soviet GVO industry in current rubles (Table A7, line 5) by this current dollar series yields a series of current ruble to current dollar ratios (Table A6)" (page 71). In step 2 Steiner takes the gross dollar-valued Soviet industrial output series "calculated" in step

TABLE A2
U.S. Industrial Output in Soviet Definition, 1960–75
(Billions of Dollars)

Year	All manu-factures (1)	Minus oil and gas well drilling and explo-ration service (2)	Minus publishing and editing (3)	Plus auto repair services (4)	Plus miscel-laneous repair services (5)	Plus railroad equipment mainte-nance (6)	Plus mining industries (7)	Plus fishing industry (8)	Plus electric power (9)	Plus gas utilities (10)	Plus water supply system (11)	Total (12)
1960	369.6	1.0	4.5	3.1	2.5	1.8	18.0	.4	11.5	5.6	1.5	408.6
1961	370.6	1.0	4.9	3.3	2.7	1.7	18.2	.4	12.2	6.0	1.6	410.7
1962	399.7	1.0	5.4	3.4	2.9	1.7	18.8	.4	13.0	6.4	1.7	441.7
1963	421.0	1.1	5.8	3.6	3.0	1.8	19.6	.4	13.7	6.7	1.9	464.7
1964	445.6	1.1	6.3	3.7	3.2	1.8	20.6	.4	14.4	7.1	1.9	491.4
1965	492.0	1.1	6.8	3.8	3.4	1.8	21.5	.4	15.2	7.4	2.0	530.7
1966	538.5	1.0	7.3	4.0	3.6	1.8	23.0	.5	16.2	7.9	2.1	589.2
1967	557.4	1.0	7.8	4.1	3.8	1.9	23.7	.4	17.2	8.3	2.2	610.2
1968	603.4	1.0	8.4	4.2	4.1	1.9	25.0	.5	18.6	8.8	2.3	659.3
1969	642.6	1.1	9.0	4.4	4.2	2.0	26.9	.5	20.1	9.5	2.4	702.5
1970	634.3	1.2	9.3	4.5	4.6	2.2	29.8	.6	22.1	10.3	2.7	700.6
1971	671.0	1.4	8.7	5.5	5.4	2.3	30.3	.7	25.0	11.3	3.2	744.6
1972	744.2	1.5	9.2	6.0	6.2	2.4	30.7	.7	27.9	12.5	3.4	823.3
1973	856.8	1.6	9.6	7.2	7.7	2.6	32.2	.9	31.7	13.0	3.7	944.6
1974	982.0	1.7	9.6	7.8	8.5	2.9	36.8	.9	39.1	15.2	4.1	1086.0
1975	993.0	1.8	9.6	8.5	9.3	3.0	55.2	1.0	46.9	19.1	4.7	1129.3

Source: See Treml and Gallik [68], pg. 26–27.
Table A2 corresponds with Steiner's Table A-3.

TABLE A3
U.S. Industrial Output in Soviet Definition, 1960–70
(Millions of Dollars)

Year	All manu-factures (1)	Minus oil and gas well drilling and exploration services (2)	Minus publishing and editing (3)	Plus auto repair services (4)	Plus miscel-laneous repair services (5)	Plus railroad equipment mainte-nance (6)	Plus mining industries (7)	Plus fishing industry (8)	Plus electric power (9)	Plus gas utilities (10)	Plus water supply system (11)	Total (12)
1960	369,600	1,000	4,500	3,101	2,542	1,760	18,032	354	11,516	5,617	1,529	408,551
1961	370,600	1,050	4,900	3,287	2,695	1,684	18,230	362	12,169	5,993	1,621	410,691
1962	399,700	1,050	5,400	3,399	2,857	1,743	18,838	396	13,025	6,445	1,725	441,678
1963	420,973	1,099	5,814	3,588	3,022	1,785	19,620	377	13,697	6,727	1,865	464,741
1964	445,600	1,100	6,300	3,710	3,218	1,764	20,612	389	14,408	7,133	1,917	491,351
1965	492,009	1,100	6,800	3,836	3,427	1,775	21,524	445	15,158	7,407	2,004	539,685
1966	538,508	1,050	7,300	3,966	3,650	1,844	22,968	472	16,196	7,870	2,115	589,239
1967	557,398	1,046	7,800	4,086	3,827	1,869	23,729	440	17,223	8,261	2,187	610,174
1968	603,379	1,050	8,400	4,225	4,076	1,914	24,971	497	18,580	8,781	2,313	659,286
1969	642,636	1,050	9,000	4,369	4,341	1,995	26,921	518	20,139	9,476	2,464	702,809
1970	630,710	1,050	9,300	4,518	4,623	2,170	29,791	613	22,066	10,283	2,687	697,111

Table A3 corresponds with Treml and Gallik's Table A-1.

TABLE A4
Wholesale Price Indices, U.S. Dollars, 1959–74

	Electrical power	Fuels	Chemical	Machinery	Pulp, Wood	Non-metal mineral	Textile	Food	Other (metal)
1959	100.1	95.3	101.6	91.3	98.05	97	98.4	89.4	92.3
1960	101.2	96.1	101.8	92	96.7	97.2	99.5	89.5	92.4
1961	101.7	97.2	100.7	91.9	93.1	97.6	97.7	91	91.9
1962	102.1	96.7	99.1	92	93.95	97.6	98.6	91.9	91.2
1963	101.3	96.3	97.9	92.2	94.55	97.1	98.5	92.5	91.3
1964	100.4	93.7	98.3	92.8	95.4	97.3	99.2	92.3	92.8
1965	100.1	95.5	99	93.9	96.05	97.5	99.8	95.5	96.4
1966	99.6	97.8	99.4	96.8	99.5	98.4	100.1	101.2	98.8
1967	100	100	100	100	100	100	100	100	100
1968	100.9	98.9	99.9	103.2	107.2	108.7	103.7	102.2	102.6
1969	101.8	100.9	99.9	106.5	114.7	107.7	106.	107.3	108.5
1970	105.9	106.2	102.2	111.4	110.9	112.9	108.1	112.1	116.6
1971	118.6	114.2	104.2	115.5	118.55	122.4	108.6	114.3	119
1972	121.5	118.6	104.2	117.9	128.85	126.1	113.6	120.8	123.5
1973	129.3	134.3	110	121.7	149.65	130.2	123.8	148.1	132.8
1974	163.1	208.3	146.8	139.4	167.65	153.2	189.1	170.9	171.9

Source: Business Statistics, 1975, pgs. 48–49.

TABLE A4 (Continued)

Share Structure of Soviet GVO Industry (%)

Year									
1959	2.32	7.84	3.78	15.98	7.1	3.98	23.6	25.6	9.8
1960	2.4	7.7	3.9	16.6	6.9	4	22.5	25.4	10.6
1961	2.48	7.56	4.12	17.26	6.7	4.02	21.4	25.1	11.36
1962	2.56	7.42	4.34	17.92	6.5	4.04	20.3	24.9	12.06
1963	2.64	7.28	4.56	18.58	6.3	4.06	19.2	24.6	12.78
1964	2.79	7.14	4.78	19.24	6.1	4.08	18.1	24.4	13.31
1965	2.8	7	5	19.9	5.9	4.1	17	24.1	14.8
1966	2.82	6.84	5.2	20.52	5.76	4.1	17	23.52	14.8
1967	2.84	6.68	5.4	21.14	5.62	4.1	17	22.94	14.8
1968	2.86	6.52	5.6	21.76	5.48	4.1	17	22.36	14.8
1969	2.88	6.36	5.8	22.38	5.34	4.1	17	21.76	14.4
1970	2.9	6.2	6	23	5.2	4.1	17	21.2	14.4
1971	2.9	6.1	6.1	23.8	5.1	4.1	16.8	20.7	14.4
1972	2.9	6	6.3	24.9	5	4.1	16.2	20.1	14.5
1973	2.9	5.9	6.5	25.9	4.9	4.1	15.7	19.6	14.5
1974	2.8	5.8	6.7	26.9	4.7	4.1	15.2	19.5	14.8

Source: 1960 entry is from NKH 72 pg 166; 1965 and 1970–1974 from NKH 74 pg 1975. Other years estimated by interpolation. Table A4 corresponds with Steiner's Table A-4.

TABLE A5
Soviet GVO Industry in Billions of Current Dollars

1960	245.2
1961	248.5
1962	278.5
1963	302.1
1964	321.9
1965	350.8
1966	385.9
1967	408.8
1968	461.5
1969	492.0
1970	526.3
1971	562.2
1972	621.6
1973	713.2
1974	874.2

Source: Ratio of USSR/US Industrial Output (Table A2) multiplied by US Industrial
Output (Table A4). See Treml and Gallik [68], p. 14.
Table A2 corresponds with Steiner's Table A-3.
Table A5 corresponds with Steiner's Table A-5.

1 and simply divides it by the official Soviet ruble-valued industrial
output series obtained from *Narodnoe Khoziaistvo SSSR*. Symbolically,
this ruble-valued gross industrial output series is:

6.
$$Q_s^* = \sum_{i=1}^{s} r_i \, q_i$$

and the ratio Steiner forms is

7.
$$R = \frac{\sum_{i=1}^{s} r_i \, q_i}{\sum_{i=1}^{s} p_i \, q_i}$$

This operation is easily checked arithmetically. Soviet gross industrial
output valued respectively in dollars and rubles for 1960 are 157.4 and
245.2. Dividing these figures yields 0.6419, which agrees with the analogous entry in Steiner's Table A6.

Step 3: "These ratios are then deflated by the dollar price index (Soviet
sector share weights) (see Table A8) to calculate a series of *current ruble*

TABLE A6
Soviet GVO Industry (Current Prices): Implicit Ruble Dollar Ratios

1960	0.642
1961	0.695
1962	0.677
1963	0.665
1964	0.66
1965	0.654
1966	0.643
1967	0.699
1968	0.699
1969	0.701
1970	0.711
1971	0.704
1972	0.676
1973	0.627
1974	0.549

Source: Table A-2, line 5 multiplied by Table A-5
N.B.: Steiner's Table A-2 is not reproduced in this appendix, see his original.
Table A6 corresponds with Steiner's Table A-6.

to *constant 1970 dollar* ratios" (page 71). In step 3 Steiner takes the ratio computed in step 2 (equation 7) and "deflates" it by a dollar price index with Soviet weights. Algebraically the operation intended is

8.
$$
\frac{\sum_{i=1}^{s} r_i^t q_i^t}{\sum_{i=1}^{s} p_i^{70} q_i^{70}} = \frac{\sum_{i=1}^{s} r_i^t q_i^t}{\sum_{i=1}^{s} p_i^t q_i^t} \cdot \frac{\sum_{i=1}^{s} p_i^t q_i^t}{\sum_{i=1}^{s} p_i^{70} q_i^{70}}
$$

(Note that the second term on the right cannot be the dollar price index Steiner specifies.) The dollar price index for Soviet industrial output employed for this purpose is reported in Table A8.

The source reference at the bottom of Table A8 explains that the price index is computed from "sector dollar price indices multiplied by Soviet output weights. See Table A4." The requisite multiplication can be performed in two alternative ways. First, the wholesale price index matrix A can be row multiplied by the Soviet industrial share matrix B

TABLE A7

Data on Official Price Indices and Indices of Comparable Prices

	1960	1961	1962	1963	1964	1965	1966	1967	1968	1969	1970	1971	1972	1973	1974
1. Official Index[1]—Industry	69	70	71	71	71	70	71	77	77	77	77	76	76	75	75
2. Indexed, 1970 = 1.00	.896	.909	.922	.922	.922	.909	.922	1.00	1.00	1.00	1.00	.987	.987	.974	.974
3. Official Index[1]—MBMW	44	44	44	43	42	41	40	40	40	39	39	36	36	34	33
4. Indexed, 1970 = 100	1.128	1.128	1.128	1.103	1.077	1.051	1.026	1.026	1.026	1.00	1.000	0.923	0.923	0.872	0.846
5. GVO Industry[2]—Current Price	157.4	172.6	188.4	201.0	212.4	229.4	248.3	285.9	322.8	345.0	374.3	395.7	420.0	447.3	479.3
6. Indexed, 1970 = 100	42.1	46.1	50.3	53.7	56.7	61.3	66.3	76.4	86.2	92.2	100.0	105.7	112.2	119.5	128.1
7. GVO Industry[3] Comparable Price Indexed, 1970 = 100	44.3	48.3	53.0	57.3	61.5	66.9	72.7	80.0	86.7	92.7	100.0	108.0	115.3	124.0	133.3
8. Implicit Index of Comparable Prices Industry*	.950	.954	.950	.937	.923	.916	.912	.955	.995	.995	1.000	.979	.973	.964	.960
9. GVO MBMW[4]—Current Price	30.9	34.9	39.1	43.3	47.0	50.6	58.7	66.2	74.4	81.1	89.8	95.0	104.3	108.8	119.7
10. Indexed, 1970 = 100	34.4	38.9	43.5	48.2	52.3	56.3	65.4	73.7	82.9	90.3	100.0	105.8	116.1	121.2	133.3
11. GVO MBMW[5] Index, Comparable,															

TABLE A7 (Continued)

Indexed, 1970 = 100	31.9	36.7	42.2	47.6	52.2	57.2	64.2	71.9	80.5	90.0	100.0	111.0	124.1	139.0	155.0
12. Implicit Index of Comparable Prices MBMW**	1.079	1.060	1.032	1.012	1.002	0.985	1.017	1.025	1.029	1.004	1.000	0.953	0.936	0.871	0.860

* Line 6 divided by line 7
** Line 10 divided by Line 11

Notes:

1. Official series from Soviet annual statistical handbooks [16] (*Naradnoe Khozlaystvo SSR—NKH*).

   1949 equals 100.

   Entries for '65, '67, '70–75 from
   NKH '75 pg 231; 60, 66 from (English)
   NKH '67 pg 226; '69 from
   NKH '70 pg 175; '64 from
   NKH '69 pg 188; 62, 63 from
   NKH '63 pg 136. Entry for 1961 is not available and was estimated by interpolating entries for 1960 and 1962.
   Billion current rubles, establishment basis.

2. Entries for 1955–1967 from (English)
   NKH 67 pg 185; 1967–75 from
   NKH 75 pg 191.

3. Entries for 1960–65 from NKH '65, pg 121 in 1 July 1955 prices.
   Entries for 1965–1975 from the growth series in NKH '75 pg 255.

4. Abbot [1]. Billion current rubles.
   Establishment basis.

5. Entries for 1960–1970 from NKH '70 pg 204; 1970–1975 from NKH '75 pg 255.

Table A7 corresponds with Steiner's Table A-1.

TABLE A8
Dollar Price Index for GVO Industry (Soviet Sector Share Weights)

1960	0.855
1961	0.852
1962	0.855
1963	0.855
1964	0.858
1965	0.872
1966	0.897
1967	0.904
1968	0.929
1969	0.963
1970	1
1971	1.033
1972	1.074
1973	1.182
1974	1.422

Source: Sector dollar price indices multiplied by Soviet output weights. See Table A4. Table A8 corresponds with Steiner's Table A-7.

a) $M = A * B$

$$\begin{bmatrix} a_{11} & a_{12} & a_{13} \\ \cdot & & \\ \cdot & & \\ \cdot & \cdot & \cdot \cdot \end{bmatrix} * \begin{bmatrix} b_{11} & b_{12} & b_{13} \\ \cdot & & \\ \cdot & & \\ \cdot & \cdot & \cdot \cdot \end{bmatrix} = \begin{bmatrix} a_{11} b_{11} & a_{12} b_{12} & a_{13} b_{13} \\ \cdot & & \\ \cdot & & \\ \cdot & \cdot & \cdot \cdot \end{bmatrix}$$

summed

10. $m = M e$ $\begin{bmatrix} a_{11}b_{11} & a_{12}b_{12} & a_{13}b_{13} \\ \cdot & & \\ \cdot & & \\ \cdot & \cdot & \cdot \cdot \end{bmatrix} \begin{bmatrix} 1 \\ 1 \\ 1 \end{bmatrix} = \begin{bmatrix} \sum_{i=1}^{n} a_{1i}b_{1i} \\ \sum_{i=1}^{n} a_{2i}b_{2i} \\ \sum_{i=1}^{n} a_{3i}b_{3i} \end{bmatrix}$

and normalized

11. $m^* = \begin{bmatrix} m_1/m_j \\ m_2/m_j \\ \cdot \\ \cdot \\ m_3/m_j \end{bmatrix}$

For these matrix operations to be legitimate the elements in the vector m* must be logically meaningful. It is easy to demonstrate that they are not by considering any two vector elements in m. Take the years 1960 and 1970 as examples. The term $\sum_{j=1}^{9} a_{1j} b_{1j}$ where the first subscript refers to a particular year can be rewritten more specifically as

12.
$$\sum_{j=1}^{9} a_{1j} b_{1j} = \sum_{i=1}^{s} \left(\frac{p_i^{60} \bar{q}_i^{67}}{p_i^{67} \bar{q}_i^{67}} \cdot \frac{r_i^{67} q_i^{60}}{\sum_{i=1}^{s} r_i^{67} q_i^{60}} \right)$$

and

13.
$$\sum_{j=1}^{9} a_{2j} b_{2j} = \sum_{i=1}^{s} \left(\frac{p_i^{70} \bar{q}_i^{67}}{p_i^{67} \bar{q}_i^{67}} \cdot \frac{r_i^{67} q_i^{70}}{\sum_{i=1}^{s} r_i^{67} q_i^{70}} \right)$$

Dividing equation 12 by equation 13 does not yield a logically consistent "dollar price index (Soviet sector share weights)"because the share weights are variable. Algebraically, Steiner's "dollar price index" cannot be construed as a price index

14.
$$\frac{\sum_{i=1}^{s} p_i^{t} q_i^{o}}{\sum_{i=1}^{s} p_i^{o} q_i^{o}} \neq \frac{\sum_{i=1}^{s} \left(\frac{p_i^{60} \bar{q}_i^{67}}{p_i^{67} \bar{q}_i^{67}} \cdot \frac{r_i^{67} q_i^{60}}{\sum_{i=1}^{s} r_i^{67} q_i^{60}} \right)}{\sum_{i=1}^{s} \left(\frac{p_i^{70} \bar{q}_i^{67}}{p_i^{67} \bar{q}_i^{67}} \cdot \frac{r_i^{67} q_i^{70}}{\sum_{i=1}^{s} r_i^{67} q_i^{70}} \right)}$$

of the conventional sort at all where t and o are time superscripts. (The superscripts 60, 67, 70, refer to the years 1960, 1967, and 1970.)

The "dollar price index" reported in Table A8 could also be computed in another way by directly normalizing the price index (matrix A) to a 1970 base and then repeating the steps indicated in equations 9 and 10. These calculations alter the precise form of the m elements, which are now prenormalized, but the result is no more logical than before.

Unfortunately due to rounding errors it is difficult to determine which of the two alternative, but nonequivalent matrix row multiplication procedures Steiner employed. Either approach, however, will produce results only trivially different than those presented in his Table A8.

It follows from this demonstration that equation 8, the ratio of gross Soviet industrial output valued in current rubles and constant 1970 dollars, is not accurately calculated with Steiner's procedures, nor had it been would it have yielded the ratio he intended. See equation 8.

Step 4: "Finally, these ratios are divided by the 1970 ruble to 1970 dollar ratio (.711) to yield an implicit ruble price index (Table A9)" (page 71). In Steiner's fourth and last step he divided what he believes is equation 8, the result of step 3, by the 1970 ruble/dollar ratio for gross Soviet industrial output to obtain what he asserts is an "implicit ruble price index."

15.
$$\frac{\sum_{i=1}^{s} r_i^t q_i^{70}}{\sum_{i=1}^{s} r_i^{70} q_i^{70}} \neq \frac{\sum_{i=1}^{s} r_i^t q_i^t}{\sum_{i=1}^{s} p_i^{70} q_i^{70}} \div \frac{\sum_{i=1}^{s} r_i^{70} q_i^{70}}{\sum_{i=1}^{s} p_i^{70} q_i^{70}}$$

The operation he performs, ignoring the error in equation 8, actually yields,

16.
$$\frac{\sum_{i=1}^{s} r_i^t q_i^t}{\sum_{i=1}^{s} r_i^{70} q_i^{70}} = \frac{\sum_{i=1}^{s} r_i^t q_i^t}{\sum_{i=1}^{s} p_i^{70} q_i^{70}} \cdot \frac{\sum_{i=1}^{s} p_i^{70} q_i^{70}}{\sum_{i=1}^{s} r_i^{70} q_i^{70}}$$

which is the ratio of Soviet gross industrial output for some current year t and 1970. To verify that this is indeed the operation Steiner has performed, all that needs to be done is to observe where he obtains the divisor, 0.711, he uses to transform "series of *current ruble* to *constant 1970 dollar* ratios" (equation 8) into his "implicit ruble price index" (equation 16) reported in Table A9.

Steiner's gross industrial ruble dollar ratio for 1970 is taken from Treml-Gallik (Table A1, column 5). The derivation of the ratio is described in the table. The numerator is Soviet gross industrial output obtained from *Narodnoe Khoziaistvo* 1970, p. 69,

17.
$$\sum_{i=1}^{s} r_i^{70} q_i^{70}$$

The denominator is Soviet gross industrial output in dollars estimated by Treml-Gallik,

TABLE A9
Approach 1: Ruble Price Index for Soviet Industrial Output

1960	0.773
1961	0.834
1962	0.815
1963	0.801
1964	0.797
1965	0.804
1966	0.812
1967	0.890
1968	0.914
1969	0.951
1970	1.000
1971	1.024
1972	1.022
1973	1.045
1974	1.099

Table A9 corresponds with Steiner's Table A-8.

18. $$\sum_{i=1}^{s} p_i^{70} q_i^{70}$$

The ratio of expression 18 to 17 is the right most term in equation 16. This means that Steiner's "implicit ruble price index" is nothing else than the ratio of the Soviet gross industrial output index taken from his Table A7, row 5 (equation 6) and Soviet gross industrial output for 1970 taken from Treml-Gallik [Table A1, column 1 (equation 17)]. Both are obtained directly from the same official Soviet statistical series. *Steiner's series therefore with or without the error in equation 8 is economically meaningless and cannot be construed as an "implicit ruble price index."*

To prove beyond a shadow of a doubt that this interpretation is correct, let us once again check Steiner's arithmetic. Column 1, Table A10 records the ratio of Soviet gross industrial output valued in rubles and dollars, the end product of step 2 (equation 7, Steiner's Table A6). Column 2, Table A10 reports Steiner's "dollar price index for GVO industry" (equations 9–14, Steiner's Table A7).

The algebraic characterization of columns 2–4 ignore the logical deficiencies of Steiner's "dollar price index" (column 2). According to Steiner, columns 1 and 2 are "deflators" (multiplied) to produce a "series of *current ruble* to *constant 1970 dollar* ratios. This product, which is not reported in Steiner's paper, is computed in Table 10, column 3. When divided by the Treml-Gallik ruble-dollar ratio, 0.711, Steiner's

TABLE A10
A Reconstruction of Steiner's Derivation of His "Implicit Ruble Price Index"

	(1)	(2)	(3)	(4)
1960	0.642	0.855	0.549	0.772
1961	0.695	0.852	0.592	0.833
1962	0.677	0.855	0.579	0.814
1963	0.665	0.855	0.569	0.800
1964	0.661	0.858	0.566	0.796
1965	0.654	0.872	0.570	0.802
1966	0.643	0.897	0.577	0.812
1967	0.699	0.904	0.632	0.889
1968	0.699	0.929	0.649	0.913
1969	0.701	0.963	0.675	0.949
1970	0.711	1.000	0.711	1.000
1971	0.704	1.033	0.727	1.023
1972	0.676	1.074	0.726	1.021
1973	0.627	1.182	0.741	1.042
1974	0.549	1.422	0.781	1.098

Column 1: Steiner's Table A-6, $\dfrac{\sum\limits_{i=1}^{s} r_i^i q_i^i}{\sum\limits_{i=1}^{s} p_i^i q_i^i}$

Column 2: Steiner's Table A-7, $\dfrac{\sum\limits_{i=1}^{s} p_i^i q_i^i}{\sum\limits_{i=1}^{s} p_i^{70} q_i^{70}} = \dfrac{\sum\limits_{i=1}^{s} \left(\dfrac{p_i^{60}\overline{q}_i^{67}}{p_i^{67}\overline{q}_i^{67}} \cdot \dfrac{r_i^{67} q_i^{60}}{\sum\limits_{i=1}^{s} r_i^{67} q_i^{60}} \right)}{\sum\limits_{i=1}^{s} \left(\dfrac{p_i^{70}\overline{q}_i^{67}}{p_i^{67}\overline{q}_i^{67}} \cdot \dfrac{r_i^{67} q_i^{70}}{\sum\limits_{i=1}^{s} r_i^{67} q_i^{70}} \right)}$

Column 3: $\dfrac{\sum\limits_{i=1}^{s} r_i^i q_i^i}{\sum\limits_{i=1}^{s} p_i^{70} q_i^{70}}$ = column 1 × column 2

Column 4: $\dfrac{\sum\limits_{i=1}^{s} r_i^i q_i^i}{\sum\limits_{i=1}^{s} r_i^{70} q_i^{70}} = \dfrac{\sum\limits_{i=1}^{s} r_i^i q_i^i}{\sum\limits_{i=1}^{s} p_i^{70} q_i^{70}} \cdot \dfrac{\sum\limits_{i=1}^{s} p_i^{70} q_i^{70}}{\sum\limits_{i=1}^{s} r_i^{70} q_i^{70}}$ = column 3/(0.711) "implicit ruble price index" Table A8 is replicated almost exactly, differing only due to rounding error.

It follows directly that the description of Steiner's computations laid out above is arithmetically valid. If my interpretation is in error, then that error can only inhere in my algebraic characterization. The reader is invited to confirm my derivation. Should no errors be found then the conclusion that Steiner's calculations are meaningless is unavoidable for at root his failure is not one of arithmetic but analytic conceptualization.

APPENDIX 3

The Office of Economic Research's Estimates of Soviet Machine Price Inflation

A third attempt by the CIA to estimate price inflation in the Soviet machinery sector appeared recently in *USSR and the United States: Price Ratios for Machinery, 1967 Rubles–1972 Dollars*, Volume 1, ER80–10410, September 1980. Working with ruble-dollar ratios for machinery computed for 1955 by Abraham Becker and for 1967/72 by the agency, John Keilty and Earl Rubenking applied the following formula to calculate Soviet machinery price inflation from 1955 to 1967:[1]

1.
$$I_s = \frac{R_{67} \cdot I_u}{R_{55}}$$

where I_s is an index of Soviet machinery ruble price change

R_{67} is the CIA's aggregate machinery ruble-dollar ratio for 1967/72

I_u is an index of American machinery dollar price change

R_{55} is Becker's aggregate machinery ruble-dollar ratio for 1955.

To evaluate the merit of this expression as a measure of Soviet machinery price inflation equation 1 can be rewritten in full index form:[2]

2.
$$\frac{\sum r_{67}q_{55}}{\sum r_{55}q_{55}} = \frac{\dfrac{\sum r_{67}q_{55}}{\sum p_{67}q_{55}} \cdot \dfrac{\sum p_{67}q_{55}}{\sum p_{55}q_{55}}}{\dfrac{\sum r_{55}q_{55}}{\sum p_{55}q_{55}}}$$

$$= \frac{\sum r_{67}q_{55}}{\sum p_{55}q_{55}} \cdot \frac{\sum p_{55}q_{55}}{\sum r_{55}q_{55}}$$

where r_i and p_i refer respectively to ruble and dollar prices of the 1955 machinery bundle, q_{55}. The right hand side of equation 2 appears to simplify to the expression on the left and these operations produce the inflation estimate reported in the text:[3]

3.
$$I_s = (.479)\,(1.542) \div .589 = 1.254$$

4.
$$i = 100\,(1.254 - 1)/12 = 1.9 \text{ percent per annum.}$$

Closer inspection reveals that the simplification achieved in equation 2 is spurious. The qs in the terms above do not pertain to the same physical quantities. Becker's qs refer to a set of Soviet machines produced in 1955.[4] The qs in the inflation index refer to Bureau of Labor Statistics domestic machinery samples;[5] the CIA's qs pertain to machinery produced in 1972, but aggregated with 1955 value added weights.[6] Since these qs clearly bear little or no coherent relationship to one another, equation 2 is really the inequality:

5.
$$\frac{\sum r_{67}q_{55}}{\sum r_{55}q_{55}} \neq \frac{\dfrac{\sum r_{67}q_{72}^A}{\sum p_{72}q_{72}^A} \cdot \dfrac{\sum p_{72}q_{55}^C}{\sum p_{55}q_{55}^C}}{\dfrac{\sum r_{55}q_{55}^B}{\sum p_{55}q_{55}^B}}$$

where

q_{72}^A is the CIA 1972 machinery product sample aggregated with 1955 value added weights

q_{55}^B is Becker's machinery sample for 1955

q_{55}^C is the Bureau of Labor Statistics sample of machines produced in the U.S. in 1955.[7]

(all consistently grouped with value added weights)[8] which does not yield a meaningful measure of price inflation in the Soviet machinery sector. The expression on the right hand side of inequality 5 confounds differences in sample, sample size, product type, and quality, with inflationary increases from 1955 to 1967 in the prices of identical machines.

The authors of the study are not entirely unaware that their measure of Soviet machinery inflation is methodologically deficient. They write:

> On balance, it is likely that a number of factors have contributed to the implied rate of Soviet price change. It may even be that problems of data and methodology account for the whole change. The results of the exercise suggest, however, that if Soviet prices of producers' durables during 1955–67 did increase, both the aggregate increase and the annual compounded rate of increase were quite small.[9]

But they are unable to identify precisely why their formula is amiss. Had they done so they would have been able to see that all the complexities associated with inequality 5 are superfluous. A proper index of Soviet machine price inflation

6.
$$I = \frac{\sum_{i=1}^{n} r_{67}q_i}{\sum_{i=1}^{n} r_{55}q_i}$$

can be computed without ruble-dollar ratios by directly comparing the ruble prices of machinery that appear both in Becker's and the CIA's product sets.[10] Of course, it might well be that the intersection of these sets is null, or insufficiently large to evaluate the inflation rate.[11] This outcome, however, cannot be prejudged, and even if it proved to be the case would have the virtue of demonstrating precisely why the inflation rate could not be computed.

Notes

1. CIA, *USSR and the United States: Price Ratios for Machinery, 1967 Rubles-1972 Dollars,* Volume I, ER80-10410, September 1980, p. 40. Private correspondence January 5, 1981, and April 8, 1981.
2. The notation used here differs from the original. The exact expressions are provided in Ibid., appendix E, p. 61. The dollar prices used by the agency actually pertain to 1972, rather than 1967. For expositional reasons, I ignore this point, which is not germane to the argument, in the text.
3. Ibid., p. 42.
4. See Abraham Becker (1959).
5. CIA, op. cit., p. 39. It is not clear whether the samples or the quantity weights (value added) refer to 1955.

6. Ibid., p. 41.
7. See note 5.
8. One of the authors of the OER study, John Keilty, informed me in a letter dated January 5, 1981 that "equation 5 does not represent the actual methodology used. We did not simply take the 1955 and 1967–72 weighted ratios computed in the main part of the study to do the inflation computations. Items from the Becker and CIA samples were grouped into U.S. machinery output categories, and entirely new ratios were developed. Similarly, individual category inflation rates were appropriately weighted. In all three cases, the same weights were used."
9. CIA, op. cit. p. 42.
10. Equation 6 is a simple unweighted index of Soviet machinery price change. If one were concerned with measuring machinery inflation in the Soviet machine sector as a whole, or the hypothetical rate that would prevail if the U.S. product mix were produced, Soviet and/or American value added weights could be introduced in the sample.
11. "The straightforward approach to computing Soviet inflation rates, outlined in your equation 6, requires information on prices for an array of Soviet machinery products in two years. Unfortunately such data are scarce because machinery models change. And to limit the inflation analysis to a handful of items would ignore the problems posed by new product pricing if years are far apart" (John Keilty, personal correspondence, January 5, 1981).

APPENDIX 4

Holzman's Hypothesis that CIA Ruble Estimates Overstate the Relative Magnitude of Soviet Defense Expenditures

Franklyn Holzman has attempted to demonstrate that the CIA's ruble estimates of Soviet defense expenditure are overstated. In his essay "Are the Soviets Really Outspending the U.S. on Defense?" he hypothesizes that the disparity between the CIA's dollar ratio of Soviet-American defense spending and its ruble ratio is a positive monotonic function of the number of subcategories used to calculate the ruble ratio.[1] This proposition can be expressed algebraically as:

1. $$D = g(X_d/X_r)$$

where D is a disparity ratio indicator

X_d is the dollar-valued ratio of Soviet and American defense expenditures

X_r is the ruble-valued ratio of Soviet and American defense expenditures

g   is the subcategory aggregation function that causes the true ruble-dollar disparity X_d/X_r to diverge from the calculated disparity.

The dollar-valued ratio of Soviet and American defense expenditures is computed in two steps. The CIA calculates the numerator according to its direct costing method by multiplying its estimate of Soviet weapons and other defense services with dollar prices obtained from parametric cost estimating relationships and data on defense service costs. The denominator is taken principally from DOD estimates of fiscal year American defense outlays. The resulting ratio produces the scalar a:

2.
$$X_d = \frac{\sum_{i=1}^{n} p_i q_i^S}{\sum_{i=1}^{m} p_i q_i^A} = a.$$

where p_i represents the dollar price of the ith good, q_i.

The ruble-valued ratio of Soviet and American defense expenditure in principle is identical to the dollar ratio, except that the dollar prices p_i in equation 2 are transformed into rubles r_i with the agency's ruble-dollar ratios r_i/p_i.

3.
$$X_r = \frac{\sum_{i=1}^{n} \frac{r_i}{p_i} p_i q_i^S}{\sum_{i=1}^{m} \frac{r_i}{p_i} p_i q_i^A} = \frac{\sum_{i=1}^{n} r_i q_i^S}{\sum_{i=1}^{m} r_i q_i^A} = b.$$

which alters the scalar quotient from a to b. The quotient of the ratio of the dollar and ruble Soviet-American defense expenditure ratios is the scalar:

4.
$$X_d/X_r = a/b = c.$$

If it is calculated with full and accurate information it necessarily expresses the true index number disparity caused by valuing Soviet and American defense expenditures alternatively in dollars and rubles.

It follows therefore that in hypothesizing that the Soviet-American defense expenditures disparity is a function not only of X_d/X_r but "subcategories" Holzman believes that the quotient c is affected by the number of elements over which the numerator and denominator of equation 3 are summed. Summation could conceivably bias the scalar quotient c in two distinctly different ways. First, the domain of the summation may be incomplete

5.
$$X_r = \frac{\sum\limits_{i=1}^{k} \frac{r_i}{p_i} p_i q_i^S}{\sum\limits_{i=1}^{1} \frac{r_i}{p_i} p_i q_i^A} = d$$

where $k < n$, $\ell < m$. If the omitted subcategories:

6.
$$\frac{\sum\limits_{i=k+1}^{n} \frac{r_i}{p_i} p_i q_i^S}{\sum\limits_{i=1+1}^{m} \frac{r_i}{p_i} p_i q_i^A} = e$$

yield a scalar quotient e, that differs from the scalar quotient d in the complete domain, then equation 5 will be a biased estimator of the true quotient b. Second, the variance of individual ruble-dollar ratios σ around c may exceed the variance of the subaggregates around d:

7.
$$(\sigma_{1,\ldots,k}; \sigma_{k+1,\ldots,n}) \lessgtr \text{ or } \sigma_1, \sigma_2, \ldots, \sigma_n$$

from which it might seem to follow that

8.
$$\frac{\sum\limits_{i=1}^{k} \frac{r_i}{p_i} p_i q_i^S + \sum\limits_{i=k+1}^{n} \frac{r_i}{p_i} p_i q_i^S}{\sum\limits_{i=1}^{1} \frac{r_i}{p_i} p_i q_i^A + \sum\limits_{i=1+1}^{m} \frac{r_i}{p_i} p_i q_i^A} <$$

$$\frac{\sum\limits_{i=1}^{g} \frac{r_i}{p_i} p_i q_i^S + \sum\limits_{i=g+1}^{k} \frac{r_i}{p_i} p_i q_i^S + \sum\limits_{i=k+1}^{n} \frac{r_i}{p_i} p_i q_i^S}{\sum\limits_{i=1}^{h} \frac{r_i}{p_i} p_i q_i^A + \sum\limits_{i=h+1}^{1} \frac{r_i}{p_i} p_i q_i^A + \sum\limits_{i=1+1}^{m} \frac{r_i}{p_i} p_i q_i^A}$$

The first explanation of the effect summation may have on the Soviet-U.S. defense expenditure ratios must be rejected because it is inconsistent with the facts. The CIA's ruble estimates of Soviet and American defense expenditures are complete. They do not omit any components of Soviet defense spending. Moreover, even if they did, there would be no a priori basis for supposing that omitted components were systematically biased above or below the true scalar quotient b.

The second explanation, which Holzman appears to favor, is technically incorrect. While it is true that the absolute value of the variance of subcategory ruble-dollars is apt to be a positive function of the number of subcategories identified, the scalar quotient on the right and left side of inequality 8 should always be a strict equality. In computing the value of the numerator and the denominator it should make no difference ✴whether the value products $\frac{r_i}{p_i} \, p_i \, q_i$ are summed individually:

9. $$X_r = \frac{r_1}{p_1} p_1 \, q_1^A + \frac{r_2}{p_2} p_2 \, q_2^A \ldots + \frac{r_m}{p_m} p_m \, q_m^A = a.$$

or by subcategory

10. $$X_r = \sum_{i=1}^{2} \frac{r_i}{p_i} p_i \, q_i^A + \frac{r_m}{p_m} p_m \, q_m^A = a$$

Holzman thus must have implicitly supposed that the CIA's ruble Soviet-U.S. defense expenditure ratio was calculated from highly aggregated subcategory ruble-dollar ratios that did not accurately reflect the true ruble-dollar ratio of the subaggregates. This interpretation appears to be consistent with his supposition that the CIA employed only a few ruble-dollar ratios in computing the aggregate Soviet-U.S. defense expenditure ratio it reported.[2] This surmise is erroneous, however. The nonpersonnel subcategory he mentions is composed of operations and maintenance, construction, RDT & E, and procurement. The number of ruble-dollar ratios employed for the procurement subcategory alone far exceeds the ten subcategories Holzman appears to believe the agency relied on in its calculations.[3]

It thus follows that neither Holzman's implicit assumption of aggregation bias, nor his hypothesis that the CIA's ruble U.S.-Soviet defense expenditure ratio is a positive monotonic function of the domain of summation is supported by the evidence. The substantial advantage the Soviets have achieved in aggregate defense spending indicated by the agency's ruble estimates and confirmed by its dollar estimates therefore cannot be dismissed because the CIA uses too few subcategories in calculating its ruble estimates.

Had Holzman's principal objective been to rigorously formulate and test the hypothesis that the CIA's Soviet-U.S. ruble defense expenditure ratio was a positive monotonic function of the domain of summation, he would have quickly discovered his error. However, the hypothesis seemed compelling to him because it appeared to resolve a derivative problem. According to the CIA the Soviet-U.S. defense dollar expenditure ratios for manpower and nonpersonnel activities in 1977 were 1.85 and 1.25 respectively.[4] Their weighted aggregate value was:

11.
$$X_d = \alpha \frac{\sum_{i=1}^{k} p_i q_i^S}{\sum_{i=1}^{1} p_i q_i^A} + (1-\alpha) \frac{\sum_{i=k+1}^{n} p_i q_i^S}{\sum_{i=1+1}^{m} p_i q_i^A}$$

$$= \alpha(1.85) + (1-\alpha)\, 1.25 = 1.40.$$

Noting that nonpersonnel costs must have a higher weight in rubles than in dollars, $(1-\beta) > (1-\alpha)$, Holzman argued that the CIA's ratio of Soviet-American defense expenditures valued in rubles which was reported by the agency to be 1.25

12.
$$X_r = \beta \frac{\sum_{i=1}^{k} \frac{r_i}{p_i} p_i q_i^S}{\sum_{i=1}^{1} \frac{r_i}{p_i} p_i q_i^A} + (1-\beta) \frac{\sum_{i=k+1}^{n} \frac{r_i}{p_i} p_i q_i^S}{\sum_{i=1+1}^{m} \frac{r_i}{p_i} p_i q_i^A} = 1.25$$

must either give zero weight to manpower expenditures:

13.
$$X_d = 0(1.85) + 1(1.25) = 1.25$$

or be computed with additional subcomponents some of which were less than 1.25.

The dichotomy posed here is a false one, however. Revaluing defense expenditures in rubles not only affects manpower and nonpersonnel weights, α and $1-\alpha$, it also reduces the aggregate expenditure ratio

14.
$$\frac{\sum_{i=1}^{n} \frac{r_i}{p_i} p_i q_i^S}{\sum_{i=1}^{m} \frac{r_i}{p_i} p_i q_i^A} < \frac{\sum_{i=1}^{n} p_i q_i^S}{\sum_{i=1}^{m} p_i q_i^A}$$

because ruble prices overstate the cost of U.S. defense activities. The ratio of Soviet-U.S. defense expenditures which Holzman calls into question does not use the *dollar* manpower, nonpersonnel ratios 1.85, 1.25 shown in equation 13, it uses other ruble ratios with a lower aggregate value. As a consequence the CIA's ruble Soviet defense expenditure ratio is not self-evidently implausible, or arithmetically inconsistent as he implies, and his own estimate of the Soviet-U.S. ruble defense expenditure ratio 1.10, which depends on the existence of subcategory summation bias has no sound conceptual foundation.

Notes

1. Franklyn D. Holzman (1980a), pp. 91–92.
2. Ibid., p. 91.
3. The exact number of ruble–dollar ratios is classified.
4. Holzman (1980a), p. 91.

APPENDIX 5

Reconciliation of the "New Information" with the CIA's Gross National Product Accounts for 1970

The validity of the hypothesis that the CIA has underestimated the Soviet arms buildup is predicated in part on the premise that the "new information" covertly obtained from the Soviet Ministry of Defense is accurate. Michael Kaser has suggested that I investigate this matter by comparing the CIA's prerevision 1970 Soviet GNP accounts with the revised accounts implied by the agency's postrevision estimates of military procurement, construction, RDT&E, operations, maintenance, and manpower to determine whether the changes entailed are plausible.

Table A11 provides most of the information required for this evaluation. It reveals that postrevision military procurement and construction expenditures are 15 billion rubles higher than prerevision outlays and explain 59 percent of the 24.9 billion ruble increase in Soviet defense spending disclosed by the "new information." This increase is easily encompassed within the machine-building metalworking (MBMW) and construction control totals established by the agency's GNP accounts. The "new information" causes the military share of MBMW to rise from 13.5 to 44.6 percent, and the military share of construction outlays to increase from 2.4 to 11.8 percent. Although these changes are large, the civilian-military mix which they imply does not seem implausible.

A more detailed examination of the structure of civilian MBMW outlays poses some difficulties. Table A12 demonstrates that after adjustment for investment durables, both the CIA's pre- and postrevision civilian MBMW estimates imply consumer durable production levels that are inconsistent with official Soviet series. OER's implicit prerevision consumer durable figure is 6.4 billion rubles too high; its postrevision estimate, 6.2 billion rubles too low. These residuals might be interpreted to suggest that pre- and postrevision CIA military procurement estimates are correspondingly too low and too high. William Lee's calculations provide an alternative explanation. They indicate that final MBMW deliveries, including net imports, exceed those estimated by the CIA by 6.2 billion rubles (see William Lee, *The Estimation of Soviet Defense Expenditures, 1955–75: An Unconventional Approach*, Table 4.3, p. 61, Table A.29, p. 209). These 6.2 billion rubles Lee believes should be added to OER's GNP estimates, bringing it to 386.9 billion rubles, and thereby justifying the agency's postrevision military procurement estimate. My own independent calculations derived from the Soviet 1966 producer price I-O table support Lee's final MBMW production estimate (see Table A12, panel E).

Military operations and maintenance outlays, the RDT&E expenditures including space research, all classified under the heading of NMP by end use in Table A11, account for another 22 percent of the disparity between the agency's pre- and postrevision defense spending estimates. Unlike MBMW and construction, funds to cover the 5.4 billion rubles of increased postrevision military expenditure need not be subtracted from corresponding civilian uses. The CIA's gross national product accounts contain 12.1 billion rubles of unidentified public outlays which are employed in Table A11 to finance 2 billion additional rubles of military RDT&E including space research, and 3.4 billion rubles of defense operations and maintenance.

The remaining 4.5 billion rubles required to explain the 24.9 billion dollar difference between the CIA's pre- and postrevision estimates is provided by military personnel costs. This category, which is classified by the agency as nonproductive services, is included in GNP, but has no corresponding entry in Soviet NMP accounts. As a consequence, funding for these revised military personnel costs is implicitly covered from unpublished budgetary sources that cannot be evaluated. Because the agency's increased estimate of Soviet military personnel outlays is not financed from the civilian sector, its estimate of real Soviet GNP for 1970 necessarily rises from 380.7 to 385.2 billion rubles measured

TABLE A11
Reconciliation of Pre- and Postrevision Soviet Defense Expenditures with the CIA's Gross National Product Accounts for 1970 (Established Prices)

	Prerevision			Postrevision		
	Civilian	Military	Total	Civilian	Military	Total
A. NMP:						
Sector of Origin						
1. MBMW	35.1	5.5	40.6	22.5	18.1	40.6
2. Construction	24.8	.6	25.4	22.4	3.0	25.4
	59.9	6.1	66	44.9	21.1	66
B. NMP						
End Use						
1. Unidentified Outlays	12.1	—	12.1	6.7	—	6.7
2. RDT&E including Space	1.9	8	9.9	1.9	10	11.9
3. Outlays, nec (defense, net exports)	3.3	5.6	8.9	3.3	9	12.3
	17.3	13.6	30.9	11.9	19	30.9
C. GNP: Nonproductive Services						
1. Military personnel	—	5.3	5.3	—	9.8	9.8
D. Other NMP			211.1			211.1
E. Other GNP			73.4			73.4
F. GNP: Established prices	355.7	25	380.7	335.3	49.9	385.2
G. GNP: Factor Cost			340.2			344.1
H. Military Burden						
a. Established Prices		6.6%			12.9%	
b. Factor Cost		7.3%			14.4%	

Sources:

I. Prerevision

A. Military Expenditures

1. MBMW: *Allocation of Resources in the Soviet Union and China, 1974,* pp. 68–69.

2. Construction: Procurement constitutes 90 percent of the agency's estimate of Soviet military investment. Prerevision construction therefore is 5.5/.9 − 5.5 = .6.

3. RDT&E: Valued in 1974 dollar prices, the CIA estimates Soviet military RDT&E to be 10 billion dollars. Deflated with the DOD RDT&E price index and converted to rubles with the agency's aggregate ruble-dollar ratio (see Table 13.11, notes to column 4), prerevision 1970 ruble RDT&E = .794(10)(.64) = 5. See *Allocation of Resources in the Soviet Union and China, 1976,* p. 18.

4. Space: Total prerevision RDT&E ruble outlays including space research is 8 billion rubles. The difference between this figure and reported military RDT&E represents space outlays. See William Lee, *The Estimation of Soviet Defense Expenditures, 1955–75: An Unconventional Approach,* p. 20.

5. Military personnel: CIA, *USSR: Gross National Product Accounts,* A(ER) 75–76, November 1975, p. 17 and Table 7, p. 9.

6. Operations and Maintenance (Outlays nec): Calculated as the residual between the prerevision total, 25 billion rubles, and the sum of items 1–5 above. See *Estimated Soviet Defense Spending in Rubles, 1970–1975,* p. 1.

B. Total Expenditures

1. MBMW: *USSR, Gross National Product Accounts, 1970,* Table 7, p. 9.

2. Construction: *USSR, Gross National Product Accounts, 1970,* Table 7, p. 9.

3. RDT&E including space: *USSR, Gross National Product Accounts, 1970,* Table 6, p. 8.

4. Operations and maintenance (outlays nec): *USSR, Gross National Product Accounts, 1970,* Table 6, p. 8, line 3c minus unidentified outlays and statistical discrepancy, (12.1 billion rubles), p. 17.

5. Unidentified Outlays: *USSR, Gross National Product Accounts, 1970,* p. 17.

6. Military personnel: *USSR, Gross National Product Accounts, 1970,* Table 7, p. 9.

C. Civilian Expenditures: Residual total minus military outlays.

II. Postrevision

A. Military Expenditures

1. MBMW: Extrapolated from the 1960 military MBMW figure, 5.5 billion rubles, with the official Soviet MBMW nominal growth rate, 12.1 percent (*Narodnoe Khoziaistvo SSSR,* 1972, p. 166), adjusted for deflation with the MBMW industrial wholesale price index (p. 199), corrected for declining trend in deliveries from GVO to final demand (Rush Greenslade, "The Real Gross National Product of the USSR, 1950–1975," in *Soviet Economy in a New Perspective,* JEC, p. 291). The real MBMW growth rate is 12.7 percent per annum.

2. Construction: The CIA retrospectively revised its dollar estimates of Soviet military construction in 1981 for its improved perception of the size of Soviet military construction programs. See *Soviet and U.S. Defense Activities, 1971–79: A Dollar Cost Comparison,* p. 6. This revision caused dollar military construction outlays in 1971 to increase from 3.9 billion dollars (10 percent of investment) to 8.2 billion dollars (the difference between the agency's estimates for 1971 made respectively in 1980 and 1981, both valued in 1979

TABLE A11 (Continued)

dollar prices). Construction as a share of investment thus rose from 10 to 19 percent. Applying the latter ratio to the CIA's 1970 estimates of Soviet procurement (in 1970 prices) yields a dollar military construction estimate of 18.5/.81 − 18.5 = 4.4 billion dollars, which converted to rubles with the agency's 1970 (geometric) ruble dollar construction ratio .695 yields a ruble military construction value of 3 billion rubles. See CIA, *Ruble-Dollar Ratios for Construction*, ER 76-10068, February 1976, p. 1.

3. RDT&E: Excluding space outlays, and adjusted with DOD RDT&E price deflators, military RDT&E for 1970, reported by the CIA in 1980, is 7.8 billion dollars (see *Soviet and U.S. Defense Activities, 1970–79: A Dollar Cost Comparison*, p. 4). Converted to rubles with the agency's average ruble-dollar ratio (see Table 13.11, notes to column 4), .64 yields a military ruble RDT&E estimate of 5 billion rubles.

4. Space: The difference between Soviet defense expenditures on U.S. and Soviet definitional basis is set at roughly 5 billion rubles, most of which is space. See *Estimated Soviet Defense Spending in Rubles, 1970–1975*, p. 7.

5. Military personnel: The cost of military personnel is stated to be 20 percent of Soviet defense outlays in *Estimated Soviet Defense Spending in Rubles, 1970–1975*, p. 15. Using the mean of the CIA's defense spending range 45 billion rubles, yields a military personnel cost estimate of 9 billion rubles. In the intervening years the agency has increased its military personnel estimate 8.3 percent for 1970 (compare *A Dollar Cost Comparison of Soviet and U.S. Defense Activities, 1967–1977*, p. 9, and *Soviet and U.S. Defense Activities, 1970–79; A Dollar Cost Comparison*, p. 7). Adjusted for this higher manpower estimate, military personnel outlays in 1970 can be put at 9.8 billion rubles.

6. Operations and maintenance (outlays nec): The agency estimated in 1976 that 1970 operations and maintenance outlays were slightly higher than estimated personnel expenditures (9 billion rubles). See *Estimated Soviet Defense Spending in Rubles, 1970–1975*, p. 15.

B. Total Expenditures
   1. MBMW: same as prerevision total.
   2. Construction: same as prerevision total.
   3. RDT&E including space, operations, and maintenance: same as prerevision total. Subtotals differ because two billion rubles of unidentified prerevision outlays have been transferred to postrevision RDT&E, and 3.4 billion rubles have been transferred to postrevision operations and maintenance.
   4. Military personnel: same as postrevision military personnel estimate.

C. Civilian Outlays: Residual, total minus military expenditures.

TABLE A12
Structure of Soviet Civilian Machine-Building Output for 1970

	(1) Investment Durables	(2) Consumer Durables	(3) Total	(4) Net Imports	(5) Domestic Durables
A. Soviet Statistics	25.3	3.4	28.7	2.7	26
B. Prerevision CIA	25.3	9.8	35.1	(2.7)	32.4
C. Postrevision CIA	25.3	-2.8	22.5	(2.7)	19.8
D. Lee	25.7	3.4	29.1	2.7	26.4
E. Rosefielde	25.3	6.8	32.1	2.7	29.4

Sources:
A.1: *Narodnoe Khoziaistvo 1972*, p. 474.
A.2: William Lee, *The Estimation of Soviet Defense Expenditures, 1955–75: An Unconventional Approach*, Tables A.24, A.26, A.29, pp. 200, 203, 209.
A.4: Lee, ibid., Table A.27, p. 204.
B.1: *USSR: Gross National Product Accounts, 1970*, Table 6, p. 8.
B.2: Prerevision Civilian MBMW output (Table A11, panel A) minus investment durables (Table A12, B.1).
B.4: Lee, ibid., Table A.27, p. 204.
C.1: *USSR: Gross National Product Accounts, 1970*, Table 6, p. 8.
C.2: Postrevision Civilian MBMW (Table A11, panel A), minus investment durables (Table A12, C.1).
C.4: Lee, ibid., Table A.27, p. 204.
D.1: Lee, ibid., Table A.29, p. 209.
D.2: Ibid.
D.3: Ibid.
E.1: *Narodnoe Khoziaistvo 1972*, p. 474.

TABLE A12 (Continued)

E.2: The 1966 Soviet I-O table valued in purchaser prices shows final MBMW deliveries of 33.9 billion rubles. MBMW GVO adjusted for price deflation 1967–70 (using the industrial wholesale price index including turnover tax: .952) and the declining trend in GVO deliveries to final demand 1966–72 (−1.25 percent compound annual decline) grew 11.7 percent per annum 1966–70. Employing this rate to extrapolate final MBMW deliveries in 1970 yields:

$$M_{70}^{67} = (1.117)^4 (33.9) = 52.7 \text{ billion rubles}$$

which deflated from 1967 to 1970 purchaser prices works out to

$$M_{70}^{70} = 52.7 (.952) = 50.2 \text{ billion rubles.}$$

See Steven Rosefielde, *The Transformation of the 1966 Soviet Input-Output Table from Producers to Adjusted Factor Cost Values*, GE75TMP-47, GE TEMPO, Washington, D.C., 1975, p. 90.

Final domestic MBMW output minus procurement minus investment durables should equal consumer durables:

$$\text{Consumer MBMW} = M_{70}^{70} - I_{70}^{70} - P_{70}^{70}$$
$$= 50.2 - 25.3 - 18.1$$
$$= 6.8 \text{ billion rubles.}$$

I use the implied CIA postrevision procurement estimate to facilitate comparison with Lee's and the CIA's consumer durable estimate. If OER's best residual procurement estimate 18.5 billion rubles is substituted, my consumer durable estimate declines to 6.4 billion rubles.

E.4: Lee, ibid., Table A.27, p. 204.

at established prices (391.4 billion if Lee's MBMW figure is accepted). The impact of these diverse changes on the Soviet military burden is illustrated in Table A11, panel G, valued alternatively at established and factor cost prices.

The changes detailed in Table A11 are summarized in Table A13 and compared with William Lee's Soviet defense expenditure estimates prepared prior to the acquisition of the new information. The correspondence between Lee's estimates and the agency's postrevision figures is remarkable, especially when it is noted that the CIA's 2.4 billion ruble adjustment in Soviet ruble construction was not made until 1981.

A close review of Tables A11 and A13 demonstrates that the postrevision adjustments necessitated by the "new information" are not only admissible; they produce more plausible accounting balances than the ones they replace. This can be verified by comparing the internal consistency of the CIA's MBMW accounts.

Table A14, panel A presents OER's *implicit* postrevision MBMW GNP account, calculated from official Soviet data, assuming that the official Soviet MBMW GVO index valued at current prices is not distorted by hidden inflation. Observe that military MBMW output extrapolated from the CIA's 1960 estimate with the official Soviet MBMW GVO growth index, adjusted for price *deflation* and the declining trend in GVO deliveries to final demand, differs only insignificantly from OER's best residual estimate, 18.5 billion rubles, derived from the "new information." Note as well that the 1960 total MBMW estimate is consistent with official Soviet statistics because it is computed with the same growth rate used to extrapolate military MBMW in 1970 (I abstract here from Lee's MBMW GNP estimate which can be accommodated without altering the conclusions drawn above by more detailed calculations).

The CIA's prerevision MBMW GNP account by contrast is glaringly inconsistent. Total MBMW production in 1960 (19.9 billion rubles), computed by backcasting the agency's 1970 estimate with OER's index of civilian MBMW, greatly exceeds the 12.3 billion ruble figure implied by official Soviet growth statistics (panel A). Likewise, accepting Greenslade's estimate of 1970 civilian MBMW outlays (27.1 billion rubles) generates an 8 billion ruble noncivilian, nonmilitary balancing entry, required to reconcile civilian and military MBMW uses (32.6 billion rubles) with total 1970 MBMW production (40.6 billion rubles).

Attempts to purge the prerevision MBMW account for these inconsistencies, while retaining the "hidden inflation" assumption, have thus far failed to produce the desired result. Panel C, for example, reports Rush Greenslade's (former OER director) abortive effort at reconciliation. Instead of relying on OER's civilian MBMW index, Greenslade

TABLE A13
Summary Reconciliation of the CIA's Pre- and Postrevision Soviet Defense Expenditure Estimates for 1970

| | CIA | | Lee |
	Prerevision	Postrevision	
1. Procurement	5.5	18.1	18.1
2. Construction	.6	3	} 10.5
3. Operations and Maintenance	5.6	9	
4. Personnel	5.3	9.8	7.4
5. RDT&E	5	5	} 10
6. Space	3	5	
7. Total	25	49.9	46

Sources: Table A11; and William Lee, *The Estimation of Soviet Defense Expenditures, 1955–75: An Unconventional Approach,* Table 4.6, p. 66, Table D.5, p. 279.

TABLE A14
Soviet Civilian and Military Machine-Building Metalworking Production (Established Prices)

A. Postrevision: OER	Civilian	Military	Other	Total
1960	6.8	5.5	—	12.3
1970	22.5	18.1	—	40.6
B. Prerevision: OER				
1960	13.3	5.5	1.1	19.9
1970	27.1	5.5	8	40.6
C. Greenslade				
1960	13.3	5.5	−1.4	17.4
1970	27.1	13.5	—	40.6

Sources:
Panel A: 1970 values: Table A11, A.1.
  1960 values:
  1. Military: *Allocation of Resources in the Soviet Union and China (1974),* pp. 68–69.
  2. Total: 1960 value, extrapolated using the official Soviet MBMW growth index adjusted for deflation and reduced GVO deliveries to final demand. See Table A11, sources, II.A.1.
  3. Civilian: Total minus military outlays.

TABLE A14 (Continued)

Panel B:

    1. Military: *Allocation of Resources in the Soviet Union and China (1974)*, pp. 68–69.

    2. Total: 1960 value extrapolated using OER's civilian MBMW real growth index. See Greenslade, "The Real Gross National Product of the USSR, 1950–1975." In *Soviet Economy in a New Perspective*, JEC, Table 1, p. 271. 1970 value: Table A11, A.1.

    3. Civilian: See panel C3.

Panel C:

    1. Military: 1960 value, *Allocations of Resources in the Soviet Union and China (1974)*, pp. 68–69. 1970 value, extrapolated with the same procedure described in panel A.1, except the adjusted MBMW growth rate 12.7 percent per annum is reduced 3.9 percent to 8.8 percent per annum to allow for "hidden inflation." See Greenslade, ibid., p. 291.

    2. Total: 1960 value extrapolated at Greenslade's estimated total MBMW growth rate. 1970 value: Table A11, A.1.

    3. Civilian: 1970 value calculated by subtracting military from total outlays. 1960 value computed by backcasting the 1970 value with OER's sample civilian machinery index. See Greenslade (1976), p. 271.

---

employed the official Soviet MBMW index, adjusted for an annual rate of hidden inflation of 3.9 percent, to extrapolate military MBMW to 1970. This expedient permitted Greenslade to probe the possibility that military MBMW grew faster than the civilian rate (whereas it had formerly been assumed not to be growing at all), while embracing OSR's supposition that the hidden MBMW inflation rate was roughly 4 percent.

The results of this compromise are edifying. Panel C demonstrates that total 1960 MBMW outlays not only continue to exceed those supportable with official Soviet statistics, including an inexplicable negative residual, but 1970 military MBMW outlays are 4 to 5.5 billion rubles below the range of procurement estimates suggested by direct costing and the "new information." The CIA's prerevision procurement estimates thus do not appear to be consistent with Soviet NMP statistics, whereas the "new information" is compatible both with the agency's implicit postrevision national product accounts and official Soviet MBMW growth indices.

This inference is readily extended to total defense expenditures. The agency's estimates of military construction, operations, maintenance, and personnel costs should be closely linked to the CIA's evaluation of Soviet procurement activities. If the revised procurement estimates are accepted it would be unreasonable to suppose that supporting expenditures should not be increased. As a consequence, the revised estimates of construction, operations, maintenance, and personnel costs derived from the "new information" not only follow logically from the postrevision procurement estimates, but simultaneously serve as a check on the agency's ex-post facto appraisal of Soviet procurement activities.

Bibliography

Alexander, Arthur. "R & D in Soviet Aviation," Rand, R-589-PR, November 1970.

Allocation of Resources in the Soviet Union and China. Joint Economic Committee of Congress, Washington, D.C., 1974.

Allocation of Resources in the Soviet Union and China—1976, Part 2. Joint Economic Committee of Congress, Executive Session, Washington, D.C., May-June, 1976.

Allocation of Resources in the Soviet Union and China—1979. Joint Economic Committee of Congress, June 26, 1979.

Allocation of Resources in the Soviet Union and China, 1981. Joint Economic Committee of Congress, Washington, D.C., July 8, 1981.

Alsop, Joseph. "A Cautionary Tale," *Washington Post*, No. 92 (March 7, 1977), pp. 7–21.

An Analysis of the Behavior of Soviet Machinery Prices, 1960–1973. National Foreign Assessment Center, CIA, ER79-10631, Washington, D.C., December 1979.

Aspin, Les. *What Are the Russians Up to? A Perspective on Soviet Military Intentions.* Mimeo, November 1977.

"Assessing the Soviet Economy: The CIA's Giant Goof," *Business Week*, 2472 (February 28, 1977), pp. 96–103.

A Study of Ship Acquisition Cost Estimating in Naval Sea Systems Command. Executive Summary, Naval Sea Systems Command, October 1977.

Barry, James. "Testimony," *CIA Estimates of Soviet Defense Spending*, Permanent Select Committee on Intelligence, House of Representatives, September 3, 1980, Washington, D.C., pp. 73–92.

Becker, Abraham. *Prices of Producers' Durables in the United States and the USSR in 1955.* Research memorandum RM-2432, Rand Corporation, Santa Monica, California, August 15, 1959.

————. *Soviet Military Outlays Since 1958.* Rand, RM-3886-PR, June 1964.

————.*Soviet National Income 1958–1964.* University of California, Berkeley, 1969.

————."National Income Accounting in the USSR," in Treml and Hardt, eds., *Soviet Economic Statistics*, Duke University Press, Durham, N.C., 1972, pp. 69–119.

————. *Ruble Price Levels and Dollar-Ruble Ratios of Soviet Machinery in the 1960s.* R-1063-DDRE, Rand Corporation, January 1973.

————. "The Price Level of Soviet Machinery in the 1960s," *Soviet Studies*, Vol. XXVI, 3, July, 1974, pp. 363–79.

————. "Dollar-Ruble Ratios of Soviet Machinery in the 1960s," *Jahrbuch der Wirtschaft Osteuropas*, Vol. 6, n.d., pp. 253–78.

————. *Military Expenditure Limitation for Arms Control: Problems and Prospects.* Ballinger, Cambridge, Mass.: 1977.

————. "The Meaning and Measure of Soviet Military Expenditure," in *Soviet Economy in a Time of Change*, Joint Economic Committee of Congress, Vol. 1, October 1979, pp. 352–68.

————. *CIA Estimates of Soviet Military Expenditure.* Rand P-6534, Santa Monica, August 1980.

Bergson, Abram. "A Reformulation of Certain Aspects of Welfare Economics," *Quarterly Journal of Economics*, 52, 1938, pp. 310–34.

————. "The Fourth Five Year Plan: Heavy Versus Consumers' Goods Industries," *Political Science Quarterly*, Vol. LXII, June 1947, pp. 195–227.

————. *The Real National Income of Soviet Russia Since 1928.* Harvard University Press, Cambridge, 1961.

————. "Soviet National Income Statistics: Summary and Assessment," in Treml and Hardt, eds., *Soviet Economic Statistics.* Duke University Press, Durham, N.C., 1972.

————. "Index Numbers and the Computation of Factor Productivity," *Review of Income and Wealth*, No. 3, September 1975, pp. 259–78.

————.*Productivity and the Social System—The USSR and the West.* Harvard University Press, Cambridge, 1978.

Berliner, Joseph. "Flexible Pricing and New Products in the USSR," *Soviet Studies*, XXVII, 4, October 1975, pp. 525–44.

––––––. *The Innovation Decision in Soviet Industry*. MIT Press, Cambridge, 1976.

––––––. "Technological Progress and the Evolution of Soviet Price Policy," in Rosefielde, ed., *Economic Welfare and the Economics of Soviet Socialism*. Cambridge University Press, New York, 1981.

Bornstein, Morris. "The Soviet Price System," *American Economic Review*, Vol. 52, 1, March 1962, pp. 64–103.

––––––. "Soviet Price Statistics," in Treml and Hardt, eds., *Soviet Economic Statistics*. Duke University Press, Durham, N.C., 1972, pp. 355–96.

––––––. "Soviet Price Policy in the 1970s," in *Soviet Economy in a New Perspective*. JEC, October 1976, pp. 17–66.

––––––. "The Administration of the Soviet Price System," *Soviet Studies*, XXX, No. 4, October 1978, pp. 466–90.

Bronson, David and Severin, Barbara. "Recent Trends in Consumption and Disposable Money Income in the USSR," in *New Directions in the Soviet Economy*. Part II-B, JEC, Washington, 1966.

––––––. "Soviet Consumer Welfare: The Brezhnev Era," in *Soviet Economic Prospects for the Seventies*. JEC, Washington, 1973.

Burton, Donald. "Soviet Defense Procurement Trends and Prospects." Testimony of Donald F. Burton, chief, Military-Economic Analysis Center, Office of Strategic Research, National Foreign Assessment Center before the Subcommittee on General Procurement, Committee on Armed Forces, United States Senate, November 1, 1979.

Bush, Keith. "Soviet Inflation," in Yves Laulan, ed., *Banking, Money and Credit in Eastern Europe*. NATO, Brussels, 1973.

Callahan, Alexander. "Industrial Engineering Estimates: Can They Be Used to Measure Procurement Cost of Operational Systems Built by a Foreign Economy?" Unpublished manuscript, Naval Postgraduate School, September 1978.

Chertko, N.T. "The Role of Machine-Building in the Formation of the Technological Structure of Capital Investment," in V. Krasovsky, ed., *Planirovanie i Arnaliz Narodnokhozyaistvennoi Struktury Kapital'nykh Vlozhenii*. Moscow, Ekonomika, 1970, pp. 228–48.

Cohn, Stanley. *Economic Development in the Soviet Union*. D.C. Heath, Lexington, Mass., 1970.

―――. "Estimation of Military Durables Procurement from Machinery Production and Sales Data." Unpublished, revised draft, August, 1977.

―――. "A Comment on Alec Nove, 'A Note on Growth, Investment and Price Indexes.' " *Soviet Studies*, vol. XXXIII, no. 2, April 1981, pp. 296–299.

―――. *Sources of Low Soviet Capital Productivity*. 1981, unpublished draft.

Collins, John and Cordesman, Anthony. *Imbalance of Power*, Presidio Press, 1978.

Daniels, James and Kreisel, George, Jr. *A Study of the Relationship Between Avionics Cost—Per Pound Factors and Design Technology Levels*. J. Watson Noah Associates, FR-1061-USN, December 1975.

David, P.A. and van de Klundert, T. "Biased Efficiency Growth in the U.S.," *American Economic Review*, Vol. LX, No. 3, June 1965, pp. 357–94.

Denison, E.F. "Theoretical Aspects of Quality Change, Capital Change and Net Capital Formation," in Franco Modigliani, ed., *Problems of Capital Formation*. Conference on Research in Income and Wealth, Princeton, New Jersey, 1957, pp. 215–61.

Denton, M. Elizabeth. "Soviet Consumer Policy: Trends and Prospects," in *Soviet Economy in a Time of Change*. Joint Economic Committee, Vol. 1, October 1979, pp. 759–89.

DIA. *U.S. and Soviet Weapon System Design Practice (U)*. May, 1980.

Desai, Padma. "The Production Function and Technical Change in Post-war Soviet Industry: A Reexamination," *American Economic Review*, 66, 1976, pp. 372–81.

―――. "On Reconstructing Price, Output, and Value-Added Indexes in Postwar Soviet Industry and Its Branches," *Oxford Bulletin of Economic Statistics*, Vol. 40, No. 1, February 1978, pp. 55–77.

A Dollar Cost Comparison of Soviet and U.S. Defense Activities, 1966–1976. SR 77-10001U, CIA, January 1977.

A Dollar Cost Comparison of Soviet and U.S. Defense Activities, 1967–1977. SR 78-10002, CIA, January 1978.

A Dollar Cost Comparison of Soviet and U.S. Defense Activities, 1968–1978. SR 79-10004, CIA, January 1979.

Domar, Evsey. "On the Measurement of Technological Change," *Economic Journal*, Vol. LXXI, December 1961.

Epstein, Jay. "The Spy War," *New York Times Magazine*, September 28, 1980, pp. 34–108.

Estimated Soviet Defense Spending in Rubles, 1970–1975. SR 76-10121U, CIA, May 1976.

Estimated Soviet Defense Spending: Trends and Prospects. SR 78-10121, CIA, June 1978.

Faltsman, Vladimir. "Mochchnostnoi Ekvivalent Osnovnykh Fondov," *Voprosy Ekonomiki,* Vol. 8, August 1980, pp. 121–32.

Fearn, Robert. "Controls over Wage Funds and Inflationary Pressures in the USSR," *Industrial and Labor Relations Review*, January 1965, pp. 186–95.

Fisher, Franklin, and Shell, Karl. *The Economic Theory of Price Indices: Two Essays on the Effects of Taste, Quality and Technical Change.* Academic Press, New York, 1972.

Fisher, Irving. *The Making of Index Numbers.* The Riverside Press, Cambridge, 1922.

Garvy, George. *Money, Financial Flows and Credit in the Soviet Union.* National Bureau of Economic Research and Ballinger Press, 1977.

Gomulka, Stanislaw. "Soviet Postwar Industrial Growth, Capital-Labor Substitution, and Technical Changes: A Reexamination," in Zbigniew Fallenbuchl, ed., *Economic Development in the Soviet Union and Eastern Europe, Volume 2: Sectoral Analysis.* Praeger, New York, 1976, pp. 3–47.

Graaf, Jan van de. *Theoretical Welfare Economics.* Cambridge University Press, 1957.

Granick, David. *Soviet Introduction of New Technology: A Depiction of the Process.* Stanford Research Institute, Menlo Park, California, 1975.

Gregory, Paul. "Economic Growth and Structural Change in Tsarist Russia and the Soviet Union: A Long Term Comparison," in Rosefielde (ed.),*Economic Welfare and the Economics of Soviet Socialism*. Cambridge University Press, New York, 1981.

Griliches, Zvi (ed.). *Price Indexes and Quality Change*. Harvard University Press, Cambridge, 1971.

Griliches, Zvi and Jorgenson, D. "The Explanation of Productivity Change," *The Review of Economic Studies*, Vol. XXXIV, No. 99, July 1967, pp. 249–83.

————. "Divisia Index Numbers and Productivity Measurement," *The Review of Income and Wealth*, Series 17, No. 2, June 1971, pp. 227–29.

Greenslade, Rush. "Industrial Production Statistics in the USSR," in Vladimir Treml and John Hardt (eds.), *Soviet Economic Statistics*. Duke University Press, 1972, pp. 155–94.

————. "The Real Gross National Product of the USSR, 1950–1975," in *Soviet Economy in a New Perspective*. JEC, Washington, 1976, pp. 269–300.

Greenslade, Rush and Wallace, Phyllis. "Industrial Production in the USSR," in *Dimensions of Soviet Economic Power*. JEC, Washington, D.C., 1962, pp. 115–36.

Grossman, Gregory. "Price Control, Incentives, and Innovation in the Soviet Economy," in Alan Abouchar (ed.), *The Socialist Price Mechanism*. Duke University Press, Durham, N.C., 1977, pp. 129–69.

Hardt, John and Cohn, Stanley. *Economic Insights on Soviet Defense Programming*. Research Analysis Corp., n.d.

Harman, Alvin. *A Methodology for Cost Factor Comparison and Prediction*. Rand RM-6269-ARPA, August 1970.

Harré, Romano. *The Principles of Scientific Thinking*. University of Chicago Press, Chicago, 1970.

Harré, R. and Secord, P.F. *The Explanation of Social Behavior*. Littlefield, Adams, Totowa, New Jersey, 1973.

Hicks, J.R. "The Valuation of Social Income," *Economica*, Vol. VII, No. 26, May 1940, pp. 105–24.

Holzman, Franklyn. *Foreign Trade Under Central Planning*. Harvard

University Press, Cambridge, 1974.

————. *Financial Checks on Soviet Defense Expenditures*. Lexington Books, Lexington, Mass., 1975.

————. "Are the Soviets Really Outspending the U.S. on Defense?" *International Security*, Vol. 4, No. 4, Spring 1980(a), pp. 86–104.

————. "Testimony," *CIA Estimates of Soviet Defense Spending*. Permanent Select Committee on Intelligence, House of Representatives, Washington, D.C., September 3, 1980(b) pp. 43–72.

Howard, David. "A Note on Hidden Inflation in the Soviet Union," *Soviet Studies*, XXVIII, 4, October 1976, pp. 599–608.

————. *The Disequilibrium Model in a Controlled Economy*. Lexington Books, Lexington, Mass., 1979.

————. "Hidden Inflation in the Soviet Union: A Reply to Professor Rosefielde," *Soviet Studies*, Vol. XXXII, No. 4, October 1980, pp. 580–82.

Huffstutler, Robert. "Testimony," *CIA Estimates of Soviet Defense Spending*. Permanent Select Committee on Intelligence, House of Representatives, September 3, 1980, Washington, D.C., pp. 73–92.

Katz, Barbara. "The Disequilibrium Model in a Controlled Economy: Comment," *American Economic Review*, Vol. 69, No. 4, September 1979, pp. 721–25.

Komin, A.N. "Problemy Sovershenstvovaniia Optovykh Tsen Promyshlennosti," *Planovoe Khozyaistvo*, No. 10, 1966.

————. *Problemy Planovia Tsenobrazovannia*. Moscow, 1971.

————. "Sovershenstvovanie Tsenobrazovaniia," *Planovoe Khozyaistvo*, no. 2, 1972(a).

————. "Novye Optovye Tseny Na Produktsiiu Machinostroeniya," *Ekonomicheskaya Gazeta*, No. 20, 1972(b).

Krasovsky, V. *Problemy Ekonomiki Kapital'nykh Volzhenii*. Moscow, 1967.

————. (editor). *Planirovanie i Analiz Narodnokhozyaistvennoi Struktury Kapital'nykh Volozhenii*. Moscow, Ekonomika, 1970.

Kuschpeta, O. *The Banking and Credit System of the USSR*. Martinus Nijhoff, Boston, 1978.

Kvasha, Ya. and Krasovsky, V. "Kapital'noe Stroitel'stvo i Problema Vozmeschcheniia," *Voprosy Ekonomiki*, No. 11, 1964.

———. "Kapital'noe Stroitel'stvo i Nakoplenie," *Voprosy Ekonomiki*, No. 7, 1965.

———."Perspektivnoe Planirovanie Khozyaistvennye Izmereniia," *Voprosy Ekonomiki*, No. 4, 1968.

Larkin, Richard and Collins, Edward. "Resource Allocation Trends in the Soviet Union and China," in *Allocation of Resources in the Soviet Union and China, 1981,* July 8, 1981.

Large, J.P. and Gillespie, K.M.S. *A Critique of Aircraft Airframe Cost Models.* Rand R-2194-AF, September 1977.

Lee, William T. *The Estimation of Soviet Defense Expenditures for 1955-75: An Unconventional Approach.* Praeger, New York, 1977(a).

———.*Understanding the Soviet Military Threat.* National Strategy Information Center, Inc., New York, 1977(b).

———. "Soviet Defense Expenditures in the 10th FYP," *Osteuropa*, December 1977, reprinted in *Current News*, No. 322, June 15, 1978, pp. 1–11.

———.Trends in Soviet Weapons Procurement and Defense Expenditures, 1955–1980." Statement presented to the Subcommittee on General Procurement of the Senate Armed Services Committee, November 1, 1979.

———. "Soviet Nuclear Targeting Strategy and SALT," in Rosefielde (ed.), *World Communism at the Crossroads*. Martinus Nijhoff, Boston, 1980(a), pp. 55–88 (a).

———. "Testimony," *CIA Estimates of Soviet Defense Spending.* Permanent Select Committee on Intelligence, House of Representatives, Washington, D.C., September 3, 1980(b), pp. 17–31, 47–72 (b).

———. "USSR Gross National Product in Established Prices, 1955–1975," *Jahrbuch der Wirtschaft Osteuropas*, Band 8, n.d., p. 429.

Leggett, Robert E. "Measuring Inflation in the Soviet Machinebuilding Sector, 1960–1973," *Journal of Comparative Economics*, Vol. 5, No. 2, June 1981, pp. 169–84.

Leontief, W. "Introduction to a Theory of the Internal Structure of

Functional Relationships," *Econometrica*, Vol. 15, No. 4, October 1947, pp. 361–73.

Luttwak, Edward. "European Insecurity and American Policy," in *Defending America*. Basic Books, New York, 1977, pp. 169–86.

Measuring Price Changes of Military Expenditures. U.S. Department of Commerce, Bureau of Economic Analysis, Washington, D.C., June 1975 (Report prepared for ACDA).

Merrilees, W. "The Case against Divisia Index Numbers as a Basis in a Social Accounting System," *The Review of Income and Wealth*, Series 17, No. 1, March 1971, pp. 81–85.

"The Metaphysics of Dollar Estimates of Soviet Defense Activities." CIA, 1978.

Michaud, Norbert. "Epagoge for an Increase in Soviet Defense Shares." Paper delivered at the Air Force conference "The Soviet Union: What Lies Ahead?" September 26, 1980, Reston, Virginia.

Millar, James and Pickersgill, Joyce. "Aggregate Economic Problems in Soviet-Type Economies," *The ACES Bulletin*, XIX, No. 1, Spring, 1977.

Mitrofanova, N. "Tendentsii Dvizheniia Kontraktnykh Tsen v Torgovlie Stran SEV," *Voprosy Ekonomiki,* Vol. 8, August 1978, pp. 101–6.

Mood, A. and Graybill, F. *Introduction to the Theory of Statistics*. McGraw-Hill, New York, 1963.

Moorsteen, Richard. "On Measuring Productive Potential and Relative Efficiency," *Quarterly Journal of Economics*, Vol. LXXV, No. 3, August 1961, pp. 451–67.

Moorsteen, Richard and Powell, Raymond. *The Soviet Capital Stock 1928–1962*. Richard D. Irwin, Homewood, Illinois, 1966.

Narodnoe Khoziaistvo SSSR (annual statistical handbook). Statistika, Moscow.

Nelson, J.R. and Timson, F. *Relating Technology to Acquisition Costs: Aircraft Turbine Engines*. Rand R-1288-PR, n.d.

Nimitz, Nancy. *Soviet Expenditures on Scientific Research*. Rand RM-3384-PR, January 1963.

———. *The Structure of Soviet Outlays on R & D in 1960 and 1968*. Rand R-1207-DDR & E, June 1974.

————. *The Structure of Soviet R & D Outlays*. Rand WN-7463-PR, n.d.

Nissanke, Machiko. "The Disequilibrium Model in a Controlled Economy: Comment," *American Economic Review*, Vol. 69, No. 4, September, 1979, pp. 726–31.

Nitze, Paul H. "Nuclear Strategy: Detente and American Survival," in *Defending America*. Basic Books, New York, 1977, pp. 97–109.

Nove, Alec. *An Economic History of the USSR*. Penguin Books, Baltimore, 1969.

————. "A Note on Growth, Investment and Price Indices," *Soviet Studies*, Vol. XXXIII, No. 1, 1981a, pp. 142–45.

————. "A Reply to Stanley Cohn," *Soviet Studies*, Vol. XXXIII, No. 2, 1981b, pp. 300–01.

Nutter, G. Warren. "On Economic Size and Growth," *Journal of Law and Economics*, Vol. IX, October 1966, pp. 163–88.

Palterovich, D.M. *Park Proizvodstvennovo Aborudovaniia*. Moscow, Nauka, 1970.

————. "Prognoz Razvitiia Orudii Truda," *Voprosy Ekonomiki*, No. 11, 1973.

Parker, Patrick. "Soviet Military Strategy in the Decade 1977–1987," in Rosefielde (ed.), *World Communism at the Crossroads*, Martinus Nijhoff, 1980, pp. 1–33.

Pickersgill, Joyce. "Soviet Inflation: Causes and Consequences," *Soviet Union*, 4, No. 2, 1977.

————. "Soviet Household Saving Behavior," *Review of Economics and Statistics*, 58, May 1978, pp. 139–47.

————. "The Political Economy of Soviet Inflation." Paper delivered at the Second World Congress for Soviet and East European Studies, Garmisch-Partenkirschen, September 30–October 4, 1980 (a).

————. "Recent Evidence on Soviet Households Savings Behavior," *The Review of Economics and Statistics*, Vol. LXII, No. 4, November 1980, pp. 629–633 (b).

Pipes, Richard. "Why the Soviet Union Thinks It Can Fight and Win a Nuclear War," *Commentary*, Vol. 64, No. 1, July 1977, pp. 21–34.

Pitzer, J. "Reconciliation of Gross National Product and Soviet National Income." Soviet Economy Branch USSR (Eastern European Division, OER*), December 1977. Paper presented at the NATO Colloquium, July 1977.

Polmar, Norman. "The U.S.-Soviet Naval Balance," in *Defending America*. Basic Books, New York, 1977, pp. 187–204.

Portes, Richard and Winter, David. "The Demand for Money and for Consumption Goods," *Review of Economics and Statistics*, 60, February 1978, pp. 8–18.

"Price Index Methodology Used for the 1978 Dollar Cost Comparison of U.S. and Soviet Defense Activities." Memorandum for the Record (CIA), July 28, 1978.

Redd, J.S. "An Examination of the CIA Economic Net Assessment of the United States and the Soviet Union." Unpublished manuscript, Naval Postgraduate School, 1978.

Rosefielde, Steven. *The Transformation of the 1966 Soviet Input-Output Table from Producers to Adjusted Factor Cost Values*. GE75TMP-47, GE TEMPO, Washington, D.C., 1975.

————. *East-West Trade and Postwar Soviet Economic Growth: A Sectoral Production Function Approach*. SRI, 1976.

————. "Economic Theory in the Excluded Middle Between Positivism and Rationalism," *Atlantic Economic Journal*, Vol. 4, No. 2, Spring 1979(a), pp. 1–9.

————. "Production Functions and the Estimation of Opportunity Costs in Centrally Planned Economies." Unpublished manuscript, June 1979(b).

————. "A Review of David Howard's *The Disequilibrium Model in a Controlled Economy*," *Russian Review*, Vol. 39, No. 4, 1980(a), p. 514.

————. "The First Great Leap Forward Reconsidered: The Lessons of Solzhenitsyn's *Gulag Archipelago*," *Slavic Review*, December 1980(b).

————. "Index Numbers and the Computation of Factor Productivity: A Further Appraisal," *Review of Income and Wealth*, 1980(c).

————. "Post Positivist Scientific Method and the Appraisal of Nonmarket Economic Behavior," *Quarterly Journal of Ideology*, Vol. 3, No. 1, Spring 1980(d).

—————. "Testimony," *CIA Estimates of Soviet Defense Spending*. Permanent Select Committee on Intelligence, House of Representatives, Washington, D.C., September 3, 1980(e), pp. 10–16, 47–72.

—————. "Was the Soviet Union Affected by the International Economic Disturbances of the 1970s?" in E. Neuberger and L. Tyson (eds.), *Transmission and Response: Impact of International Economic Disturbances on the Soviet Union and Eastern Europe*. Pergamon Press, Elsford, New York, 1980(f).

—————. *World Communism at the Crossroads: Military Ascendancy, Political Economy and Human Welfare*. Martinus Nijhoff, Boston, 1980(g).

—————. "A Comment on David Howard's Estimate of Hidden Inflation in the Soviet Retail Sales Sector," *Soviet Studies*, Vol. 33, No. 3, 1980(h), pp. 425–26.

—————(ed). *Economic Welfare and the Economics of Soviet Socialism*. Cambridge University Press, New York, 1981(a).

—————. "Hidden Inflation in the Soviet Union: A Rejoinder to David Howard," *Soviet Studies*, Vol. 33, No. 4, 1981(b).

—————. "A Comment on Robert Leggett's Hedonic Measures of Open and Hidden Inflation in the Soviet Machinebuilding Sector, 1960–1973," *Journal of Comparative Economics,"* forthcoming 1982(a).

—————. "Disguised Inflation in Soviet Industry: A Reply to James Steiner," *Journal of Comparative Economics,* forthcoming 1982(b).

—————. "The Measurement of Soviet Weapons Growth: Learning Curve Distortion," unpublished manuscript, January 1982(c).

—————. "The Soviet Defense Burden: Measurement Problems Posed by the Impending 1982 Ruble Price Reform: Summary of the Proceedings of the CIA Conference, 'Price Change in the Soviet Defense Sector,' December 7–8, 1981, Northern Virginia," unpublished manuscript, January 1982(d).

Rosefielde, S. and Lovell, C.A. Knox. "The Impact of Adjusted Factor Cost Valuation on the CES Interpretation of Postwar Soviet Economic Growth," *Economica*, 44, November 1977, pp. 381–92.

Rothstein, A.I. *Problemy promyshlennoi statistiki SSSR*. Leningrad, 1936.

Royal United Services Institute and Brassey's (eds.). *Defense Yearbook, 1981.* Brassey's Publishers Ltd., Oxford, 1981.

Ruble-Dollar Ratios for Construction. CIA, ER 76-10068, February 1976.

Samuelson, P.A. "The Evaluation of Real National Income," *Oxford Economic Papers,* Vol. II, No. 1, January 1950, pp. 1–29.

———. "Bergsonian Welfare Economics," in Rosefielde (1981a).

Samuelson, P.A. and Swamy, Subramanian. "Invariant Economic Index Numbers and Canonical Duality: Survey and Synthesis," *American Economic Review*, Vol. 64, No. 4, September 1974, pp. 566–93.

Schroeder, Gertrude. "An Appraisal of Soviet Wage and Income Statistics," in Treml and Hardt (eds.), *Soviet Economic Statistics.* Duke University Press, Durham, 1972, pp. 288–314.

———."Consumer Goods Availability and Repressed Inflation in the Soviet Union," in *Economic Aspects of Life In the USSR.* Main Finding of Colloquium held 29th-31st January, 1975 in Brussels by NATO Directorate of Economic Affairs.

Schroeder, Gertrude and Severin, Barbara. "Soviet Consumption and Income Policies in Perspective," *Soviet Economy in a New Perspective.* JEC, October 14, 1976, pp. 644–45.

Shisko, Robert. *Technological Change Through Product Improvement in Aircraft Turbine Engines*, Rand R-1061, May 1973.

Sitnin, V. "Itogi Reformy Optovykh Tsen i Zadachi Dal'neishnovo Sovershenstvovaniia Tsenobrazovaniia SSSR," *Voprosy Ekonomiki*, No. 5, 1968.

Soviet and U.S. Defense Activities, 1970–1970: A Dollar Cost Comparison. National Foreign Assessment Center, CIA, SR80-10005, January, 1980.

Soviet Economy in 1978–79 and Prospects for 1980. CIA, ER80-10328, June 1980.

Soviet Military Power. DOD, September 1981.

Soviet and U.S. Defense Activities, 1971–80: A Dollar Cost Comparison. National Foreign Assessment Center, CIA, SR81-10005, January 1981.

Spechler, Martin. "Decentralizing the Soviet Economy: Legal Regulation of Price and Quality," *Soviet Studies*, Vol. XXII, No. 2, October 1970, pp. 222–54.

———. "The Pattern of Technological Achievement in the Soviet Enterprise," *ACES Bulletin*, Vol. XVII, No. 1, Summer 1975, pp. 63–87.

Stanley, William. *Performance Advances in Fighter Aircraft: Measuring and Predicting Progress*. Rand P-6500, July 1980.

Stanley, William and Miller, Michael. *Measuring Technological Change in Jet Fighter Aircraft*. Rand R-2249-AF, September 1979.

Steiner, James. *Inflation in Soviet Industry and Machine-Building and Metalworking (MBMW) 1960–1975*. Military-Economic Analysis Center, OSR, CIA, SRM 78-10142, July 1978 (a).

———. "Price Deflators for the Output of Defense Oriented Industries." Unpublished manuscript, 1978(b).

———. "Disguised Inflation in Soviet Industry: A Rejoinder," *Journal of Comparative Economics*, forthcoming 1982.

Sullivan, Leonard. "Five Year Defense Topline Projections," *Military Posture*. House Armed Services Committee, Washington, D.C., 1975(a), pp. 1817–60.

———. "Force-Structure and Long-Range Projections," House Budget Committee, Part 1, July 1975(b), pp. 1–54.

———. "Defense Economics: Modernization Through Left-Overs." Paper presented at the USAFA-Rand Conference on Economics of National Security, U.S. Air Force Academy, August 16, 1979.

———. "Correlating National Security Strategy and Defense Investment," in Nitze, et al., *National Security in the 1980s: From Weakness to Strength*. Transaction Books–Institute for Contemporary Studies, 1980(a), pp. 337–74.

———. "Strategic Top-Down Planning," Systems Planning Corporation, October 1980(b).

Tighe, Jr., Eugene. "Testimony," *Allocation of Resources in the Soviet Union and China*. Joint Economic Committee of Congress, July 1979, Washington, D.C., pp. 74–131.

Timson, F.S. and Tikhansky, D.F. *Confidence in Estimated Airframe Costs: Uncertainty in Aggregate Prediction* (R-903-PR). Santa Monica, Calif.: Rand Corporation, October 1972.

Treml, Vladimir. *The Structure of the Soviet Economy*. Praeger, New York, 1972.

————. "Foreign Trade and the Soviet Economy," in Neuberger and Tyson (eds.), *Transmission and Response: The Impact of International Disturbances on the Soviet Union and Eastern Europe*. Pergamon Press, New York, 1980.

Treml, V. and Gallik, D.M. *Soviet Studies on Ruble-Dollar Parity Ratios*. Department of Commerce, Foreign Demographic Analysis Division, Washington, D.C., 1973.

USSR: Gross National Product Accounts, 1970, Research Aid. CIA, Washington, D.C., 1975.

USSR: Toward a Reconciliation of Marxist and Western Measures of National Income. ER 78-10505, CIA, October, 1978.

Vartia, Yrjo. "Ideal Log-Change Index Numbers," *Scandinavian Journal of Statistics*, No. 3, 1976(a), pp. 121–26.

————. *Relative Changes and Index Numbers*. The Research Institute of the Finnish Economy, Helsinki, 1976(b).

Weitzman, Martin. "Soviet Postwar Economic Growth and Capital Labor Substitution," *American Economic Review*, Vol. IX, No. 4, September 1970, pp. 676–92.

Wohlstetter, Albert. "Optimal Ways to Confuse Ourselves," *Foreign Policy*, No. 20, Fall 1975. 170–98.

————. "Racing Forward or Ambling Back," in *Defending America*. Basic Books, New York, 1977, pp. 110–68.

Yergin, Daniel. "The Arms Zealots," *Harper's*, Vol. 254, June 1977, pp. 64–76.

Zwass, Adam. *Money, Banking and Credit in the Soviet Union and Eastern Europe*. M.E. Sharpe, White Plains, 1979.

Index

American arms procurement, dollar estimates: CIA, 9–10, 13–14, 19, 162–64, 166–82; mission-specific estimates, 168–82; Rosefielde, 162–64, 166–82

American arms procurement, ruble estimates: CIA, 14–15, 17, 157–61; Rosefielde, 14–15, 157–61

American defense burden, 11, 206–10

American intervintage technological progress, 15, 19, 63, 67–68, 70, 73, 154, 165, 168–70, 196, 257–63, 265–67

American national security policy: false perceptions, 11, 231; options, 27

Arms control: Soviet revealed preference, 11, 231, 233; Carter initiative, 11, 233

Arms parity, 10, 231–34

Arms race, 10, 11, 231–34; Richardson-Cournot-Stackelberg model, 10

American social cost of defense, 207–09

Arms superiority, 9, 10, 211–28, 231; dollar comparison, 217, 224–27; ordinality, 10, 213–17; potential military utility, 213–14, 224; quality, 10, 217, 223–24; ruble comparisons,

219–23; "Sovietizing," 10, 223–24

Barry, James, 56–57, 99, 248

Becker, Abraham, 125–39; hidden inflation, 113, 125–38; influence on CIA costing effort, 136; "new information," 39n–40n; new product bias, 127–29; prerevision ruble series, 37n, 255; ruble-dollar ratios, 192, 284–87; Soviet MBMW price index, 127–29, 136; Soviet defense spending, 255; special order item bias, 129–35

Bergson, Abram, 72, 202

Berliner, Joseph, 103

Bornstein, Morris, 110

Bronson-Severin index, 141–45

Burden of defense, see Soviet procurement burden, Soviet defense burden, American procurement burden, American defense burden

Burton, Donald, 37–40, 50–52, 54, 57

Carter, James, 233

Chertko, N. T., 126, 128–29

CIA, contradictions explained: Colby's testimony, 38, 50, 54; handling of "new information," 38–39; hidden

317